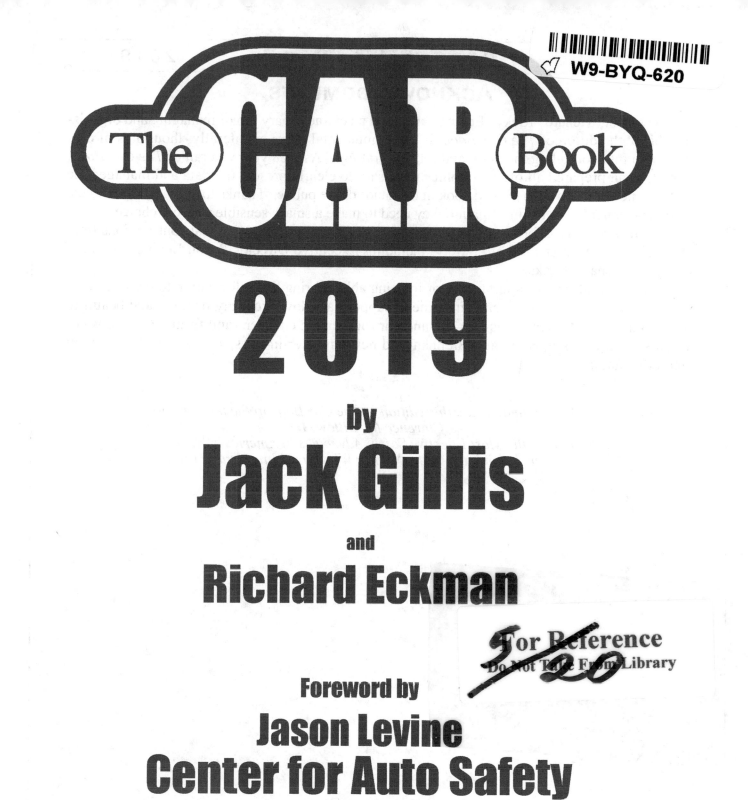

The CAR Book

2019

by

Jack Gillis

and

Richard Eckman

Foreword by

Jason Levine
Center for Auto Safety

A Center for Auto Safety Publication

ACKNOWLEDGMENTS

Co-author, Richard "Ricky" Eckman again did an extraordinary job of managing and organizing this 39th edition of *The Car Book*. It is a monumental effort as, literally, thousands of data points go into compiling the book and all of its ratings. As a 28 year veteran of *The Car Book*, Amy Curran prepared all of the graphics necessary to clearly present the data and managed the logistics necessary to get a printed book in the hands of the public. Thanks to Amy, Ricky, and the team, consumers have the information they need to make a smart, sensible new car choice.

For 38 years, this effort would not have been possible without the essential contributions from the staff of the Center for Auto Safety, including Executive Director, Jason Levine and Chief Counsel, Michael Brooks.

As always, the most important factor in being able to bring this information to the American car buyer for 39 years is the encouragement, support, and love from my brilliant and beautiful wife, Marilyn Mohrman-Gillis. For her and our four terrific children (and former *Car Book* co-authors!)–Katie, John, Brian and Brennan–and new daughter-in-laws, Jessie and Marine, I am eternally grateful.

—J.G.

We again dedicate this edition of The Car Book to the memory of
Clarence M. Ditlow, III
One of the Most Effective Safety Advocates in America's History
A True Friend and Great Mentor Who Saved Inumerable Lives

Contents

JASON LEVINE, CENTER FOR AUTO SAFETY

When the Center for Auto Safety was founded in 1970 there was a real problem: deaths associated with cars were on the rise and our government could not, or would not, exercise its duty to stand up for the interests of the American consumer over the desires of auto manufacturers. Into this void stepped the Center to serve as a watchdog over both the industry and the federal government, on behalf of our members and all drivers, passengers, and pedestrians. The more things change the more they stay the same. Today, decades of falling death rates have been reversed, auto manufacturers and technology companies have run roughshod over regulators, and the federal government appears to have absolved itself of its law enforcement responsibilities when it comes to auto safety. The need for the Center as an independent watchdog has never been more acute.

The National Highway Traffic Safety Administration (NHTSA) is tasked with writing safety regulations for cars and enforcing the law when it comes to auto safety. However, the current leadership of NHTSA, perhaps taking its cues from the White House, has chosen a path of deregulation and has brought enforcement efforts to a crawl that feels like bumper-to-bumper traffic. What NHTSA has apparently misunderstood is that traffic-related crashes and deaths didn't decrease by 80% over the last 5 decades because of the kindness and charity of the car manufacturers. The safety features now commonplace in modern vehicles, from seatbelts to airbags, from rollover-preventing electronic stability control to backup cameras, are only there because each and every one of them was mandated by the government, at the urging of public safety advocates, over the objections of the auto companies.

Unfortunately, today's NHTSA has chosen a path that emphasizes the burdens being placed on manufacturers by these regulations and remains focused exclusively on removing regulations instead of writing needed rules, such as mandating automatic emergency braking, or writing rules required by Congress, such as mandating a warning alarm when rear seat passengers fail to wear their seatbelt. The Center, on your behalf, has sued the Department of Transportation to try and accelerate these and other rulemakings.

When it comes to recalls and investigations, too often these days, NHTSA has taken a hands-off approach. Despite the tens of millions of recalled Takata airbags remaining unrepaired on the road, the government has chosen to ask these companies nicely to live up to their end of the bargain instead of enforcing the binding terms of the consent orders. Those 19 manufacturers signed on the line that they were responsible for replacing more than 60 million defective airbags. Yet, three years later, when certain manufacturers are failing to do what's right, and there are 25 million unrepaired recalled airbags still on the road, NHTSA is a mere bystander.

The truth is, recall rates are far from where they should be across the board. This is why the Center created www.FixAutoRecalls.com, a website dedicated to closing the recall completion gap, which numbers close to 70 million vehicles on the road today. In the year ahead, the Center will work to make it illegal to sell a used car with an open recall; will advocate for policy changes by ride-share companies like Uber and Lyft so that the car that picks you up isn't under recall; and we'll continue to pressure NHTSA to write a rule required by Congress that will force manufacturers to use electronic communication in addition to letters when notifying you about a recall.

There's no reason to wait for the information to come to you when it comes to auto safety. To be an effective advocate for yourself and your family all you need is information. That's why we built the CAS Vehicle Safety Check where you can see recalls, complaints, investigations and more about your car. To get regular updates, visit our website at www.autosafety.org, and sign up for electronic Monthly Safety Tune-Up Reports, which will include the latest Service Alerts for your car that you should be aware of when you bring it in for service. Contact your members of Congress and tell them how important car safety is to you, both in the cars of today and the ones yet to be built. When you shop for a new car, of course be sure to use The Car Book to understand how your options rate against each other. Finally, your continued financial support of the Center makes it possible for us to fight on your behalf fighting for safer, higher quality, and more fuel-efficient vehicles. There's no doubt that cars are safer today than they once were. But, recent increases in road deaths and pedestrian fatalities point to a system that is far from perfect and needs an independent watchdog like the Center to keep a look out for you! Please visit www.autosafety.org to learn more.

CENTER FOR AUTO SAFETY

Every year, car manufacturers spend tens of millions of dollars to influence government decision making. General Motors, Ford, and all the other major automakers have large staffs in Washington to represent their interests. But who looks out for the consumer? Who works on behalf of safety and not shareholders?

For 48 years, the independent, member supported, non-profit Center for Auto Safety has been the voice for consumers before government agencies, in Congress, and in the courts. The Center was established in 1970 by Ralph Nader and Consumers Union, publishers of Consumer Reports. As consumer concerns about auto safety issues expanded, so did the work of the Center. Center accomplishments include:

Initiating Safety Recalls: Annually, the Center analyzes thousands of consumer complaints. Based on these complaints and other reports, the Center requests government investigations and pursues recalls by manufacturers of defective vehicles. Center advocacy has resulted in the recall of millions of vehicles, including the deadly GM faulty ignition switches, Jeep fuel tank fires, and exploding Takata airbags.

Representing the Consumer in Washington: The Center monitors the activities of our government to ensure it carries out its responsibilities to the American taxpayer. The Center's fulltime job is to see the consumer's point of view represented in vehicle safety policies and rules. Over the course of our history, the Center has submitted hundreds of comments on government safety standards, and testified repeatedly before Congress on auto safety, consumer protection, and fuel economy.

One major Center success was the fight to get airbags in every car. Another was working to change the practice of manufacturers using weak roofs that crush vehicle occupants in rollovers. Since 2013, vehicle roofs are more than twice as strong as before, and rollover deaths and injuries have been dramatically reduced.

Exposing Secret Warranties and Making Repair Bulletins Public: The Center played a prominent role in the disclosure of secret warranties — or "policy adjustments," as manufacturers call them. These occur when an automaker agrees to pay for certain repairs beyond the warranty period but refuses to notify consumers. More recently, the Center went to court to make Technical Service Bulletins sent by manufacturers to their dealers publicly available — and we won!

Lemon Laws: The Center's work on Lemon Laws aided in the enactment of laws in all 50 states making it easier to return a defective new car and get your money back. Before Lemon Laws, automakers would refuse to buy back vehicles. Today, it is your legal right in every state to have a bad car bought back by the manufacturer.

Tire Ratings: Thanks to a Center lawsuit overturning the Department of Transportation's revocation of a valuable tire information program, consumers have reliable treadwear ratings to help them get the most miles for their dollar.

Legal Action: When the Center has exhausted other means of obtaining relief for consumers, we go to court. Currently we are suing DOT seeking implementation of a rear seat belt warnings law and we have brought an action against the Federal Trade Commission to overturn its policy allowing used cars with unrepaired recalls to be sold as "safe." The Center has also challenged class action settlements that don't deliver for consumers.

CENTER FOR AUTO SAFETY ONLINE

The Center is your representative fighting for auto safety, quality, and fuel economy every day. We depend on public support to keep us running. Learn more about at our advocacy efforts at our website: www.autosafety.org. Once there you can sign up for our member-only CAS Safety Tune-Up Reports, including customized email updates about your car. To become a member, or make a tax-deductible contribution to auto safety, at: www.autosafety.org/make-donation/. To contribute by mail, send a check to: Center for Auto Safety, 1825 Connecticut Ave., NW #330, Washington, DC 20009-5708.

WWW.AUTOSAFETY.ORG

JACK GILLIS

After three years of record sales, the 2019 models are expected to keep pace. Rear cameras are now standard and advanced safety features are making their way into the more reasonably priced models. Thanks to a fuel efficiency standard that will be in jeopardy by 2021, the 2019 models are more fuel efficient than ever.

Probably the biggest news is that automakers are beginning to phase out sedans. Crossovers and SUVs have taken over as the most popular vehicle types. Finally, as you can see from the pages in the back of the book, electric vehicles are becoming more and more available.

In order to make you both a smarter and safer car buyer, *The Car Book* documents these changes and puts them at your fingertips. We've rated the 2019s for the number of safety features they have so you can easily find the top performers.

This is the 39th year we've been bringing consumers the information they need to make a smart and safe vehicle choice. Not only are vehicles getting better, so is the buying experience. More dealers are abandoning the difficult negotiation process in favor of a straightforward posted price. So with lots of new electronics, improved safety features, and some improvements in the showroom, *The Car Book* is ready to guide you to a great new 2019 vehicle!

Working closely with the Center for Auto Safety, our goal is to sift through the myriad of government and industry data on cars and present the information so you can actually use it. Thirty-nine years ago, *The Car Book* was the first publication to give you the ability to make an informed choice on one of the most important and complex items that you will ever purchase. In setting out to change the way people buy their cars, *The Car Book* was able to change the way car companies made them.

In keeping with *The Car Book*'s philosophy of making it as easy as possible to identify the truly good performers in the government crash tests, we provide a unique *Car Book* Combined Crash Test Rating which combines all of the complex government testing into a simple, straightforward number. In addition, we take the step of comparing the vehicles on a relative basis to each other so you can easily tell which ones are truly the best performers.

Before *The Car Book*, consumers had no idea which warranties were better, what you could expect to pay for typical repairs, which cars cost the most and least to insure, or how they stacked up in government complaints. Now you have this information all in one place.

Our exclusive car-by-car ratings at the end of the book provide an overview of all the criteria you need to make a good choice. Here, you'll be able to quickly assess key features and see how the car you're interested in stacks up against its competition so you can make sure your selection is the best car for you.

While the choices get better each year, it's still a challenge to separate the lemons from the peaches. There are differences in how cars protect you in a crash, how much they cost to maintain, and the benefits of their warranties. Nevertheless, by using *The Car Book*, there's no reason why your next car shouldn't last at least 150,000 miles. Finally, our "Showroom Strategies" section will give you the keys to getting the best deal.

The information in *The Car Book* is based on data collected and developed by our staff, the U.S. Department of Transportation, and the Center for Auto Safety. With all of this information in hand, you'll find some great choices for 2019.

Once you've bought your new car, congratulations on a great choice!

—Jack

USING THE BUYING GUIDE

The "Buying Guide" provides a quick comparison of the 2019 cars in terms of their safety, warranty, fuel economy, complaint rating, and price range—arranged by size class. To fully understand the information in the charts, it is important to read the related section in the book.

Overall Rating: This shows how well this car stacks up on a scale of 1 to 10 when compared to all others on the market. We have adopted the Olympic rating system with "10" being the best. Because safety is the most important component of our ratings, cars with no crash test results at the time of printing are not given an overall rating.

Combined Crash Test Rating: This indicates how well the car performed in the government's frontal and side crash test programs compared to this year's vehicles tested to date. See pages 21-27 for details. Note: In order to qualify for a *Best Bet*, the vehicle may not have any Poor or Vry. Pr. crash test or safety feature ratings.

Safety Feature Rating: This is an evaluation of how many extra safety features are available in comparison to all the vehicles. See pages 64-66.

Warranty Rating: This is an overall comparative assessment of the car's warranty. See pages 31-33.

Fuel Economy: This is the EPA city/highway mpg for, what is expected to be, the most popular version of each model. See pages 29-30.

Complaint Rating: This is based on complaints received by the U.S. Department of Transportation. If not rated, the vehicle is too new to have a complaint rating. See page 45.

Price Range: This will give you a general idea of the "sticker," or manufacturer's suggested retail price (MSRP).

 Indicates a *Car Book* Best Bet. See pages 14-19.

ABOUT THE CAR BOOK BEST BETS

It is important to consult the specific chapters to learn more about how *The Car Book* ratings are developed and to look on the car pages, beginning on page 67, for more details on these vehicles. In order to be considered as a "Best Bet" the vehicle must have a crash test rating as safety is a critical factor in gaining that recognition. *Vehicles with "Poor" (3 or 4) or "Vry. Pr." (1 or 2) in Combined Crash Tests, or Front or Side Crash Test Ratings, or an additional injury warning will not qualify as a "Best Bet." In addition, vehicles with a poor or Vry. Pr. safety feature rating will not qualify as a "Best Bet."* Because most people are considering vehicles in the same size category, the "Best Bets" beginning on page 14 are by size—indicating how these vehicles compared against others in the same size class. You will note that some of our "Best Bets" have some "not so good" ratings on the next pages. Nevertheless, these vehicles still rise to the top in their size class. This points to the trade offs we often make when buying a new vehicle.

Vehicle	Pg #	Overall Rating	Combined Crash Test Rating	Safety Features Rating	Warranty Rating	Fuel Economy Rating	Complaint Rating	Price Range
Intermediate (cont.)								
Toyota Avalon	**233**	**8**	Good	**Very Good**	**Very Poor**	21/31	Good	**$33-$42,000**
Toyota Camry	**234**	**8**	**Very Good**	**Very Good**	**Very Poor**	28/39	Good	**$24-$34,000**
Volkswagen Passat	251	4	Average	Very Poor	Very Good	25/36	Poor	$22-$33,000
Volvo S60	253			Average	Good	25/36		$33-$47,000
Volvo V60	254			Average	Good	25/36		$38-$49,000
Large								
BMW 7 Series	82			Very Good	Very Good	21/29	Average	$83-$96,000
Buick LaCrosse	92	5	Average	Very Good	Good	21/31	Good	$30-$43,000
Cadillac CT6	95			Very Good	Very Good	18/27	Good	$54-$88,000
Cadillac XTS	**99**	**8**	**Very Good**	**Good**	**Very Good**	**18/28**	Good	**$45-$72,000**
Chevrolet Impala	106	4	Average	Average	Average	18/28	Good	$27-$36,000
Chrysler 300	116	1	Very Poor	Average	Poor	19/30	Poor	$28-$40,000
Dodge Challenger	118	4	Good	Very Poor	Poor	19/30	Very Good	$26-$63,000
Dodge Charger	119	2	Poor	Average	Poor	19/31	Poor	$28-$66,000
Ford Taurus	136	3	Average	Poor	Poor	19/29	Good	$27-$42,000
Genesis G80	137			Very Good	Very Good	19/27	Very Good	$41-$59,000
Lincoln Continental	185	6	Very Good	Good	Very Good	17/26	Poor	$44-$64,000
Mercedes-Benz E	198	3	Average	Very Good	Poor	22/30	Average	$52-$69,000
Mercedes-Benz S	203			Very Good	Poor	19/28	Good	$89-$147,000
Tesla Model S	**229**	**10**	**Very Good**	**Very Good**	**Very Good**	88/90	Poor	**$69-$135,000**
Minivan								
Chrysler Pacifica	117	8	Good	Good	Poor	18/28	Very Poor	$26-$43,000
Honda Odyssey	**148**	**9**	Good	**Very Good**	**Very Poor**	19/28	Poor	**$29-$44,000**
Kia Sedona	171			Poor	Very Good	18/25	Good	$26-$41,000
Toyota Sienna	243	2	Average	Good	Very Poor	18/25	Poor	$29-$47,000
Small SUV								
Acura RDX	**69**	**9**	**Very Good**	**Very Good**	**Average**	19/27	Good	**$35-$40,000**
Audi Q3	75			Very Poor	Good	20/28	Very Good	$32-$37,000
BMW X1	84			Average	Very Good	22/32	Poor	$34-$36,000
Buick Encore	**90**	**10**	Good	Good	Good	23/30	Very Good	**$23-$31,000**
Chevrolet Equinox	105	4	Average	Average	Average	26/32	Average	$23-$37,000
Chevrolet Trax	**114**	**10**	Good	Good	**Average**	24/30	Very Good	**$21-$28,000**
Fiat 500X	123			Poor	Average	22/31	Poor	$19-$27,000
Ford EcoSport	124			Poor	Poor	27/29	Good	$19-$26,000
Ford Escape	126	6	Very Good	Average	Poor	22/31	Average	$23-$33,000
GMC Terrain	141	5	Average	Poor	Average	26/30	Good	$24-$39,000
Honda CR-V	**145**	**10**	**Very Good**	Good	**Very Poor**	26/32	Good	**$24-$33,000**
Honda HR-V	147	5	Poor	Very Poor	Very Poor	28/34	Average	$19-$26,000

Vehicle	Pg #	Overall Rating	Combined Crash Test Rating	Safety Features Rating	Warranty Rating	Fuel Economy Rating	Complaint Rating	Price Range
Small SUV (cont.)								
Hyundai Kona	152			Good	Very Good	28/32	Very Good	$20-29,000
Hyundai Tucson	**156**	**8**	**Average**	**Good**	**Very Good**	**24/28**	**Poor**	**$22-$31,000**
Infiniti QX30	159			Good	Very Good	24/33	Very Poor	$29-$38,000
Infiniti QX50	160			Poor	Very Good	17/24		$34-$36,000
Jeep Compass	164	4	Very Poor	Very Poor	Poor	22/30	Poor	$20-$29,000
Jeep Renegade	166	1	Very Poor	Poor	Poor	22/31	Very Poor	$17-$27,000
Jeep Wrangler	167			Very Poor	Poor	17/21	Very Poor	$23-$37,000
Kia Sportage	**174**	**9**	**Good**	**Average**	**Very Good**	**22/29**	**Good**	**$23-$34,000**
Lnd Rvr Rng Rvr Evoque	176			Average	Good	21/30	Average	$41-$54,000
Lexus NX	182	5	Good	Good	Good	22/28	Good	$35-$39,000
Lincoln MKC	186	6	Poor	Average	Very Good	19/26	Good	$33-$48,000
Mazda CX-3	**192**	**10**	**Very Good**	**Average**	**Very Poor**	**29/34**	**Very Good**	**$19-$26,000**
Mazda CX-5	193	4	Average	Poor	Very Poor	26/32	Average	$24-$30,000
Mercedes-Benz GLA	199			Good	Poor	23/31	Average	$32-$49,000
Mercedes-Benz GLC	200			Very Good	Poor	21/28	Very Poor	$39-$54,000
Mitsu. Outlander Sport	208	3	Poor	Very Poor	Very Good	23/29	Good	$19-$27,000
Subaru Crosstrek	223	5	Average	Good	Poor	27/33	Average	$21-$26,000
Subaru Forester	224			Good	Poor	24/32		$22-$36,000
Toyota RAV4	241			Good	Very Poor	22/29		$24-$32,000
Volkswagen Tiguan	252			Poor	Very Good	22/27	Poor	$25-$37,000
Mid-Size SUV								
Acura MDX	**68**	**7**	**Good**	**Very Good**	**Average**	**18/27**	**Poor**	**$44-$61,000**
Audi Q5	76			Poor	Good	23/27	Average	$41-$50,000
Audi Q7	77	3	Average	Good	Good	19/25	Poor	$49-$65,000
BMW X3	85			Good	Very Good	22/29	Very Good	$41-$55,000
BMW X5	86			Good	Very Good	18/27		$55-$72,000
BMW X6	87			Average	Very Good	18/24	Poor	$64-$106,000
Buick Envision	91			Very Good	Good	21/27	Poor	$36-$45,000
Cadillac XT5	98	3	Poor	Good	Very Good	19/25	Very Poor	$40-$63,000
Dodge Durango	120	2	Poor	Good	Poor	18/25	Very Poor	$29-$62,000
Dodge Journey	121	1	Very Poor	Poor	Poor	19/25	Very Poor	$22-$34,000
Ford Edge	**125**	**9**	**Very Good**	**Good**	**Poor**	**20/30**	**Poor**	**$29-$40,000**
Ford Explorer	128	3	Average	Average	Poor	17/23	Very Poor	$31-$53,000
GMC Acadia	138	2	Poor	Good	Average	18/25	Poor	$32-$47,000
Honda Pilot	**149**	**8**	**Good**	**Average**	**Very Poor**	**19/27**	**Poor**	**$30-$43,000**
Hyundai Santa Fe	153			Very Good	Very Good	21/27		$24-$37,000
Hyundai Santa Fe XL	154			Good	Very Good	18/25	Very Poor	$30-$41,000
Infiniti QX60	161	5	Average	Average	Very Good	19/26	Average	$43-$44,000

Vehicle	Pg #	Overall Rating	Combined Crash Test Rating	Safety Features Rating	Warranty Rating	Fuel Economy Rating	Complaint Rating	Price Range
Mid-Size SUV (cont.)								
Jeep Cherokee	163	5	Average	Good	Poor	21/28	Very Poor	$24-$37,000
Jeep Grand Cherokee	165	4	Average	Very Poor	Poor	14/22	Very Poor	$30-$47,000
Kia Sorento	172	6	Good	Poor	Very Good	21/28	Poor	$25-$45,000
Lnd Rvr Rng Rvr Sport	177			Average	Good	14/19	Very Good	$65-$94,000
Lexus RX	184	4	Poor	Good	Good	20/28	Very Good	$43-$53,000
Lincoln Nautilis	188	5	Very Poor	Average	Very Good	17/25	Poor	$39-$56,000
Mazda CX-9	194			Average	Very Poor	20/26	Very Good	$31-$44,000
Mercedes-Benz GLE	201			Very Good	Poor	18/23	Average	$53-$101,000
Mitsubishi Outlander	207	4	Average	Average	Very Good	24/29	Poor	$23-$31,000
Nissan Murano	214			Poor	Very Poor	21/28	Good	$29-$40,000
Nissan Pathfinder	215			Poor	Very Poor	19/26	Poor	$29-$43,000
Nissan Rogue	216	3	Very Poor	Average	Very Poor	25/32	Very Good	$23-$31,000
Porsche Macan	220			Average	Good	17/23	Very Good	$47-$77,000
Subaru Outback	**227**	**8**	**Very Good**	**Good**	**Poor**	**25/33**	**Poor**	**$25-$35,000**
Tesla Model X	**230**	**10**	**Very Good**	**Very Good**	**Very Good**	**89/90**	**Poor**	**$79-$140,000**
Toyota 4Runner	231	2	Very Poor	Poor	Very Poor	17/21	Very Good	$34-$44,000
Toyota Highlander	**237**	**8**	**Good**	**Very Good**	**Very Poor**	**18/24**	**Very Good**	**$30-$47,000**
Volkswagen Atlas	248	6	Very Good	Good	Very Good	18/25	Poor	$30-$48,000
Volvo XC60	255			Very Good	Good	22/28	Very Good	$40-$51,000
Large SUV								
Buick Enclave	89	4	Average	Average	Good	18/26	Average	$39-$55,000
Cadillac Escalade	96	3	Good	Average	Very Good	14/21	Good	$76-$97,000
Cadillac Escalade ESV	97	4	Average	Average	Very Good	14/20	Very Good	$80-$99,000
Chevrolet Suburban	111	2	Average	Poor	Average	15/22	Poor	$50-$67,000
Chevrolet Tahoe	112	4	Good	Poor	Average	16/22	Average	$47-$65,000
Chevrolet Traverse	113	4	Average	Average	Average	18/27	Average	$32-$52,000
Ford Expedition	127			Good	Poor	17/22	Good	$48-$75,000
Ford Flex	131			Very Poor	Poor	16/23	Poor	$30-$40,000
GMC Yukon	142	5	Very Good	Average	Poor	16/22	Good	$49-$69,000
GMC Yukon XL	111	4	Average	Average	Poor	15/22	Good	$52-$72,000
Infiniti QX80	162			Good	Very Good	14/20	Good	$63-$89,000

Vehicle	Pg #	Overall Rating	Combined Crash Test Rating	Safety Features Rating	Warranty Rating	Fuel Economy Rating	Complaint Rating	Price Range
Large SUV (cont.)								
Lnd Rvr Range Rover	175			Average	Good	14/19	Good	$85-$140,000
Lincoln Navigator	189			Average	Very Good	16/21	Very Good	$72-$93,000
Mercedes-Benz GLS	202			Very Good	Poor	17/22	Good	$67-$124,000
Nissan Armada	210			Good	Very Poor	14/19	Good	$44-$60,000
Subaru Ascent	222			Very Good	Poor	21/27		$32-45,000
Toyota Sequoia	242			Poor	Very Poor	13/17	Very Good	$48-$67,000
Volvo XC90	**256**	**8**	**Very Good**	**Very Good**	**Good**	**22/28**	**Very Poor**	**$45-$104,000**
Compact Pickup								
Chevrolet Colorado	102	2	Poor	Very Poor	Average	20/27	Average	$20-$33,000
Ford Ranger	135			Very Good	Poor	21/28		$25-36,000
GMC Canyon	139			Very Poor	Poor	20/26	Very Poor	$20-$43,000
Nissan Frontier	211	1	Poor	Very Poor	Very Poor	15/21	Average	$18-$35,000
Toyota Tacoma	244	1	Very Poor	Poor	Very Poor	19/23	Poor	$24-$39,000
Standard Pickup								
Chevrolet Silverado	108			Poor	Average	16/22		$28-$55,000
Ford F-150	**129**	**8**	**Very Good**	**Average**	**Poor**	**17/23**	**Average**	**$27-$57,000**
GMC Sierra	140			Poor	Average	16/22		$29-$56,000
Nissan Titan	218	1	Good	Very Poor	Very Poor	15/21	Very Poor	$35-$55,000
Ram 1500	221	5	Poor	Average	Very Poor	17/22		$27-$53,000
Toyota Tundra	245			Average	Very Poor	13/18	Very Good	$32-$50,000

F ollowing is our list of the highest rated 2019 vehicles in each size category. The ratings are based on expected performance in nine important categories–Combined Crash Rating, Safety Features, Rollover, Preventive Maintenance, Repair Costs, Warranty, Fuel Economy, Complaints, and Insurance Costs–with the heaviest emphasis placed on safety. We have adopted the Olympic rating system with "10" being the best. (See box on page 7.)

KIA SOUL — COMPACT

Page 173

Combo Crash Tests	8	Warranty	9
Safety Features	5	Fuel Economy	6
Rollover	4	Complaints	6
PM	4	Insurance	1
Repair Costs	8	**OVERALL RATING... 7**	

TOYOTA PRIUS — COMPACT

Page 239

Combo Crash Tests	5	Warranty	2
Safety Features	7	Fuel Economy	10
Rollover	7	Complaints	4
PM	9	Insurance	5
Repair Costs	5	**OVERALL RATING... 7**	

ACURA TLX — INTERMEDIATE

Page 70

Combo Crash Tests	10	Warranty	6
Safety Features	8	Fuel Economy	6
Rollover	8	Complaints	3
PM	5	Insurance	10
Repair Costs	3	**OVERALL RATING... 9**	

HYUNDAI SONATA

INTERMEDIATE

Combo Crash Tests 9	Warranty 10
Safety Features 6	Fuel Economy 7
Rollover 7	Complaints 5
PM 5	Insurance 5
Repair Costs 8	**OVERALL RATING. . . 9**

Page 155

TOYOTA AVALON

INTERMEDIATE

Combo Crash Tests 8	Warranty 2
Safety Features 10	Fuel Economy 5
Rollover 7	Complaints 8
PM 6	Insurance 5
Repair Costs 4	**OVERALL RATING. . . 8**

Page 233

TOYOTA CAMRY

INTERMEDIATE

Combo Crash Tests 9	Warranty 2
Safety Features 10	Fuel Economy 8
Rollover 8	Complaints 7
PM 6	Insurance 5
Repair Costs 3	**OVERALL RATING. . . 8**

Page 234

SUBARU LEGACY

INTERMEDIATE

Combo Crash Tests 9	Warranty 3
Safety Features 7	Fuel Economy 7
Rollover 8	Complaints 5
PM 2	Insurance 1
Repair Costs 9	**OVERALL RATING. . . 7**

Page 226

TESLA MODEL S — LARGE

Combo Crash Tests	9	Warranty	10
Safety Features	9	Fuel Economy	10
Rollover	10	Complaints	1
PM	8	Insurance	1
Repair Costs	10	**OVERALL RATING**	**10**

Page 229

CADILLAC XTS — LARGE

Combo Crash Tests	9	Warranty	10
Safety Features	7	Fuel Economy	3
Rollover	6	Complaints	8
PM	1	Insurance	8
Repair Costs	3	**OVERALL RATING**	**8**

Page 99

HONDA ODYSSEY — MINIVAN

Combo Crash Tests	7	Warranty	2
Safety Features	10	Fuel Economy	3
Rollover	5	Complaints	4
PM	9	Insurance	10
Repair Costs	8	**OVERALL RATING**	**9**

Page 148

BUICK ENCORE — SMALL SUV

Combo Crash Tests	8	Warranty	8
Safety Features	7	Fuel Economy	6
Rollover	3	Complaints	10
PM	7	Insurance	5
Repair Costs	8	**OVERALL RATING**	**10**

Page 90

CHEVROLET TRAX — SMALL SUV

Combo Crash Tests	8	Warranty	6
Safety Features	7	Fuel Economy	6
Rollover	3	Complaints	10
PM	7	Insurance	10
Repair Costs	5	**OVERALL RATING**	**10**

Page 114

HONDA CR-V
SMALL SUV

Page 145

Combo Crash Tests	9	Warranty	2
Safety Features	7	Fuel Economy	7
Rollover	4	Complaints	7
PM	10	Insurance	10
Repair Costs	8	**OVERALL RATING**	**10**

MAZDA CX-3
SMALL SUV

Page 192

Combo Crash Tests	9	Warranty	1
Safety Features	5	Fuel Economy	8
Rollover	5	Complaints	9
PM	7	Insurance	8
Repair Costs	9	**OVERALL RATING**	**10**

ACURA RDX
SMALL SUV

Page 69

Combo Crash Tests	9	Warranty	6
Safety Features	10	Fuel Economy	3
Rollover	4	Complaints	-
PM	5	Insurance	10
Repair Costs	5	**OVERALL RATING**	**9**

KIA SPORTAGE
SMALL SUV

Page 174

Combo Crash Tests	7	Warranty	9
Safety Features	6	Fuel Economy	5
Rollover	4	Complaints	8
PM	5	Insurance	8
Repair Costs	7	**OVERALL RATING**	**9**

HYUNDAI TUCSON
SMALL SUV

Page 156

Combo Crash Tests	5	Warranty	10
Safety Features	8	Fuel Economy	6
Rollover	4	Complaints	3
PM	4	Insurance	10
Repair Costs	10	**OVERALL RATING**	**8**

ACURA MDX

MID-SIZE SUV

Combo Crash Tests 8	Warranty 6
Safety Features 10	Fuel Economy 3
Rollover 4	Complaints 4
PM 5	Insurance 10
Repair Costs 2	**OVERALL RATING. . . 7**

Page 68

TESLA MODEL X

MID-SIZE SUV

Combo Crash Tests 10	Warranty 10
Safety Features 9	Fuel Economy 10
Rollover 9	Complaints 2
PM 8	Insurance 8
Repair Costs 10	**OVERALL RATING. . 10**

Page 230

HONDA PILOT

MID-SIZE SUV

Combo Crash Tests 8	Warranty 2
Safety Features 6	Fuel Economy 3
Rollover 4	Complaints 4
PM 10	Insurance 10
Repair Costs 7	**OVERALL RATING. . . 8**

Page 149

SUBARU OUTBACK

MID-SIZE SUV

Combo Crash Tests 10	Warranty 3
Safety Features 7	Fuel Economy 7
Rollover 3	Complaints 4
PM 2	Insurance 5
Repair Costs 9	**OVERALL RATING. . . 8**

Page 227

TOYOTA HIGHLANDER

MID-SIZE SUV

Combo Crash Tests 8
Safety Features 9
Rollover 3
PM 7
Repair Costs 6

Warranty 2
Fuel Economy 2
Complaints 10
Insurance 8
OVERALL RATING. . . 8

Page 237

FORD EDGE

MID-SIZE SUV

Combo Crash Tests 10
Safety Features 8
Rollover 4
PM 6
Repair Costs 6

Warranty 4
Fuel Economy 4
Complaints 4
Insurance 10
OVERALL RATING. . . 7

Page 125

VOLVO XC90

LARGE SUV

Combo Crash Tests 9
Safety Features 10
Rollover 3
PM 3
Repair Costs 2

Warranty 8
Fuel Economy 5
Complaints 2
Insurance 10
OVERALL RATING. . . 8

Page 256

FORD F-150

STANDARD PICKUP

Combo Crash Tests 10
Safety Features 6
Rollover 2
PM 8
Repair Costs 8

Warranty 4
Fuel Economy 2
Complaints 5
Insurance 8
OVERALL RATING. . . 8

Page 129

CRASH TESTS

Safety is likely the most important factor that most of us consider when choosing a new car. In the past, evaluating safety was difficult. Now, thanks to the information in *The Car Book*, it's much easier to pick a safe vehicle. The bottom line: For the greatest protection, you'll want the maximum number of safety features (See Safety Checklist, pages 64-66) and good crash test results (the following tables).

A key factor in occupant protection is how well the car protects you in a crash. This depends on its ability to absorb the force of the impact rather than transfer it to the occupant. In the frontal test, the vehicle impacts a solid barrier at 35 mph. In the side test, a moving barrier is crashed into the side of the vehicle at 38.5 mph. A second side test simulates hitting a tree or roadside pole by smashing a vehicle onto a vertical pole at the driver's door at 20 mph. The only occupant in this side pole test is a small female dummy in the driver seat.

The dummies measure the impact on the head, chest, neck and thighs.

Not all 2019 vehicles have undergone a crash test. The good news is that by carrying forward previous tests from cars that haven't changed, we have results for 115 2019 models. The bad news is that there are 82 models for which we don't have crash test results.

How the Cars are Rated: The combined crash test ratings are based on the _relative_ performance of the 2019 vehicles tested to date. *This is a big difference from the government's "star" program.* Rather than large groups of undifferentiated vehicles in the government's star ratings, *The Car Book* rates them from best to worst. This means that those manufacturers really working on safety each year will rise to the top.

The first column provides *The Car Book's* Combined Crash Test Rating. The cars are rated from 10 Best to 1 Worst. The front is weighted 60%, the side 36%, and the pole test 4% with results compared among all new 2019 crash tests to date.

Next are the individual front and side tests. Again, relative to all other 2019 vehicles with crash test results, we indicate if the vehicle was Vry. Gd., Good, Average, Poor or Vry. Pr.. For side tests, the cars are rated separately from the trucks. Because of their construction, the dynamics of a side test are different in cars and light trucks.

The next five columns indicate the likelihood of the occupant sustaining a life-threatening injury. The percent likelihood is listed for the driver and front passenger in the front test, the driver and rear passenger in the side test, and the driver in the side pole test. Lower percentages mean a lower likelihood of being seriously injured if there is a crash test of this type. This information is taken directly from the government's analysis of the crash test results.

USING CRASH TEST DATA

TIP One of the most important results of our being the first to publish crash test data, and later develop our relative comparative ratings, is that it has put enormous pressure on the manufacturers to improve. Whereas years ago, when competition was based on style and horsepower, thanks to *The Car Book*, today's manufacturers are feverously competing on safety features. While the most important factors in evaluating the safety of today's vehicles are crash test performance and advanced safety features, size and weight do play a role. It is important to compare vehicles in the size classes that follow. For example, in a frontal collision between a subcompact and SUV rated 'Vry. Gd.," you'll be better off in the SUV. Nevertheless, selecting the best performers in whatever size class you are buying, is fundamental to protecting yourself. And remember, these tests are conducted with fully belted dummies, if you are not wearing your safety belt, then test results do not really apply.

CRASH TESTS

Crash Test Performance (10=Best, 1=Worst)	Combined Car Book Crash Test Rating	Test Type	Car Book Crash Test Rating-Index (Lower numbers are better)	Likelihood of Life Threatening Injury				
				Front Fixed Barrier		Side Moving Barrier		Side Pole
				Front Driver	Front Pass.	Side Driver	Side Pass.	Pole Driver
Subcompact								
Chevrolet Sonic	7	Front	Very Good-165	8.3%	8.1%			
		Side	Very Poor-153			9.5%	7.6%	3.8%
Chevrolet Spark	2	Front	Very Poor-228	13.6%	10.7%			
		Side	Poor-147			9.2%	6.8%	5.6%
Fiat 500	1	Front	Very Poor-256	11.4%	16.0%			
		Side	Poor-148			5.3%	8.0%	15.8%
Ford Fiesta	3	Front	Average-199	8.2%	12.8%			
		Side	Very Poor-154			8.9%	8.2%	3.6%
Honda Fit	9	Front	Good-175	9.2%	9.1%			
		Side	Good-85			6.8%	2.5%	3.5%
Mini Hardtop	4	Front	Average-194	10.7%	9.7%			
		Side	Very Poor-250			7.5%	18.7%	8.6%
Mitsubishi Mirage	2	Front	Poor-218	12.6%	10.5%			
		Side	Very Poor-210			7.5%	11.8%	22.1%
Nissan Versa	1	Front	Very Poor-241	12.6%	13.1%			
		Side	Very Poor-206			11.2%	12.1%	3.5%
Toyota Prius C	2	Front	Poor-206	11.7%	10.1%			
		Side	Very Poor-196			17.7%	5.2%	5.1%
Toyota Yaris	2	Front	Poor-217	9.9%	13.1%			
		Side	Average-111			7.7%	4.6%	2.9%
Compact								
Audi A3	6	Front	Average-197	11.2%	9.6%			
		Side	Average-113			7.0%	5.1%	4.2%
Audi A4	2	Front	Very Poor-276	12.9%	16.9%			
		Side	Average-119			4.3%	8.2%	2.6%
Cadillac ATS	2	Front	Very Poor-237	10.3%	14.9%			
		Side	Poor-138			7.5%	7.4%	4.8%
Chevrolet Cruze	5	Front	Good-176	9.0%	9.5%			
		Side	Very Poor-192			8.7%	12.7%	2.6%
Chevrolet Volt	4	Front	Poor-216	8.4%	14.5%			
		Side	Good-95			6.0%	4.7%	1.4%
Honda Civic	5	Front	Average-197	9.3%	11.5%			
		Side	Poor-153			4.9%	10.0%	9.6%
Kia Soul	8	Front	Good-180	7.6%	11.2%			
		Side	Good-81			4.7%	4.0%	2.6%

CRASH TESTS

Crash Test Performance (10=Best, 1=Worst)	Combined Car Book Crash Test Rating	Test Type	Car Book Crash Test Rating-Index (Lower numbers are better)	Likelihood of Life Threatening Injury				
				Front Fixed Barrier		Side Moving Barrier		Side Pole
				Front Driver	Front Pass.	Side Driver	Side Pass.	Pole Driver
Compact (cont.)								
Lexus IS	5	Front	Poor-219	12.4%	10.9%			
		Side	Good-85			5.6%	2.8%	7.1%
Mazda Mazda3 (2018)	4	Front	Poor-209	10.3%	11.7%			
		Side	Poor-119			11.5%	2.4%	2.8%
Mercedes-Benz C-Class	3	Front	Average-203	7.8%	13.6%			
		Side	Very Poor-170			5.7%	12.2%	4.8%
Nissan Sentra	2	Front	Very Poor-242	11.8%	14.%			
		Side	Average-118			6.6%	6.5%	1.7%
Subaru Impreza	6	Front	Good-172	9.5%	9.0%			
		Side	Poor-127			8.5%	5.2%	5.6%
Toyota Corolla	4	Front	Poor-217	9.6%	13.4%			
		Side	Average-105			3.6%	6.7%	5.6%
Toyota Prius (2018)	5	Front	Average-203	10.3%	11.1%			
		Side	Average-116			6.5%	2.0%	23.2%
Toyota Yaris iA	5	Front	Poor-205	9.9%	11.7%			
		Side	Average-111			7.7%	4.6%	2.9%
Volkswagen Golf	5	Front	Average-198	9.8%	11.1%			
		Side	Average-116			9.1%	3.9%	3.6%
Intermediate								
Acura TLX	10	Front	Very Good-156	7.3%	8.9%			
		Side	Very Good-58			4.4%	1.7%	3.4%
BMW 5 Series	4	Front	Very Poor-233	13.1%	11.7%			
		Side	Good-85			8.4%	0.8%	5.5%
Chevrolet Camaro	7	Front	Average-201	10.7%	10.5%			
		Side	Very Good-78			5.9%	2.3%	4.7%
Chevrolet Malibu	5	Front	Poor-223	10.4%	13.3%			
		Side	Very Good-73			6.0%	1.2%	6.4%
Ford Fusion	3	Front	Very Poor-226	8.7%	15.2%			
		Side	Average-117			6.3%	6.2%	4.1%
Ford Fusion Energi	7	Front	Very Good-154	7.3%	8.7%			
		Side	Very Poor-158			14.6%	3.6%	4.7%
Ford Mustang	8	Front	Very Good-162	7.0%	9.9%			
		Side	Poor-140			3.3%	10.4%	7.0%
Hyundai Sonata	9	Front	Very Good-147	7.5%	7.8%			
		Side	Average-114			5.8%	6.2%	4.6%
Infiniti Q50	4	Front	Very Poor-246	10.7%	15.6%			
		Side	Very Good-68			6.5%	1.2%	2.6%

CRASH TESTS

Crash Test Performance (10=Best, 1=Worst)	Combined Car Book Crash Test Rating	Test Type	Car Book Crash Test Rating-Index (Lower numbers are better)	Likelihood of Life Threatening Injury				
				Front Fixed Barrier		Side Moving Barrier		Side Pole
				Front Driver	Front Pass.	Side Driver	Side Pass.	Pole Driver
Intermediate (cont.)								
Kia Optima	7	Front	Good-175	7.3%	11.0%			
		Side	Poor-128			4.2%	9.3%	2.2%
Lincoln MKZ	3	Front	Very Poor-226	8.7%	15.2%			
		Side	Average-117			6.3%	6.2%	4.1%
Mazda Mazda6	7	Front	Good-185	7.6%	11.7%			
		Side	Good-96			8.2%	2.5%	3.5%
Nissan Maxima	7	Front	Good-185	8.7%	10.8%			
		Side	Average-111		6.0%	4.3%	11.4%	
Subaru Legacy	9	Front	Very Good-168	9.1%	8.5%			
		Side	Good-80			3.3%	4.7%	4.0%
Toyota Avalon	8	Front	Average-194	10.1%	10.4%			
		Side	Very Good-63			4.1%	1.2%	9.1%
Toyota Camry	9	Front	Very Good-170	8.4%	9.3%			
		Side	Good-80			3.5%	4.8%	2.5%
Toyota Prius V	6	Front	Poor-211	10.3%	12.0%			
		Side	Very Good-70			4.3%	1.5%	10.5%
Volkswagen Passat	5	Front	Very Poor-238	12.6%	12.8%			
		Side	Very Good-76			4.4%	3.1%	5.3%
Large								
Buick LaCrosse	5	Front	Good-188	8.1%	11.6%			
		Side	Very Poor-168			11.6%	7.7%	2.9%
Cadillac XTS	9	Front	Very Good-160	7.6%	9.1%			
		Side	Good-88			4.2%	4.3%	6.7%
Chevrolet Impala	6	Front	Good-173	7.5%	10.6%			
		Side	Poor-142			10.1%	6.1%	2.9%
Chrysler 300	2	Front	Very Poor-236	12.7%	12.5%			
		Side	Poor-120			12.9%	0.8%	5.1%
Dodge Challenger	7	Front	Average-204	11.7%	9.8%			
		Side	Very Good-56			4.7%	1.4%	2.6%
Dodge Charger	3	Front	Very Poor-232	14.3%	10.4%			
		Side	Average-110			12.2%	0.6%	3.8%
Ford Taurus	6	Front	Very Good-164	8.4%	8.7%			
		Side	Very Poor-154			8.3%	8.3%	5.8%
Lincoln Continental	10	Front	Very Good-158	7.6%	8.9%			
		Side	Very Good-67			3.9%	3.0%	3.4%
Mercedes-Benz E-Class	5	Front	Poor-206	9.6%	12.1%			
		Side	Good-87			6.4%	2.4%	6.8%

CRASH TESTS

Crash Test Performance (10=Best, 1=Worst)	Combined Car Book Crash Test Rating	Test Type	Car Book Crash Test Rating-Index (Lower numbers are better)	Likelihood of Life Threatening Injury				
				Front Fixed Barrier		Side Moving Barrier		Side Pole
				Front Driver	Front Pass.	Side Driver	Side Pass.	Pole Driver
Large (cont.)								
Tesla Model S	9	Front	Good-180	9.4%	9.5%			
		Side	Very Good-58			3.5%	1.5%	7.9%
Minivan								
Chrysler Pacifica	8	Front	Very Good-159	8.7%	7.9%			
		Side	Poor-93			5.8%	4.3%	3.2%
Honda Odyssey	7	Front	Good-180	9.5%	9.4%			
		Side	Good-58			2.3%	3.4%	3.1%
Toyota Sienna	6	Front	Average-197	8.6%	12.1%			
		Side	Average-71			2.9%	4.0%	4.5%
Small SUV								
Acura RDX	9	Front	Average-202	11.1%	10.4%			
		Side	Very Good-50			2.8%	1.3%	0.8%
Buick Encore	8	Front	Very Good-165	8.3%	9.0%			
		Side	Average-66			3.3%	3.0%	5.4%
Chevrolet Equinox	6	Front	Very Good-166	7.6%	9.8%			
		Side	Very Poor-230			6.2%	18.0%	5.6%
Chevrolet Trax	8	Front	Very Good-165	8.3%	9.0%			
		Side	Average-66			3.3%	3.0%	5.4%
Ford Escape	9	Front	Good-179	8.3%	10.5%			
		Side	Very Good-60			2.0%	3.5%	5.0%
GMC Terrain	6	Front	Very Good-166	7.6%	9.8%			
		Side	Very Poor-230			6.2%	18.%	5.6%
Honda CR-V	9	Front	Very Good-155	7.5%	8.6%			
		Side	Good-58			2.9%	2.3%	6.1%
Honda HR-V	3	Front	Poor-214	11.9%	10.8%			
		Side	Average-70			4.4%	2.6%	5.1%
Hyundai Tucson	4	Front	Poor-210	11.2%	11.1%			
		Side	Average-72			3.7%	1.7%	12.8%
Jeep Compass	2	Front	Poor-211	11.3%	11.1%			
		Side	Very Poor-120			4.1%	8.1%	4.4%
Jeep Renegade	2	Front	Poor-207	10.4%	11.6%			
		Side	Very Poor-187			3.8%	15.8%	2.4%
Kia Sportage	7	Front	Average-195	10.9%	9.6%			
		Side	Good-59			3.5%	1.6%	7.4%
Lexus NX	7	Front	Very Good-153	7.7%	8.3%			
		Side	Very Poor-108			10.9%	0.9%	6.5%

CRASH TESTS

Crash Test Performance (10=Best, 1=Worst)	Combined Car Book Crash Test Rating	Test Type	Car Book Crash Test Rating-Index (Lower numbers are better)	Likelihood of Life Threatening Injury				
				Front Fixed Barrier		Side Moving Barrier		Side Pole
				Front Driver	Front Pass.	Side Driver	Side Pass.	Pole Driver
Small SUV (cont.)								
Lincoln MKC	3	Front	Poor-213	8.9%	13.7%			
		Side	Poor-84			2.5%	5.8%	3.4%
Mazda CX-3	9	Front	Very Good-169	8.5%	9.2%			
		Side	Good-62			4.8%	1.8%	3.2%
Mazda CX-5	6	Front	Good-173	8.6%	9.5%			
		Side	Very Poor-128			2.7%	10.1%	4.5%
Mitsubishi Outlander Sport	4	Front	Average-203	10.0%	11.3%			
		Side	Poor-97			2.8%	6.3%	6.8%
Subaru Crosstrek	5	Front	Average-201	10.0%	11.2%			
		Side	Average-65			4.3%	2.0%	5.6%
Mid-Size SUV								
Acura MDX	7	Front	Very Good-168	8.3%	9.2%			
		Side	Average-68			2.5%	4.2%	3.6%
Audi Q7	6	Front	Average-195	10.0%	10.6%			
		Side	Average-67			3.7%	3.5%	2.0%
Cadillac XT5	3	Front	Average-199	8.2%	12.7%			
		Side	Very Poor-104			4.7%	5.6%	7.2%
Dodge Durango	3	Front	Very Poor-226	14.1%	9.9%			
		Side	Average-63			6.4%	.6%	2.9%
Dodge Journey	2	Front	Poor-222	9.6%	14.0%			
		Side	Very Poor-154			5.7%	9.7%	9.1%
Ford Edge	10	Front	Very Good-161	8.3%	8.5%			
		Side	Good-53			2.6%	2.7%	2.9%
Ford Explorer	5	Front	Good-183	10.4%	8.8%			
		Side	Poor-94			5.1%	3.5%	9.9%
GMC Acadia	3	Front	Poor-204	9.1%	12.4%			
		Side	Very Poor-121			5.0%	7.7%	4.0%
Honda Pilot	8	Front	Good-189	9.9%	10.0%			
		Side	Very Good-46			2.5%	1.0%	8.1%
Infiniti QX60	6	Front	Average-196	11.2%	9.5%			
		Side	Average-64			4.9%	1.8%	4.2%
Jeep Cherokee	5	Front	Very Poor-228	11.2%	13.1%			
		Side	Very Good-45			3.2%	1.7%	1.6%
Jeep Grand Cherokee	6	Front	Good-178	9.4%	9.3%			
		Side	Poor-93			8.3%	2.3%	2.4%

CRASH TESTS

Crash Test Performance (10=Best, 1=Worst)	Combined Car Book Crash Test Rating	Test Type	Car Book Crash Test Rating-Index (Lower numbers are better)	Likelihood of Life Threatening Injury				
				Front Fixed Barrier		Side Moving Barrier		Side Pole
				Front Driver	Front Pass.	Side Driver	Side Pass.	Pole Driver
Mid-Size SUV (cont.)								
Kia Sorento	7	Front	Good-177	8.8%	9.7%			
		Side	Poor-84			3.2%	5.3%	3.7%
Lexus RX	3	Front	Very Poor-251	13.7%	13.2%			
		Side	Good-54			3.1%	2.2%	3.7%
Lincoln MKX	2	Front	Very Poor-313	16.1%	18.1%			
		Side	Poor-81			5.3%	2.3%	8.3%
Mitsubishi Outlander	5	Front	Average-195	12.4%	8.0%			
		Side	Poor-91			3.8%	4.7%	7.8%
Nissan Rogue	1	Front	Very Poor-240	10.5%	15.0%			
		Side	Very Poor-116			6.5%	4.6%	10.4%
Subaru Outback	10	Front	Very Good-168	9.1%	8.5%			
		Side	Very Good-50			2.9%	1.9%	4.0%
Tesla Model X	10	Front	Very Good-152	8.3%	7.5%			
		Side	Very Good-43			3.3%	1.1%	3.1%
Toyota 4Runner	1	Front	Very Poor-255	11.9%	15.5%			
		Side	Poor-88			7.1%	0.9%	11.7%
Toyota Highlander	8	Front	Average-192	11.2%	9.0%			
		Side	Very Good-45			2.4%	1.1%	7.3%
Volkswagen Atlas	9	Front	Good-182	10.1%	9.0%			
		Side	Very Good-43			2.0%	1.7%	5.6%
Large SUV								
Buick Enclave	5	Front	Average-191	7.1%	12.9%			
		Side	Poor-74			4.4%	3.5%	2.3%
Cadillac Escalade	7	Front	Poor-209	10.1%	12.0%			
		Side	Very Good-45			3.0%	0.4%	8.6%
Cadillac Escalade ESV	5	Front	Average-199	9.5%	11.5%			
		Side	Average-69			4.5%	1.0%	12.2%
Chevrolet Suburban	6	Front	Average-195	10.4%	10.2%			
		Side	Average-69			4.5%	1.0%	12.2%
Chevrolet Tahoe	8	Front	Good-185	9.7%	9.7%			
		Side	Very Good-45			3.0%	0.4%	8.6%
Chevrolet Traverse	5	Front	Average-191	7.1%	12.9%			
		Side	Poor-74			4.4%	3.5%	2.3%
GMC Yukon	9	Front	Good-185	9.7%	9.7%			
		Side	Very Good-45			3.0%	0.4%	8.6%
GMC Yukon XL	6	Front	Average-195	10.4%	10.2%			
		Side	Average-69			4.5%	1.0%	12.2%

Crash Test Performance (10=Best, 1=Worst)	Combined Car Book Crash Test Rating	Test Type	Car Book Crash Test Rating-Index (Lower numbers are better)	Likelihood of Life Threatening Injury				
				Front Fixed Barrier		Side Moving Barrier		Side Pole
				Front Driver	Front Pass.	Side Driver	Side Pass.	Pole Driver
Large SUV (cont.)								
Subaru Ascent	10	Front	Very Good-158	7.6%	8.9%			
		Side	Very Good-39			8.9%	0.7%	2.6%
Volvo XC90	9	Front	Very Good-170	9.3%	8.5%			
		Side	Good-54			3.7%	2.3%	1.1%
Compact Pickup								
Chevrolet Colorado	3	Front	Poor-223	10.4%	13.3%			
		Side	Poor-73			6.0%	1.2%	6.4%
GMC Canyon	3	Front	Poor-223	10.4%	13.3%			
		Side	Average-73			6.0%	1.2%	6.4%
Nissan Frontier	4	Front	Very Poor-357	18.5%	21.1%			
		Side	Very Good-37			3.0%	0.5%	4.1%
Toyota Tacoma	1	Front	Very Poor-258	14.2%	13.5%			
		Side	Very Poor-115			10.1%	1.0%	12.7%
Standard Pickup								
Ford F-150	10	Front	Very Good-167	8.1%	9.4%			
		Side	Very Good-43			3.6%	0.7%	3.9%
Nissan Titan	7	Front	Average-200	11.5%	9.7%			
		Side	Very Good-46			4.1%	0.9%	2.0%
Ram 1500	5	Front	Poor-214	10.8%	11.9%			
		Side	Good-59			5.2%	0.3%	7.3%
Toyota Tundra		Front	Very Poor-236	12.0%	13.2%			
		Side	No Index-			2.7%		7.5%

2019 CRASH TESTS AND THE GOVERNMENT SHUTDOWN

Unfortunately, The Car Book 2019 contains about 15% fewer crash tests this year. This is due to the 2018-2019 federal government shutdown. Due to the absence of staff at the National Highway Traffic Safety Administration during this period, on-going and planned crash tests on 2019 model year vehicles were halted. Because The Car Book prioritizes safety, and does not give Overall Ratings to vehicles without crash tests, there are fewer vehicles in vehicles with Overall Ratings in this year's edition. As new results become available, you can find them at TheCarBook.org.

BUYING FOR SAFETY

So how do you buy for safety? Many consumers mistakenly believe that handling and performance are the key elements in the safety of a car. While an extremely unresponsive car could cause an accident, most new cars have adequately safe handling. In fact, many people actually feel uncomfortable driving high performance cars because the highly responsive steering, acceleration, and suspension systems can be difficult to get used to. But the main reason handling is overrated as a safety measure is that automobile collisions are, by nature, accidents. Once they've begun, they are beyond human capacity to prevent, no matter how well your car handles. So the key to protecting yourself is to purchase a car that offers a high degree of crash protection and automatic crash avoidance features.

When it comes to crash protection, here's a general list of what you should look for:

Dynamic Head Restraints: They adjust to give better protection in an accident.

Air Belts: Belts that blow up like long, soft balloons in a crash. Just being introduced in rear seats on some Ford vehicles.

Lane Keeping Assist: Keeps you within the white lines.

Automatic Braking: Applies the brakes faster than you can.

Blind Spot Detection: Keeps you from hitting another vehicle that you may not see.

Rear View Camera: Keeps children behind your car safe and helps with parking.

Adaptive Cruise Control: Adjusts your speed based on surrounding highway traffic.

Roll Sensing Airbags: Offer extra protection in a rollover–standard in many new cars.

Bicycle Detection: Alerts you when a bicycle has been detected.

Left Turn Crash Avoidance: Prevents a crash if turning left into the path of another car.

Adaptive Headlights: Increases vision by turning headlights when steering wheel turns.

FUEL ECONOMY

As gas prices bounce up and down, regular driving still takes a big bite out of our pocketbooks. Even at today's lower gas prices, the average household spends $1,500 a year on gas. The good news is that higher fuel efficiency standards are forcing car companies to provide more fuel efficient vehicles. Listed below are the best and worst of this year's ratings according to annual fuel cost. The complete EPA fuel economy guide is available at www.fueleconomy.gov.

FUEL ECONOMY MISERS AND GUZZLERS

Vehicle	Specifications	MPG (city/hwy)	Annual Fuel Cost
THE BEST			
Electric Vehicles (EV)*			
BMW I3 BEV	Automatic, RWD	137/111	$550
Chevrolet Bolt EV	Automatic, FWD	128/110	$550
Hyundai Ioniq Electric	Automatic, FWD	150/122	$500
Nissan LEAF	Automatic, FWD	124/101	$600
Kia Soul Electric	Automatic, FWD	124/93	$600
Plug In Hybrid Electric Vehicles (PHEVs)*			
Chevrolet Volt	1.5L, 4 cyl., Continuously Variable, FWD	43/42	$650
Ford Fusion Energi Plug-in Hybrid	2.0L, 4 cyl., Continuously Variable, FWD	43/41	$750
Chrysler Pacifica Hybrid	3.6L, 6 cyl., Continuously Variable, FWD	32/33	$900
Audi A3 e-tron ultra	1.4L, 4 cyl., 6-sp. Automated Manual - Selectable, FWD	34/39	$1,000
Gas			
Hyundai Ioniq Blue	1.6L, 4 cyl., 6-sp. Automated Manual, FWD	57/59	$635
Honda Insight	1.5L, 4 cyl., 1-sp. Continuously Variable, FWD	55/49	$703
Hyundai Ioniq	1.6L, 4 cyl., 6-sp. Automated Manual, FWD	55/54	$674
Kia Niro FE	1.6L, 4 cyl., 6-sp. Automated Manual, FWD	52/49	$726
Honda Insight Touring	1.5L, 4 cyl., 1-sp. Continuously Variable, FWD	51/45	$761
Toyota Camry Hybrid LE	2.5L, 4 cyl., 6-sp. Selectable Cont. Variable, FWD	51/53	$708
Kia Niro	1.6L, 4 cyl., 6-sp. Automated Manual, FWD	51/46	$754
Chevrolet Malibu	1.8L, 4 cyl., 1-sp. Continuously Variable, FWD	49/43	$794
Toyota PRIUS c	1.5L, 4 cyl., 1-sp. Continuously Variable, FWD	48/43	$803
Honda ACCORD	2.0L, 4 cyl., 1-sp. Continuously Variable, FWD	48/48	$766
Kia Niro Touring	1.6L, 4 cyl., 6-sp. Automated Manual, FWD	46/40	$849
Toyota Camry Hybrid XLE/SE	2.5L, 4 cyl., 6-sp. Selectable Cont. Variable, FWD	44/47	$810
Ford Fusion Hybrid FWD	2.0L, 4 cyl., 1-sp. Continuously Variable, FWD	43/41	$873
Lexus ES 300h	2.5L, 4 cyl., 6-sp. Selectable Cont. Variable, FWD	43/45	$837
Toyota Avalon Hybrid	2.5L, 4 cyl., 6-sp. Selectable Cont. Variable, FWD	43/43	$855
Lincoln MKZ Hybrid FWD	2.0L, 4 cyl., 1-sp. Continuously Variable, FWD	42/39	$904
Hyundai Sonata Hybrid	2.0L, 4 cyl., 6-sp. Automated Manual, FWD	40/46	$861
Kia Optima Hybrid	2.0L, 4 cyl., 6-sp. Automated Manual, FWD	39/45	$881
Mitsubishi Mirage	1.2L, 3 cyl., 1-sp. Continuously Variable, FWD	36/43	$939
Mitsubichi Mirage	1.2L, 3 cyl., 5-sp. Manual, FWD	33/41	$1,004
THE WORST**			
Jeep Grand Cherokee Trackhawk 4x4	6.2L, 8 cyl., 8-sp. Automatic, AWD	11/17	$3,252
Mercedes-Benz AMG GLE 63	5.5L, 8 cyl., 7-sp. Automatic, 4WD	12/18	$3,031
Toyota Tundra 4WD	5.7L, 8 cyl., 6-sp. Semi-Automatic, 4WD	13/17	$2,483
Toyota Sequoia 2WD	5.7L, 8 cyl., 6-sp. Semi-Automatic, RWD	13/17	$2,483
Toyota Tundra 2WD	5.7L, 8 cyl., 6-sp. Semi-Automatic, RWD	13/18	$2,410
Lexus LX 570	5.7L, 8 cyl., 8-sp. Semi-Automatic, 4WD	13/18	$2,410
Mercedes-Benz AMG GLS 63	5.5L, 8 cyl., 7-sp. Automatic, 4WD	13/18	$2,410
Chevrolet Corvette	6.2L, 8 cyl., 8-sp. Semi-Automatic, RWD	12/20	$2,856
Chevrolet Corvette	6.2L, 8 cyl., 7-sp. Manual, RWD	13/19	$2,838
Dodge Durango SRT AWD	6.4L, 8 cyl., 8-sp. Automatic, AWD	13/19	$2,341
Infiniti QX80 4WD	5.6L, 8 cyl., 7-sp. Semi-Automatic, 4WD	13/19	$2,341
Jeep Grand Cherokee SRT 4x4	6.4L, 8 cyl., 8-sp. Automatic, AWD	13/19	$2,341
Land Rover Range Rover LWB SVA	5.0L, 8 cyl., 8-sp. Semi-Automatic, 4WD	13/19	$2,341
BMW M760i xDrive	6.6L, 12 cyl., 8-sp. Semi-Automatic, AWD	13/20	$2,759
Chevrolet Camaro	6.2L, 8 cyl., 10-sp. Semi-Automatic, RWD	13/21	$2,684
Mercedes-Benz AMG S 65 (coupe)	6L, 12 cyl., 7-sp. Automatic, RWD	13/21	$2,684
Dodge Challenger SRT	6.2L, 8 cyl., 6-sp. Manual, RWD	13/21	$2,684
Dodge Challenger SRT	6.2L, 8 cyl., 8-sp. Automatic, RWD	13/22	$2,613
Dodge Charger SRT	6.2L, 8 cyl., 8-sp. Automatic, RWD	13/22	$2,613
Mercedes-Benz AMG S 65	6.0L, 12 cyl., 7-sp. Automatic, RWD	13/22	$2,613

Note: 2019 annual fuel cost based on driving 15,000 miles and a projected regular gas price of $2.15; #=Premium Required; *=Annual cost based on epa estimate for electric use;
=Fuel Economy rating based on Hybrid function only; annual cost based on epa estimate for gas and electric use; *=Low volume exotic vehicles (over $120,000) and cargo vans were excluded.

TWELVE WAYS TO SAVE MONEY AT THE PUMP

Here are a few simple things you can do that will save you a lot of money. Specific savings are based on gas at $2.45.

1. Pump 'Em Up: 27% of vehicles have tires that are under-inflated. Properly inflated tires can improve mileage by 3%, which is like getting 7 cents off a gallon of gas. Check the label on your door or glove box to find out what the pressure range should be for your tires. Don't use the "max pressure" written on your tire. Electronic gauges are fast, easy to use and accurate. Don't rely on the numbers on the air pump. The good news–all new cars must have a low tire pressure warning on the dash.

2. Check Your Air Filter: A dirty air filter by itself can rob a car by as much as 10% percent of its mileage. If an engine doesn't get enough air, it will burn too much gasoline. Replacing a dirty filter can in effect knock up to 25 cents off a gallon of gas.

3. Straighten Out: Not only does poor wheel alignment cause your tires to wear out faster and cause poor handling, but it can cause your engine to work harder and reduce your fuel efficiency by 10%.

4. Be A Regular: Check your owner's manual. Very, very few cars actually need high-octane gas. Using 87-octane (regular) gas can save you over 28 cents per gallon over mid-grade and 52 cents over premium.

5. Tune Up: A properly tuned engine is a fuel saver. Have a trusted mechanic tune your engine to factory specifications and you could save up to 8 cents a gallon.

6. Check Your Cap: It is estimated that nearly 15% of the cars on the road have broken or missing gasoline caps. This hurts your mileage and can harm the environment by allowing your gasoline to evaporate. Many Ford products have a capless gas filler, which is a great convenience.

7. Don't Speed: A car moving at 55 mph gets better fuel economy than the same car at 65 mph. For every 5 mph you reduce your highway speed, you can reduce fuel consumption by 7%, which is like getting 17 cents off a gallon of gas.

8. Don't Idle: An idling car gets 0 mpg. Cars with larger engines typically waste more gas at idle than cars with smaller engines. If you're stopped for more than a minute, consider turning your engine off. Some new cars do that automatically.

9. Drive Smoother: The smoother your accelerations and decelerations, the better your mileage. A smooth foot can save 38 cents a gallon.

10. Combo Trips: Short trips can be expensive because they usually involve a "cold" vehicle. For the first mile or two before the engine gets warmed up, a cold vehicle only gets 30 to 40% of the mileage it gets at full efficiency. Combine your trips.

11. Lose Weight: For every 100 pounds you carry around, you lose 1 to 2% in fuel efficiency. Remove extra items from your trunk or the rear of your SUV. Empty your roof rack—50% of engine power, traveling at highway speed, is used in overcoming aerodynamic drag or wind resistance.

12. Choose Your Gas Miser: If you own more than one vehicle, choosing to drive the one with better gas mileage will save you money. If you drive 15,000 miles per year, half in a vehicle with 20 mpg and half with a 30 mpg vehicle and switch to driving 75% of your trips in the 30 mpg vehicle, you will save $153 annually with gas at $2.45.

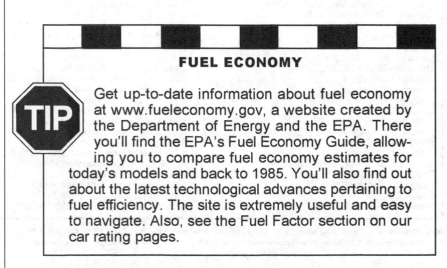

FUEL ECONOMY

Get up-to-date information about fuel economy at www.fueleconomy.gov, a website created by the Department of Energy and the EPA. There you'll find the EPA's Fuel Economy Guide, allowing you to compare fuel economy estimates for today's models and back to 1985. You'll also find out about the latest technological advances pertaining to fuel efficiency. The site is extremely useful and easy to navigate. Also, see the Fuel Factor section on our car rating pages.

COMPARING WARRANTIES

After buying your car, maintenance will be a significant portion of your operating costs. The strength of your warranty and the cost of repairs after the warranty expires will determine these costs. Comparing warranties and repair costs, before you buy, can save you thousands of dollars down the road.

Along with your new car comes a warranty which is a promise from the manufacturer that the car will perform as it should. Most of us never read the warranty until it is too late. In fact, because warranties are often difficult to read and understand, most of us don't really know what our warranty covers.

To keep your warranty in effect, you must operate and maintain your car according to the instructions in your owner's manual. It is important to keep a record of all maintenance performed on your car.

Do not confuse a warranty with a service contract. A service contract must be purchased separately while a warranty is yours at no extra cost when you buy the car.

Warranties are difficult to compare because they contain fine print and confusing language. The following table will help you compare this year's warranties. Because the table does not contain all the details about each warranty, review the actual warranty to understand its fine points. You have the right to inspect a warranty before you buy—it's the law.

The table provides information on five critical items in a warranty:

The **Basic Warranty** covers most parts against manufacturer's defects. Tires, batteries, and items added to the car at the time of sale are covered under

separate warranties. The table describes coverage in terms of months and miles. For example, 48/50 means the warranty is good for 48 months or 50,000 miles, whichever comes first. This is the most important part of your warranty because it covers the items most likely to fail. We give the basic warranty the most weight.

The **Power Train Warranty** often lasts longer than the basic warranty. Because each manufacturer's definition of the power train is different, it is important to find out exactly what your warranty will cover. Power train coverage should include the engine, transmission, and drive train. Some luxury cars will cover additional systems such as steering, suspension, and electrical systems. We give the powertrain warranty less weight than the basic because it doesn't cover as much as the basic warranty. Even with less weight in our rating, it can have a lot of influence in the overall index if it is very long.

The **Corrosion Warranty** usually applies only to actual holes due to rust. Read this section carefully because many corrosion warranties do not apply to what the manufacturer may describe as cosmetic rust or bad paint.

The **Roadside Assistance** column indicates whether or not the manufacturer offers a program for helping with break-

downs, lockouts, jump starts, flat tires, running out of gas, and towing. Some have special limitations or added features. Because each one is different, check yours carefully.

The **Scheduled Maint. (Free)** column indicates whether or not free scheduled maintenance is included and for how long. These programs cover parts scheduled to be replaced such as filters. If there is an asterisk next to the coverage, that means the manufacturer also covers the cost of any parts that need to be replaced because of wear. Covering the cost of "wear" parts is a terrific feature and offered by very few manufacturers.

The last column, the **Warranty Rating Index**, provides an overall assessment of this year's warranties. **The higher the Index number, the better the warranty.** We give the most weight to the basic and power train components of the warranties. Roadside assistance was weighted somewhat less, and the corrosion warranty received the least weight.

Finally, we also considered special features such as extra coverage on batteries or wheel alignment. These benefits added to the overall ratings, whereas certain limitations (shortened transferability) took away from the rating.

The best ratings are in *BOLD*.

BEST AND WORST WARRANTIES

Manufacturer Warranty	Basic Warranty	Power Train Warranty	Corrosion Assistance	Roadside Maint. (Free)	Scheduled Index		Warranty Rating
Acura[1]	48/50	72/70	60/75	48/50		1106	Average
Audi	48/50	48/50	144/180	48/Unlimited	12/5	1203	Good
BMW[2]	48/50	48/50	144/180	48/Unlimited	48/50	1288	Vry. Gd.
Buick	48/50	72/70	72/90	72/90	24/24	1259	Good
Cadillac[3]	48/50	72/70	72/90[4]	72/70	48/50	1320	Vry. Gd.
Chevrolet	36/36	60/60[5]	72/90	60/60	24/24	1062	Average
Chrysler[6]	36/36	60/60[7]	60/75	60/60		1010	Poor
Dodge[8]	36/36	60/60[9]	60/75	60/60		1010	Poor
Fiat[10]	48/50	48/50	60/75[11]	48/50		1014	Average
Ford[12]	36/36	60/60	60/Unlimited	60/60		989	Poor
Genesis[13]	60/60	120/100	72/Unlimited	60/60	36/36	1578	Vry. Gd.
GMC	36/36	60/60	72/90	60/60	24/24	1026	Average
Honda[14]	36/36	60/60	60/Unlimited	36/36		912	Vry. Pr.
Hyundai[15]	60/60	120/100[16]	84/Unlimited	60/Unlimited		1469	Vry. Gd.
Infiniti[17]	48/60	72/70	84/Unlimited	60/Unlimited		1299	Vry. Gd.
Jeep[18]	36/36	60/60[19]	36/Unlimited	60/60		964	Poor
Kia[20]	60/60	120/100[21]	60/10	60/60		1276	Vry. Gd.
Land Rover	60/60	60/60	72/Unlimited	36/50	12/15	1169	Good
Lexus[22]	48/50	72/70	72/Unlimited	48/Unlimited	12/10	1200	Good
Lincoln[23]	48/50	72/70	60/Unlimited	72/70[24]	24/24	1271	Vry. Gd.
Mazda	36/36	60/60	36/Unlimited	36/36		846	Vry. Pr.
Mercedes-Benz[25]	48/50	48/50	48/50	48/50		937	Poor
Mini	48/50	48/50	144/Unlimited	48/Unlimited	36/36	1280	Vry. Gd.
Mitsubishi	60/60	120/100	84/100[26]	60/Unlimited		1429	Vry. Gd.
Nissan	36/36	60/60	60/Unlimited			798	Vry. Pr.
Porsche	48/50	48/50	144/180	48/50		1157	Good
Ram	60/60	60/60	36/Unlimited			930	Vry. Pr.
Subaru[27]	36/36	60/60	60/Unlimited	48/50		972	Poor
Tesla	48/50	96/Unlimited	48/50	48/50		1357	Vry. Gd.
Toyota	36/36	60/60	60/Unlimited	24/Unlimited	25/25	926	Vry. Pr.
Volkswagen	72/72	72/72	120/120	36/36	12/12	1374	Vry. Gd.
Volvo	48/50	48/50	120/Unlimited	48/Unlimited	36/36	1220	Good

[1] Wheel Alignment and Balancing 12/12
[2] Free Scheduled Maintenance includes wear parts but is not transferable
[3] Wheel Alignment and Balancing 12/7.5
[4] All Corrosion 48/50
[5] All Corrosion 36/36
[6] Wheel Alignment and Balancing 12/12
[7] All Corrosion 36/Unlimited
[8] Wheel Alignment and Balancing 12/12
[9] All Corrosion 36/Unlimited
[10] Wheel Alignment and Balancing 12/12
[11] All Corrosion 36/Unlimited

[12] Wheel Alignment and Balancing 12/12; Brake Pads 12/18
[13] Free Scheduled Maintenance includes wear parts but is not transferable
[14] Wheel Alignment and Balancing 12/12
[15] Wheel Alignment and Balancing 12/12; Wear Items 12/12
[16] Only transferable up to 60/60
[17] Wheel Alignment and Balancing 12/12
[18] Wheel Alignment and Balancing 12/12
[19] All Corrosion 36/Unlimited
[20] Wheel Alignment and Balancing 12/12

[21] Transferable only to 60/60
[22] Wheel Alignement and Balancing 12/12
[23] Wheel Alignment and Balancing 12/12; Brake Pads 12/18
[24] Lifetime for original owner
[25] Wheel Alignment and Balancing 12/12
[26] Transferable only up to 60/60
[27] Wear Items 36/36

SECRET WARRANTIES AND TECHNICAL SERVICE BULLETINS

If dealers report a lot of complaints about a certain part or system and the manufacturer determines that the problem is due to faulty design or assembly, the manufacturer may permit dealers to repair the problem at no charge to the customer, even though the warranty is expired. In the past, this practice was often reserved for customers who made a big fuss. The availability of the free repair was never publicized, which is why we call these "secret warranties."

Manufacturers deny the existence of secret warranties. They call these free repairs "policy adjustments" or "goodwill service." Whatever they are called, most consumers never hear about them. Many secret warranties are disclosed in technical service bulletins that the manufacturers send to dealers. These bulletins outline free repair or reimbursement programs, as well as other problems and their possible causes and solutions.

Technical service bulletins from manufacturers must, by law, be sent to, and be on file at, the National Highway Traffic Safety Administration (NHTSA). In 2012, Congress required NHTSA to make all of these bulletins, and an accompanying index, publicly available through NHTSA's website. However, the agency did not take sufficient steps to fulfill this obligation, so in 2016, the Center for Auto Safety sued the Department of Transportation to force the DOT to comply with the congressional mandate to begin publishing all service bulletins and related manufacturer communications. The court ruled for the Center, on behalf of consumers and forced NHTSA to publish all service bulletins online. The Center for Auto Safety continues to monitor the agency's progress to ensure the up-to-date service bulletins are posted in a timely fashion.

To view service bulletins on your vehicle, visit www.nhtsa.gov/recall to look up your vehicle by VIN, or make and model, and then click on "Manufacturer Communications" to view a list of all available communications between the automaker and dealers, the great majority of which are service bulletins.

Additionally, you can look up all service bulletins relating to your car at the Center's website at https://www.autosafety.org/vehicle-safety-check/. While there, take advantage of a members-only feature which enables you to get a customized monthly email Safety Tune-Up Report, listing all new service bulletins on your car!

Secret Warranty Disclosure Laws: Spurred by the proliferation of secret warranties and the failure of the FTC to take action, California, Connecticut, Virginia, Wisconsin, and Maryland have passed legislation that requires consumers to be notified of secret warranties on their cars. Several other states have introduced similar warranty bills. You can find out more online through your state attorney general or consumer protection division website.

Typically, disclosure laws require the following: direct notice to consumers within a specified time after the adoption of a warranty adjustment policy; notice of the disclosure law to new car buyers; reimbursement within a number of years after payment to owners who paid for covered repairs before they learned of the extended warranty service; and dealers must inform consumers who complain about a covered defect that it is eligible for repair under warranty.

If you live in a state with a secret warranty law already in effect, write your state attorney general's office (in care of your state capitol) for information. To encourage passage of such a bill, contact your state representatives (in care of your state capitol).

LITTLE SECRETS OF THE AUTO INDUSTRY

Some state lemon laws require dealers and manufacturers to give you copies of technical service bulletins on problems affecting your vehicle. These bulletins may alert you to a secret warranty on your vehicle or help you make the case for a free repair if there isn't a secret warranty. See page 48 for an overview of your state's lemon law. If you would like to see the complete law, go to www.autosafety.org/lemon-laws-state to view your state's lemon laws. To see technical service bulletins on your vehicle you can also use the Center for Auto Safety's "Vehicle Safety Check" features at www.autosafety.org.

KEEPING IT GOING

Comparing maintenance costs before you buy can help decide which car to purchase. These costs include preventive maintenance servicing—such as changing the oil and filters—as well as the cost of repairs after your warranty expires. The following tables enable you to compare the costs of preventive maintenance and nine likely repairs.

Preventive Maintenance: The first column in the table is the periodic servicing, specified by the manufacturer, that keeps your car running properly. For example, regularly changing the oil and oil filter. Every owner's manual specifies a schedule of recommended servicing for at least the first 60,000 miles and many now go to 100,000 miles. The tables on the following pages estimate the labor cost of following this preventive maintenance schedule for 60,000 miles, the length of a typical warranty. Service parts are not included in this total.

Repair Costs: The tables also list the costs for nine repairs that typically occur during the first 100,000 miles. There is no precise way to predict exactly when a repair will be needed. But if you keep a car for 75,000 to 100,000 miles, it is likely that you will experience many of these repairs at least once. The last column provides a relative indication of how expensive these nine repairs are for many cars. Repair cost is rated as Vry. Gd. if the total for nine repairs is in the lowest fifth of

all the cars rated, and Vry. Pr. if the total is in the highest fifth.

Most repair shops use "flat-rate manuals" to estimate repair costs. These manuals list the approximate time required for repairing many items. Each automobile manufacturer publishes its own manual and there are several independent manuals as well. For many repairs, the time varies from one manual to another. Some repair shops even use different manuals for different repairs. To determine a repair bill, a shop multiplies the time listed in its manual by its hourly labor rate and then adds the cost of parts.

Some dealers and repair shops create their own maintenance schedules which call for more frequent (and thus more expensive) servicing than the manufacturer's recommendations. If the service recom-

mended by your dealer or repair shop doesn't match what the manufacturer recommends, make sure you understand and agree to the extra items. Our cost estimates are based on published repair times multiplied by a nationwide average labor rate of $90 per hour and include the cost of replaced parts and related adjustments.

Prices in the following tables may not predict the exact costs of these repairs. For example, labor rates for your area may be more or less than the national average. However, the prices will provide you with a relative comparison of costs for various automobiles.

Finally, for many of the electric vehicles you'll see a $0. That's because the EV doesn't have that part. This is one reason why EVs can be less expensive to maintain.

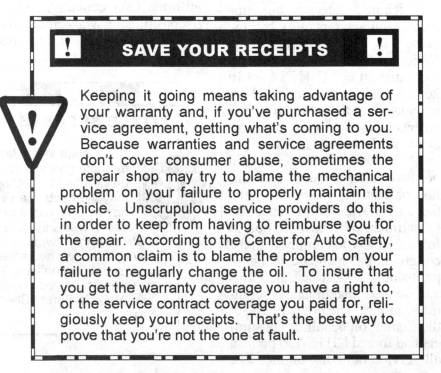

! SAVE YOUR RECEIPTS !

Keeping it going means taking advantage of your warranty and, if you've purchased a service agreement, getting what's coming to you. Because warranties and service agreements don't cover consumer abuse, sometimes the repair shop may try to blame the mechanical problem on your failure to properly maintain the vehicle. Unscrupulous service providers do this in order to keep from having to reimburse you for the repair. According to the Center for Auto Safety, a common claim is to blame the problem on your failure to regularly change the oil. To insure that you get the warranty coverage you have a right to, or the service contract coverage you paid for, religiously keep your receipts. That's the best way to prove that you're not the one at fault.

	PM Costs to 60,000 Miles	Front Brake Pads	Starter	Fuel Injector	Fuel Pump	Struts/ Shocks	Timing Belt/Chain	Water Pump	Muffler	Headlamps	Relative Repair Cost*
Subcompact											
BMW i3	1009	162	0	0	0	232	0	885	0	1494	Vry. Gd.
Chevrolet Sonic	545	231	344	127	420	159	416	404	717	798	Vry. Gd.
Chevrolet Spark	545	214	284	170	442	181	871	442	475	881	Good
Fiat 500	636	179	328	420	598	98	372	469	339	711	Vry. Gd.
Ford Escape	764	194	435	200	394	219	1085	316	1666	936	Poor
Ford Fiesta	836	172	292	132	298	154	427	283	480	686	Vry. Gd.
Honda Fit	482	159	412	282	461	398	521	295	267	681	Vry. Gd.
Hyundai Accent	873	156	380	357	440	121	462	243	385	342	Vry. Gd.
Hyundai Veloster	891	166	374	177	453	289	374	306	430	773	Vry. Gd.
Kia Rio	782	173	395	239	351	197	463	284	449	640	Vry. Gd.
Mazda MX-5	873	201	377	249	497	349	488	274	653	1498	Average
Mini Cooper	927	215	577	218	605	358	822	484	527	1365	Poor
Mitsubishi Mirage	618	191	535	292	139	226	468	475	442	1344	Good
Nissan Versa	600	201	427	296	528	196	445	220	391	705	Vry. Gd.
Toyota Prius C	564	169	0	516	536	149	1211	739	288	1154	Average
Toyota Yaris	491	185	433	272	479	149	633	255	288	344	Vry. Gd.
Compact											
Acura ILX	582	179	633	510	560	349	452	369	374	938	Good
Audi A3	1391	201	590	382	383	468	518	574	630	1075	Average
Audi A4	982	233	863	375	617	821	736	733	699	608	Vry. Pr.
BMW 2 Series	1009	259	654	510	300	311	1218	777	847	754	Poor
BMW 3 Series	954	259	654	510	294	588	1223	777	933	930	Vry. Pr.
BMW 4 Series	954	259	654	510	294	588	1223	777	933	930	Vry. Pr.
Buick Cascada	1264	287	368	342	369	312	518	609	1124	1090	Average
Cadillac ATS	1191	281	731	670	602	341	661	750	1245	1083	Vry. Pr.
Chevrolet Bolt	836	193	0	0	0	130	0	388	0	1034	Vry. Gd.
Chevrolet Cruze	973	185	480	303	409	184	487	684	643	827	Good
Chevrolet Volt	1091	208	0	145	489	155	903	442	692	1018	Good
Honda Civic	427	159	649	200	549	200	580	313	336	700	Good
Hyundai Elantra	991	138	362	237	318	190	502	255	388	830	Vry. Gd.
Kia Forte	591	173	227	212	330	174	508	320	337	595	Vry. Gd.
Kia Soul	964	173	414	277	310	170	600	341	455	1010	Good
Lexus IS	764	164	1021	670	475	351	1347	566	469	1512	Vry. Pr.
Lexus RC	809	164	839	595	532	297	1375	659	460	1709	Vry. Pr.
Mazda Mazda3	800	186	360	294	604	208	470	302	450	730	Vry. Gd.
Mercedes-Benz C-Class	1300	202	567	361	881	423	412	689	975	1075	Poor
Mercedes-Benz CLA-Class	1282	160	1021	648	713	250	440	486	646	1021	Poor
Mini Countryman	927	231	509	225	427	362	868	452	651	868	Average
Nissan Leaf	673	172	0	0	0	232	0	681	0	1400	Vry. Gd.
Nissan Sentra	709	184	365	371	530	168	603	329	442	656	Vry. Gd.
Subaru Impreza	1018	184	575	240	452	382	578	381	410	469	Good
Toyota 86	982	200	684	609	731	355	702	403	648	994	Poor
Toyota Corolla	554	161	448	338	481	188	1128	294	431	658	Good
Toyota Corolla iM	518	164	507	322	449	333	652	268	405	539	Vry. Gd.
Toyota Prius	564	192	0	675	517	164	1222	371	492	1277	Average
Toyota Prius Prime	564	169	0	304	465	351	1322	717	298	707	Good
Toyota Yaris iA	541	146	428	227	168	286	514	248	261	694	Vry. Gd.
Volkswagen Golf	1100	191	732	223	388	421	564	482	489	613	Good
Volkswagen Jetta	927	179	714	449	571	410	611	703	755	750	Poor
AVERAGE OF ALL VEHICLES	$912	$218	$484	$367	$506	$309	$817	$492	$673	$964	

	PM Costs to 60,000 Miles	REPAIR COSTS									
		Front Brake Pads	Starter	Fuel Injector	Fuel Pump	Struts/Shocks	Timing Belt/Chain	Water Pump	Muffler	Headlamps	Relative Repair Cost*
Intermediate											
Acura TLX	945	160	852	664	513	335	426	323	742	1473	Poor
Audi A5	982	233	720	366	540	471	732	739	828	669	Poor
Audi A6	982	260	937	1688	601	426	662	684	712	621	Vry. Pr.
BMW 5 Series	573	261	643	442	571	492	1355	731	1111	1060	Vry. Pr.
Buick Regal	1264	321	657	346	421	279	524	816	1162	1070	Poor
Chevrolet Camaro	1264	315	357	396	650	282	715	450	914	713	Average
Chevrolet Corvette	1291	351	388	539	675	232	1325	314	1432	1400	Vry. Pr.
Chevrolet Malibu	718	263	393	351	437	247	542	509	687	500	Good
Ford Fusion	691	272	277	325	274	113	650	191	595	941	Vry. Gd.
Ford Fusion Energi	854	171	0	130	321	132	589	220	420	1037	Vry. Gd.
Ford Mustang	609	219	203	216	243	166	840	269	960	1462	Average
Honda Accord	509	167	553	495	598	263	431	333	476	1100	Average
Hyundai Sonata	900	166	313	251	353	154	725	324	675	830	Good
Infiniti Q50	891	176	519	422	519	547	757	272	642	1458	Poor
Kia Optima	873	173	246	277	339	165	609	264	337	632	Vry. Gd.
Lexus ES	873	198	563	445	491	458	1531	417	538	1437	Vry. Pr.
Lexus GS	664	163	881	751	489	243	1835	614	577	1695	Vry. Pr.
Lincoln MKZ	691	205	295	393	497	300	1201	358	1104	1439	Vry. Pr.
Mazda Mazda6	807	193	256	571	555	239	559	234	377	707	Good
Nissan Altima	964	196	351	349	424	237	660	277	429	708	Vry. Gd.
Nissan Maxima	836	182	426	435	480	234	902	425	691	921	Average
Subaru Legacy	1200	179	469	229	448	330	633	381	281	503	Vry. Gd.
Tesla Model 3	709	197	0	0	0	278	0	911	0	1328	Vry. Gd.
Toyota Avalon	873	209	563	445	491	359	1558	417	407	618	Poor
Toyota Camry	873	198	583	473	500	323	1521	473	410	1121	Poor
Volkswagen Passat	927	180	767	264	504	384	962	478	749	678	Average
Volvo S60	918	240	540	415	877	226	506	504	700	572	Average
Volvo V60	1127	232	482	415	877	234	605	504	576	609	Average
Large											
BMW 7 Series	1264	318	767	622	609	2104	1397	858	1101	2001	Vry. Pr.
Buick LaCrosse	1264	287	461	209	506	774	1181	450	636	1118	Vry. Pr.
Cadillac CT6	1191	321	685	590	592	367	671	676	828	1055	Vry. Pr.
Cadillac XTS	1254	263	440	401	606	279	976	521	739	1389	Poor
Chevrolet Impala	1264	258	400	453	524	205	775	511	651	711	Average
Chrysler 300	636	218	251	234	449	879	760	374	1810	1250	Vry. Pr.
Dodge Challenger	636	436	307	215	768	263	683	279	1004	1461	Poor
Dodge Charger	636	280	252	215	616	155	646	308	1135	667	Good
Ford Flex	809	162	220	216	270	187	1043	539	1007	820	Average
Ford Taurus	918	171	220	188	359	179	1032	592	800	768	Good
Genesis G80	1054	245	480	224	444	341	1254	385	612	1103	Poor
Lincoln Continental	909	219	276	318	438	490	1156	507	1134	1460	Vry. Pr.
Mercedes-Benz E-Class	1027	196	880	531	513	311	1161	785	1174	1236	Vry. Pr.
Mercedes-Benz S-Class	1027	228	721	461	544	763	407	978	1535	1651	Vry. Pr.
Tesla Model S	709	223	0	0	0	306	0	1053	0	1438	Vry. Gd.
Minivan											
Chrysler Pacifica	509	286	477	200	510	309	903	351	995	620	Average
Honda Odyssey	545	175	579	208	512	146	359	484	678	725	Good
Kia Sedona	1000	173	264	334	414	218	756	327	574	405	Vry. Gd.
Toyota Sienna	1127	161	564	436	700	176	1393	557	577	705	Poor
AVERAGE OF ALL VEHICLES	$912	$218	$484	$367	$506	$309	$817	$492	$673	$964	

	PM Costs to 60,000 Miles	REPAIR COSTS									
		Front Brake Pads	Starter	Fuel Injector	Fuel Pump	Struts/ Shocks	Timing Belt/ Chain	Water Pump	Muffler	Headlamps	Relative Repair Cost*
Small SUV											
Acura RDX	918	406	569	273	558	268	338	428	545	1397	Average
Audi Q3	982	201	751	413	337	660	772	663	402	1280	Poor
BMW X1	791	256	743	562	651	425	1315	797	1092	1365	Vry. Pr.
Buick Encore	727	336	285	116	454	198	737	373	636	671	Good
Chevrolet Equinox	1291	321	474	478	763	161	826	485	1065	819	Poor
Chevrolet Trax	782	189	329	120	580	222	1050	513	834	1016	Average
Fiat 500X	636	179	328	420	598	98	372	469	339	711	Vry. Gd.
Ford EcoSport	764	192	354	222	466	278	994	209	511	1062	Good
GMC Terrain	1291	321	474	478	763	161	826	485	1065	931	Poor
Honda CR-V	509	159	639	359	510	234	424	266	426	777	Good
Honda HR-V	754	167	672	155	485	211	451	328	414	796	Good
Hyundai Kona	809	142	407	154	328	220	473	442	656	713	Vry. Gd.
Hyundai Tucson	982	169	372	318	344	189	312	343	607	650	Vry. Gd.
Infiniti QX30	727	181	459	388	487	298	814	762	719	1623	Vry. Pr.
Infiniti QX50	600	184	586	324	523	298	814	772	719	1519	Vry. Pr.
Jeep Compass	455	189	391	132	462	356	511	349	487	390	Vry. Gd.
Jeep Renegade	954	319	774	142	406	484	556	390	566	464	Good
Jeep Wrangler	409	235	252	303	591	139	756	394	404	270	Vry. Gd.
Kia Sportage	936	173	246	247	338	241	536	361	653	1488	Good
Land Rover Range Rover Evoque	864	294	612	532	723	604	626	308	749	538	Average
Lexus NX	1445	151	602	600	519	241	1330	542	865	671	Poor
Lincoln MKC	864	214	258	194	405	181	999	564	837	1433	Poor
Mazda CX-3	a782	192	388	373	337	226	425	256	421	741	Vry. Gd.
Mazda CX-5	718	173	408	365	347	224	404	248	495	633	Vry. Gd.
Mercedes-Benz GLA-Class	491	339	771	574	574	435	404	913	869	1387	Vry. Pr.
Mercedes-Benz GLC-Class	1073	349	711	564	547	484	390	866	869	1410	Vry. Pr.
Mitsubishi Outlander Sport	800	183	537	366	718	274	520	511	481	1178	Average
Subaru Crosstrek	1018	179	575	240	452	373	578	381	413	473	Good
Subaru Forester	1036	184	623	550	473	339	633	471	423	510	Good
Toyota RAV4	973	204	544	300	604	125	1092	332	314	610	Good
Volkswagen Tiguan	1064	179	714	427	571	420	621	702	774	742	Poor
Medium SUV											
Acura MDX	945	323	599	1383	716	284	385	526	762	1239	Vry. Pr.
Audi Q5	982	271	773	478	622	431	795	719	936	668	Vry. Pr.
Audi Q7	1091	281	1071	785	490	728	1437	395	1030	760	Vry. Pr.
BMW X3	1254	259	767	556	616	515	1089	886	1219	1716	Vry. Pr.
BMW X5	1064	323	728	552	656	568	1841	776	2157	2287	Vry. Pr.
BMW X6	1118	352	681	458	821	491	833	1197	1705	2487	Vry. Pr.
Buick Envision	1182	292	465	215	511	766	809	455	640	1123	Poor
Cadillac XT5	1264	216	430	443	385	168	1064	534	979	985	Poor
Dodge Durango	927	235	506	243	545	426	949	317	564	877	Average
Dodge Journey	591	235	430	247	765	330	940	430	1477	335	Poor
Ford Edge	864	231	190	243	409	254	1018	308	862	1079	Average
Ford Explorer	918	171	240	216	488	142	858	502	864	1219	Average
GMC Acadia	1218	289	407	317	535	179	1172	482	646	1315	Poor
Honda Pilot	527	177	527	293	653	218	432	550	676	866	Good
Hyundai Santa Fe	982	186	323	266	592	224	1291	331	599	1120	Average
Hyundai Santa Fe Sport	982	183	313	294	465	245	548	313	618	1258	Good
Infiniti QX60	1100	182	513	424	503	350	1078	263	739	1508	Poor
Jeep Cherokee	436	235	547	195	699	304	976	434	936	548	Average
AVERAGE OF ALL VEHICLES	$912	$218	$484	$367	$506	$309	$817	$492	$673	$964	

37

	PM Costs to 60,000 Miles	Front Brake Pads	Starter	Fuel Injector	Fuel Pump	Struts/ Shocks	Timing Belt/ Chain	Water Pump	Muffler	Headlamps	Relative Repair Cost*
REPAIR COSTS											
Jeep Grand Cherokee	636	235	506	243	482	244	949	302	870	621	Average
Kia Sorento	945	182	245	278	507	215	564	300	600	1029	Good
Land Rover Range Rover Sport	1291	254	703	669	663	413	1315	394	498	298	Poor
Lexus RX	909	236	766	323	489	133	2026	1158	725	2315	Vry. Pr.
Lincoln MKX	764	212	190	216	390	250	1009	507	732	1183	Average
Mazda CX-9	800	195	328	237	597	313	1117	1097	638	907	Poor
Mercedes-Benz GLE-Class	1064	338	709	596	584	465	377	885	903	1387	Vry. Pr.
Mitsubishi Outlander	991	182	428	309	652	242	520	459	424	783	Good
Nissan Murano	709	203	523	437	632	304	904	506	659	1209	Poor
Nissan Pathfinder	1454	203	648	437	618	213	965	522	708	832	Poor
Nissan Rogue	1064	182	458	435	524	162	943	349	615	1391	Poor
Porsche Macan	1091	399	575	442	550	576	1162	519	1268	1041	Vry. Pr.
Subaru Outback	1200	184	469	230	461	339	624	381	299	503	Vry. Gd.
Tesla Model X	709	223	0	0	0	306	0	1053	0	1438	Vry. Gd.
Toyota 4Runner	564	159	612	384	631	132	1677	626	575	509	Poor
Toyota Highlander	727	161	531	464	593	107	1778	277	271	552	Average
Volkswagen Atlas	1091	243	761	535	486	480	1409	777	955	1343	Vry. Pr.
Volvo XC60	918	293	636	470	891	274	357	504	521	655	Average
Volvo XC90	1054	254	655	433	736	324	546	1000	602	1282	Vry. Pr.
Large SUV											
Buick Enclave	1218	298	430	432	613	156	797	702	664	1409	Poor
Cadillac Escalade	1291	229	337	377	622	809	999	418	1245	1642	Vry. Pr.
Cadillac Escalade ESV	1291	229	337	377	646	809	999	418	1288	1642	Vry. Pr.
Chevrolet Suburban	1291	229	346	383	650	211	1242	384	736	646	Average
Chevrolet Tahoe	1291	214	346	383	675	205	1242	530	1140	637	Poor
Chevrolet Traverse	1218	286	421	451	610	153	1238	581	553	739	Average
Ford Expedition	1109	174	242	158	390	191	730	206	492	986	Vry. Gd.
GMC Yukon	1291	214	346	383	675	205	1242	530	1140	765	Poor
Infiniti QX80	1091	204	504	340	480	222	1292	315	537	1384	Poor
Land Rover Range Rover	882	254	703	669	663	491	1223	394	498	297	Poor
Lexus GX	827	159	812	441	621	120	1254	489	785	1361	Vry. Pr.
Lincoln Navigator	1136	174	213	243	409	290	941	293	520	1387	Average
Mercedes-Benz GLS-Class	1073	320	731	589	584	484	386	832	826	1420	Vry. Pr.
Nissan Armada	1091	182	525	314	531	376	1116	306	655	947	Average
Subaru Ascent	1073	195	595	237	477	547	296	475	346	476	Vry. Gd.
Toyota Sequoia	827	198	980	319	715	379	1356	471	366	395	Poor
Compact Pickup											
Chevrolet Colorado	1291	235	504	393	429	179	501	434	363	697	Good
Ford Ranger	1185	202	558	471	585	126	578	510	490	728	Average
GMC Canyon	1291	235	504	393	429	179	501	434	363	734	Good
Nissan Frontier	1091	203	558	390	703	163	895	373	465	452	Good
Toyota Tacoma	564	184	649	547	609	101	1457	518	530	573	Poor
Standard Pickup											
Chevrolet Silverado	1291	260	456	402	635	168	1255	384	750	650	Average
Ford F-150	618	174	223	525	413	114	833	530	386	629	Good
GMC Sierra	1291	260	456	402	635	168	1255	384	787	790	Average
Nissan Titan	1127	177	591	313	571	199	1295	318	620	769	Average
Ram 1500	673	160	308	149	427	177	528	422	419	475	Vry. Gd.
Toyota Tundra	827	176	1032	319	552	121	1255	434	649	430	Average
	$912	$218	$484	$367	$506	$309	$817	$492	$673	$964	
AVERAGE OF ALL VEHICLES	$912	$218	$484	$367	$506	$309	$817	$492	$673	$964	

38

SERVICE CONTRACTS

Service contracts are one of the most expensive options you can buy. In fact, service contracts are a major profit source for many dealers.

A service contract is not a warranty. It is more like an insurance plan that, in theory, covers repairs that are not covered by your warranty or that occur after the warranty runs out. They are often inaccurately referred to as "extended warranties."

Service contracts are generally a poor value. The companies who sell contracts are very sure that, on average, your repairs will cost considerably less than what you pay for the contract—if not, they wouldn't be in business.

Here are some important questions to ask before buying a service contract:

How reputable is the company responsible for the contract? If the company offering the contract goes out of business, you will be out of luck. The company may be required to be insured, but find out if they actually are and by whom. Check with your Better Business Bureau or office of consumer affairs if you are not sure of a company's reputation. Service contracts from car and insurance companies are more likely to remain in effect than those from independent companies.

Exactly what does the contract cover and for how long? Service contracts vary considerably—different items are covered and different time limits are offered. This is true even among service contracts offered by the same company. For example, one company has plans that range from 4 years/36,000 miles maximum coverage to 6 years/100,000 miles maximum coverage, with other options for only power train coverage. Make sure you know what components are covered because if a breakdown occurs on a part that is not covered, you are responsible for the repairs.

If you plan to resell your car in a few years, you won't want to purchase a long-running service contract. Some service contracts automatically cancel when you resell the car, while others require a hefty transfer fee before extending privileges to the new owner. Check out the transferability of the service contract.

Some automakers offer a "menu" format, which lets you pick the items you want covered in your service contract. Find out if the contract pays for preventive maintenance, towing, and rental car expenses. If not written into the contract, assume they are not covered.

Make sure the contract clearly specifies how you can reach the company. Knowing this before you purchase a service contract can save you time and aggravation in the future.

How will the repair bills be paid? It is best to have the service contractor pay bills directly. Some contracts require you to pay the repair bill, and reimburse you later. This can be a major hassle.

Where can the car be serviced? Can you take the car to any mechanic if you have trouble on the road? What if you move?

What other costs can be expected? Most service contracts will have a deductible expense, which means you will have to pay part of the repair cost. Compare deductibles on various plans. Also, some companies charge the deductible for each individual repair while other companies pay per visit, regardless of the number of repairs being made.

What are your responsibilities? Make sure you know what you have to do to uphold the contract. For example if you have to follow the manufacturer's recommended maintenance, keep detailed records or the contract could be voided. You will find your specific responsibilities in the contact. Be sure to have the seller point them out.

SERVICE CONTRACTS VS. SAVINGS ACCOUNT

TIP One alternative to buying a service contract is to deposit the cost of the contract into a savings account. If the car needs a major repair not covered by your warranty, the money in your account is likely to cover the cost. Most likely, you'll be building up a down payment for your next car!

INSURANCE

Insurance is a big part of ownership expenses, yet it's often forgotten in the showroom. As you shop, remember that the car's design and accident history may affect your insurance rates. Some cars cost less to insure because experience has shown that they are damaged less, less expensive to fix after a collision, or stolen less.

Auto insurance covers different aspects of damage and injury. The term "first party" means you and "third party" means someone else who was involved in a crash with your vehicle. The critical parts of your insurance are:

Liability (third party): This pays for damage or injury you or your vehicle may inflict on others. It is generally limited (in some cases to only $10,000 but may be several hundred thousand dollars) so that if you severely or fatally injure someone, the liability insurance will not be adequate to pay the costs. For minor or moderate damage or injury, insurance companies generally negotiate payments, but for major ones, there may be lawsuits.

Collision Damage (first party): This pays for crash damage to your own car when no other party is found to be at fault for the accident. If you lease your vehicle or have an outstanding loan on it, you will be required to have collision damage insurance.

Uninsured or Underinsured drivers: This pays your expenses when someone else is at fault, but lacks sufficient insurance or personal resources to pay for the damage or injury. The amount typically covers property damage, but may not cover serious injuries.

Comprehensive (first party): This covers the cost of some types of damage not related to crashes including theft.

Supplementary Insurance: Additional forms of insurance that may apply when auto insurance doesn't cover loss are health insurance, which may pay the cost of more serious injuries, life insurance which pays if you are killed in a crash and umbrella policy insurance which may pay liability costs beyond what is covered by your auto policy. An umbrella policy may be important if you want to protect assets such as savings, your house or business, or other major assets.

Shop Around: You can save hundreds of dollars by shopping around for insurance.

There are a number of factors that determine what coverage will cost you. A car's design can affect both the chances and severity of an accident. For example, a well-designed bumper, which few cars have, may escape damage in a low-speed crash. Some cars are easier to repair than others or may have less expensive parts. Cars with four doors tend to be damaged less than cars with two doors.

Other factors that affect your insurance costs include:

Your Annual Mileage: The more you drive, the more your vehicle will be "exposed" to a potential accident. Driving less

than 5,000 to 7,500 miles per year often gets a discount. Ask your insurer if they offer this option.

Where You Drive and Park: If you regularly drive and park in the city, you will most likely pay more than if you drive in rural areas. You may get a discount if you garage your car.

Youthful Drivers: Usually the highest premiums are paid by male drivers under the age of 25. Whether or not the under-25-year-old male is married also affects insurance rates. (Married males pay less.) As the driver gets older, and if he or she has good driving record, rates are lowered.

Insurance discounts and surcharges depend upon the way a vehicle is traditionally driven. Sports cars, for example, are usually surcharged due, in part, to the typical driving habits of their owners. Four-door sedans and station wagons generally merit discounts. Not all companies offer discounts or surcharges, and many cars receive neither. Some companies offer a discount or impose a surcharge on collision premiums only. Others apply discounts and surcharges on both collision and comprehensive coverage. Discounts and surcharges usually range from 10 to 30 percent. Remember that

REDUCING INSURANCE COSTS

one company may offer a discount on a particular car while another may not.

Major crashes are rare events for individuals, but more than 37,000 people are killed and double that number suffer serious injuries in crashes each year. In a very severe crash with major injury or death, the limits on first and third party auto insurance will be inadequate to cover the costs. NHTSA estimates that the economic cost of a fatality may range from several million to more than ten million dollars, and injuries such as quadriplegia and serious brain damage could easily have a lifetime cost of ten million dollars for each individual. If a crash is not deemed to be the fault of another motorist (such as with a single vehicle crash), your health insurance may cover the cost of your injuries, but is unlikely to cover such things as long term rehabilitation and loss of income.

Get Your Discounts: After you have shopped around and found the best deal by comparing the costs of different coverages, be sure you get all the discounts you are entitled to.

Most insurance companies offer discounts of 5 to 30 percent on various parts of your insurance bill. Ask your insurance company for a complete list of the discounts that it offers. These can vary by company and from state to state.

Here are some of the most common insurance discounts:

Driver Education/Defensive Driving Courses: Discounts for completing a state-approved driver education course can mean a $40 reduction in the cost of coverage. Discounts of 5 to 15 percent are available in some states to those who complete a defensive driving course.

Good Student Discounts of up to 25 percent for full-time high school or college students who are in the upper 20 percent of their class, on the dean's list, or have a B or better grade point average.

Good Driver Discounts are available to drivers with an accident and violation-free record, (or no incidents in the past 3 years).

Mature Driver Credit: Drivers ages 50 and older may qualify for up to a 10 percent discount or a lower price bracket.

Sole Female Driver: Some companies offer discounts of 10 percent for females, ages 30 to 64, who are the only driver in a household.

Non-Drinkers and Non-Smokers: A few companies offer incentives ranging from 10–25 percent to those who abstain.

Farmer Discounts: Many companies offer farmers either a 10 to 30 percent discount or a lower price bracket.

Car Pooling: Commuters sharing driving may qualify for discounts of 5 to 25 percent or a lower price bracket.

Children away at school don't drive the family car very often, so if they're on your policy and they're at school, let your company know. If you insure them separately,

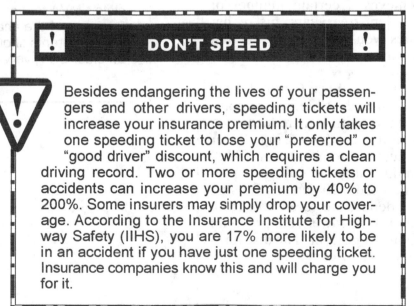

! DON'T SPEED !

Besides endangering the lives of your passengers and other drivers, speeding tickets will increase your insurance premium. It only takes one speeding ticket to lose your "preferred" or "good driver" discount, which requires a clean driving record. Two or more speeding tickets or accidents can increase your premium by 40% to 200%. Some insurers may simply drop your coverage. According to the Insurance Institute for Highway Safety (IIHS), you are 17% more likely to be in an accident if you have just one speeding ticket. Insurance companies know this and will charge you for it.

discounts of 10–40 percent or a lower price bracket are available.

Desirable Cars: Premiums are usually much higher for cars that are the favorite target of thieves.

Anti-Theft Device Credits: Discounts of 5-15 percent are offered in some states for cars equipped with a hood lock and an alarm or a disabling device (active or passive) that prevents the car from being started without a key.

Multi-policy and Multicar Policy Discount: Some companies offer discounts of up to 10–20 percent for insuring your home and auto with the same company, or more than one car.

First Accident Allowance: Some insurers offer a "first accident allowance," which guarantees that if a customer achieves a certain number of accident-free years, his or her rates won't go up after the first at-fault accident.

Deductibles: Opting for the largest deductible you're comfortable with will reduce your premiums. Increasing your deductible to $500 from $200 could cut your collision premium about 20 percent. Raising the deductible to $1,000 from $200 could lower your premium about 45 percent. The discounts may vary by company.

Collision Coverage: The older the car, the less the need for collision insurance. Consider dropping collision insurance entirely on an older car. Regardless of how much coverage you carry, the insurance company will only pay up to the car's "book value." For example, if your car requires $1,000 in repairs, but its "book value" is only $500, the insurance company is required to pay only $500.

Organizations: If you are a member of AARP, AAA, the military, a union, a professional group, an alumni association, or similar organization, you may be able to get lower cost insurance or a discount.

YOUNG DRIVERS

TIP

Each year, teenagers account for about 15 percent of highway deaths. According to the Insurance Institute for Highway Safety (IIHS), the highest driver death rate per 100,000 people is among 18-year-olds. Parents need to make sure their children are fully prepared to be competent, safe drivers before letting them out on the road. All states issue learner's permits. However, only 35 states and the District of Columbia require permits before getting a driver's license. It isn't difficult for teenagers to get a license and only 14 states prohibit teenagers from driving during night and early morning. Call your state's MVA for young driver laws.

Because of the challenges in learning how to drive safely, parents should not to let their teenagers drive an older SUV, very small car, or one without airbags.

Americans spend billions of dollars on vehicle repairs every year. While many of those repairs are satisfactory, there are times when getting your vehicle fixed can be a very difficult process. In fact, vehicle defects and repairs are the number one cause of consumer complaints, according to the Federal Trade Commission. This chapter is designed to help you if you have a complaint, whether it's for a new vehicle still under warranty or for one you've had for years. In addition, we offer a guide to arbitration, the names and addresses of consumer groups, federal agencies, and the manufacturers themselves. Finally, we tell you how to take the important step of registering your complaint, particularly if it involves safety, with the U.S. Department of Transportation.

No matter what your complaint, keep accurate records. Copies of the following items are indispensable in helping to resolve your problems:

☑ your original purchase papers

☑ your service invoices

☑ bills you have paid

☑ letters or emails you have written to the manufacturer or the repair facility owner

☑ written repair estimates from your independent mechanic.

☑ notes on discussion with company representatives including names and dates.

RESOLVING COMPLAINTS

Here are some basic steps to help you resolve your problem:

1 First, return your vehicle to the repair facility that did the work. Bring a written list of the problems and make sure that you keep a copy of the list. Give the repair facility a reasonable opportunity to examine your vehicle and attempt to fix it. Speak directly to the service manager (not to the service writer who wrote up your repair order), and ask him or her to test drive the vehicle with you so that you can point out the problem.

2 If that doesn't resolve the problem, take the vehicle to a diagnostic center or another mechanic for an independent examination. This may cost $45 to $60. Get a written statement defining the problem and outlining how it may be fixed. Give your repair shop a copy. If your vehicle is under warranty, do not allow any warranty repair by an independent mechanic; you may not be reimbursed by the manufacturer.

3 If your repair shop does not respond to the independent assessment, present your problem to an arbitration panel. These panels hear both sides of the story and try to come to a resolution.

If the problem is with a new vehicle dealer, or if you feel that the manufacturer is responsible, you may be able to use one of the manufacturer's arbitration programs.

If the problem is solely with an independent dealer, a local Better Business Bureau (BBB) may be able to mediate your complaint. It may also offer an arbitration hearing. In any case, the BBB should enter your complaint into its files on that establishment.

When contacting any arbitration program, determine how long the process takes, who makes the final decision, whether you are bound by that decision, and whether the program handles all problems or only warranty complaints.

Beware of "binding arbitration" because you give up your right to later pursue legal action.

4 If there are no arbitration programs in your area, contact private consumer groups, local government agencies, or your local "action line" newspaper columnist, newspaper editor, or radio/TV broadcaster. A phone call or letter from them may persuade a repair facility to take action. Send a copy of your letter to the repair shop.

5 One of your last resorts is to bring a lawsuit against the dealer, manufacturer, or repair facility in small claims court. The fee for filing such an action is usually small, and you generally act as your own attorney, saving attorney's fees. There is a monetary limit on the amount you can claim, which varies from state to state. Your local consumer affairs office, state attorney general's office, or the clerk of the court can tell you how to file such a suit.

6 Finally, talk with an attorney. It's best to select an attorney who is familiar with handling automotive problems and has no ties to the local business community. Lawyer referral services can provide names of attorneys who deal with automobile problems. If you can't afford an attorney, contact the Legal Aid Society.

WARRANTY COMPLAINTS

If your vehicle is under warranty or you are having problems with a factory-authorized dealership, here are some guidelines:

1 Have the warranty available to show the dealer. Make sure you call the problem to the dealer's attention before the end of the warranty period.

2 If you are still dissatisfied after giving the dealer a reasonable opportunity to fix your vehicle, contact the manufacturer's representative (also called the zone representative) in your area. This person can authorize the dealer to make repairs or take other steps to resolve the dispute. Your dealer will have your zone representative's name and telephone number. Explain the problem and ask for a meeting and a personal inspection of your vehicle.

3 If you can't get satisfaction from the zone representative, call or write the manufacturer's owner relations department. Your owner's manual contains this phone number and address. In each case, as you move up the chain, indicate the steps you have already taken and keep careful records of your efforts.

4 Your next option is to present your problem to a complaint handling arbitration program. Beware of "binding arbitration" because you give up your right to later pursue legal action and beware of arbitrators selected by a manufacturer, dealer or repair shop.

If you complain of a problem during the warranty period, you have a right to have the problem fixed even after the warranty runs out. If your warranty has not been honored, you may be able to "revoke acceptance," which means that you return the vehicle to the dealer. If you are successful, you may be entitled to a replacement vehicle or to a full refund of the purchase price and reimbursement of legal fees under the Magnuson-Moss Warranty Act. Or, if you are covered by one of the state lemon laws, you may be able to return the vehicle and receive a refund or replacement from the manufacturer.

NEED HELP?

If you need assistance with a vehicle safety issue or repair problem, the Center for Auto Safety is here to help! The Center collects consumer complaints in an effort to force automakers and the government to address safety defects and to prevent consumers from being ripped off on repairs. To file a complaint with the Center, visit www.autosafety.org/submit-complaint and provide as much detail as you can on your vehicle problem. To stay up to date on Center for Auto Safety vehicle safety activities, sign up by visiting www.autosafety.org and clicking on the "Stay Informed" button.

VEHICLE SAFETY HOT LINE: 800-424-9393
TTY FOR HEARING IMPAIRED: 800-424-9153
WWW.SAFERCAR.GOV

The toll-free Auto Safety Hot Line can provide information on recalls, record information about safety problems, and refer you to the appropriate government experts on other vehicle related problems. You can even have recall information mailed to you within 24 hours of your call at no charge. Most importantly, you can call the hot line to report safety problems which will become part of the National Highway - Traffic Safety Administration's complaint database. If you have access to the internet, www.safercar.gov is a more efficient way to register complaints and obtain recall and safety information. You can also look up the individual complaints about a particular vehicle.

Thanks to the efforts of the Center for Auto Safety, we are able to provide you with a car by car index of vehicle complaints on file with the National Highway Traffic Safety Administration (NHTSA). Each year, thousands of Americans file online, or call the government, to register complaints about their vehicles.

The Car Book Complaint Index is the result of our analysis of these complaints. It is based on a ratio of the number of complaints for each vehicle to the sales of that vehicle. In order to predict the expected complaint performance of the 2019 models, we have examined the complaint history of that car's series. The term series refers to the fact that when a manufacturer introduces a new model, that vehicle remains essentially unchanged, on average, for four to six years. For example, the Ford Explorer was redesigned in 2011 and remains essentially the same car for 2019. As such, we have compiled the complaint experience for that series in order to give you some information to use in deciding which car to buy. For vehicles introduced or significantly changed in 2019, we do not yet have enough data to develop a complaint index.

The following table presents the projected best and worst complaint ratings for the 2019 models for which we can develop ratings. Higher index numbers mean the vehicle generated a greater number of complaints. Lower numbers indicate fewer complaints.

2019 PROJECTED COMPLAINT INDEX

THE BEST	INDEX*
Audi A5	385
Lexus RC	452
Toyota Corolla iM	493
Genesis G80	671
Cadillac Escalade ESV	683
BMW X3	715
Infiniti QX50	801
BMW 2 Series	889
Audi Q3	927
Chevrolet Cruze	1001
Mazda 3	1051
Lexus RX	1215
Porsche Macan	1217
Toyota Highlander	1259
Lexus IS	1263
Buick Encore	1279
Toyota Corolla	1289
Chevrolet Trax	1301
Chevrolet Malibu	1342
Nissan Rogue	1356
Mazda CX-9	1453

THE WORST	INDEX*
Chevrolet Volt	>20,000
Hyundai Santa Fe	>20,000
Chrysler Pacifica	>20,000
Tesla Model S	>20,000
Hyundai Tucson	14,561
Ford Fusion Energi	12,242
Jeep Cherokee	11,755
Dodge Journey	9,852
Mercedes-Benz GLC	9,674
Mercedes-Benz CLA	9,329
Dodge Durango	9,143
Jeep Grand Cherokee	8,796
Chevrolet Bolt	8,425
Ford Fiesta	8,124
Volvo XC90	7,453
Jeep Renegade	7,415
Ford Explorer	7,382
Nissan Titan	7,021
Tesla Model X	6,952
Fiat 500	6,512

*IMPORTANT NOTE: The numbers represent relative index scores, not the number of complaints received. The complaint index score considers sales volume and years on the road. Lower index numbers are better. We capped the complaint index at 20,000 for excessively high complaint indices.

Consumer Groups and Government Contacts

Advocates for Highway and Auto Safety
750 First St., NE, Suite 1130
Washington, DC 20002
(202) 408-1711/408-1699 fax
www.saferoads.org
An alliance of consumer, health and safety groups and insurance companies. A great resource for state laws governing auto safety. A leading organization fighting for safer cars before the U.S. Congress and the National Highway Traffic Safety Administration.

Consumer Action
1170 Market St., Suite 500
San Francisco, CA 94102
(415) 777-9635
www.consumer-action.org
Complaint handling and advocacy related to consumer rights. A great resource for non-English consumer information.

Consumers for Auto Reliability and Safety
1303 J St., Suite 270
Sacramento, CA 95814
(530) 759-9440
www.carconsumers.org
Auto safety, airbags, and lemon laws. A leader in exposing the sale and rental of cars with open safety recalls.

KIDS AND CARS
(816) 216-7085
www.kidsandcars.org
email@kidsandcars.org
Safety and advocacy related to protecting children in and around motor vehicles. They lead the effort to require already available technology to prevent the death of unattended children in hot cars or from tragic back over accidents.

SafetyBelt Safe, U.S.A.
P.O. Box 553
Altadena, CA 91003
(800) 745-SAFE
www.carseat.org
stombrella@carseat.org
Excellent information and training on child safety seats and safety belt usage. The majority of parents do not use child seats correctly.

National Highway Traffic Safety Administration
1200 New Jersey Ave., SE, West Bldg.
Washington, DC 20590
(888) 327-4236
www.nhtsa.gov
www.safercar.gov
NHTSA issues safety and fuel economy standards for new motor vehicles; investigates safety defects and enforces recall of defective vehicles and equipment; conducts research and demonstration programs on vehicle safety, fuel economy, driver safety, and automobile inspection and repair; provides grants for state highway safety programs in areas such as police traffic services, driver education and licensing, emergency medical services, pedestrian safety, and alcohol abuse.
In addition with the EPA, they are in charge of setting fuel economy standards. They have a huge job, are woefully underfunded and need consumers to support their efforts in Congress.

Environmental Protection Agency
1200 Pennsylvania Ave., NW
Washington, DC 20460
(202) 272-0167/www.epa.gov
www.fueleconomy.gov
EPA's responsibilities include setting and enforcing air and noise emission standards for motor vehicles and measuring fuel economy in new vehicles (EPA Fuel Economy Guide).

Federal Trade Commission
600 Pennsylvania Ave., NW
Washington, DC 20580
(202) 326-2222
www.ftc.gov
The FTC regulates advertising, credit practices, marketing abuses, and professional services and ensures that products are properly labeled (as in fuel economy ratings). The commission covers unfair or deceptive trade practices in motor vehicle sales and repairs, as well as non-safety defects.

U.S. Department of Justice
Civil Division
950 Pennsylvania Ave., NW
Washington, DC 20530
(202) 307-0066
www.justice.gov/civil
feedback@doj.gov
The DOJ enforces federal law that requires manufacturers to label new automobiles and forbids removal or alteration of labels before delivery to consumers. Labels must contain make, model, vehicle identification number, dealer's name, suggested base price, manufacturer option costs, and manufacturer's suggested retail price.

AUTOMOBILE MANUFACTURERS

Acura (Division of Honda)
John Ikeda, Vice President-General
Manager
See Honda for address
Customer Relations: 800-382-2238

Audi (Division of Volkswagen)
Scott Keogh, President
See Volkswagen for address
Customer Relations: 800-822-2834

BMW
Bernhard Kuhnt, President and CEO
300 Chestnut Ridge Road
Woodcliff Lake, NJ 07677-7731
Customer Relations: 800-831-1117

Buick (Division of General Motors)
P.O. Box 33136
Detroit, MI 48232-5136
Customer Relations: 800-521-7300

Cadillac (Division of General Motors)
P.O. Box 33169
Detroit, MI 48232-5169
Customer Relations: 800-458-8006

Chevrolet (Division of General Motors)
P.O. Box 33136
Detroit, MI 48323-5136
Customer Relations: 800-222-1020

Chrysler (Chrysler, Dodge, Fiat, Jeep, Ram)
Michael Manley, CEO
1000 Chrysler Drive
Auburn Hills, MI 48326
Customer Relations: 800-247-9753

Dodge (Division of Chrysler)
P.O. Box 21-8004
Auburn Hills, MI 48321-8004
Customer Relations: 800-423-6343

Fiat (Division of Chrysler)
P.O. Box 21-8004
Auburn Hills, MI 48321-8004
Customer Relations: 888-242-6342

Ford (Ford, Lincoln)
James Hackett, President and CEO
P.O. Box 6248
Dearborn, MI 48126
Customer Relations 800-392-3673

General Motors (Buick, Cadillac, Chev., GMC)
Mary Barra, Chairman and CEO
300 Renaisance Center
Detorit, MI 48265

Genesis (Division of Hyundai)
Erwin Raphael, General Manager
10550 Talbert Ave.
Fountain Valley, CA 92708
Customer Relations: 844-340-9741

GMC (Division of General Motors)
P.O. Box 33172
Detroit, MI 48232
Customer Relations: 800-462-8782

Honda (Honda, Acura)
Toshiaki Mikoshiba, President and CEO
1919 Torrance Blvd.
Torrance, CA 90501
Customer Relations: 800-999-1009

Hyundai (Hyundai, Genesis)
Kyung Soo Lee, President and CEO
P.O. Box 20850
Fountain Valley, CA 92728-0850
Customer Relations: 800-633-5151
Email: consumeraffairs@hmausa.com

Infiniti (Division of Nissan)
Roland Krueger, President
See Nissan for address
Customer Relations: 800-662-6200

Jaguar, Land Rover
Joachim Eberhardt, President
555 MacArthur Blvd.
Mahwah, NJ 07430
Jaguar Customer Relations: 800-452-4827
Land Rover Cust. Relations: 800-637-6837

Jeep (Division of Chrysler)
P.O. Box 21-8004
Auburn Hills, MI 48321-8004
Customer Relations: 877-426-5337

Kia
SeungKyu Yoon, President and CEO
P.O. Box 52410
Irvine, CA 92619-2410
Customer Relations: 800-333-4542

Lexus (Division of Toyota)
Jeff Bracken, Vice President and General
Manager
P.O. Box 2991-Mail Drop L201
Torrance, CA 90509-2991
Customer Relations: 800-255-3987

Lincoln (Division of Ford)
Joy Falotico, President
See Ford for address
Customer Relations: 800-521-4140

Mazda
Masahiro Moro, President and CEO
P.O. Box 19734
Irvine, CA 92623-9734
Customer Relations: 800-222-5500

Mercedes-Benz
Dietmar Exler, President and CEO
1 Mercedes Drive
Montvale, NJ 07645
Customer Relations 800-367-6372

Mini (Division of BMW)
Thomas Felbermair, Vice President
See BMW for address
Customer Relations: 866-275-6464

Mitsubishi
Fred Diaz, President and CEO
P.O. Box 6400
Cypress, CA 90630-9998
Customer Reloations: 800-648-7820

Nissan
Hiroto Saikawa, President and CEO
P.O. Box 685003
Franklin, TN 37068-5003
Customer Relations: 800-647-7261

Porsche
Klaus Zellmer, President and CEO
980 Hammond Dr., Suite 1000
Atlanta, GA 30328
Customer Relations: 800-767-7243

Ram (Division of Chrysler)
P.O. Box 21-8007
Auburn Hills, MI 48321-8004
Customer Relations: 866-726-4636

Smart (Division of Mercedes-Benz)
Bart Herring, General Manager
1 Mercedes Drive
Montvale, NJ 07645
Customer Relations 800-762-2466

Subaru
Thomas Doll, President & CEO
One Subaru Drive
Camden, NJ 08103
Customer Relations: 800-782-2783

Telsa
Elon Musk, CEO
3500 Deer Creek
Palo Alto, CA 94304
Customer Relations: 877-798-3752

Toyota (Toyota, Lexus)
Jim Lentz, President and CEO
19001 South Western Ave. Dept. WC11
Torrance, CA 90501
Customer Relations: 800-331-4331

Volkswagen
Hinrich Woebcken, President and CEO
2200 Ferdinand Porsche Dr.
Herndon, VA 20171
Customer Relations: 800-822-8987

Volvo
Anders Gustafsson, President and CEO
One Volvo Drive
P.O. Box 914
Rockleigh, NJ 07647
Customer Relations: 800-458-1552

LEMON LAWS

Sometimes, despite our being an educated shopper, we buy a new vehicle that just doesn't work right. There may be little problem after little problem, or perhaps one big problem that the dealer cannot seem to fix. Because of the "sour" taste that such vehicles leave in the mouths of consumers who buy them, these vehicles are known as "lemons."

In the past, it was difficult to obtain a refund or replacement if a vehicle was a lemon. The burden of proof was left to the consumer. Because it is hard to define exactly what constitutes a lemon, many lemon owners were unable to win a case against a manufacturer. And when they won, consumers had to pay for their attorneys giving them less than if they had traded in their lemon.

Thanks to the urging of the Center for Auto Safety "Lemon Laws" have been passed by all states, making help available when consumers get stuck with a lemon. Although there are some important state-to-state varia-tions, all of the laws have simi-larities: They establish a period of coverage, usually two years from delivery or the written warranty period, whichever is shorter; they may require some form of non-court arbitration; and most impor-tantly they define what qualifies as a lemon. In most states a new car, truck, or van is "presumed" to be a lemon when it has been taken back to the shop 3 to 4 times for the same problem or is out of service for a total of 30 days dur-ing the covered period. This time does not mean consecutive days and can be for different prob-lems. Twenty states have safety lemon provisions which presume a vehicle is a lemon after only 1 to 2 repairs of a defect likely to cause death or serious injury. Be sure to keep careful records of your repairs since some states now require only one of the repairs to be within the specified time period. Thirty-three states provide for the award of attorney fees to consumers, with the other 17 relying on the Federal lemon law (the Magnuson-Moss War-ranty Act) for fees. A vehicle may be covered by the federal lemon law even though it doesn't meet the specific state requirements.

Specific information about your state's lemon law can be obtained at the Center for Auto Safety's Lemon Law Library, which has helpful links to state laws and information from your state attorney general or con-sumer protection office. The Center's Lemon Law Library may be found at http://www.auto-safety.org/lemon-law-library.

The following table offers a general description of the Lemon Law in every state and what you need to do to set it in motion (Notification/Trigger). We indi-cate where state-run arbitration programs are available. State-run programs are the best type of arbitration. Be aware, a few state lemon laws are so bad con-sumers should also consider rely-ing on the Federal lemon law and state contract law. We have marked these bad laws with a ☒ while the best laws have a ☑.

Alabama	Qualification: 3 unsuccessful repairs or 30 calendar days within shorter of 24 months or 24,000 miles, provided 1 repair attempt or 1 day out of service is within shorter of 1 year or 12,000 miles. Notice/Trigger: Certified mail to manufacturer + opportunity for final repair attempt within 14 calendar days.
Alaska	Qualification: 3 unsuccessful repairs or 30 business days out of service within shorter of 1 year or warranty. Notice/Trigger: Certified mail to manufacturer + dealer (or repair agent) that problem has not been corrected in reasonable number of attempts + refund or replacement demanded within 60 days. Manufacturer has 30 calendar days for final repair attempt.
Arizona	Qualification: 4 unsuccessful repairs or 30 calendar days out of service within warranty period or shorter of 2 years or 24,000 miles. Notice/Trigger: Written notice + opportunity to repair to manufacturer.
Arkansas	Qualification: 3 unsuccessful repairs, 5 total repairs of any nonconformity, or 1 unsuc-cessful repair of problem likely to cause death or serious bodily injury within longer of 24 months or 24,000 miles. Notice/Trigger: Certified or registered mail to manufacturer who has 10 days to notify consumer of repair facility. Facility has 10 days to repair.

L—Law specifically applies to leased vehicles; S-C—State has certified guidelines for arbitration; S-R—State-run arbitration mechanism available

California	Qualification: 4 repair attempts or 30 calendar days out of service or 2 repair attempts for defect likely to cause death or serious bodily injury within shorter of 18 months or 18,000 miles, or "reasonable" number of attempts during entire express warranty period. Notice/Trigger: Direct written notice to manufacturer at address clearly specified in owner's manual. Covers small businesses with up to 5 vehicles under 10,000 pounds GVWR.
Colorado ☒ WORST	Qualification: 4 unsuccessful repairs or 30 business days out of service within shorter of 1 year or warranty. Notice/Trigger: Prior certified mail notice + opportunity to repair for manufacturer.
Connecticut	Qualification: 4 unsuccessful repairs or 30 calendar days out of service within shorter of 2 years or 24,000 miles, or 2 unsuccessful repairs of problem likely to cause death or serious bodily injury within warranty period or 1 year. Notice/Trigger: Report t o manufacturer, agent, or dealer. Written notice to manufacturer only if required in owner's manual or warranty. S-R
Delaware	Qualification: 4 unsuccessful repairs or 30 calendar days out of service within shorter of 1 year or warranty. Notice/Trigger: Written notice + opportunity to repair to manufacturer.
D.C.	Qualification: 4 unsuccessful repairs or 30 calendar days out of service or 1 unsuccessful repair of safety-related defect, within shorter of 2 years or 18,000 miles. Notice/Trigger: Report to manufacturer, agent, or dealer.
Florida	Qualification: 3 unsuccessful repairs or 15 calendar days within 24 months from delivery. Notice/Trigger: Certified or express mail notice to manufacturer who has 10 days to notify consumer of repair facility plus 10 more calendar day s for final repair attempt after delivery to designated dealer. S-R
Georgia	Qualification: 1 unsuccessful repair of serious safety defect or 3 unsuccessful repair attempts or 30 calendar days out of service within shorter of 24,000 miles or 24 months. Notification/Trigger: Overnight or certified mail notice return receipt requested. Manufacturer has 7 days to notify consumer of re pair facility & consumer has 14 days from manufacturer receipt of original notice to deliver vehicle to repair facility. Facility has 28 calendar days from manufacturer receipt of original notice to repair. State-run arbitration mechanism available.
Hawaii ☑ BEST	Qualification: 3 unsuccessful repair attempts, or 1 unsuccessful repair attempt of defect likely to cause death or serious bodily injury, or out of service for total of 30 days within shorter of 2 years or 24,000 miles. Notice/Trigger: Written notice + opportunity to repair to manufacturer. S-R
Idaho	Qualification: 4 repair attempts or 30 business days out of service within shorter of 2 years or 24,000 miles, or 1 repair of complete failure of braking or steering likely to cause death or serious bodily injury. Notice/ Trigger: Written notice to manufacturer or dealer + one opportunity to repair to manufacturer. S-R.
Illinois ☒ WORST	Qualification: 4 unsuccessful repairs or 30 business days out of service within shorter of 1 yea r or 12,000 miles. Notice/Trigger: Written notice + opportunity to repair to manufacturer.
Indiana	Qualification: 4 unsuccessful repairs or 30 business days out of service within shorter of 18 months or 18,000 miles. Notice/Trigger: Written notice to manufacturer only if required in the warranty.
Iowa	Qualification: 3 unsuccessful repairs, or 1 unsuccessful repair of nonconformity likely to cause death or serious bodily injury, or 30 calendar days out of service within shorter of 2 years or 24,000 miles. Notice/Trigger: Certified registered mail + final opportunity to repair within 10 calendar days of receipt of notice to manufacturer.

Kansas	Qualification: 4 unsuccessful repairs or 30 calendar days out of service or 10 total repairs within shorter of 1 year or warranty. Notice/Trigger: Actual notice to manufacturer.
Kentucky	Qualification: 4 unsuccessful repairs or 30 calendar days out of service within shorter of 1 year or 12,000 miles. Notice/Trigger: Written notice to manufacturer.
Louisiana **[X] WORST**	Qualification: 4 unsuccessful repairs or 90 calendar days out of service within shorter of 1 year or warranty. Notice/Trigger: Report to manufacturer or dealer.
Maine	Qualification: 3 unsuccessful repairs (or 1 unsuccessful repair of serious failure of brakes or steering) or 15 business days out of service within shorter of warranty or 3 years or 18,000 miles. Applies to vehicles within first 18,000 miles or 3 years regardless of whether claimant is original owner. Notice/Trigger: Written notice to manufacturer or dealer. Manufacturer has 7 business days after receipt for final repair attempt. S-R
Maryland	Qualification: 4 unsuccessful repairs, 30 calendar days out of service or 1 unsuccessful repair of braking or steering system within shorter of 15 months or 15,000 miles. Notice/Trigger: Certified mail return receipt requested + opportunity to repair within 30 calendar days of receipt of notice to manufacturer or factory branch.
Massachusetts	Qualification: 3 unsuccessful repairs or 10 business days out of service within shorter of 1 year or 15,000 miles. Notice/Trigger: Notice to manufacturer or dealer who has 7 business days to attempt final repair. S-R
Michigan	Qualification: 4 unsuccessful repairs within 2 years from date of first unsuccessful repair or 30 calendar days within shorter of 1 year or warranty. Notice/Trigger: Certified mail return receipt requested to manufacturer who has 5 business days to repair after delivery. Consumer may notify manufacturer after third repair attempt.
Minnesota	Qualification: 4 unsuccessful repairs or 30 business days or 1 unsuccessful repair of total braking or steering loss likely to cause death or serious bodily injury within shorter of 2 years or warranty. Notice/Trigger: Written notice + opportunity to repair to manufacturer, agent, or dealer.
Mississippi	Qualification: 3 unsuccessful repairs or 15 business days out of service within shorter of 1 year or warranty. Notice/Trigger: Written notice to manufacturer who has 10 business days to repair after delivery to designated dealer.
Missouri **[X] WORST**	Qualification: 4 unsuccessful repairs or 30 business days out of service within shorter of 1 year or warranty. Notice/Trigger: Written notice to manufacturer who has 10 calendar days to repair after delivery to designated dealer.
Montana	Qualification: 4 unsuccessful repairs or 30 business days out of service after notice within shorter of 2 years or 18,000 miles. Notice/Trigger: Written notice + opportunity to repair to manufacturer. S-R
Nebraska	Qualification: 4 unsuccessful repairs or 40 calendar days out of service within shorter of 1 year or warranty. Notice/Trigger: Certified mail + opportunity to repair to manufacturer.
Nevada	Qualification: 4 unsuccessful repairs or 30 calendar days out of service within shorter of 1 year or warranty. Notice/Trigger: Written notice to manufacturer.
New Hampshire	Qualification: 3 unsuccessful repairs by same dealer or 30 business days out of service within warranty. Notice/Trigger: Report to manufacturer, distributor, agent, or dealer (on forms provided by manufacturer) + final opportunity to repair before arbitration. S-R

50

L—Law specifically applies to leased vehicles; S-C—State has certified guidelines for arbitration; S-R—State-run arbitration mechanism available

New Jersey ☑ BEST	Qualification: 3 Unsuccessful repairs or 20 calendar days out of service within shorter of 2 years or 24,000 miles; or 1 unsuccessful repair of a serious safety defect likely to cause death or serious bodily injury. Notice/Trigger: Certified mail notice, return receipt requested to manufacturer who has 10 days to repair. Consumer may notify manufacturer at any time after the second repair attempt, or after the first repair attempt in the case of a serious safety defect.
New Mexico	Qualification: 4 unsuccessful repairs or 30 business days out of service within shorter of 1 year or warranty. Notice/Trigger: Written notice + opportunity to repair to manufacturer, agent, or dealer.
New York ☑ BEST	Qualification: 4 unsuccessful repairs or 30 calendar days out of service within shorter of 2 years or 18,000 miles. Notice/Trigger: Notice to manufacturer, agent, or dealer.
North Carolina	Qualification: 4 unsuccessful repairs within shorter of 24 months, 24,000 miles or warranty or 20 business days out of service during any 12 month period of warranty. Notice/Trigger: Written notice to manufacturer + opportunity to repair within 15 calendar days of receipt only if required in warranty or owner's manual.
North Dakota ☒ WORST	Qualification: 3 unsuccessful repairs or 30 business days out of service within shorter of 1 year or warranty. Notice/Trigger: Direct written notice + opportunity to repair to manufacturer. (Manufacturer's informal arbitration process serves as prerequisite to consumer refund or replacement.)
Ohio ☑ BEST	Qualification: 3 unsuccessful repairs of same nonconformity, 30 calendar days out of service, 8 total repairs of any nonconformity, or 1 unsuccessful repair of problem likely to cause death or serious bodily injury within shorter of 1 year or 18,000 miles. Notice/Trigger: Report to manufacturer, its agent, or dealer.
Oklahoma	Qualification: 4 unsuccessful repairs or 30 calendar days out of service within shorter of 1 year or warranty Notice/Trigger: Written notice + opportunity to repair to manufacturer.
Oregon	Qualification: 3 unsuccessful repairs or 30 business days within shorter of 2 years or 24,000 miles, or 1 unsuccessful repair of a serious safety defect likely to cause death or injury. Notice/Trigger: Direct written notice + opportunity to repair to manufacturer.
Pennsylvania	Qualification: 3 unsuccessful repairs or 30 calendar days within shorter of 1 year, 12,000 miles, or warranty. Notice/Trigger: Delivery to authorized service + repair facility. If delivery impossible, written notice to manufacturer or its repair facility obligates them to pay for delivery.
Rhode Island ☑ BEST	Qualification: 4 unsuccessful repairs or 30 calendar days out of service within shorter of 1 year or 15,000 miles. Notice/Trigger: Report to dealer or manufacturer who has 7 days for final repair opportunity.
South Carolina	Qualification: 3 unsuccessful repairs or 30 calendar days out of service within shorter of 1 year or 12,000 miles. Notice/Trigger: Certified mail + opportunity to repair (not more than 10 business days) to manufacturer only if manufacturer informed consumer of such at time of sale.

L—Law specifically applies to leased vehicles; S-C—State has certified guidelines for arbitration; S-R—State-run arbitration mechanism available

South Dakota	Qualification: 4 unsuccessful repairs, 1 of which occurred during shorter of 1 year or 12,000 miles, or 30 calendar days out of service during shorter of 24 months or 24,000 miles. Notice/Trigger: Certified mail to manufacturer + final opportunity to repair + 7 calendar days to notify consumer of repair facility.
Tennessee	Qualification: 4 unsuccessful repairs or 30 calendar days out of service within shorter of 1 year or warranty. Notice/Trigger: Certified mail notice to manufacturer + final opportunity to repair within 10 calendar days.
Texas	Qualification: 4 unsuccessful repair attempts, 30 days out of service, 2 unsuccessful repair attempts of a serious safety hazard within shorter of manufacturer warranty, 24 months or 24,000 miles. Notice/Trigger: Written notice to manufacturer. S-R
Utah	Qualification: 4 unsuccessful repairs or 30 business days out of service within shorter of 1 year or warranty. Notice/Trigger: Report to manufacturer, agent, or dealer. S-R
Vermont	Qualification: 3 unsuccessful repairs when at least first repair was within warranty, or 30 calendar days out of service within warranty. Notice/Trigger: Written notice to manufacturer (on provided forms) after third repair attempt, or 30 days. Arbitration must be held within 45 days after notice, during which time manufacturer has 1 final repair. S-R Note: Repairs must be done by same authorized agent or dealer, unless consumer shows good cause for taking vehicle to different agent or dealer.
Virginia	Qualification: 3 unsuccessful repairs, or 1 repair attempt of serious safety defect, or 30 calendar days out of service within 18 months. Notice/Trigger: Written notice to manufacturer. If 3 unsuccessful repairs or 30 days already exhausted before notice, manufacturer has 1 more repair attempt not to exceed 15 days.
Washington ☑ BEST	Qualification: 4 unsuccessful repairs, 30 calendar days out of service (15 during warranty period), or 2 repairs of serious safety defects, first reported within shorter of warranty or 24 months or 24,000 miles. One repair attempt + 15 of 30 days must fall within manufacturer's express warranty of at least 1 year of 12,000 miles. Notice/ Trigger: Written notice to manufacturer. S-R Note: Consumer should receive replacement or refund within 40 calendar days of request.
West Virginia	Qualification: 3 unsuccessful repairs or 30 calendar days out o f service or 1 unsuccessful repair of problem likely to cause death or serious bodily injury within shorter of 1 year or warranty. Notice/Trigger: Written notice + opportunity to repair to manufacturer.
Wisconsin	Qualification: 4 unsuccessful repairs or 30 calendar days out of service within shorter of 1 year or warranty. Notice/Trigger: Report to manufacturer or dealer. Note: Consumer should receive replacement or refund within 30 calendar days after offer to return title.
Wyoming	Qualification: 3 unsuccessful repairs or 30 business days out of service within 1 year. Notice/Trigger: Direct written notice + opportunity to repair to manufacturer. S-R

L—Law specifically applies to leased vehicles; S-C—State has certified guidelines for arbitration; S-R—State-run arbitration mechanism available

5 BASIC STEPS TO CAR BUYING

Buying a car means matching wits with a seasoned professional. But if you know what to expect, you'll have a much better chance of getting a really good deal!

There's no question that buying a car can be an intimidating experience. But it doesn't have to be. First of all, you have in your hands all of the information you need to make an informed choice. Secondly, if you approach the purchase logically, you'll always maintain control of the decision. Start with the following basic steps:

1 Consider your needs and how you will use a vehicle, and based on that, narrow your choice down to a particular class of car—sports, station wagon, minivan, sedan, large luxury, SUV, truck, or economy car. These are general classifications and some cars may fit into more than one category. In most cases, *The Car Book* presents the vehicles by size class.

2 Determine what features are really important to you. Most buyers consider safety on the top of their list, which is why the "Safety Chapter" is right up front in *The Car Book*. Specifically items such as blind spot detection, automatic braking, and lane keeping assist along with airbags, power options, the general size, fuel economy, number of passengers, as well as "hidden" elements such as maintenance and insurance costs, should be considered at this stage in your selection process.

3 Find three or four cars that meet the needs you outlined above and your pocketbook. It's important not to narrow your choice down to one car because then you lose all your bargaining power in the showroom. (Why? Because you might lose the psychological ability to walk away from a bad deal!) In fact, because cars today are more similar than dissimilar, it's not hard to keep three or four choices in mind. In the "Car Rating Pages" in the back of the book, we suggest some competitive choices for your consideration. For example, if you are interested in the Honda Accord, you should also consider the Toyota Camry, Ford Fusion, and Hyundai Sonata.

4 Make sure you take a good, long test drive. The biggest car buying mistake most of us make is to overlook those nagging problems that seem to surface only after we've brought the car home. Spend at least an hour driving the car and preferably without a salesperson. If a dealership won't allow you to test drive a car without a salesperson, go somewhere else. The test drive should include time on the highway, parking, taking the car in and out of your driveway or garage, sitting in the back seat, and using the trunk or storage area. Renting the car you're interested in for a day can be very insightful.

TIP: Whatever you do, don't talk price until you're ready to buy!

5 This is the stage most of us dread—negotiating the price. While price negotiation is a car buying tradition, a few dealers are trying to break tradition by offering so-called "no-haggle" or "posted" pricing. Since they're still in the minority and because it's very hard for an individual to establish true competition between dealers, we recommend avoiding negotiating altogether by using the nonprofit CarBargains pricing service described on page 56.

THE 180-DEGREE TURN

When buying a car, you have the most important tool in the bargaining process: the 180-degree turn. Be prepared to walk away from a deal, even at the risk of losing the "very best deal" your salesperson has ever offered, and you will be in the best position to get a real "best deal." Remember: Dealerships need you, the buyer, to survive.

IN THE SHOWROOM

Being prepared in the showroom is the best way to turn a potentially intimidating showroom experience into a profitable one. Here's some advice on handling what you'll find in the showroom.

Beware of silence. Silence is often used to intimidate, so be prepared for long periods of time when the salesperson is "talking with the manager." This tactic is designed to make you want to "just get the negotiation over with." Instead of becoming a victim, do something that indicates you are serious about looking elsewhere. Bring the classified section of the newspaper and begin circling other cars or review brochures from other manufacturers. By sending the message that you have other options, you increase your bargaining power and speed up the process.

Don't fall in love with a car. Never look too interested in any particular car. Advise family members or friends who go with you against being too enthusiastic about any one car. Tip: Beat the dealers at their own game—bring along a friend who tells you that the price is "too much compared to the other deal," or "I really liked that other car much better," or "wasn't that other car much cheaper?"

Keep your wallet in your pocket. Don't leave a deposit, even if it's refundable. You'll feel pressure to rush your shopping, and you'll have to return and face the salesperson again before you are ready.

Shop at the end of the month. Salespeople anxious to meet sales goals are more willing to negotiate a lower price at this time.

Buy last year's model. The majority of new cars are the same as the previous year, with minor cosmetic changes. You can save considerably by buying in early fall when dealers are clearing space for "new" models. The important trade-off you make using this technique is that the carmaker may have added a new safety feature to an otherwise unchanged vehicle.

Buying from stock. You can often get a better deal on a car that the dealer has on the lot. However, these cars often have expensive options you may not want or need. Do not hesitate to ask the dealer to remove an option (and its accompanying charge) or sell you the car without charging for the option. The longer the car sits there, the more interest the dealer pays on the car, which increases the dealer's incentive to sell.

Ordering a car. Cars can be ordered from the manufacturer with exactly the options you want. Simply offering a fixed amount over invoice may be attractive because it's a sure sale and the dealership has not invested in the car. All the salesperson has to do is take your order.

If you do order a car, make sure when it arrives that it includes only the options you requested. Don't fall for the trick where the dealer offers you unordered options at a "special price," because it was their mistake. If you didn't order an option, don't pay for it.

BEWARE OF MANDATORY ARBITRATION AGREEMENTS

More and more dealers are adding mandatory binding arbitration agreements, which they often call "dispute resolution mechanisms," to your purchase contract. What this means is that you waive the right to sue or appeal any problem you have with the vehicle. In addition, the dealer often gets to choose the arbitrator. Before you start negotiating the price, ask if the dealer requires Mandatory Binding Arbitration. If so, and they won't remove that requirement, you should buy elsewhere. Many dealers do not have this requirement.

GETTING THE BEST PRICE

One of the most difficult aspects of buying a new car is getting the best price. Most of us are at a disadvantage negotiating because we don't know how much the car actually cost the dealer. The difference between what the dealer paid and the sticker price represents the negotiable amount.

Beware, now that most savvy consumers know to check the so-called "dealer invoice," the industry has camouflaged this number. Special incentives, rebates, and kickbacks can account for $500 to $2,000 worth of extra profit to a dealer selling a car at "dealer invoice." The non-profit Center for the Study of Services recently discovered that in 37 percent of cases when dealers are forced to bid against each other, they offered the buyer a price below the "dealer invoice"—an unlikely event if the dealer was actually losing money. The bottom line is that "dealer invoice" doesn't really mean dealer cost.

You can't really negotiate with only one dealer, you need to get two or three bidding against each other. Introducing competition is the best way to get the lowest price on a new car. To do this you have to convince two or three dealers that you are, in fact, prepared to buy a car; that you have decided on the make, model, and features; and that your decision now rests solely on which dealer will give you the best price. You can try to do this by phone, but often dealers will not give you the best price, or will quote you a price over the phone that they will not honor later. Instead, you should try to do this in person. As anyone knows who has ventured into an auto showroom simply to get the best price, the process can be lengthy and terribly arduous. Nevertheless, if you can convince the dealer that you are serious and are willing to take the time to go to a number of dealers, it will pay off. Be sure the dealer knows that you simply want the best price for the particular make, model and options. Otherwise, we suggest you use the CarBargains service described on page 56.

Here are some other showroom strategies:

Shop away from home. If you find a big savings at a dealership far from your home or on the Internet, call a local dealer with the price. They may match it. If not, pick up the car from the distant dealer, knowing your trip has saved you hundreds of dollars. You can still bring it to your local dealer for warranty work and repairs.

Beware of misleading advertising. New car ads are meant to get you into the showroom. They usually promise low prices, big rebates, high trade-in, and spotless integrity—don't be deceived. Advertised prices are rarely the true selling price. They usually exclude transportation charges, service fees, or document fees. And always look out for the asterisk, both in advertisements and on invoices. It can be a signal that the advertiser has something to hide.

Don't talk price until you're ready to buy. On your first few trips to the showroom, simply look over the cars, decide what options you want, and do your test-driving.

Shop the corporate twins. Page 61 contains a list of corporate twins—nearly identical cars that carry different name plates. Check the price and options of the twins of the car you like. A higher-priced twin may have more options, so it may be a better deal than the lower-priced car with the added options you want.

Watch out for dealer preparation overcharges. Before paying the dealer to clean your car, make sure that preparation is not included in the basic price. The price sticker will state: "Manu-facturer's suggested retail price of this model includes dealer preparation."

If you must negotiate . . . negotiate up from the "invoice" price rather than down from the sticker price. Simply make an offer close to or at the "invoice" price. If the salesperson says that your offer is too low to make a profit, ask to see the factory invoice.

Don't trade in. Although it is more work, you can usually do better by selling your old car yourself than by trading it in. To determine what you'll gain by selling the car yourself, check the NADA Official Used Car Guide at your credit union or library. On the web, the Kelly Blue Book website at kbb.com is a good source for determining the value of your used car. The difference between the trade-in price (what the dealer will give you) and the retail price (what you typically can sell it for) is your extra payment for selling the car yourself. Another option is to get a bid for your car from one of the national used car chains, such as CarMax. They do buy used cars with no obligation for you to buy from them.

If you do decide to trade your car in at the dealership, keep the buying and selling separate. First, negotiate the best price for your new car, then find out how much the dealer will give you for your old car. Keeping the two deals separate ensures that you know what you're paying for your new car and simplifies the entire transaction.

Question everything the dealer writes down. Nothing is etched in stone. Because things are written down, we tend not to question them. This is wrong—always assume that anything written down, or printed, is negotiable.

CARBARGAINS' BEST PRICE SERVICE

Even with the information that we provide you in this chapter of *The Car Book*, many of us still will not be comfortable negotiating for a fair price. In fact, as we indicated on the previous page, we believe it's really very difficult to negotiate the best price with a single dealer. The key to getting the best price is to get dealers to compete with each other.

CarBargains is a service of the non-profit Consumers' CHECKBOOK, a consumer group that provides comparative price and quality information for many products and services.

CarBargains will "shop" the dealerships in your area and obtain at least five price quotes for the make and model of the car that you want to buy. The dealers who submit quotes know that they are competing with other area dealerships and have agreed to honor the prices that they submit. It is important to note that CarBargains is not an auto broker or "car buying" service; they have no affiliation with dealers.

Here's how the service works:

1. You provide CarBargains with the specific make, model, and style of car you wish to buy (Toyota Camry XLE, for example).

2. Within two weeks, CarBar-gains will send you dealer quote sheets from at least five local dealers who have bid against one another to sell you that car. You get the name and phone number of the manager responsible for handling the quote.

When you receive your quotes, you will also get some suggestions on low-cost sources of financing and a valuation of your used car (trade-in).

The price for this service ($250, or $225 if you become a member) may seem expensive, but when you consider the savings that will result by having dealers bid against each other, as well as the time and effort of trying to get these bids yourself, we believe it's a great value. The dealers know they have a bona fide buyer; they know they are bidding against 5-7 of their competitors; and, you have CarBargains' experts on your side.

To obtain CarBargains' competitive price quotes, call them at 800-475-7283 or visit their website at www.carbargains.org.   , model, style, and year of the car you want to buy. You should receive your report within two weeks.

FINANCING

You've done your test-drive, researched prices, studied crash tests, determined the options you want, and haggled to get the best price. Now you have to decide how to pay for the car.

If you have the cash, pay for the car right away. You avoid finance charges, you won't have a large debt haunting you, and the full value of the car is yours. You can then make the monthly payments to yourself to save up for your next car.

However, most of us cannot afford to pay cash for a car, which leaves two options: financing or leasing. While leasing may seem more affordable, financing will actually cost you less and give you flexibility. When you finance a car, you own it after you finish your payments. At the end of a lease, you have nothing. We don't recommend leasing, but if you want more information, see page 59.

Shop around for interest rates. Most banks and credit unions will knock off at least a quarter of a percent for their customers. Have these quotes handy when you talk financing with the dealer.

The higher your down payment, the less you'll have to finance. This will not only reduce your overall interest charges, but often qualifies you for a lower interest rate.

Avoid long car loans. The monthly payments are lower, but you'll pay far more in overall interest charges. For example, a two-year, $25,000 loan at 4 percent will cost you $1,055 in interest; the same amount at five years will cost you $2,625—well over twice as much!

Beware of manufacturer promotional rates—the 0 to 1 percent rates you see advertised. These low rates are usually only valid on two or three-year loans and only for the most credit-worthy customers.

Read everything you are asked to sign and ask questions about anything you don't fully understand.

Make sure that an extended warranty has not been added to the purchase price. Dealers will sometimes do this without telling you. Extended warranties are generally a bad value. See the "Warranties" chapter for more information.

Credit Unions vs. Banks: Credit unions generally charge fewer and lower fees and offer better rates than banks. In addition, credit unions offer counseling services where consumers can find pricing information on cars or compare monthly payments for financing. You can join a credit union either through your employer, an organization or club, or if you have a relative who is part of a credit union.

DON'T BE TONGUE-TIED

TIP

Beware of high-pressure phrases like "I've talked to the manager and this is really the best we can do. As it is, we're losing money on this deal." Rarely is this true. Dealers are in the business to make money and most do very well. Don't tolerate a take-it-or-leave-it attitude. Simply repeat that you will only buy when you see the deal you want and that you don't appreciate the dealer pressuring you. Threaten to leave if the dealer continues to pressure you to buy today.

Don't let the dealer answer your questions with a question. If you ask, "Can I get this same car with leather seats?" and the salesperson answers, "If I get you leather seats in this car, will you buy today?" this response tries to force you to decide to buy before you are ready. Ask the dealer to just answer your question and say that you'll buy when you're ready. It's the dealer's job to answer questions, not yours.

If you are having a difficult time getting what you want, ask the dealer: "Why won't you let me buy a car today?" Most salespeople will be thrown off by this phrase as they are often too busy trying to use it on you. If they respond in frustration, "OK, what do you want?" you can simply say "straightforward answers to simple questions."

Get a price; don't settle for: "If you're shopping price, go to the other dealers first and then come back." This technique ensures that they don't have to truly negotiate. Your best response is: "I only plan to come back if your price is the lowest, so that's what I need today, your lowest price."

LEASING VS. BUYING

About 25% of new car transactions are actually leases. Unfortunately, most leasees don't realize that, in spite of the low monthly payments, leasing costs more than buying.

When you pay cash or finance a car, you own an asset; leasing leaves you with nothing except all the headaches and responsibilities of ownership with none of the benefits. When you lease you pay a monthly fee for a predetermined time in exchange for the use of a car. However, you also pay for maintenance, insurance, and repairs as if you owned the car. Finally, when it comes time to turn in the car, it has to be in top shape—otherwise, you'll have to pay for repairs, clean up, or body work. One of the most important things to remember about a lease is that it is very difficult and expensive to end it early.

If you are considering a lease, here are some leasing terms you need to know and some tips to get you through the process:

Capitalized Cost is the price of the car on which the lease is based. Negotiate this as if you were buying the car. Capitalized Cost Reduction is your down payment.

Know the make and model of the vehicle you want. Tell the agent exactly how you want the car equipped. You don't have to pay for options you don't request. Decide in advance how long you will keep the car.

Find out the price of the options on which the lease is based. Typically, they will be full retail price. Their cost can be negotiated (albeit with some difficulty) before you settle on the monthly payment.

Find out how much you are required to pay at delivery. Most leases require at least the first month's payment. Others have a security deposit, registration fees, or other "hidden costs." When shopping around, make sure price quotes include security deposit and taxes—sales tax, monthly use tax, or gross receipt tax. Ask how the length of the lease affects your monthly cost.

Find out how the lease price was determined. Lease prices are generally based on the manufacturer's suggested retail price, less the predetermined residual value. (Residual value is how much the seller expects the vehicle to be worth at the end of the lease.) The best lease values are cars with a high expected residual value. To protect themselves, leasers tend to underestimate residual value, but there is little you can do about this estimate.

Find out the annual mileage limit. Don't accept a contract with a lower limit than you need. Most standard contracts allow 15,000 to 18,000 miles per year. If you go under the allowance one year, you can go over it the next. Watch out for excess mileage fees. If you go over, you'll get charged per mile.

Avoid "capitalized cost reduction" or "equity leases." Here the leaser offers to lower the monthly payment by asking you for more money up front—in other words, a down payment.

Ask about early termination. Between 30 and 40 percent of two-year leases are terminated early and 40–60 percent of four-year leases terminate early—this means expensive early termination fees. If you terminate the lease before it is up, what are the financial penalties? Typically, they are very high so watch out. Ask the dealer exactly what you would owe at the end of each year if you wanted out of the lease. Remember, if your car is stolen, the lease will typically be terminated. While your insur-

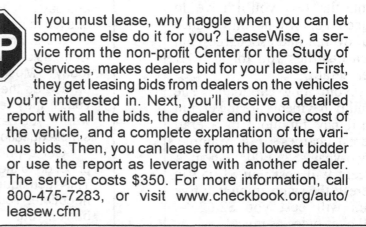

LEASEWISE

TIP

If you must lease, why haggle when you can let someone else do it for you? LeaseWise, a service from the non-profit Center for the Study of Services, makes dealers bid for your lease. First, they get leasing bids from dealers on the vehicles you're interested in. Next, you'll receive a detailed report with all the bids, the dealer and invoice cost of the vehicle, and a complete explanation of the various bids. Then, you can lease from the lowest bidder or use the report as leverage with another dealer. The service costs $350. For more information, call 800-475-7283, or visit www.checkbook.org/auto/leasew.cfm

ance should cover the value of the car, you still may owe additional amounts per your lease contract.

Avoid maintenance contracts. Getting work done privately is cheaper in the long run. And don't forget, this is a new car with a standard warranty.

Arrange for your own insurance. By shopping around, you can generally find less expensive insurance than what's offered by the lessor.

Ask how quickly you can expect delivery. If your agent can't deliver in a reasonable time, maybe he or she can't meet the price quoted.

Retain your option to buy the car at the end of the lease at a predetermined price. The price should equal the residual value; if it is more then the leaser is trying to make an additional profit. Regardless of how the end-of-lease value is determined, if you want the car, make an offer based on the current "Blue Book" value of the car at the end of the lease.

Again, residual value is the value of your car at the end of the lease. The Automotive Lease Guide is often used by leasing companies to determine the residual value. Because determining the residual value means predicting what the car is going to be worth some time in the future, it is a very difficult thing to do. As such, leasing companies often underestimate the residual value which means you'll absorb more of the cost of the vehicle in the lease. On the other hand, if the residual value at the end of the lease is very low, consider buying the vehicle for that amount.

LEASING VS. BUYING

The following table compares the costs of leasing vs. buying the same car over three and six years. Your actual costs may vary, but you can use this format to compare the cars you are considering. Our example assumes the residual value of the purchased vehicle to be 55 percent after three years and 40 percent after six years.

3 Years	Lease 36 Month	Finance 5 Yr Loan-3.6% Sell in 3 Yrs.
MSRP	$33,500	$33,500
Lease Value/Purchase Cost of Car[1]	$30,150	$30,150
Initial Payment/Down Payment[2]	$3,015	$3,015
Loan Amount		$27,135
Monthly Payments[3]	$320	$495
Total Payments (first 3 years of loan)[4]	$11,520	$17,662
Amount Left on Loan		$11,385
Excess Miles and Disposition Fees[5]	$480	
Total Cost[6]	$15,015	$32,062
Less Value of Vehicle .55 Residual[7]		$18,425
Overall Cost, First 3 years	**$15,015**	**$13,637**
Savings over Leasing 3 Years		**$1,378**

6 Years	Lease 2nd 36 Month	Finance 5 Yr Loan-3.6% Keep Car 6 Yrs.
MSRP-2nd Car 5% Increase in Cost[8]	$35,175	$33,500
Lease Value/Purchase Cost of Car	$31,658	$30,150
Initial Payment/Down Payment[2]	$3,166	$3,015
Loan Amount		$27,135
Monthly Payment[9]	$340	$495
Total Payments[10]	$12,240	$29,700
Amount Left on Loan		$0
Excess Miles and Disposition Fees[5]	$480	
Total Cost of Second Lease	$15,886	
Total Cost[11]	$30,901	$32,715
Less Value of Vehicle .40 Residual 6 yrs[12]		$13,400
Total Cost, 6 years	**$30,901**	**$19,315**
Savings Over Leasing 6 Years		**$11,586**

1. Purchase price reflects that most buyer's pay about 90% of the MSRP.
2. Initial lease payment based on leases with 10% due at signing and loans with 10% down payment.
3. Monthly lease payments based on typical leases as reported by US News and World Report. Monthly finance payments based on a 5 year, 3.59% loan.
4. Total payments (lease and finance) paid for 3 years.
5. Average excess mileage fee of $480 based on a 12000 mile limit and averages 3 typical situations: 25% going 1500 mile over the limit at $0.15/mile; 50% pre-paying for 1500 in mile overages at $0.10/mile, and 25% not exceeding the mileage limit–plus a typical disposition fee of $350.
6. Total amount paid; includes down payment, monthly payments, and end of lease fees.
7. Three-year residual value of 55 percent based on average actual 36-month residual value for the top 10 selling vehicles for model year 2019.
8. Represents the expected 5% increase in the cost of a similar leased vehicle 3 years later.
9. Estimated increase in lease payment.
10. Total payments for the second 3 year lease and total payments for the 5 year loan at 3.59%.
11. Total cost of 2 3-year leases and total cost for 5 year loan purchase.
12. Six-year residual value of 40 percent based on average actual 72-month residual value for the top 10 selling vehicles for model year 2019.

DEPRECIATION

Over the past 20 years, new vehicle depreciation costs have steadily increased. A study conducted by Runzheimer International shows that depreciation and interest now account for just over 50 percent of the costs of owning and operating a vehicle. Recently, however, the increasing cost of depreciation has slowed down. This is due to the increased prices of new vehicles and the stabilization in finance rates.

While there is no foolproof method for predicting retained vehicle value, your best bet is to purchase a popular vehicle model. Chances are, though not always, it will also be a popular used vehicle, meaning that it will retain more of its value when you go to sell it.

Most new cars are traded in within four years and are then available on the used car market. The priciest used cars may not be the highest quality. Supply and demand, as well as appearance, are important factors in determining used car prices.

The table indicates which of the top-selling 2015 cars held their value the best and which did not.

2015 VEHICLES WITH THE BEST AND WORST RESALE VALUE

THE BEST

Model	2015 Price	2018 Price	Retain. Value
Toyota Tacoma	$27,785	$26,950	97.0%
Jeep Wrangler	$30,995	$29,650	95.7%
Toyota 4Runner	$32,820	$28,600	87.1%
Chevrolet Equinox	$26,190	$21,820	83.3%
Toyota Tundra	$31,825	$26,500	83.3%
Jeep Patriot	$18,295	$14,550	79.5%
Jeep Grand Cherokee	$29,195	$23,150	79.3%
Nissan Murano	$30,230	$23,785	78.7%
Chevrolet Silverado	$31,310	$23,875	76.3%
GMC Acadia	$34,335	$25,650	74.7%
Cadillac SRX	$42,880	$31,650	73.8%
Subaru Forester	$22,995	$16,820	73.2%
BMW 3 Series	$43,200	$31,600	73.2%
Chevrolet Camaro	$23,555	$17,100	72.6%
Ford F-150	$31,555	$22,750	72.1%
Hyundai Santa Fe	$29,800	$21,400	71.8%
Honda Accord	$21,955	$15,750	71.7%
Honda CR-V	$24,195	$17,300	71.5%
Toyota Highlander	$30,520	$21,650	70.9%
Ram Pickup	$31,750	$22,500	70.9%
Toyota Prius	$24,200	$17,150	70.9%
Nissan Frontier	$26,000	$18,300	70.4%
BMW X5	$52,800	$36,975	70.0%
Mercedes-Benz E	$51,400	$35,980	70.0%
Honda Odyssey	$28,825	$20,120	69.8%

THE WORST

Model	2015 Price	2018 Price	Retain. Value
Chrysler 200	$21,700	$11,560	53.3%
Ford Focus	$18,515	$9,950	53.7%
Chevrolet Malibu	$23,510	$12,650	53.8%
Chevrolet Impala	$29,135	$15,850	54.4%
Volkswagen Passat	$23,945	$13,250	55.3%
Chevrolet Cruze	$23,805	$13,250	55.7%
Ford Fusion	$23,855	$13,465	56.5%
Toyota Sienna	$30,490	$17,350	56.9%
Kia Forte	$16,100	$9,250	57.5%
Ford Taurus	$28,900	$16,625	57.5%
Nissan Maxima	$31,200	$17,975	57.6%
Cadillac CTS	$41,495	$24,150	58.2%
Mini Cooper	$19,950	$11,970	60.0%
Nissan Altima	$22,110	$13,450	60.8%
Volkswagen Jetta	$17,820	$10,865	61.0%
Subaru Legacy	$23,295	$14,275	61.3%
Nissan Versa	$13,790	$8,550	62.0%
Dodge Charger	$26,995	$16,750	62.1%
Buick LaCrosse	$33,135	$20,650	62.3%
Hyundai Elantra	$19,600	$12,250	62.5%
Hyundai Accent	$14,645	$9,175	62.7%
Fiat 500	$16,195	$10,155	62.7%
Hyundai Sonata	$21,450	$13,550	63.2%
Volkswagen Golf	$19,995	$12,650	63.3%
Ford Fiesta	$14,600	$9,250	63.4%

CORPORATE TWINS

"Corporate twins" refers to vehicles that have different names but share the same mechanics, drivetrain, and chassis. In many cases the vehicles are identical. Sometimes the difference is in body style, price, or options as with the Chevrolet Tahoe and the Cadillac Escalade.

While corporate twins share the same basic structure and running gear, some will drive and feel different because of the tuning of the suspension, the standard equipment and options available, and the the comfort and convenience features. One twin may stress a soft ride and

luxury while another a tighter, sportier feel.

Historically, corporate twins have been limited mainly to domestic car companies. Today, several Asian and European car companies have started the practice.

CORPORATE TWINS

Chrysler
Chrysler 300
Dodge Charger

Ford
Ford Escape
Lincoln MKC

Ford Expedition
Lincoln Navigator

Ford Fusion
Lincoln MKZ

General Motors
Buick Encore
Chevrolet Trax

Buick Enclave
Chevrolet Traverse

Buick Regal
Chevrolet Malibu

Cadillac Escalade
Chevrolet Tahoe
GMC Yukon

General Motors (cont.)
Cadillac Escalade ESV
Chevrolet Suburban
GMC Yukon XL

Cadillac XTS
Chevrolet Impala

Cadillac XT5
GMC Acadia

Chevrolet Colorado
GMC Canyon

Chevrolet Equinox
GMC Terrain

Chevrolet Silverado
GMC Sierra

Honda
Acura MDX
Honda Pilot

Hyundai–Kia
Hyundai Accent
Kia Rio

Nissan
Nissan Pathfinder
Infiniti QX60

Toyota
Lexus GX
Toyota 4Runner

Lexus RX
Toyota Highlander

Volkswagen-Audi
Audi A3
Volkswagen Golf

Cadillac Escalade

Chevrolet Tahoe

GMC Yukon

This section provides an overview of the most important features of this year's new models. Nearly all the information you'll need to make a smart choice is concisely presented on one page. (The data are collected for the model expected to be the most popular.) Here's what you'll find and how to interpret the data we've provided:

The Ratings

These are the ratings in nine important categories, as well as an overall comparative rating. We have adopted the Olympic rating system with "10" being the best.

Overall Crash Test: This rating represents a combination of the front and side crash test ratings and provides a relative comparison of how this year's models did against each other. We give the best performers a 10 and the worst a 1. Remember to compare crash test results relative to other cars in the same size class. For details, see page 20.

Safety Features: This is an evaluation of how much extra safety is built into the car. We give credit for torso and pelvis side airbags, roll-sensing side airbags, a knee bolster bag, crash imminent braking, daytime running lamps, adjustable upper seat belt anchorages, lane keeping assist, pedestrian crash avoidance, automatic crash notification, lane departure warning, dynamic brake support, and frontal collision warning. We also include dynamic head restraints, and blind spot detection among other important safety features. See the "Safety Checklist" descriptions on the following pages.

Rollover: Electronic Stability Control has dramatically reduced the likelihood of roll-overs. Because of that, we've reduced the "weight" that the rollover rating has in the vehicle's overall rating. When ESC is not able to prevent the vehicle from getting into a position where a rollover is possible, the vehicle's center of gravity plays a major role in whether or not that vehicle will actually rollover. The government uses a formula which estimates the "risk of rollover" in percentages. Using those percentages, we rated the 2019 vehicles on a relative basis. Again, the good news is that ESC is often able to prevent a vehicle from getting into a position where it is likely to roll over.

Preventive Maintenance: Each manufacturer suggests a preventive maintenance schedule designed to keep the car in good shape and to protect your rights under the warranty. Those with the lowest estimated PM costs get a 10 and the highest a 1. See pages 35-38 for the estimated costs and more information.

Repair Costs: It is virtually impossible to predict exactly what any new car will cost you in repairs. As such, we take nine typical repairs that you are likely to experience after your warranty expires and compare those costs among this year's models. Those with the lowest cost get a 10 and the highest a 1. See pages 35-38 for specific part repair cost and more information.

Warranty: This is an overall assessment of the manufacturer's basic, powertrain, corrosion, and roadside assistance warranties compared to all other manufacturer warranties. We also give credit for perks like free scheduled maintenance. We give the highest-rated warranties a 10 and the lowest a 1. For details, see page 32.

Fuel Economy: Here we compare the EPA mileage ratings of each car. The misers get a 10 and the guzzlers get a 1. For the purposes of the overall rating we pick the fuel economy rating of what is expected to be the most popular engine and drive train configuration. See pages 29-30 for details.

Complaints: This is where you'll find how each vehicle stacks up against hundreds of others on the road, based on the U.S. government complaint data for that vehicle. If the car has not been around long enough to have developed a complaint history, it is given a 5 (average). The least complained about cars get a 10 and the most problematic a 1. See page 45 for details.

Insurance Costs: Insurance companies rate vehicles to determine how much they plan to charge for insurance. While each insurer may have slightly different methods of rating, vehicles typically get a discount (max and min), a surcharge (max and min) or neither (average or typical). We looked at data from the insurance rating program of the largest insurer in America. This rating can predict the cost of insuring that vehicle, however, your location, age, driving record, and other factors also play a significant role in your cost of insurance. (See The Insurance Section pages 40-42.) Vehicles with a low rating (1 or 3) are more expensive to insure than other vehicles in that class or category. On the other hand, vehicles with a high rating (8 or 10) would be less expensive to insure in that particular class of vehicles. Because insurance companies may rate vehicles differently, it's important to compare prices between companies before you buy the car.

Overall Rating: This is the "bottom line." Using a combination of all of the key ratings, this tells how this vehicle stacks up against the others on a scale of 1 to 10. Due to the importance of safety, the combined crash test rating is 20 percent of the overall rating while the other eight ratings are 10 percent each. Vehicles with no front or side crash test results, as of our publication date, cannot be given an overall rating. In other categories, if information is unavailable, an "average" is included in order to develop an overall rating.

At-a-Glance

Status: Here we tell you if a vehicle is all-new, unchanged, or has received appearance change. All-new vehicles (the minority) are brand new from the ground up. Unchanged vehicles are essentially the same, but could have some different color or feature options. Vehicles with an appearance change are those whose internal workings stayed essentially the same, but have updated body panels.

Year Series Started: Each year the model is made, the production usually improves and as a result there are fewer defects. Therefore, the longer a car has been made, the less likely you are to be plagued with manufacturing and design defects. On the other hand, the newer a car is, the more likely it is to have the latest in features and safety.

Twins: These are cars with different make and model names but share the same mechanics, drive train, and chassis. In some cases the vehicles are identical, in other cases the body style, pricing or options are different.

Body Styles: This is a listing of the various body styles available such as coupe, sedan, wagon, etc. SUVs and minivans are only offered in one body style. Data on the page are for the first style listed.

Seating: This is the number of seating positions in the most popular model. When more than one number is listed (for example, 5/6) it means that different seat configurations are available.

Anti-theft Device: This lists the anti-theft devices standard for the vehicle. An immobilizer is an electronic device fitted to an automobile which prevents the engine from running unless the correct key (or other token) is present. This prevents the car from being "hot-wired" and driven away. A car alarm is an electronic device that emits high-volume sound and can sometimes flash the vehicles headlights in an attempt to discourage theft of the vehicle itself, its contents, or both. Passive devices automatically enter an armed state after the ignition is turned off and doors are closed. Active devices require

the user to perform some action like pressing a button to arm and disarm the system.

Parking Index Rating: Using the car's length, wheelbase, and turning circle, we have calculated how easy it will be to maneuver this car in tight spots. This rating of "very easy" to "very hard" is an indicator of how much difficulty you may have parking.

Where Made: Here we tell you where the car was assembled. You'll find that traditional domestic companies often build their vehicles in other countries. Also, many foreign companies build their cars in the U.S.

Fuel Factor

MPG Rating (city/hwy): This is the EPA-rated fuel economy for city and highway driving measured in miles per gallon. Most models have a variety of fuel economy ratings because of different engine and transmission options. We've selected the combination expected to be most popular.

Driving Range: Given the car's expected fuel economy and gas tank size, this value gives you an idea of the number of miles you can expect to go on a tank of gas.

Fuel: The type of fuel specified by the manufacturer: regular, premium, E85.

Annual Fuel Cost: This is an estimate based on driving 15,000 miles per year at $2.15/gallon for regular and $2.68/gallon for premium. If the vehicle takes E85 (85% ethanol and 15% gasoline) or gasoline we calculated the annual cost using regular gasoline.

Gas Guzzler Tax: Auto companies are required to pay a gas guzzler tax on the sale of cars with exceptionally low fuel economy. This tax does not apply to light trucks.

Greenhouse Gas Emissions: This shows the amount (in tons) of greenhouse gases (carbon dioxide, nitrous oxide, and methane) that a vehicle emits per year along with the CO_2 emitted in producing and distributing the fuel.

Barrels of Oil Used Per Year: This is the number of barrels of petroleum the vehicle will likely use each year. One barrel, once refined, makes about 19.5 gallons of gas.

Competition

Here we tell you how the car stacks up with some of its key competitors. Use this information to broaden your choice of new car possibilities. This list is only a guideline, not an all-inclusive list of every possible alternative.

Price Range

This box contains information on the MSRP. When available, we offer a variety of prices between the base and the most luxurious version of the car. The difference is often substantial. Usually the more expensive versions have fancy trim, larger engines, and lots of automatic equipment. The least expensive versions usually have manual transmissions and few extra features. In addition to the price range, we provide the estimated dealer markup. Remember, prices and dealer costs can change during the year. Use these figures for general reference and comparisons, not as

a precise indication of exactly how much the car you are interested in will cost. See page 56 for a buying service designed to ensure that you get the very best price

Safety Checklist

Crash Tests

Frontal and Side Crash Test Ratings: Here's where we tell you if the front or side crash test index was Vry. Gd., good, average, poor or Vry. Pr. when compared to 2019 cars tested to date. To provide this rating we use the crash test for the vehicles with the best available safety equipment among the models when multiple models were tested. Unfortunately, not all of the 2019 models have been crash tested. If the car has been previously tested and the 2019 model is unchanged, we can carry those results forward. For details about the crash test programs, see page 20.

Airbags

All vehicles have dual front airbags and head airbags that deploy across the side windows. We've identified three additional types of airbags that the

TYPES OF AIRBAGS

Airbags were introduced over 40 years ago and have been so successful in saving lives that car makers now include a variety of types. Here's a rundown of the basic types of airbags you'll find in today's vehicles. Manufacturers have various marketing names for these airbags.

Front: These deploy toward the front occupants and are now standard in all vehicles.

Head: These deploy from above the doors and are often called curtain airbags. They can reduce head injuries, shield from spraying glass, and provide protection in rollovers. Some form of these are in all vehicles.

Side: These deploy from the side of the seat or door and protect both the front and rear passengers in a side impact. Bags mounted in seats offer protection in a wider range of seating positions. Not all vehicles have these.

Rollover Protection: These head curtain airbags remain inflated for five seconds to protect in a sustained rollover. Not all vehicles have these.

Knee Bolster: These fill space between the front occupant's knees and instrument panel protecting the knees and legs. Not all vehicles have these.

vehicle may have. The Side Airbags have historically been two separate bag systems. Recently, most manufacturers have been combining torso and pelvis protection into one bag. When the two are combined, we list *Front Pelvis/Torso from Seat* after each airbag type. Otherwise we identify specific bag type (or not) that comes with the vehicle.

Torso Side Airbag: This airbag protects the chest from serious injury in a side impact crash.

Pelvis Side Airbag: Provides extra protection around the pelvis and hip area, the portion of the body is usually closest to the vehicles exterior.

Rollover Sensing Airbags: This is a special side airbag system which keeps the side airbags inflated longer in the event of a rollover. These are standard in many 2019 models.

Knee Bolster Airbag: This airbag fills the space between the front passenger's knees and the dashboard.

Crash Avoidance

Collision Avoidance: Great new technology is available that can react faster than you in the event of a frontal collision. There are three basic systems available: Crash Imminent Braking (CIB), Dynamic Brake Support (DBS), and Frontal Collision Warning (FCW). All of these systems use radar or laser sensors to either alert the driver (FCW) or actively intervene to apply the brakes prior to a crash. CIB will actually apply the brakes if you are about to experience a frontal crash. DBS will increase your braking force if the sensors determine that you are not applying enough force to stop in time. FCW will merely sound an alarm in the event of an imminent frontal collision. Whenever a vehicle has CIB or DBS, it will also have a Frontal Crash Warning. We believe that Crash Imminent Braking and Dynamic Brake Support are more useful than just a Frontal Collision Warning (and thus rated higher), however FCW is still a useful safety feature. The government has set standards for FCW and we've used a ^ to indicate which systems DON'T meet the FCW requirements.

Blind Spot Detection: This is a blind spot monitor that uses radar or other technologies to detect objects in the driver's blind spot. When switching lanes a visible, audible, or vibrating alert warns if a vehicle has entered your blind spot.

Lane Keeping Assist: Going one step beyond a Lane Departure Warning, cars with Lane Keeping Assist will actually apply pressure to the brakes or adjust the steering when it senses that a car is drifting out of its lane. Lane Departure Warning (LDW) will simply alert the driver. If the vehicle has Land Keeping Assist, it will also have LDW. We have combined the two since the technology for Lane Departure Warning is required for Lane Keeping Assist, which we believe to be a better technology. The government has set standards for LDW and we've used an ^ to indicate which systems DON'T meet the low requirements.

Pedestrian Crash Avoidance: These systems utilize a variety of technologies (infrared,

THE BEST SAFETY FEATURES

TIP

The good news: automatic crash avoidance features are becoming more available. The bad news: it is hard to determine which ones work the best. Currently, the National Highway Traffic Safety Administration has standards for three important safety features: Back up cameras, Lane Depature Warning, and Frontal Collision Warning. Compliance to these standards is voluntary. In the tradition of *The Car Book*, exposing differences to stimulate market changes, in 2016 we published for the first time which of these three safety features meets the government standards and we continue to do so this year. However, it is important to note that having one of these features that doesn't meet government standards is better than not having it at all. Unfortunately, in order to get some of these features you often have to buy expensive "option packages" or a more expensive model which may include things you don't necessarily need or want.

camera, radar) to detect pedestrians and adjust the car's course to avoid a collision.

General

Automatic Crash Notification: Using cellular technology and global positioning systems, some vehicles have the ability to send a call for help in the event of airbag deployment or accident. Often free initially, you'll have to pay extra later for this feature. There are several different types of ACN systems. Some simply dial 911 in the event of a crash while others connect your car to a call center which can determine the severity of the crash and dispatch emergency services. Some systems even send information about the crash to the call center.

Daytime Running Lights: Some cars offer daytime running lights that can reduce your chances of being in a crash by up to 40 percent by increasing the visibility of your vehicle. We indicate whether daytime running lights are standard, optional, or not available.

Safety Belts/Restraints

Dynamic Head Restraints: Many people position their seat and head restraint according to their own body and comfort requirements. This may not be the best position to protect you in a crash. These adjustors, sensing a crash, will automatically move the seat and headrest to the optimal position to help reduce injury during a rear-end crash. The IIHS has rated the performance of many headrests.

Adjustable Belts: Proper positioning of the safety belt across your chest is critical to obtaining the benefits of buckling up. Some systems allow you to adjust the height of the belt so it crosses your chest properly.

Specifications

Drive: This indicates the type of drive the manufacturer offers. This could be two wheel drive in the front (FWD) or rear (RWD) or all or four wheel drive (AWD/4WD).

Engine: This is the engine size (liters) and type that is expected to be the most popular. The engine types specify V6 or V8 for six or eight cylinders and I3, I4 or I6 for engines with cylinders in-line. For electric vehicles, we indicate the type of auxiliary power offered.

Transmission: This is the type of transmission expected to be the most popular. Most drivers today prefer automatic transmissions. The number listed with the transmission (5-sp.) is the number of gears or speeds. Then we list whether it's automatic or manual and if the transmission is a continuously variable transmission (CVT). CVT changes smoothly and efficiently between ratios of engine to car speeds and can provide better fuel economy.

Tow Rating: Ratings of very low, low, average, high, and very high indicate the vehicle's relative ability to tow trailers or other loads. Some manufacturers do not provide a tow rating.

Head/Leg Room: This tells how roomy the front seat is. The values are given in inches and rated in comparison to all other vehicles.

Interior Space: This tells how roomy the car's passenger area should feel. This value is given in cubic feet and rated in comparison to all other vehicles. Many SUVs do not provide interior space specifications.

Cargo Space: This gives you the cubic feet available for cargo. For minivans, the volume is behind the last row of seats. In cars, it's the trunk space. We rate the roominess of the cargo space compared to all trucks, SUVs, and cars.

Wheelbase/Length: The distance between the centers of the front and rear wheels is the wheelbase and the length is the distance from front bumper to rear bumper. Wheelbase can affect the ride and length affects how big the car "feels."

Acura ILX   Compact

Ratings—10 Best, 1 Worst

Combo Crash Tests	—
Safety Features	7
Rollover	6
Preventive Maintenance	9
Repair Costs	7
Warranty	6
Fuel Economy	7
Complaints	5
Insurance Costs	10
OVERALL RATING	—

Acura ILX

Safety Checklist

Crash Test:
- Frontal . . . . —
- Side . . . . —

Airbags:
- Torso . . . Std. Front Pelvis/Torso from Seat
- Roll Sensing . . . . Yes
- Knee Bolster . . . . None

Crash Avoidance:
- Collision Avoidance . . . Optional CIB & DBS
- Blind Spot Detection . . . . Optional
- Lane Keeping Assist . . . . Optional
- Pedestrian Crash Avoidance . . . . . Optional

General:
- Auto. Crash Notification Operat. Assist.-Fee
- Day Running Lamps . . . . Standard

Safety Belt/Restraint:
- Dynamic Head Restraints . . . . None
- Adjustable Belt . . . . Standard Front

^Warning feature does not meet government standards.

Acura ILX

At-a-Glance

Status/Year Series Started	Unchanged/2018
Twins	—
Body Styles	Sedan
Seating	5
Anti-Theft Device	Std. Pass. Immobil. & Alarm
Parking Index Rating	Easy
Where Made	Marysville, OH

Fuel Factor
MPG Rating (city/hwy)	Good-25/35
Driving Range (mi.)	Short-379
Fuel Type	Premium
Annual Fuel Cost	Average-$1553
Gas Guzzler Tax	No
Greenhouse Gas Emissions (tons/yr.)	Low-5.1
Barrels of Oil Used per year	Average-11.4

Acura ILX

How the Competition Rates

Competitors	Rating	Pg.
Audi A3	5	71
Cadillac ATS	4	94
Lexus IS	8	181

Price Range

Price Range	Retail	Markup
Base	$27,990	6%
Premium Package	$29,990	6%
Technology Package	$32,990	6%
Technology Pkg. w/A-SPEC	$34,980	6%

Specifications

Drive	FWD
Engine	2.4-liter I4
Transmission	8-sp. Automatic
Tow Rating (lbs.)	—
Head/Leg Room (in.)	Cramped-38/42.3
Interior Space (cu. ft.)	Very Cramped-89.3
Cargo Space (cu. ft.)	Very Cramped-12.3
Wheelbase/Length (in.)	105.1/181.9

Ratings—10 Best, 1 Worst

Combo Crash Tests	8
Safety Features	10
Rollover	4
Preventive Maintenance	5
Repair Costs	2
Warranty	6
Fuel Economy	3
Complaints	4
Insurance Costs	10
OVERALL RATING	**7**

Acura MDX

Acura MDX

At-a-Glance

Status/Year Series Started	Unchanged/2014
Twins	Honda Pilot
Body Styles	SUV
Seating	7
Anti-Theft Device	Std. Pass. Immobil. & Alarm
Parking Index Rating	Hard
Where Made	Lincoln, AL
Fuel Factor	
MPG Rating (city/hwy)	Poor-18/27
Driving Range (mi.)	Average-413
Fuel Type	Premium
Annual Fuel Cost	Very High-$2104
Gas Guzzler Tax	No
Greenhouse Gas Emissions (tons/yr.)	High-8.6
Barrels of Oil Used per year	High-15.7

How the Competition Rates

Competitors	Rating	Pg.
Cadillac XT5	3	98
Infiniti QX60	5	161
Volkswagen Atlas	6	248

Price Range

	Retail	Markup
Base	$44,050	7%
SH-AWD w/Tech. Package	$50,460	7%
Advance w/RES	$56,500	7%
SH-AWD Advance w/RES	$58,500	7%

Safety Checklist

Crash Test:
  Frontal . . . . Very Good
  Side . . . . Average
Airbags:
  Torso . . . Std. Front Pelvis/Torso from Seat
  Roll Sensing . . . . Yes
  Knee Bolster . . . . Standard Driver
Crash Avoidance:
  Collision Avoidance . . Standard CIB & DBS
  Blind Spot Detection . . . . Optional
  Lane Keeping Assist . . . . Standard
  Pedestrian Crash Avoidance . . . . . Optional
General:
  Auto. Crash Notification Operat. Assist.-Fee
  Day Running Lamps . . . . Standard
Safety Belt/Restraint:
  Dynamic Head Restraints . . . . None
  Adjustable Belt . . . . Standard Front

^Warning feature does not meet government standards.

Acura MDX

Specifications

Drive	AWD
Engine	3.5-liter V6
Transmission	6-sp. Automatic
Tow Rating (lbs.)	Low-3500
Head/Leg Room (in.)	Very Cramped-38.1/41.4
Interior Space (cu. ft.)	Very Roomy-132.3
Cargo Space (cu. ft.)	Cramped-14.8
Wheelbase/Length (in.)	111/193.6

Ratings—10 Best, 1 Worst

Combo Crash Tests	9
Safety Features	10
Rollover	4
Preventive Maintenance	5
Repair Costs	5
Warranty	6
Fuel Economy	3
Complaints	—
Insurance Costs	10
OVERALL RATING	**9**

Acura RDX

Acura RDX

At-a-Glance

Status/Year Series Started	All New/2019
Twins	—
Body Styles	SUV
Seating	5
Anti-Theft Device	Std. Pass. Immobil. & Alarm
Parking Index Rating	Hard
Where Made	East Liberty, OH
Fuel Factor	
MPG Rating (city/hwy)	Poor-21/27
Driving Range (mi.)	Short-393
Fuel Type	Premium
Annual Fuel Cost	Very High-$2032
Gas Guzzler Tax	No
Greenhouse Gas Emissions (tons/yr.)	High-6.4
Barrels of Oil Used per year	High-14.3

How the Competition Rates

Competitors	Rating	Pg.
Buick Encore	10	90
Lexus NX	5	182
Lincoln MKC	6	186

Price Range

	Retail	Markup
FWD	$37,300	5%
AWD	$39,300	5%
Advance FWD	$45,400	5%
Advance AWD	$47,400	5%

Safety Checklist

Crash Test:
- Frontal . . . . Average
- Side . . . . Very Good

Airbags:
- Torso . . . Std. Front Pelvis/Torso from Seat
- Roll Sensing . . . . Yes
- Knee Bolster . . . . Standard Front

Crash Avoidance:
- Collision Avoidance . . Standard CIB & DBS
- Blind Spot Detection . . . . Optional
- Lane Keeping Assist . . . . Standard
- Pedestrian Crash Avoidance . . . . . Optional

General:
- Auto. Crash Notification Operat. Assist.-Fee
- Day Running Lamps . . . . Standard

Safety Belt/Restraint:
- Dynamic Head Restraints . . . . None
- Adjustable Belt . . . . Standard Front

^Warning feature does not meet government standards.

Acura RDX

Specifications

Drive	AWD
Engine	2.0-liter I4
Transmission	10-sp. Automatic
Tow Rating (lbs.)	—
Head/Leg Room (in.)	Cramped-39.6/41.6
Interior Space (cu. ft.)	Roomy-104
Cargo Space (cu. ft.)	Roomy-31.1
Wheelbase/Length (in.)	108.3/186.8

Ratings—10 Best, 1 Worst

Combo Crash Tests	10
Safety Features	8
Rollover	8
Preventive Maintenance	5
Repair Costs	3
Warranty	6
Fuel Economy	6
Complaints	3
Insurance Costs	10
OVERALL RATING	**9**

Acura TLX

Acura TLX

At-a-Glance

Status/Year Series Started	Unchanged/2015
Twins	—
Body Styles	Sedan
Seating	5
Anti-Theft Device	Std. Pass. Immobil. & Alarm
Parking Index Rating	Hard
Where Made	Marysville, OH

Fuel Factor

MPG Rating (city/hwy)	Average-23/33
Driving Range (mi.)	Very Long-458
Fuel Type	Premium
Annual Fuel Cost	High-$1673
Gas Guzzler Tax	No
Greenhouse Gas Emissions (tons/yr.)	Average-6.5
Barrels of Oil Used per year	Average-12.2

How the Competition Rates

Competitors	Rating	Pg.
BMW 5 Series	6	81
Hyundai Sonata	9	155
Volkswagen Passat	4	251

Price Range

	Retail	Markup
Base 2.4L	$33,000	5%
Base 3.5L	$36,200	5%
3.5L w/Tech. Package	$39,900	5%
SH-AWD w/Advance Package	$45,750	5%

Safety Checklist

Crash Test:
  Frontal . . . . Very Good
  Side . . . . Very Good
Airbags:
  Torso . . . Std. Front Pelvis/Torso from Seat
  Roll Sensing . . . . Yes
  Knee Bolster . . . . Standard Driver
Crash Avoidance:
  Collision Avoidance . . . Optional CIB & DBS
  Blind Spot Detection . . . . Optional
  Lane Keeping Assist . . . . Optional
  Pedestrian Crash Avoidance . . . . . Optional
General:
  Auto. Crash Notification Operat. Assist.-Fee
  Day Running Lamps . . . . Standard
Safety Belt/Restraint:
  Dynamic Head Restraints . . . . None
  Adjustable Belt . . . . Standard Front

^Warning feature does not meet government standards.

Acura TLX

Specifications

Drive	FWD
Engine	2.4-liter I4
Transmission	8-sp. Automatic
Tow Rating (lbs.)	—
Head/Leg Room (in.)	Cramped-37.2/42.6
Interior Space (cu. ft.)	Cramped-93.3
Cargo Space (cu. ft.)	Very Cramped-13.2
Wheelbase/Length (in.)	109.3/190.3

Ratings—10 Best, 1 Worst

Combo Crash Tests	6
Safety Features	7
Rollover	7
Preventive Maintenance	1
Repair Costs	5
Warranty	7
Fuel Economy	6
Complaints	4
Insurance Costs	5
OVERALL RATING	**5**

Audi A3

At-a-Glance

Status/Year Series Started	Unchanged/2015
Twins	Volkswagen Golf
Body Styles	Sedan, Wagon
Seating	5
Anti-Theft Device	Std. Pass. Immobil. & Alarm
Parking Index Rating	Easy
Where Made	Gyor, Hungary
Fuel Factor	
MPG Rating (city/hwy)	Average-24/33
Driving Range (mi.)	Short-397
Fuel Type	Premium
Annual Fuel Cost	Average-$1628
Gas Guzzler Tax	No
Greenhouse Gas Emissions (tons/yr.)	Average-6.6
Barrels of Oil Used per year	Average-12.2

How the Competition Rates

Competitors	Rating	Pg.
Cadillac ATS	4	94
Lexus IS	8	181
Mercedes-Benz C-Class	1	196

Price Range	Retail	Markup
Premium Sedan	$31,950	8%
Premium Plus Sedan Quattro	$38,200	8%
Premium Cabrio	$38,350	8%
Prestige Cabriolet Quattro	$49,500	8%

Audi A3

Safety Checklist

Crash Test:
- Frontal . . . . Average
- Side . . . . Average

Airbags:
- Torso Std. Fr. & Opt. Rr. Pelvis/Torso from Seat
- Roll Sensing . . . . Yes
- Knee Bolster . . . . Standard Front

Crash Avoidance:
- Collision Avoidance . . . Optional CIB & DBS
- Blind Spot Detection . . . . Optional
- Lane Keeping Assist . . . . Optional
- Pedestrian Crash Avoidance . . . . None

General:
- Auto. Crash Notification . . . . None
- Day Running Lamps . . . . Standard

Safety Belt/Restraint:
- Dynamic Head Restraints . . . . None
- Adjustable Belt . . . . Standard Front

^Warning feature does not meet government standards.

Audi A3

Specifications

Drive	AWD
Engine	2.0-liter I4
Transmission	6-sp. Automatic
Tow Rating (lbs.)	—
Head/Leg Room (in.)	Very Cramped-36.5/41.2
Interior Space (cu. ft.)	Very Cramped-86
Cargo Space (cu. ft.)	Very Cramped-10.03
Wheelbase/Length (in.)	103.8/175.4

Ratings—10 Best, 1 Worst

Combo Crash Tests	2
Safety Features	5
Rollover	8
Preventive Maintenance	4
Repair Costs	2
Warranty	7
Fuel Economy	7
Complaints	3
Insurance Costs	5
OVERALL RATING	**2**

Audi A4

Audi A4

At-a-Glance

Status/Year Series Started	Unchanged/2017
Twins	—
Body Styles	Sedan
Seating	5
Anti-Theft Device	Std. Pass. Immobil. & Alarm
Parking Index Rating	Average
Where Made	Ingolstadt, Germany
Fuel Factor	
MPG Rating (city/hwy)	Good-25/33
Driving Range (mi.)	Long-429
Fuel Type	Premium
Annual Fuel Cost	Average-$1588
Gas Guzzler Tax	No
Greenhouse Gas Emissions (tons/yr.)	Low-5.2
Barrels of Oil Used per year	Average-11.8

How the Competition Rates

Competitors	Rating	Pg.
Audi A3	5	71
Cadillac ATS	4	94
Mercedes-Benz C-Class	1	196

Price Range	Retail	Markup
2.0T Premium Sedan	$36,000	8%
2.0T Premium Sedan Quattro	$40,500	8%
2.0T Prem. Plus Sedan Quattro	$43,700	8%
2.0T Prestige Sedan Quattro	$50,000	8%

Safety Checklist

Crash Test:
   Frontal................Very Poor
   Side.....................Average
Airbags:
   Torso Std. Fr. & Opt. Rr. Pelvis/Torso from Seat
   Roll Sensing..................No
   Knee Bolster ....None
Crash Avoidance:
   Collision Avoidance .. Std. CIB & Opt. DBS
   Blind Spot Detection .... Optional
   Lane Keeping Assist .... Optional^
   Pedestrian Crash Avoidance .....Standard
General:
   Auto. Crash Notification.... Dial Assist-Fee
   Day Running Lamps ....Standard
Safety Belt/Restraint:
   Dynamic Head Restraints ....None
   Adjustable Belt..........Standard Front

^Warning feature does not meet government standards.

Audi A4

Specifications

Drive	AWD
Engine	2.0-liter I4
Transmission	8-sp. Automatic
Tow Rating (lbs.)	—
Head/Leg Room (in.)	Cramped-38.9/41.3
Interior Space (cu. ft.)	Cramped-92
Cargo Space (cu. ft.)	Very Cramped-13
Wheelbase/Length (in.)	111/186.1

Ratings—10 Best, 1 Worst

Combo Crash Tests	—
Safety Features	9
Rollover	8
Preventive Maintenance	4
Repair Costs	4
Warranty	7
Fuel Economy	7
Complaints	10
Insurance Costs	3
OVERALL RATING	**—**

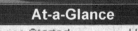

Audi A5

At-a-Glance

Status/Year Series Started	Unchanged/2018
Twins	—
Body Styles	Coupe
Seating	4
Anti-Theft Device	Std. Pass. Immobil. & Alarm
Parking Index Rating	Average
Where Made	Ingolstadt, Germany
Fuel Factor	
MPG Rating (city/hwy)	Good-24/34
Driving Range (mi.)	Long-423
Fuel Type	Premium
Annual Fuel Cost	Average-$1611
Gas Guzzler Tax	No
Greenhouse Gas Emissions (tons/yr.)	Low-5.4
Barrels of Oil Used per year	Average-12.2

How the Competition Rates

Competitors	Rating	Pg.
BMW 5 Series	6	81
Infiniti Q50	3	158
Volkswagen Passat	4	251

Price Range

	Retail	Markup
2.0T Premium Coupe Quattro	$42,800	8%
2.0T Pre. Plus Coupe Quattro	$45,800	8%
2.0T Premium Cabrio Quattro	$49,600	8%
2.0T Prem. Plus Cabrio Quattro	$52,600	8%

Audi A5

Safety Checklist

Crash Test:
- Frontal . . . . —
- Side . . . . —

Airbags:
- Torso . . . Std. Front Pelvis/Torso from Seat
- Roll Sensing . . . . Yes
- Knee Bolster . . . . Standard Front

Crash Avoidance:
- Collision Avoidance . Standard CIB & DBS^
- Blind Spot Detection . . . . Optional
- Lane Keeping Assist . . Warn. Only Optional
- Pedestrian Crash Avoidance . . . . . Standard

General:
- Auto. Crash Notification . . . . Dial Assist-Fee
- Day Running Lamps . . . . Standard

Safety Belt/Restraint:
- Dynamic Head Restraints . . . . None
- Adjustable Belt . . . . Standard Front

^Warning feature does not meet government standards.

Audi A5

Specifications

Drive	AWD
Engine	2.0-liter I4
Transmission	7-sp. Automatic
Tow Rating (lbs.)	—
Head/Leg Room (in.)	Cramped-39.4/41.3
Interior Space (cu. ft.)	Very Cramped-84
Cargo Space (cu. ft.)	Very Cramped-11.6
Wheelbase/Length (in.)	111.2/186.3

Audi A6 Intermediate

Audi A6

Ratings—10 Best, 1 Worst

Combo Crash Tests	—
Safety Features	—
Rollover	9
Preventive Maintenance	4
Repair Costs	1
Warranty	7
Fuel Economy	4
Complaints	—
Insurance Costs	3
OVERALL RATING	**7**

Audi A6

At-a-Glance

Status/Year Series Started	All New/2019
Twins	—
Body Styles	Sedan
Seating	5
Anti-Theft Device	Std. Pass. Immobil. & Alarm
Parking Index Rating	Average
Where Made	Neckarsulm, Germany
Fuel Factor	
MPG Rating (city/hwy)	Average-22/29
Driving Range (mi.)	Very Long-482
Fuel Type	Premium
Annual Fuel Cost	High-$1862
Gas Guzzler Tax	No
Greenhouse Gas Emissions (tons/yr.)	Average-6.0
Barrels of Oil Used per year	High-13.2

How the Competition Rates

Competitors	Rating	Pg.
Acura TLX	9	70
Infiniti Q50	3	158
Lincoln MKZ	4	187

Price Range

	Retail	Markup
3.0T Premium	$58,900	7%
3.0 Premium Plus Quattro	$62,700	8%
3.0 Prestige Quattro	$67,100	8%

Safety Checklist

Crash Test:
  Frontal . . . . —
  Side . . . . —
Airbags:
  Torso Std. Front & Rear Pelvis/Torso from Seat
  Roll Sensing . . . . Yes
  Knee Bolster . . . . Standard Front
Crash Avoidance:
  Collision Avoidance . . Standard CIB & DBS
  Blind Spot Detection . . . . Optional
  Lane Keeping Assist . . . . Optional^
  Pedestrian Crash Avoidance . . . . None
General:
  Auto. Crash Notification . . . . None
  Day Running Lamps . . . . Standard
Safety Belt/Restraint:
  Dynamic Head Restraints . . . . None
  Adjustable Belt . . . . Standard Front

^Warning feature does not meet government standards.

Audi A6

Specifications

Drive	AWD
Engine	3.0-liter V6
Transmission	7-sp. Automatic
Tow Rating (lbs.)	—
Head/Leg Room (in.)	Very Cramped-38/41.3
Interior Space (cu. ft.)	Average-99
Cargo Space (cu. ft.)	Cramped-13.7
Wheelbase/Length (in.)	115.1/194.4

Ratings—10 Best, 1 Worst

Combo Crash Tests	—
Safety Features	2
Rollover	4
Preventive Maintenance	4
Repair Costs	3
Warranty	7
Fuel Economy	4
Complaints	10
Insurance Costs	10

OVERALL RATING — —

Audi Q3

At-a-Glance

Status/Year Series Started	Unchanged/2015
Twins	—
Body Styles	SUV
Seating	5
Anti-Theft Device	Std. Pass. Immobil. & Alarm
Parking Index Rating	Average
Where Made	Martorell, Spain
Fuel Factor	
MPG Rating (city/hwy)	Poor-20/28
Driving Range (mi.)	Short-388
Fuel Type	Premium
Annual Fuel Cost	High-$1941
Gas Guzzler Tax	No
Greenhouse Gas Emissions (tons/yr.)	High-7.8
Barrels of Oil Used per year	High-14.3

How the Competition Rates

Competitors	Rating	Pg.
Acura RDX	9	68
Buick Encore	10	90
Lexus NX	5	182

Price Range

	Retail	Markup
2.0T Premium	$32,900	8%
2.0T Premium Quattro	$35,000	8%
2.0T Premium Plus	$35,800	8%
2.0T Premium Plus Quattro	$37,900	8%

Audi Q3

Safety Checklist

Crash Test:
- Frontal . . . . —
- Side . . . . —

Airbags:
- Torso . . . Std. Front Pelvis/Torso from Seat
- Roll Sensing . . . . Yes
- Knee Bolster . . . . None

Crash Avoidance:
- Collision Avoidance . . . . None
- Blind Spot Detection . . . . Optional
- Lane Keeping Assist . . . . None
- Pedestrian Crash Avoidance . . . . None

General:
- Auto. Crash Notification . . . . None
- Day Running Lamps . . . . Standard

Safety Belt/Restraint:
- Dynamic Head Restraints . . . . None
- Adjustable Belt . . . . Standard Front

^Warning feature does not meet government standards.

Audi Q3

Specifications

Drive	AWD
Engine	2.0-liter I4
Transmission	6-sp. Automatic
Tow Rating (lbs.)	—
Head/Leg Room (in.)	Very Cramped-37/40
Interior Space (cu. ft.)	Very Cramped-84
Cargo Space (cu. ft.)	Cramped-16.7
Wheelbase/Length (in.)	102.5/172.6

Ratings—10 Best, 1 Worst

Combo Crash Tests	—
Safety Features	4
Rollover	4
Preventive Maintenance	4
Repair Costs	2
Warranty	7
Fuel Economy	5
Complaints	—
Insurance Costs	5
OVERALL RATING	—

Audi Q5

Audi Q5

At-a-Glance

Status/Year Series Started	Unchanged/2018
Twins	—
Body Styles	SUV
Seating	5
Anti-Theft Device	Std. Pass. Immobil. & Alarm
Parking Index Rating	Average
Where Made	Ingolstadt, Germany
Fuel Factor	
MPG Rating (city/hwy)	Average-23/27
Driving Range (mi.)	Long-456
Fuel Type	Premium
Annual Fuel Cost	High-$1808
Gas Guzzler Tax	No
Greenhouse Gas Emissions (tons/yr.)	Average-6.0
Barrels of Oil Used per year	High-13.2

How the Competition Rates

Competitors	Rating	Pg.
Acura MDX	7	67
Lexus RX	4	184
Lincoln Nautilis	5	188

Price Range

	Retail	Markup
2.0T Premium	$41,500	8%
2.0T Premium Plus	$45,500	8%
2.0 Prestige	$50,800	8%

Safety Checklist

Crash Test:
  Frontal . . . . —
  Side . . . . —
Airbags:
  Torso Std. Fr. & Opt. Rr. Pelvis/Torso from Seat
  Roll Sensing . . . . Yes
  Knee Bolster . . . . None
Crash Avoidance:
  Collision Avoidance . . . Optional CIB & DBS
  Blind Spot Detection . . . . Optional
  Lane Keeping Assist .Warn. Only Optional^
  Pedestrian Crash Avoidance . . . . None
General:
  Auto. Crash Notification . . . . None
  Day Running Lamps . . . . Standard
Safety Belt/Restraint:
  Dynamic Head Restraints . . . . Optional
  Adjustable Belt . . . . Standard Front

^Warning feature does not meet government standards.

Specifications

Drive	AWD
Engine	2.0-liter I4
Transmission	7-sp. Automatic
Tow Rating (lbs.)	—
Head/Leg Room (in.)	Roomy-41.7/40.9
Interior Space (cu. ft.)	—
Cargo Space (cu. ft.)	Roomy-26.8
Wheelbase/Length (in.)	111/183.6

Audi Q7

Ratings—10 Best, 1 Worst	
Combo Crash Tests	6
Safety Features	8
Rollover	4
Preventive Maintenance	3
Repair Costs	1
Warranty	7
Fuel Economy	3
Complaints	4
Insurance Costs	5
OVERALL RATING	**3**

Audi Q7

At-a-Glance

Status/Year Series Started	Unchanged/2016
Twins	—
Body Styles	SUV
Sealing	7
Anti-Theft Device	Std. Pass. Immobil. & Alarm
Parking Index Rating	Very Hard
Where Made	Bratislava, Slovakia
Fuel Factor	
MPG Rating (city/hwy)	Poor-19/25
Driving Range (mi.)	Very Long-479
Fuel Type	Premium
Annual Fuel Cost	Very High-$2092
Gas Guzzler Tax	No
Greenhouse Gas Emissions (tons/yr.)	Average-6.9
Barrels of Oil Used per year	High-15.7

How the Competition Rates

Competitors	Rating	Pg.
Acura MDX	7	68
Cadillac XT5	3	98
Lexus RX	4	184

Price Range	Retail	Markup
2.0T Premium	$49,900	8%
2.0T Premium Plus	$53,900	8%
3.0T Premium Plus	$60,400	8%
3.0T Prestige	$65,400	8%

Safety Checklist

Crash Test:
- Frontal......................... Average
- Side.............................. Average

Airbags:
- Torso Std. Fr. & Opt. Rr. Pelvis/Torso from Seat
- Roll Sensing........................Yes
- Knee Bolster ....None

Crash Avoidance:
- Collision Avoidance .. Std. CIB & Opt. DBS
- Blind Spot Detection ....Optional
- Lane Keeping Assist ....Optional
- Pedestrian Crash Avoidance.....Standard

General:
- Auto. Crash Notification.... Dial Assist-Fee
- Day Running Lamps ....Standard

Safety Belt/Restraint:
- Dynamic Head Restraints ....None
- Adjustable Belt............ Standard Front

^Warning feature does not meet government standards.

Audi Q7

Specifications

Drive	AWD
Engine	3.0-liter V6
Transmission	8-sp. Automatic
Tow Rating (lbs.)	High-7700
Head/Leg Room (in.)	Cramped-38.4/41.7
Interior Space (cu. ft.)	—
Cargo Space (cu. ft.)	Cramped-14.8
Wheelbase/Length (in.)	117.9/199.6

Ratings—10 Best, 1 Worst

Combo Crash Tests	—
Safety Features	6
Rollover	7
Preventive Maintenance	4
Repair Costs	3
Warranty	9
Fuel Economy	6
Complaints	1
Insurance Costs	1
OVERALL RATING	**—**

BMW 2 Series

BMW 2 Series

BMW 2 Series

At-a-Glance

Status/Year Series Started	Unchanged/2016
Twins	—
Body Styles	Coupe
Seating	4
Anti-Theft Device	Std. Pass. Immobil. & Active Alarm
Parking Index Rating	Easy
Where Made	Leipzig, Germany
Fuel Factor	
MPG Rating (city/hwy)	Average-23/35
Driving Range (mi.)	Very Short-373
Fuel Type	Premium
Annual Fuel Cost	Average-$1638
Gas Guzzler Tax	No
Greenhouse Gas Emissions (tons/yr.)	Average-6.4
Barrels of Oil Used per year	Average-12.2

How the Competition Rates

Competitors	Rating	Pg.
Audi A3	5	71
Cadillac ATS	4	94
Lexus IS	8	181

Price Range

	Retail	Markup
230i Coupe	$34,800	6%
230xi Convertible	$42,600	6%
M240i Coupe	$45,300	6%
M 240xi Coupe	$47,300	6%

Safety Checklist

Crash Test:
- Frontal . . . . —
- Side . . . . —

Airbags:
- Torso . . . . Std. Front Torso from Seat
- Roll Sensing . . . . Yes
- Knee Bolster . . . . Standard Front

Crash Avoidance:
- Collision Avoidance . . Optional CIB & DBS^
- Blind Spot Detection . . . . None
- Lane Keeping Assist . Warn. Only Optional^
- Pedestrian Crash Avoidance . . . . . Optional

General:
- Auto. Crash Notif. . . Op. Assist. & Crash Info-Free
- Day Running Lamps . . . . Standard

Safety Belt/Restraint:
- Dynamic Head Restraints . . . . None
- Adjustable Belt . . . . None

^Warning feature does not meet government standards.

BMW 2 Series

Specifications

Drive	RWD
Engine	2.0-liter I4
Transmission	8-sp. Automatic
Tow Rating (lbs.)	—
Head/Leg Room (in.)	Average-40.1/41.5
Interior Space (cu. ft.)	Very Cramped-90
Cargo Space (cu. ft.)	Cramped-13.8
Wheelbase/Length (in.)	105.9/174.7

Ratings—10 Best, 1 Worst

Combo Crash Tests	—
Safety Features	7
Rollover	9
Preventive Maintenance	4
Repair Costs	2
Warranty	9
Fuel Economy	7
Complaints	—
Insurance Costs	3
OVERALL RATING	**—**

BMW 3 Series

BMW 3 Series

At-a-Glance

Status/Year Series Started	All New/2019
Twins	—
Body Styles	Sedan, Wagon, Convertible
Seating	5
Anti-Theft Device	Std. Pass. Immobil. & Active Alarm
Parking Index Rating	Average
Where Made	Munich, Germany / Toluca, Mexico

Fuel Factor
MPG Rating (city/hwy)	Good-23/33
Driving Range (mi.)	Average-427
Fuel Type	Premium
Annual Fuel Cost	Average-$1685
Gas Guzzler Tax	No
Greenhouse Gas Emissions (tons/yr.)	Low-5.5
Barrels of Oil Used per year	Average-12.2

How the Competition Rates

Competitors	Rating	Pg.
Audi A4	2	72
Cadillac ATS	4	94
Mercedes-Benz C-Class	1	196

Price Range	Retail	Markup
320i	$34,900	6%
328d	$41,750	6%
330xi	$42,250	6%
340xi	$50,950	6%

Safety Checklist

Crash Test:
Frontal	—
Side	—

Airbags:
Torso	Std. Front Torso from Seat
Roll Sensing	Yes
Knee Bolster	Standard Front

Crash Avoidance:
Collision Avoidance	Optional CIB & DBS^
Blind Spot Detection	Optional
Lane Keeping Assist	Optional
Pedestrian Crash Avoidance	Optional

General:
Auto. Crash Notif.	Op. Assist. & Crash Info-Free
Day Running Lamps	Standard

Safety Belt/Restraint:
Dynamic Head Restraints	None
Adjustable Belt	None

^Warning feature does not meet government standards.

BMW 3 Series

Specifications

Drive	RWD
Engine	2.0-liter I4
Transmission	8-sp. Automatic
Tow Rating (lbs.)	—
Head/Leg Room (in.)	Cramped-38.7/42
Interior Space (cu. ft.)	Average-102
Cargo Space (cu. ft.)	—
Wheelbase/Length (in.)	112.2/185.7

Ratings—10 Best, 1 Worst

Combo Crash Tests	—
Safety Features	7
Rollover	9
Preventive Maintenance	4
Repair Costs	2
Warranty	9
Fuel Economy	6
Complaints	8
Insurance Costs	1
OVERALL RATING	**—**

BMW 4 Series

BMW 4 Series

At-a-Glance

Status/Year Series Started. Unchanged/2014
Twins . . . . —
Body Styles . . . . Coupe, Convertible
Seating 4
Anti-Theft Device . Std. Pass. Immobil. & Active Alarm
Parking Index Rating . . . . Average
Where Made. . . . . .Munich, Germany
Fuel Factor
  MPG Rating (city/hwy) Average-23/35
  Driving Range (mi.) Long-430
  Fuel Type . . . . .Premium
  Annual Fuel Cost . . . . .Average-$1638
  Gas Guzzler Tax . . . . .No
  Greenhouse Gas Emissions (tons/yr.) . . Average-6.7
  Barrels of Oil Used per year Average-12.2

How the Competition Rates

Competitors	Rating	Pg.
Cadillac ATS	4	94
Lexus IS	8	181
Mercedes-Benz C-Class	1	196

Price Range

Price Range	Retail	Markup
430i Coupe	$42,200	6%
430xi Gran Coupe	$44,200	6%
440i Convertible	$57,500	7%
440xi Convertible	$59,500	7%

Safety Checklist

Crash Test:
  Frontal. . . . . —
  Side. . . . . —
Airbags:
  Torso . . . . Std. Front Torso from Seat
  Roll Sensing. .Yes
  Knee Bolster . . . . Standard Front
Crash Avoidance:
  Collision Avoidance . . Optional CIB & DBS^
  Blind Spot Detection . . . . Optional
  Lane Keeping Assist . Warn. Only Optional^
  Pedestrian Crash Avoidance . . . . . Optional
General:
  Auto. Crash Notif. Op. Assist. & Crash Info-Free
  Day Running Lamps . . . . .Standard
Safety Belt/Restraint:
  Dynamic Head Restraints . . . . .None
  Adjustable Belt. . . . . .None

^Warning feature does not meet government standards.

BMW 4 Series

Specifications

Drive. . . . . .RWD
Engine 2.0-liter I4
Transmission . . . . 8-sp. Automatic
Tow Rating (lbs.) . . . . —
Head/Leg Room (in.) Average-39.8/42.2
Interior Space (cu. ft.). . . . . Very Cramped-90
Cargo Space (cu. ft.) Cramped-15.7
Wheelbase/Length (in.) 110.6/182.6

Ratings—10 Best, 1 Worst	
Combo Crash Tests	4
Safety Features	7
Rollover	9
Preventive Maintenance	9
Repair Costs	1
Warranty	9
Fuel Economy	6
Complaints	7
Insurance Costs	1
OVERALL RATING	**6**

BMW 5 Series

BMW 5 Series

At-a-Glance

Status/Year Series Started	Unchanged/2011
Twins	—
Body Styles	Sedan, Wagon
Seating	5
Anti-Theft Device	Std. Pass. Immobil. & Active Alarm
Parking Index Rating	Hard
Where Made	Dingolfing, Germany / Toluca, Mexico
Fuel Factor	
MPG Rating (city/hwy)	Average-23/34
Driving Range (mi.)	Very Long-498
Fuel Type	Premium
Annual Fuel Cost	Average-$1655
Gas Guzzler Tax	No
Greenhouse Gas Emissions (tons/yr.)	Average-6.6
Barrels of Oil Used per year	Average-12.2

How the Competition Rates

Competitors	Rating	Pg.
Infiniti Q50	3	158
Lexus ES		178
Volvo S60		253

Price Range

	Retail	Markup
530i	$52,400	6%
530xe	$54,700	6%
540xi	$60,000	7%
M550i	$73,400	7%

Safety Checklist

Crash Test:
  Frontal . . . . Very Poor
  Side . . . . Good
Airbags:
  Torso . . . . Std. Front Torso from Seat
  Roll Sensing . . . . Yes
  Knee Bolster . . . . None
Crash Avoidance:
  Collision Avoidance . . Optional CIB & DBS^
  Blind Spot Detection . . . . Optional
  Lane Keeping Assist . Warn. Only Optional^
  Pedestrian Crash Avoidance . . . . . Optional
General:
  Auto. Crash Notif. Op. Assist. & Crash Info-Free
  Day Running Lamps . . . . Standard
Safety Belt/Restraint:
  Dynamic Head Restraints . . Standard Front
  Adjustable Belt . . . . None

^Warning feature does not meet government standards.

BMW 5 Series

Specifications

Drive	RWD
Engine	2.0-liter I4
Transmission	8-sp. Automatic
Tow Rating (lbs.)	—
Head/Leg Room (in.)	Average-40.5/41.4
Interior Space (cu. ft.)	Average-102
Cargo Space (cu. ft.)	Average-18.4
Wheelbase/Length (in.)	116.9/193.4

Ratings—10 Best, 1 Worst

Combo Crash Tests	—
Safety Features	10
Rollover	7
Preventive Maintenance	1
Repair Costs	1
Warranty	9
Fuel Economy	4
Complaints	5
Insurance Costs	1
OVERALL RATING	—

BMW 7 Series

BMW 7 Series

At-a-Glance

Status/Year Series Started. Unchanged/2016
Twins . . . . —
Body Styles . . . . .Sedan
Seating. 5
Anti-Theft Device . Std. Pass. Immobil. & Active Alarm
Parking Index Rating . . . . .Very Hard
Where Made. . .Dingolfing, Germany / Toluca, Mexico
Fuel Factor
  MPG Rating (city/hwy) Poor-21/29
  Driving Range (mi.) . . . . Very Long-494
  Fuel Type. . . . . .Premium
  Annual Fuel Cost . . . . .High-$1858
  Gas Guzzler Tax . . . . .No
  Greenhouse Gas Emissions (tons/yr.) . . Average-6.1
  Barrels of Oil Used per year High-13.7

How the Competition Rates

Competitors	Rating	Pg.
Buick LaCrosse	5	92
Mercedes-Benz E-Class	3	198
Tesla Model S	10	229

Price Range	Retail	Markup
740i	$83,100	8%
740i xDrive	$86,100	8%
750i	$96,400	8%
750i xDrive	$99,400	8%

Safety Checklist

Crash Test:
  Frontal. . . . . —
  Side. . . . . —
Airbags:
  Torso . . . . Std. Front Torso from Seat
  Roll Sensing. . . . . .Yes
  Knee Bolster . . . . Standard Front
Crash Avoidance:
  Collision Avoidance . . Optional CIB & DBS^
  Blind Spot Detection . . . . Optional
  Lane Keeping Assist . . . . Optional^
  Pedestrian Crash Avoidance . . . . . Optional
General:
  Auto. Crash Notif. Op. Assist. & Crash Info-Free
  Day Running Lamps . . . . Standard
Safety Belt/Restraint:
  Dynamic Head Restraints . . Standard Front
  Adjustable Belt. . . . . .None

^Warning feature does not meet government standards.

BMW 7 Series

Specifications

Drive. . . . . .RWD
Engine 6.0-liter V8
Transmission . . . . 8-sp. Automatic
Tow Rating (lbs.) . . . . —
Head/Leg Room (in.) Average-39.9/41.4
Interior Space (cu. ft.). Roomy-107
Cargo Space (cu. ft.) Average-18.2
Wheelbase/Length (in.) 126.4/206.6

Ratings—10 Best, 1 Worst

Combo Crash Tests	—
Safety Features	6
Rollover	4
Preventive Maintenance	4
Repair Costs	10
Warranty	9
Fuel Economy	10
Complaints	4
Insurance Costs	10
OVERALL RATING	**—**

BMW i3

BMW i3

At-a-Glance

Status/Year Series Started Unchanged/2016
Twins . . . . —
Body Styles . . . . .Coupe
Seating 4
Anti-Theft Device . Std. Pass. Immobil. & Active Alarm
Parking Index Rating . . . . .Very Easy
Where Made . . . . Leipzig, Germany
Fuel Factor
  MPG Rating (city/hwy) . . . . Very Good-137/111
  Driving Range (mi.) 200
  Fuel Type . . . . .Premium
  Annual Fuel Cost . . . . .Very Low-$650
  Gas Guzzler Tax . . . . .No
  Greenhouse Gas Emissions (tons/yr.) . Very Low-0.5
  Barrels of Oil Used per year . . . . Very Low-1.2

How the Competition Rates

Competitors	Rating	Pg.
Chevrolet Bolt		100
Nissan Leaf		212
Tesla Model 3		228

Price Range

	Retail	Markup
i3	$44,450	6%
i3s	$47,650	6%
i3 w/Range Extender	$48,300	6%
i3s w/Range Extender	$51,500	6%

Safety Checklist

Crash Test:
  Frontal . . . . —
  Side . . . . —
Airbags:
  Torso . . . . Std. Front Torso from Seat
  Roll Sensing . . . . .Yes
  Knee Bolster . . . . Standard Front
Crash Avoidance:
  Collision Avoidance . . Optional CIB & DBS^
  Blind Spot Detection . . . . .None
  Lane Keeping Assist . Warn. Only Optional^
  Pedestrian Crash Avoidance . . . . . Optional
General:
  Auto. Crash Notif. . Op. Assist. & Crash Info-Free
  Day Running Lamps . . . . .Standard
Safety Belt/Restraint:
  Dynamic Head Restraints . . . . .None
  Adjustable Belt . . . . .None

^Warning feature does not meet government standards.

BMW i3

Specifications

Drive . . . . .RWD
Engine . . . . Electric
Transmission . . . . CVT
Tow Rating (lbs.) . . . . —
Head/Leg Room (in.) Cramped-39.6/40.5
Interior Space (cu. ft.) . . . . Very Cramped-83.1
Cargo Space (cu. ft.) . . . . Very Cramped-11.8
Wheelbase/Length (in.) 101/157

Ratings—10 Best, 1 Worst

Combo Crash Tests	—
Safety Features	6
Rollover	4
Preventive Maintenance	7
Repair Costs	1
Warranty	9
Fuel Economy	6
Complaints	4
Insurance Costs	3
OVERALL RATING	**—**

BMW X1

BMW X1

At-a-Glance

Status/Year Series Started Unchanged/2016
Twins . . . . —
Body Styles . . . . SUV
Seating 5
Anti-Theft Device . Std. Pass. Immobil. & Active Alarm
Parking Index Rating . . . . Easy
Where Made. . . . . Leipzig, Germany
Fuel Factor
　MPG Rating (city/hwy) Average-22/32
　Driving Range (mi.) Average-412
　Fuel Type. . . . . .Premium
　Annual Fuel Cost . . . . .High-$1740
　Gas Guzzler Tax . . . . .No
　Greenhouse Gas Emissions (tons/yr.) Low-5.7
　Barrels of Oil Used per year Average-12.7

How the Competition Rates

Competitors	Rating	Pg.
Buick Encore	10	90
Lexus NX	5	182
Lincoln MKC	6	186

Price Range	Retail	Markup
sDrive28i	$33,900	6%
XDrive28i	$35,900	6%

Safety Checklist

Crash Test:
　Frontal. . . . . —
　Side. . . . . —
Airbags:
　Torso . . . . Std. Front Torso from Seat
　Roll Sensing. .Yes
　Knee Bolster . . . . Standard Front
Crash Avoidance:
　Collision Avoidance . . .Optional CIB & DBS
　Blind Spot Detection . . . . .None
　Lane Keeping Assist . Warn. Only Optional^
　Pedestrian Crash Avoidance . . . . . Optional
General:
　Auto. Crash Notif. . Op. Assist. & Crash Info-Free
　Day Running Lamps . . . . .Standard
Safety Belt/Restraint:
　Dynamic Head Restraints . . . . .None
　Adjustable Belt. . . . . .None

^Warning feature does not meet government standards.

BMW X1

Specifications

Drive. . . . . .RWD
Engine 2.0-liter I4
Transmission . . . . 8-sp. Automatic
Tow Rating (lbs.) Low-4400
Head/Leg Room (in.) Average-41.9/40.4
Interior Space (cu. ft.). Average-101
Cargo Space (cu. ft.) Roomy-27.1
Wheelbase/Length (in.) 105.1/174.8

Ratings—10 Best, 1 Worst

Combo Crash Tests	—
Safety Features	8
Rollover	—
Preventive Maintenance	1
Repair Costs	1
Warranty	9
Fuel Economy	5
Complaints	10
Insurance Costs	5
OVERALL RATING	—

BMW X3

At-a-Glance

Status/Year Series Started	Unchanged/2018
Twins	—
Body Styles	SUV
Seating	5
Anti-Theft Device	Std. Pass. Immobil. & Active Alarm
Parking Index Rating	Hard
Where Made	—
Fuel Factor	
MPG Rating (city/hwy)	Average-22/29
Driving Range (mi.)	Long-425
Fuel Type	Premium
Annual Fuel Cost	High-$1805
Gas Guzzler Tax	No
Greenhouse Gas Emissions (tons/yr.)	Average-5.9
Barrels of Oil Used per year	High-13.2

How the Competition Rates

Competitors	Rating	Pg.
Acura MDX	7	67
Infiniti QX60	5	161
Lexus RX	4	184

Price Range	Retail	Markup
sDrive28i	$39,250	6%
XDrive28i	$41,250	6%
XDrive28d	$42,750	6%
XDrive35i	$47,950	6%

BMW X3

Safety Checklist

Crash Test:
  Frontal . . . . —
  Side . . . . —
Airbags:
  Torso . . . . Std. Front Torso from Seat
  Roll Sensing . . . . Yes
  Knee Bolster . . . . Standard Driver
Crash Avoidance:
  Collision Avoidance . . Optional CIB & DBS^
  Blind Spot Detection . . . . Optional
  Lane Keeping Assist . Warn. Only Optional^
  Pedestrian Crash Avoidance . . . . . Optional
General:
  Auto. Crash Notif. . Op. Assist. & Crash Info-Free
  Day Running Lamps . . . . Standard
Safety Belt/Restraint:
  Dynamic Head Restraints . . Standard Front
  Adjustable Belt . . . . None

^Warning feature does not meet government standards.

BMW X3

Specifications

Drive	AWD
Engine	2.0-liter I4
Transmission	5-sp. Automatic
Tow Rating (lbs.)	Very Low-1000
Head/Leg Room (in.)	Average-41.1/40.3
Interior Space (cu. ft.)	Cramped-93.7
Cargo Space (cu. ft.)	Roomy-28.7
Wheelbase/Length (in.)	112.8/185.9

Ratings—10 Best, 1 Worst

Combo Crash Tests	—
Safety Features	8
Rollover	3
Preventive Maintenance	3
Repair Costs	1
Warranty	9
Fuel Economy	3
Complaints	9
Insurance Costs	1

OVERALL RATING   —

BMW X5

BMW X5

At-a-Glance

Status/Year Series Started. . . . . All New/2019
Twins . . . . —
Body Styles . . . . SUV
Seating 5
Anti-Theft Device . Std. Pass. Immobil. & Active Alarm
Parking Index Rating . . . . Very Hard
Where Made. . . . . .Spartanburg, SC / Toluca, Mexico
Fuel Factor
  MPG Rating (city/hwy) Averge-20/26
  Driving Range (mi.) . . . . Very Long-481
  Fuel Type. . . . . .Premium
  Annual Fuel Cost . . . . Very High-$2052
  Gas Guzzler Tax . . . . .No
  Greenhouse Gas Emissions (tons/yr.) . . Average-6.5
  Barrels of Oil Used per year High-15

How the Competition Rates

Competitors	Rating	Pg.
Acura MDX	7	67
Audi Q7	3	77
Cadillac XT5	3	98

Price Range	Retail	Markup
XDrive40i	$60,700	7%
XDrive50i	$75,750	7%

Safety Checklist

Crash Test:
  Frontal. . . . . —
  Side. . . . . —
Airbags:
  Torso . . . . Std. Front Torso from Seat
  Roll Sensing. . . . . .Yes
  Knee Bolster . . . . Standard Front
Crash Avoidance:
  Collision Avoidance . . Optional CIB & DBS^
  Blind Spot Detection . . . . .None
  Lane Keeping Assist . . . . Optional
  Pedestrian Crash Avoidance . . . . . Optional
General:
  Auto. Crash Notif. . Op. Assist. & Crash Info-Free
  Day Running Lamps . . . . .Standard
Safety Belt/Restraint:
  Dynamic Head Restraints . . Standard Front
  Adjustable Belt . . . . .None

^Warning feature does not meet government standards.

BMW X5

Specifications

Drive. . . . . .AWD
Engine 3.0-liter V6
Transmission . . . . 8-sp. Automatic
Tow Rating (lbs.) Average-6600
Head/Leg Room (in.) Cramped-40.8/39.8
Interior Space (cu. ft.). . . . . —
Cargo Space (cu. ft.) . . . . Very Roomy-33.9
Wheelbase/Length (in.) 117.1/194.3

BMW X6

Ratings—10 Best, 1 Worst

Combo Crash Tests	—
Safety Features	6
Rollover	—
Preventive Maintenance	2
Repair Costs	1
Warranty	9
Fuel Economy	2
Complaints	3
Insurance Costs	1
OVERALL RATING	**—**

BMW X6

At-a-Glance

Status/Year Series Started	Unchanged/2010
Twins	—
Body Styles	SUV
Seating	5
Anti-Theft Device	Std. Pass. Immobil. & Active Alarm
Parking Index Rating	Very Hard
Where Made	Spartanburg, SC
Fuel Factor	
MPG Rating (city/hwy)	Very Poor-18/24
Driving Range (mi.)	Long-454
Fuel Type	Premium
Annual Fuel Cost	Very High-$2197
Gas Guzzler Tax	No
Greenhouse Gas Emissions (tons/yr.)	Average-7.0
Barrels of Oil Used per year	High-15.7

How the Competition Rates

Competitors	Rating	Pg.
Audi Q7	3	77
Cadillac XT5	3	98
Lincoln Nautilis	5	188

Price Range	Retail	Markup
XDrive35i	$60,500	7%
sDrive35i	$62,700	7%
XDrive50i	$77,450	7%
M	$104,100	7%

Safety Checklist

Crash Test:
- Frontal . . . . —
- Side . . . . —

Airbags:
- Torso . . . . Std. Front Torso from Seat
- Roll Sensing . . . . Yes
- Knee Bolster . . . . None

Crash Avoidance:
- Collision Avoidance . . Optional CIB & DBS^
- Blind Spot Detection . . . . None
- Lane Keeping Assist . Warn. Only Optional^
- Pedestrian Crash Avoidance . . . . . Optional

General:
- Auto. Crash Notif. . Op. Assist. & Crash Info-Free
- Day Running Lamps . . . . Standard

Safety Belt/Restraint:
- Dynamic Head Restraints . . Standard Front
- Adjustable Belt . . . . None

^Warning feature does not meet government standards.

BMW X6

Specifications

Drive	AWD
Engine	3.0-liter V6
Transmission	8-sp. Automatic
Tow Rating (lbs.)	Average-6000
Head/Leg Room (in.)	Cramped-39.9/40.3
Interior Space (cu. ft.)	Average-101.4
Cargo Space (cu. ft.)	Roomy-26.6
Wheelbase/Length (in.)	115/193.8

Ratings—10 Best, 1 Worst

Combo Crash Tests	—
Safety Features	2
Rollover	7
Preventive Maintenance	1
Repair Costs	5
Warranty	8
Fuel Economy	4
Complaints	5
Insurance Costs	10

OVERALL RATING   —

Buick Cascada

Buick Cascada

At-a-Glance

```
Status/Year Series Started. . . . . . . Unchanged/2017
Twins . . . . . . . . . . . . . . . . . . . . . . . . . . . . . —
Body Styles . . . . . . . . . . . . . . . . . . . . . Convertible
Seating . . . . . . . . . . . . . . . . . . . . . . . . . . . . . 4
Anti-Theft Device . Std. Pass. Immobil. & Active Alarm
Parking Index Rating . . . . . . . . . . . . . . . . . Average
Where Made. . . . . . . . . . . . . . . . . Gliwice, Poland
Fuel Factor
  MPG Rating (city/hwy) . . . . . . . . . . . . . . Poor-20/27
  Driving Range (mi.) . . . . . . . . . . . . . Very Short-324
  Fuel Type . . . . . . . . . . . . . . . . . . . . . . . . Regular
  Annual Fuel Cost . . . . . . . . . . . . . . . Average-$1623
  Gas Guzzler Tax . . . . . . . . . . . . . . . . . . . . . . . No
  Greenhouse Gas Emissions (tons/yr.) . . Average-6.5
  Barrels of Oil Used per year . . . . . . . . . . High-14.3
```

How the Competition Rates

Competitors	Rating	Pg.
Audi A3	5	71
Cadillac ATS	4	94
Lexus IS	8	181

Price Range

	Retail	Markup
Convertible	$33,065	1%
Convertible Premium	$36,065	4%
Convertible Sport Touring	$37,065	4%

Safety Checklist

```
Crash Test:
  Frontal. . . . . . . . . . . . . . . . . . . . . . . . . . . —
  Side. . . . . . . . . . . . . . . . . . . . . . . . . . . . . —
Airbags:
  Torso . . . . . . . . Std. Front Torso from Seat
  Roll Sensing. . . . . . . . . . . . . . . . . . . . . . No
  Knee Bolster . . . . . . . . . . . Standard Front
Crash Avoidance:
  Collision Avoidance Warning Only Optional^
  Blind Spot Detection . . . . . . . . . . . . . None
  Lane Keeping Assist . Warn. Only Optional^
  Pedestrian Crash Avoidance . . . . . . . None
General:
  Auto. Crash Notif. . . Op. Assist. & Crash Info-Fee
  Day Running Lamps . . . . . . . . . . Standard
Safety Belt/Restraint:
  Dynamic Head Restraints . . . . . . . . . None
  Adjustable Belt. . . . . . . . . . . Optional Rear
```
^Warning feature does not meet government standards.

Buick Cascada

Specifications

```
Drive. . . . . . . . . . . . . . . . . . . . . . . . . . . . . . . . FWD
Engine . . . . . . . . . . . . . . . . . . . . . . . . 1.6-liter I4
Transmission . . . . . . . . . . . . . . . 6-sp. Automatic
Tow Rating (lbs.) . . . . . . . . . . . . . . . . . . . . . . . . —
Head/Leg Room (in.) . . . . . . . . . . .Cramped-37.8/42.2
Interior Space (cu. ft.). . . . . . . . . . .Very Cramped-82
Cargo Space (cu. ft.) . . . . . . Very Cramped-13.4
Wheelbase/Length (in.) . . . . . . . . . .106.1/184.9
```

Ratings—10 Best, 1 Worst

Combo Crash Tests	5
Safety Features	5
Rollover	4
Preventive Maintenance	2
Repair Costs	3
Warranty	8
Fuel Economy	3
Complaints	6
Insurance Costs	10
OVERALL RATING	**4**

Buick Enclave

Buick Enclave

At-a-Glance

Status/Year Series Started	Unchanged/2018
Twins	Chevrolet Traverse
Body Styles	SUV
Seating	7
Anti-Theft Device	Std. Pass. Immobil. & Active Alarm
Parking Index Rating	Very Hard
Where Made	Lansing, MI
Fuel Factor	
MPG Rating (city/hwy)	Poor-18/26
Driving Range (mi.)	Average-405
Fuel Type	Regular
Annual Fuel Cost	High-$1759
Gas Guzzler Tax	No
Greenhouse Gas Emissions (tons/yr.)	Average-7.0
Barrels of Oil Used per year	High-15.7

How the Competition Rates

Competitors	Rating	Pg.
Chevrolet Tahoe	4	112
Chevrolet Traverse	4	113
Volvo XC90	8	256

Price Range	Retail	Markup
Base FWD	$39,995	1%
Essence FWD	$44,215	5%
Premium AWD	$50,315	5%
Avenir AWD	$55,715	5%

Safety Checklist

Crash Test:
  Frontal . . . . Average
  Side . . . . Poor
Airbags:
  Torso . . . Std. Front Pelvis/Torso from Seat
  Roll Sensing . . . . Yes
  Knee Bolster . . . . None
Crash Avoidance:
  Collision Avoidance . . . Optional CIB & DBS
  Blind Spot Detection . . . . Optional
  Lane Keeping Assist . . Warn. Only Optional
  Pedestrian Crash Avoidance . . . . . Optional
General:
  Auto. Crash Notif. . . Op. Assist. & Crash Info-Fee
  Day Running Lamps . . . . Standard
Safety Belt/Restraint:
  Dynamic Head Restraints . . . . None
  Adjustable Belt . . . . Optional Rear

^Warning feature does not meet government standards

Buick Enclave

Specifications

Drive	FWD
Engine	3.6-liter V6
Transmission	9-sp. Automatic
Tow Rating (lbs.)	Low-5000
Head/Leg Room (in.)	Average-41/41.2
Interior Space (cu. ft.)	—
Cargo Space (cu. ft.)	Roomy-23.6
Wheelbase/Length (in.)	120.9/204.3

Ratings—10 Best, 1 Worst

Combo Crash Tests	8
Safety Features	7
Rollover	3
Preventive Maintenance	7
Repair Costs	8
Warranty	8
Fuel Economy	6
Complaints	10
Insurance Costs	5
OVERALL RATING	**1**

Buick Encore

Buick Encore

At-a-Glance

Status/Year Series Started	Unchanged/2013
Twins	Chevrolet Trax
Body Styles	SUV
Seating	5
Anti-Theft Device	Std. Pass. Immobil. & Active Alarm
Parking Index Rating	Easy
Where Made	Bupyeong, South Korea

Fuel Factor
MPG Rating (city/hwy)	Average-23/30
Driving Range (mi.)	Very Short-360
Fuel Type	Regular
Annual Fuel Cost	Low-$1430
Gas Guzzler Tax	No
Greenhouse Gas Emissions (tons/yr.)	Average-6.9
Barrels of Oil Used per year	Average-12.7

How the Competition Rates

Competitors	Rating	Pg.
Acura RDX	9	68
Ford Escape	5	126
Lincoln MKC	6	186

Price Range

	Retail	Markup
Preferred FWD	$24,365	4%
Sport Touring FWD	$25,565	4%
Essence AWD	$30,565	4%
Premium AWD	$32,015	4%

Safety Checklist

Crash Test:
- Frontal . . . . Very Good
- Side . . . . Average

Airbags:
- Torso Std. Front & Rear Pelvis/Torso from Seat
- Roll Sensing . . . . Yes
- Knee Bolster . . . . Standard Front

Crash Avoidance:
- Collision Avoidance . Warning Only Optional
- Blind Spot Detection . . . . Optional
- Lane Keeping Assist . . Warn. Only Optional
- Pedestrian Crash Avoidance . . . . None

General:
- Auto. Crash Notif. . . Op. Assist. & Crash Info-Fee
- Day Running Lamps . . . . Standard

Safety Belt/Restraint:
- Dynamic Head Restraints . . . . None
- Adjustable Belt . . . . . Optional Front & Rear

^Warning feature does not meet government standards.

Buick Encore

Specifications

Drive	AWD
Engine	1.4-liter I4
Transmission	6-sp. Automatic
Tow Rating (lbs.)	—
Head/Leg Room (in.)	Cramped-39.6/40.8
Interior Space (cu. ft.)	Cramped-92.8
Cargo Space (cu. ft.)	Average-18.8
Wheelbase/Length (in.)	100.6/168.4

Ratings—10 Best, 1 Worst

Combo Crash Tests	—
Safety Features	10
Rollover	2
Preventive Maintenance	2
Repair Costs	4
Warranty	8
Fuel Economy	4
Complaints	4
Insurance Costs	8
OVERALL RATING	**—**

Buick Envision

Buick Envision

At-a-Glance

Status/Year Series Started	Unchanged/2016
Twins	—
Body Styles	SUV
Seating	5
Anti-Theft Device	Std. Pass. Immobil. & Active Alarm
Parking Index Rating	Hard
Where Made	Yantai, Shandong
Fuel Factor	
MPG Rating (city/hwy)	Poor-21/27
Driving Range (mi.)	Average-404
Fuel Type	Regular
Annual Fuel Cost	Average-$1575
Gas Guzzler Tax	No
Greenhouse Gas Emissions (tons/yr.)	Average-6.2
Barrels of Oil Used per year	High-13.7

How the Competition Rates

Competitors	Rating	Pg.
Acura MDX	7	67
Audi Q7	3	77
BMW X5		86

Price Range

	Retail	Markup
Preferred FWD	$35,870	5%
Essence FWD	$37,720	5%
Premium I AWD	$42,320	5%
Premium II AWD	$44,960	5%

Buick Envision

Safety Checklist

Crash Test:
  Frontal . . . . —
  Side . . . . —
Airbags:
  Torso Std. Front & Rear Pelvis/Torso from Seat
  Roll Sensing . . . . Yes
  Knee Bolster . . . . Standard Front
Crash Avoidance:
  Collision Avoidance . . Optional CIB & DBS^
  Blind Spot Detection . . . . Optional
  Lane Keeping Assist . . Warn. Only Optional
  Pedestrian Crash Avoidance . . . . . Optional
General:
  Auto. Crash Notif. . . Op. Assist. & Crash Info-Fee
  Day Running Lamps . . . . Standard
Safety Belt/Restraint:
  Dynamic Head Restraints . . . . None
  Adjustable Belt . . . . . Optional Front & Rear

^Warning feature does not meet government standards.

Buick Envision

Specifications

Drive	AWD
Engine	2.5-liter I4
Transmission	6-sp. Automatic
Tow Rating (lbs.)	Very Low-1500
Head/Leg Room (in.)	Cramped-40/40.9
Interior Space (cu. ft.)	Average-100.6
Cargo Space (cu. ft.)	Roomy-26.9
Wheelbase/Length (in.)	108.2/183.7

Ratings—10 Best, 1 Worst

Combo Crash Tests	5
Safety Features	9
Rollover	8
Preventive Maintenance	1
Repair Costs	2
Warranty	8
Fuel Economy	5
Complaints	8
Insurance Costs	5
OVERALL RATING	**5**

Buick LaCrosse

Buick LaCrosse

At-a-Glance

Status/Year Series Started	Unchanged/2017
Twins	—
Body Styles	Sedan
Seating	5
Anti-Theft Device	Std. Pass. Immobil. & Active Alarm
Parking Index Rating	Hard
Where Made	Fairfax, KS

Fuel Factor

MPG Rating (city/hwy)	Average-21/31
Driving Range (mi.)	Short-388
Fuel Type	Regular
Annual Fuel Cost	Average-$1496
Gas Guzzler Tax	No
Greenhouse Gas Emissions (tons/yr.)	Average-6.0
Barrels of Oil Used per year	High-13.2

How the Competition Rates

Competitors	Rating	Pg.
Cadillac XTS	8	99
Ford Taurus	3	136
Toyota Avalon	8	233

Price Range	Retail	Markup
1SV	$29,565	1%
Preferred	$33,665	4%
Essence	$36,365	4%
Premium AWD	$43,425	4%

Safety Checklist

Crash Test:
- Frontal . . . . Good
- Side . . . . Very Poor

Airbags:
- Torso Std. Fr. & Opt. Rr. Pelvis/Torso from Seat
- Roll Sensing . . . . Yes
- Knee Bolster . . . . Standard Front

Crash Avoidance:
- Collision Avoidance . . . Optional CIB & DBS
- Blind Spot Detection . . . . Optional
- Lane Keeping Assist . . . . Optional
- Pedestrian Crash Avoidance . . . . . Optional

General:
- Auto. Crash Notif. . . Op. Assist. & Crash Info-Fee
- Day Running Lamps . . . . Standard

Safety Belt/Restraint:
- Dynamic Head Restraints . . . . None
- Adjustable Belt . . . . . Optional Front & Rear

^Warning feature does not meet government standards.

Buick LaCrosse

Specifications

Drive	FWD
Engine	3.6-liter V6
Transmission	8-sp. Automatic
Tow Rating (lbs.)	—
Head/Leg Room (in.)	Cramped-38.4/42
Interior Space (cu. ft.)	Average-100
Cargo Space (cu. ft.)	Cramped-15
Wheelbase/Length (in.)	114.4/197.5

Ratings—10 Best, 1 Worst

Combo Crash Tests	—
Safety Features	10
Rollover	7
Preventive Maintenance	1
Repair Costs	3
Warranty	8
Fuel Economy	6
Complaints	7
Insurance Costs	8
OVERALL RATING	**—**

Buick Regal

At-a-Glance

Status/Year Series Started	Unchanged/2018
Twins	Chevrolet Malibu
Body Styles	Sedan, Wagon
Seating	5
Anti-Theft Device	Std. Pass. Immobil. & Active Alarm
Parking Index Rating	Average
Where Made	Oshawa, Ontario
Fuel Factor	
MPG Rating (city/hwy)	Average-22/32
Driving Range (mi.)	Average-417
Fuel Type	Premium
Annual Fuel Cost	High-$1740
Gas Guzzler Tax	No
Greenhouse Gas Emissions (tons/yr.)	Average-6.7
Barrels of Oil Used per year	High-15.0

How the Competition Rates

Competitors	Rating	Pg.
Acura TLX	9	70
Lincoln MKZ	4	187
Mazda 6	5	194

Price Range	Retail	Markup
1SV	$27,065	1%
Sport Touring	$28,615	4%
Leather	$31,465	4%
GS AWD	$36,540	4%

Buick Regal

Safety Checklist

Crash Test:
  Frontal................................. —
  Side..................................... —
Airbags:
  Torso Std. Front & Rear Pelvis/Torso from Seat
  Roll Sensing........................Yes
  Knee Bolster ....Standard Front
Crash Avoidance:
  Collision Avoidance . . .Optional CIB & DBS
  Blind Spot Detection ....Optional
  Lane Keeping Assist ....Optional
  Pedestrian Crash Avoidance..... Optional
General:
  Auto. Crash Notif. . . Op. Assist. & Crash Info-Fee
  Day Running Lamps ....Standard
Safety Belt/Restraint:
  Dynamic Head Restraints ....None
  Adjustable Belt.............Optional Rear

^Warning feature does not meet government standards.

Buick Regal

Specifications

Drive	FWD
Engine	3.6-liter V6
Transmission	9-sp. Automatic
Tow Rating (lbs.)	—
Head/Leg Room (in.)	Cramped-38.8/42.1
Interior Space (cu. ft.)	Average-98
Cargo Space (cu. ft.)	Very Roomy-31.5
Wheelbase/Length (in.)	111.4/192.9

Ratings—10 Best, 1 Worst

Combo Crash Tests	2
Safety Features	8
Rollover	8
Preventive Maintenance	2
Repair Costs	2
Warranty	10
Fuel Economy	5
Complaints	6
Insurance Costs	8
OVERALL RATING	**4**

Cadillac ATS

Cadillac ATS

At-a-Glance

Status/Year Series Started	Unchanged/2013
Twins	—
Body Styles	Sedan, Coupe
Seating	5
Anti-Theft Device	Std. Pass. Immobil. & Active Alarm
Parking Index Rating	Easy
Where Made	Lansing, MI

Fuel Factor
MPG Rating (city/hwy)	Average-21/33
Driving Range (mi.)	Average-402
Fuel Type	Regular
Annual Fuel Cost	Average-$1464
Gas Guzzler Tax	No
Greenhouse Gas Emissions (tons/yr.)	Average-7.2
Barrels of Oil Used per year	High-13.2

How the Competition Rates

Competitors	Rating	Pg.
Audi A3	5	71
Infiniti Q50	3	158
Lexus IS	8	181

Price Range	Retail	Markup
Base 2.0L Sedan RWD	$34,895	5%
Luxury 2.0L Sedan AWD	$40,695	5%
Performance 3.6L Sedan RWD	$47,295	5%
Premium 3.6L Coupe AWD	$49,295	5%

Safety Checklist

Crash Test:
Frontal	Very Poor
Side	Poor

Airbags:
Torso	Std. Fr. & Opt. Rr. Pelvis/Torso from Seat
Roll Sensing	Yes
Knee Bolster	Standard Front

Crash Avoidance:
Collision Avoidance	Optional CIB & DBS
Blind Spot Detection	Optional
Lane Keeping Assist	Optional
Pedestrian Crash Avoidance	None

General:
Auto. Crash Notif.	Op. Assist. & Crash Info-Fee
Day Running Lamps	Standard

Safety Belt/Restraint:
Dynamic Head Restraints	None
Adjustable Belt	Optional Rear

^Warning feature does not meet government standards.

Cadillac ATS

Specifications

Drive	RWD
Engine	2.0-liter I4
Transmission	6-sp. Automatic
Tow Rating (lbs.)	—
Head/Leg Room (in.)	Average-38.6/42.5
Interior Space (cu. ft.)	Cramped-90.9
Cargo Space (cu. ft.)	Very Cramped-10.4
Wheelbase/Length (in.)	109.3/182.8

Ratings—10 Best, 1 Worst

Combo Crash Tests	—
Safety Features	9
Rollover	7
Preventive Maintenance	2
Repair Costs	2
Warranty	10
Fuel Economy	3
Complaints	8
Insurance Costs	3
OVERALL RATING	**—**

Cadillac CT6

At-a-Glance

Status/Year Series Started........ Unchanged/2016
Twins . . . . —
Body Styles . . . . Sedan
Seating 5
Anti-Theft Device . Std. Pass. Immobil. & Active Alarm
Parking Index Rating . . . . Very Hard
Where Made. . . . . .Hamtramck, MI
Fuel Factor
  MPG Rating (city/hwy) Poor-18/27
  Driving Range (mi.) Average-413
  Fuel Type . . . . .Regular
  Annual Fuel Cost . . . . .High-$1735
  Gas Guzzler Tax . . . . .No
  Greenhouse Gas Emissions (tons/yr.) . . Average-6.9
  Barrels of Oil Used per year High-15.7

How the Competition Rates

Competitors	Rating	Pg.
Lincoln Continental	6	185
Mercedes-Benz E-Class	3	198
Tesla Model S	10	229

Price Range

Price Range	Retail	Markup
Base 2.0L RWD	$54,095	5%
Luxury 3.6L AWD	$61,195	5%
Premium Luxury 3.6L AWD	$65,295	5%
Platinum 3.0L TT AWD	$88,295	5%

Cadillac CT6

Safety Checklist

Crash Test:
  Frontal. . . . . —
  Side. . . . . —
Airbags:
  Torso . . . Std. Front Pelvis/Torso from Seat
  Roll Sensing. . . . . .Yes
  Knee Bolster . . . . .Standard Front
Crash Avoidance:
  Collision Avoidance . . .Optional CIB & DBS
  Blind Spot Detection . . . . Optional
  Lane Keeping Assist . . . . Optional
  Pedestrian Crash Avoidance . . . . . Optional
General:
  Auto. Crash Notif. . . Op. Assist. & Crash Info-Fee
  Day Running Lamps . . . . .Standard
Safety Belt/Restraint:
  Dynamic Head Restraints . . . . .None
  Adjustable Belt. . . . . Optional Front & Rear

^Warning feature does not meet government standards.

Cadillac CT6

Specifications

Drive. . . . . .AWD
Engine 3.6-liter V6
Transmission . . . . 5-sp. Automatic
Tow Rating (lbs.) . . . . —
Head/Leg Room (in.) Average-40.1/42.3
Interior Space (cu. ft.). Roomy-110
Cargo Space (cu. ft.) Cramped-15.3
Wheelbase/Length (in.) 122.4/204

Ratings—10 Best, 1 Worst	
Combo Crash Tests	7
Safety Features	5
Rollover	2
Preventive Maintenance	1
Repair Costs	3
Warranty	10
Fuel Economy	2
Complaints	7
Insurance Costs	5
OVERALL RATING	**3**

Cadillac Escalade

Cadillac Escalade

At-a-Glance

Status/Year Series Started	Unchanged/2015
Twins	Chevrolet Suburban, GMC Yukon
Body Styles	SUV
Seating	6/9
Anti-Theft Device	Std. Pass. Immobil. & Active Alarm
Parking Index Rating	Very Hard
Where Made	Arlington, TX

Fuel Factor
MPG Rating (city/hwy)	Very Poor-16/22
Driving Range (mi.)	Very Long-474
Fuel Type	Regular
Annual Fuel Cost	Very High-$2015
Gas Guzzler Tax	No
Greenhouse Gas Emissions (tons/yr.)	High-8.2
Barrels of Oil Used per year	Very High-18.3

How the Competition Rates

Competitors	Rating	Pg.
Ford Expedition		217
GMC Yukon	5	142
Volvo XC90	8	256

Price Range	Retail	Markup
Base 2WD	$76,995	7%
Luxury 2WD	$83,690	7%
Premium Luxury 4WD	$88,290	7%
Platinum 4WD	$97,390	7%

Safety Checklist

Crash Test:
- Frontal . . . . Poor
- Side . . . . Very Good

Airbags:
- Torso . . . Std. Front Pelvis/Torso from Seat
- Roll Sensing . . . . Yes
- Knee Bolster . . . . None

Crash Avoidance:
- Collision Avoidance . . . Optional CIB & DBS
- Blind Spot Detection . . . . Optional
- Lane Keeping Assist . . . . Optional
- Pedestrian Crash Avoidance . . . . None

General:
- Auto. Crash Notif. . . Op. Assist. & Crash Info-Fee
- Day Running Lamps . . . . Standard

Safety Belt/Restraint:
- Dynamic Head Restraints . . . . None
- Adjustable Belt . . . . . Optional Front & Rear

^Warning feature does not meet government standards.

Cadillac Escalade

Specifications

Drive	AWD
Engine	6.2-liter V8
Transmission	6-sp. Automatic
Tow Rating (lbs.)	High-8100
Head/Leg Room (in.)	Very Roomy-42.8/45.3
Interior Space (cu. ft.)	Roomy-120.8
Cargo Space (cu. ft.)	Cramped-15.2
Wheelbase/Length (in.)	116/203.9

Ratings—10 Best, 1 Worst

Combo Crash Tests	5
Safety Features	5
Rollover	2
Preventive Maintenance	1
Repair Costs	5
Warranty	10
Fuel Economy	1
Complaints	10
Insurance Costs	10
OVERALL RATING	**4**

Cadillac Escalade ESV

Cadillac Escalade ESV

At-a-Glance

Status/Year Series Started Unchanged/2015
Twins . . . . Chevrolet Tahoe, GMC Yukon XL
Body Styles . . . . SUV
Seating 6/9
Anti-Theft Device . Std. Pass. Immobil. & Active Alarm
Parking Index Rating . . . . Very Hard
Where Made . . . . Arlington, TX
Fuel Factor
  MPG Rating (city/hwy) . . . . Very Poor-15/22
  Driving Range (mi.) . . . . Very Long-543
  Fuel Type . . . . Regular
  Annual Fuel Cost . . . . Very High-$2099
  Gas Guzzler Tax . . . . No
  Greenhouse Gas Emissions (tons/yr.)Very High-10.0
  Barrels of Oil Used per year . . . . Very High-18.3

How the Competition Rates

Competitors	Rating	Pg.
Ford Expedition		217
GMC Yukon XL	4	111
Volvo XC90	8	256

Price Range

Price Range	Retail	Markup
Base 2WD	$79,490	7%
Luxury 2WD	$85,090	7%
Premium Luxury 4WD	$92,490	7%
Platinum 4WD	$101,590	7%

Safety Checklist

Crash Test:
  Frontal . . . . Average
  Side . . . . Average
Airbags:
  Torso . . . Std. Front Pelvis/Torso from Seat
  Roll Sensing . . . . Yes
  Knee Bolster . . . . None
Crash Avoidance:
  Collision Avoidance . . . Optional CIB & DBS
  Blind Spot Detection . . . . Optional
  Lane Keeping Assist . . . . Optional
  Pedestrian Crash Avoidance . . . . None
General:
  Auto. Crash Notif. . . Op. Assist. & Crash Info-Fee
  Day Running Lamps . . . . Standard
Safety Belt/Restraint:
  Dynamic Head Restraints . . . . None
  Adjustable Belt . . . . . Optional Front & Rear

^Warning feature does not meet government standards.

Cadillac Escalade ESV

Specifications

Drive . . . . AWD
Engine 6.2-liter V8
Transmission . . . . 6-sp. Automatic
Tow Rating (lbs.) High-7900
Head/Leg Room (in.) . . . . Very Roomy-42.8/45.3
Interior Space (cu. ft.) Roomy-122.4
Cargo Space (cu. ft.) . . . . Very Roomy-39.3
Wheelbase/Length (in.) 130/224.3

Ratings—10 Best, 1 Worst

Combo Crash Tests	3
Safety Features	8
Rollover	3
Preventive Maintenance	1
Repair Costs	4
Warranty	10
Fuel Economy	3
Complaints	2
Insurance Costs	8
OVERALL RATING	**3**

Cadillac XT5

Cadillac XT5

At-a-Glance

Status/Year Series Started	Unchanged/2017
Twins	GMC Acadia
Body Styles	SUV
Seating	5
Anti-Theft Device	Std. Pass. Immobil. & Active Alarm
Parking Index Rating	Very Easy
Where Made	Spring Hill, TN
Fuel Factor	
MPG Rating (city/hwy)	Poor-19/25
Driving Range (mi.)	Average-405
Fuel Type	Regular
Annual Fuel Cost	High-$1725
Gas Guzzler Tax	No
Greenhouse Gas Emissions (tons/yr.)	Average-6.5
Barrels of Oil Used per year	High-15.0

How the Competition Rates

Competitors	Rating	Pg.
Acura MDX	7	67
Audi Q7	3	77
Lexus RX	4	184

Price Range	Retail	Markup
Base FWD	$39,995	5%
Luxury FWD	$45,995	5%
Premium Luxury AWD	$54,995	5%
Platinum AWD	$62,995	5%

Safety Checklist

Crash Test:
  Frontal . . . . Average
  Side . . . . Very Poor
Airbags:
  Torso . . . Std. Front Pelvis/Torso from Seat
  Roll Sensing . . . . Yes
  Knee Bolster . . . . Standard Driver
Crash Avoidance:
  Collision Avoidance . . . Optional CIB & DBS
  Blind Spot Detection . . . . Optional
  Lane Keeping Assist . . . . Optional
  Pedestrian Crash Avoidance . . . . . Optional
General:
  Auto. Crash Notif. . . Op. Assist. & Crash Info-Fee
  Day Running Lamps . . . . Standard
Safety Belt/Restraint:
  Dynamic Head Restraints . . . . None
  Adjustable Belt . . . . . Standard Front & Rear

^Warning feature does not meet government standards.

Cadillac XT5

Specifications

Drive	FWD
Engine	3.6-liter V6
Transmission	8-sp. Automatic
Tow Rating (lbs.)	Low-3500
Head/Leg Room (in.)	Cramped-38.4/41.2
Interior Space (cu. ft.)	Roomy-104.5
Cargo Space (cu. ft.)	Roomy-30
Wheelbase/Length (in.)	112.5/189.5

Ratings—10 Best, 1 Worst

Combo Crash Tests	9
Safety Features	7
Rollover	6
Preventive Maintenance	1
Repair Costs	3
Warranty	10
Fuel Economy	3
Complaints	8
Insurance Costs	8
OVERALL RATING	**8**

Cadillac XTS

Cadillac XTS

At-a-Glance

Status/Year Series Started	Unchanged/2013
Twins	Chevrolet Impala
Body Styles	Sedan
Seating	5
Anti-Theft Device	Std. Pass. Immobil. & Active Alarm
Parking Index Rating	Hard
Where Made	Oshawa, Ontario
Fuel Factor	
MPG Rating (city/hwy)	Poor-18/28
Driving Range (mi.)	Average-407
Fuel Type	Regular
Annual Fuel Cost	High-$1714
Gas Guzzler Tax	No
Greenhouse Gas Emissions (tons/yr.)	High-8.6
Barrels of Oil Used per year	High-15.7

How the Competition Rates

Competitors	Rating	Pg.
Buick LaCrosse	5	92
Chrysler 300	1	116
Ford Taurus	3	136

Price Range

	Retail	Markup
Base	$45,595	6%
Luxury AWD	$51,595	6%
Platinum	$64,895	7%
Platinum Vsport AWD	$72,695	7%

Safety Checklist

Crash Test:
  Frontal . . . . Very Good
  Side . . . . Good
Airbags:
  Torso Std. Fr. & Opt. Rr. Pelvis/Torso from Seat
  Roll Sensing . . . . Yes
  Knee Bolster . . . . Standard Front
Crash Avoidance:
  Collision Avoidance . . . Optional CIB & DBS
  Blind Spot Detection . . . . Optional
  Lane Keeping Assist . . . . Optional
  Pedestrian Crash Avoidance . . . . None
General:
  Auto. Crash Notif . . . Op. Assist. & Crash Info-Fee
  Day Running Lamps . . . . Standard
Safety Belt/Restraint:
  Dynamic Head Restraints . . . . None
  Adjustable Belt . . . . . Optional Front & Rear

^Warning feature does not meet government standards.

Cadillac XTS

Specifications

Drive	FWD
Engine	3.6-liter V6
Transmission	6-sp. Automatic
Tow Rating (lbs.)	Very Low-1000
Head/Leg Room (in.)	Very Roomy-39/45.8
Interior Space (cu. ft.)	Average-104.2
Cargo Space (cu. ft.)	Average-18
Wheelbase/Length (in.)	111.7/202

Ratings—10 Best, 1 Worst

Combo Crash Tests	—
Safety Features	9
Rollover	3
Preventive Maintenance	6
Repair Costs	10
Warranty	6
Fuel Economy	10
Complaints	2
Insurance Costs	5
OVERALL RATING	**—**

Chevrolet Bolt EV

Chevrolet Bolt EV

At-a-Glance

Status/Year Series Started	Unchanged/2017
Twins	—
Body Styles	Hatchback
Seating	5
Anti-Theft Device	Std. Pass. Immobil. & Alarm
Parking Index Rating	Very Easy
Where Made	Orion Township, MI
Fuel Factor	
MPG Rating (city/hwy)	Very Good-128/110
Driving Range (mi.)	—
Fuel Type	Electricity
Annual Fuel Cost	Very Low-$550
Gas Guzzler Tax	No
Greenhouse Gas Emissions (tons/yr.)	Very Low-0.0
Barrels of Oil Used per year	Very Low-0.0

How the Competition Rates

Competitors	Rating	Pg.
BMW i3		83
Nissan Leaf		212
Tesla Model 3		228

Price Range

	Retail	Markup
LT	$37,495	4%
Premier	$41,895	4%

Safety Checklist

Crash Test:
  Frontal............................ —
  Side.............................. —
Airbags:
  Torso . . . Std. Front Pelvis/Torso from Seat
  Roll Sensing......................Yes
  Knee Bolster .... Standard Front
Crash Avoidance:
  Collision Avoidance . . .Optional CIB & DBS
  Blind Spot Detection .... Optional
  Lane Keeping Assist .... Optional^
  Pedestrian Crash Avoidance ..... Optional
General:
  Auto. Crash Notif. . . Op. Assist. & Crash Info-Fee
  Day Running Lamps ....Standard
Safety Belt/Restraint:
  Dynamic Head Restraints ....None
  Adjustable Belt...........Optional Rear

^Warning feature does not meet government standards.

Chevrolet Bolt EV

Specifications

Drive	FWD
Engine	Electric
Transmission	1-sp. Automatic
Tow Rating (lbs.)	Very Low-0
Head/Leg Room (in.)	Average-39.7/41.6
Interior Space (cu. ft.)	Cramped-95
Cargo Space (cu. ft.)	Average-16.9
Wheelbase/Length (in.)	102.4/164

Chevrolet Camaro Intermediate

Ratings—10 Best, 1 Worst	
Combo Crash Tests	7
Safety Features	4
Rollover	10
Preventive Maintenance	1
Repair Costs	5
Warranty	6
Fuel Economy	3
Complaints	8
Insurance Costs	1
OVERALL RATING	**4**

Chevrolet Camaro

Chevrolet Camaro

At-a-Glance

Status/Year Series Started	Unchanged/2016
Twins	—
Body Styles	Coupe, Convertible
Seating	4
Anti-Theft Device	Std. Pass. Immobil. & Active Alarm
Parking Index Rating	Hard
Where Made	Lansing, MI
Fuel Factor	
MPG Rating (city/hwy)	Poor-19/28
Driving Range (mi.)	Average-422
Fuel Type	Premium
Annual Fuel Cost	Very High-$2006
Gas Guzzler Tax	No
Greenhouse Gas Emissions (tons/yr.)	Average-6.5
Barrels of Oil Used per year	High-14.3

How the Competition Rates

Competitors	Rating	Pg.
Chevrolet Corvette		103
Dodge Challenger	4	118
Ford Mustang	6	134

Price Range

	Retail	Markup
1LT Coupe	$26,700	4%
2LT Convertible	$35,700	4%
1SS Coupe	$37,000	4%
2SS Coupe	$42,000	4%

Safety Checklist

Crash Test:
  Frontal . . . . Average
  Side . . . . Very Good
Airbags:
  Torso . . . Std. Front Pelvis/Torso from Seat
  Roll Sensing . . . . Yes
  Knee Bolster . . . . Standard Front
Crash Avoidance:
  Collision Avoidance . . . . None
  Blind Spot Detection . . . . Optional
  Lane Keeping Assist . . . . None
  Pedestrian Crash Avoidance . . . . None
General:
  Auto. Crash Notif. . . Op. Assist. & Crash Info-Fee
  Day Running Lamps . . . . Standard
Safety Belt/Restraint:
  Dynamic Head Restraints . . . . None
  Adjustable Belt . . . . Optional Rear

^Warning feature does not meet government standards.

Chevrolet Camaro

Specifications

Drive	RWD
Engine	3.6-liter V6
Transmission	8-sp. Automatic
Tow Rating (lbs.)	—
Head/Leg Room (in.)	Very Cramped-36.6/42.6
Interior Space (cu. ft.)	Very Cramped-77
Cargo Space (cu. ft.)	Very Cramped-9.1
Wheelbase/Length (in.)	110.7/188.3

Chevrolet Colorado

Ratings—10 Best, 1 Worst	
Combo Crash Tests	3
Safety Features	2
Rollover	2
Preventive Maintenance	1
Repair Costs	8
Warranty	6
Fuel Economy	4
Complaints	5
Insurance Costs	10
OVERALL RATING	**2**

Chevrolet Colorado

At-a-Glance

Status/Year Series Started	Unchanged/2015
Twins	GMC Canyon
Body Styles	Pickup
Seating	5
Anti-Theft Device	Std. Pass. Immobil. & Active Alarm
Parking Index Rating	Very Hard
Where Made	Wentzville, MO
Fuel Factor	
MPG Rating (city/hwy)	Poor-20/27
Driving Range (mi.)	Very Long-475
Fuel Type	Regular
Annual Fuel Cost	Average-$1623
Gas Guzzler Tax	No
Greenhouse Gas Emissions (tons/yr.)	High-8.2
Barrels of Oil Used per year	High-15.0

How the Competition Rates

Competitors	Rating	Pg.
Ford Ranger		135
Nissan Frontier	1	211
Toyota Tacoma	1	244

Price Range	Retail	Markup
Base Ext. Cab 2WD	$20,000	1%
W/T Crew Cab 4WD	$31,220	5%
Z71 Crew Cab 4WD	$32,775	5%
LT Crew Cab 4WD	$33,775	5%

Safety Checklist

Crash Test:
  Frontal . . . . Poor
  Side . . . . Poor
Airbags:
  Torso . . . Std. Front Pelvis/Torso from Seat
  Roll Sensing . . . . Yes
  Knee Bolster . . . . None
Crash Avoidance:
  Collision Avoidance . Warning Only Optional
  Blind Spot Detection . . . . None
  Lane Keeping Assist . . Warn. Only Optional
  Pedestrian Crash Avoidance . . . . None
General:
  Auto. Crash Notif . . . Op. Assist. & Crash Info-Fee
  Day Running Lamps . . . . Standard
Safety Belt/Restraint:
  Dynamic Head Restraints . . . . None
  Adjustable Belt . . . . . Optional Front & Rear

Chevrolet Colorado

Specifications

Drive	RWD
Engine	2.5-liter I4
Transmission	6-sp. Automatic
Tow Rating (lbs.)	Low-3500
Head/Leg Room (in.)	Very Roomy-41.4/45
Interior Space (cu. ft.)	—
Cargo Space (cu. ft.)	Very Roomy-49.9
Wheelbase/Length (in.)	128.3/212.7

Ratings—10 Best, 1 Worst

Combo Crash Tests	—
Safety Features	1
Rollover	10
Preventive Maintenance	1
Repair Costs	1
Warranty	6
Fuel Economy	2
Complaints	6
Insurance Costs	10
OVERALL RATING	**—**

Chevrolet Corvette

Chevrolet Corvette

At-a-Glance

Status/Year Series Started	Unchanged/2014
Twins	—
Body Styles	Coupe, Convertible
Seating	2
Anti-Theft Device	Std. Pass. Immobil. & Active Alarm
Parking Index Rating	Average
Where Made	Bowling Green, KY
Fuel Factor	
MPG Rating (city/hwy)	Very Poor-15/25
Driving Range (mi.)	Very Short-338
Fuel Type	Premium
Annual Fuel Cost	Very High-$2435
Gas Guzzler Tax	No
Greenhouse Gas Emissions (tons/yr.)	High-8.1
Barrels of Oil Used per year	Very High-18.3

How the Competition Rates

Competitors	Rating	Pg.
Chevrolet Camaro	4	101
Dodge Challenger	4	118
Ford Mustang	6	134

Price Range

	Retail	Markup
Base Coupe	$55,495	8%
Z51 Convertible	$64,495	8%
Grand Sport Coupe	$65,495	8%
Z06 Convertible	$83,495	8%

Safety Checklist

Crash Test:
Frontal . . . . —
Side . . . . —
Airbags:
Torso . . . . Std. Front Torso from Seat
Roll Sensing . . . . No
Knee Bolster . . . . None
Crash Avoidance:
Collision Avoidance . . . . None
Blind Spot Detection . . . . None
Lane Keeping Assist . . . . None
Pedestrian Crash Avoidance . . . . None
General:
Auto. Crash Notif. . . Op. Assist. & Crash Info-Fee
Day Running Lamps . . . . Standard
Safety Belt/Restraint:
Dynamic Head Restraints . . . . None
Adjustable Belt . . . . None

Chevrolet Corvette

Specifications

Drive	RWD
Engine	6.2-liter V8
Transmission	8-sp. Automatic
Tow Rating (lbs.)	—
Head/Leg Room (in.)	Average-38/43
Interior Space (cu. ft.)	Very Cramped-52
Cargo Space (cu. ft.)	Cramped-15
Wheelbase/Length (in.)	106.7/176.9

Ratings—10 Best, 1 Worst

Combo Crash Tests	5
Safety Features	8
Rollover	7
Preventive Maintenance	4
Repair Costs	8
Warranty	6
Fuel Economy	9
Complaints	10
Insurance Costs	1
OVERALL RATING	**8**

Chevrolet Cruze

Chevrolet Cruze

At-a-Glance

Status/Year Series Started. Unchanged/2016
Twins . . . . —
Body Styles . . . . Sedan, Hatchback
Seating 5
Anti-Theft Device . Std. Pass. Immobil. & Active Alarm
Parking Index Rating . . . . Average
Where Made. Lordstown, OH
Fuel Factor
  MPG Rating (city/hwy) . . . . Very Good-29/40
  Driving Range (mi.) Long-453
  Fuel Type. . . . . .Regular
  Annual Fuel Cost . . . . .Very Low-$1110
  Gas Guzzler Tax . . . . .No
  Greenhouse Gas Emissions (tons/yr.). Very Low-4.4
  Barrels of Oil Used per year Low-10.0

How the Competition Rates

Competitors	Rating	Pg.
Honda Civic	10	144
Mazda 3	6	190
Toyota Corolla	7	235

Price Range	Retail	Markup
L MT	$16,975	1%
LS AT	$19,525	4%
LT AT	$21,450	4%
Premier Sedan AT	$23,475	4%

Safety Checklist

Crash Test:
  Frontal. . . . . .Good
  Side. . . . . Very Poor
Airbags:
  Torso Std. Front & Rear Pelvis/Torso from Seat
  Roll Sensing. .Yes
  Knee Bolster . . . . Standard Front
Crash Avoidance:
  Collision Avoidance . Warning Only Optional
  Blind Spot Detection . . . . Optional
  Lane Keeping Assist . . . . Optional
  Pedestrian Crash Avoidance . . . . .None
General:
  Auto. Crash Notif. . . Op. Assist. & Crash Info-Fee
  Day Running Lamps . . . . .Standard
Safety Belt/Restraint:
  Dynamic Head Restraints . . . . .None
  Adjustable Belt. . . . . .Optional Rear

^Warning feature does not meet government standards.

Chevrolet Cruze

Specifications

Drive. . . . . .FWD
Engine 1.4-liter I4
Transmission . . . . 6-sp. Autonatic
Tow Rating (lbs.) . . . . —
Head/Leg Room (in.) Cramped-38.9/42
Interior Space (cu. ft.). Cramped-94
Cargo Space (cu. ft.) Cramped-14.8
Wheelbase/Length (in.) 106.3/183.7

Chevrolet Equinox — Small SUV

Ratings—10 Best, 1 Worst

Combo Crash Tests	6
Safety Features	5
Rollover	2
Preventive Maintenance	1
Repair Costs	3
Warranty	6
Fuel Economy	7
Complaints	5
Insurance Costs	8
OVERALL RATING	**4**

Chevrolet Equinox

Chevrolet Equinox

At-a-Glance

Status/Year Series Started Unchanged/2018
Twins . . . . GMC Terrain
Body Styles . . . . SUV
Seating 5
Anti-Theft Device . Std. Pass. Immobil. & Active Alarm
Parking Index Rating . . . . Average
Where Made . . . . . . Oshawa, Ontario / Spring Hill, TN
Fuel Factor
  MPG Rating (city/hwy) Good-26/32
  Driving Range (mi.) Average-417
  Fuel Type . . . . Regular
  Annual Fuel Cost . . . . Low-$1294
  Gas Guzzler Tax . . . . No
  Greenhouse Gas Emissions (tons/yr.) Low-5.2
  Barrels of Oil Used per year Average-11.8

How the Competition Rates

Competitors	Rating	Pg.
Dodge Journey	1	121
Ford Escape	5	126
Honda Pilot	8	149

Price Range

	Retail	Markup
L FWD	$23,580	1%
LS FWD	$25,510	5%
LT AWD 2.0	$32,840	5%
Premier AWD 2.0	$37,230	5%

Safety Checklist

Crash Test:
  Frontal . . . . Very Good
  Side . . . . Very Poor
Airbags:
  Torso . . . Std. Front Pelvis/Torso from Seat
  Roll Sensing . . . . Yes
  Knee Bolster . . . . None
Crash Avoidance:
  Collision Avoidance . . . . Optional CIB
  Blind Spot Detection . . . . Optional
  Lane Keeping Assist . . . . Optional
  Pedestrian Crash Avoidance . . . . None
General:
  Auto. Crash Notif . . . Op. Assist. & Crash Info-Fee
  Day Running Lamps . . . . Standard
Safety Belt/Restraint:
  Dynamic Head Restraints . . . . None
  Adjustable Belt . . . . . Optional Front & Rear

^Warning feature does not meet government standards.

Chevrolet Equinox

Specifications

Drive . . . . FWD
Engine 1.5-liter I4
Transmission . . . . 6-sp. Automatic
Tow Rating (lbs.) Low-3500
Head/Leg Room (in.) Cramped-40/40.9
Interior Space (cu. ft.) Average-103.2
Cargo Space (cu. ft.) Roomy-29.9
Wheelbase/Length (in.) 107.3/183.1

Ratings—10 Best, 1 Worst

Combo Crash Tests	6
Safety Features	6
Rollover	6
Preventive Maintenance	1
Repair Costs	6
Warranty	6
Fuel Economy	3
Complaints	8
Insurance Costs	3
OVERALL RATING	**4**

Chevrolet Impala

Chevrolet Impala

At-a-Glance

Status/Year Series Started	Unchanged/2014
Twins	Cadillac XTS
Body Styles	Sedan
Seating	5
Anti-Theft Device	Std. Pass. Immobil. & Active Alarm
Parking Index Rating	Hard
Where Made	Detroit, MI / Oshawa, Ontario

Fuel Factor

MPG Rating (city/hwy)	Poor-18/28
Driving Range (mi.)	Short-397
Fuel Type	Regular
Annual Fuel Cost	High-$1714
Gas Guzzler Tax	No
Greenhouse Gas Emissions (tons/yr.)	High-8.6
Barrels of Oil Used per year	High-15.7

How the Competition Rates

Competitors	Rating	Pg.
Buick LaCrosse	5	92
Ford Taurus	3	136
Toyota Avalon	8	233

Price Range	Retail	Markup
LS	$27,985	5%
LT	$30,220	4%
Premier	$36,420	4%

Safety Checklist

Crash Test:
- Frontal . . . . .Good
- Side . . . . Poor

Airbags:
- Torso Std. Fr. & Opt. Rr. Pelvis/Torso from Seat
- Roll Sensing . . . . .Yes
- Knee Bolster . . . . Standard Front

Crash Avoidance:
- Collision Avoidance . . . . .Optional CIB
- Blind Spot Detection . . . . Optional
- Lane Keeping Assist . .Warn. Only Optional
- Pedestrian Crash Avoidance . . . . . . .None

General:
- Auto. Crash Notif. . . Op. Assist. & Crash Info-Fee
- Day Running Lamps . . . . .Standard

Safety Belt/Restraint:
- Dynamic Head Restraints . . . . .None
- Adjustable Belt . . . . . Optional Front & Rear

^Warning feature does not meet government standards.

Chevrolet Impala

Specifications

Drive	FWD
Engine	3.6-liter V6
Transmission	6-sp. Automatic
Tow Rating (lbs.)	Very Low-1000
Head/Leg Room (in.)	Very Roomy-39.9/45.8
Interior Space (cu. ft.)	Roomy-105
Cargo Space (cu. ft.)	Average-18.8
Wheelbase/Length (in.)	111.7/201.3

Ratings—10 Best, 1 Worst	
Combo Crash Tests	5
Safety Features	9
Rollover	8
Preventive Maintenance	7
Repair Costs	8
Warranty	6
Fuel Economy	8
Complaints	10
Insurance Costs	3
OVERALL RATING	**9**

Chevrolet Malibu

Chevrolet Malibu

At-a-Glance

Status/Year Series Started	Unchanged/2016
Twins	Buick Regal
Body Styles	Sedan
Seating	5
Anti-Theft Device	Std. Pass. Immobil. & Active Alarm
Parking Index Rating	Average
Where Made	Fairfax, KS
Fuel Factor	
MPG Rating (city/hwy)	Good-27/36
Driving Range (mi.)	Short-395
Fuel Type	Regular
Annual Fuel Cost	Low-$1208
Gas Guzzler Tax	No
Greenhouse Gas Emissions (tons/yr.)	Low-4.8
Barrels of Oil Used per year	Average-11.0

How the Competition Rates

Competitors	Rating	Pg.
Ford Fusion	4	132
Nissan Altima		209
Toyota Camry	8	234

Price Range	Retail	Markup
L	$21,680	1%
LS	$23,225	4%
LT	$25,125	4%
Hybrid	$27,875	4%

Safety Checklist

Crash Test:
- Frontal . . . . Poor
- Side . . . . Very Good

Airbags:
- Torso   Std. Front & Rear Pelvis/Torso from Seat
- Roll Sensing . . . . Yes
- Knee Bolster . . . . Standard Front

Crash Avoidance:
- Collision Avoidance . . . Optional CIB & DBS
- Blind Spot Detection . . . . Optional
- Lane Keeping Assist . . . . Optional
- Pedestrian Crash Avoidance . . . . . Optional

General:
- Auto. Crash Notif. . . Op. Assist. & Crash Info-Fee
- Day Running Lamps . . . . Standard

Safety Belt/Restraint:
- Dynamic Head Restraints . . . . None
- Adjustable Belt . . . . Optional Rear

^Warning feature does not meet government standards.

Chevrolet Malibu

Specifications

Drive	FWD
Engine	1.5-liter I4
Transmission	6-sp. Automatic
Tow Rating (lbs.)	—
Head/Leg Room (in.)	Average-39.1/42
Interior Space (cu. ft.)	Average-102.9
Cargo Space (cu. ft.)	Cramped-15.8
Wheelbase/Length (in.)	111.4/193.8

Ratings—10 Best, 1 Worst

Combo Crash Tests	—
Safety Features	3
Rollover	3
Preventive Maintenance	1
Repair Costs	5
Warranty	6
Fuel Economy	2
Complaints	—
Insurance Costs	10
OVERALL RATING	—

Chevrolet Silverado

Chevrolet Silverado

At-a-Glance

Status/Year Series Started	All New/2019
Twins	GMC Sierra
Body Styles	Pickup
Seating	5/6
Anti-Theft Device	Std. Pass. Immobil. & Active Alarm
Parking Index Rating	Very Hard
Where Made	Fort Wayne, IN
Fuel Factor	
MPG Rating (city/hwy)	Very Poor-16/22
Driving Range (mi.)	Long-432
Fuel Type	Regular
Annual Fuel Cost	Very High-$2015
Gas Guzzler Tax	No
Greenhouse Gas Emissions (tons/yr.)	High-8.1
Barrels of Oil Used per year	Very High-18.3

How the Competition Rates

Competitors	Rating	Pg.
Ford F-150	8	129
Nissan Titan	1	218
Ram 1500	5	221

Price Range

	Retail	Markup
W/T Reg. Cab 2WD	$28,300	5%
LT Dbl. Cab 4WD	$40,200	7%
LTZ Crew Cab 4WD	$48,700	7%
High Country Crew Cab 4WD	$56,600	7%

Safety Checklist

Crash Test:
  Frontal . . . . —
  Side . . . . —
Airbags:
  Torso . . . Std. Front Pelvis/Torso from Seat
  Roll Sensing . . . . Yes
  Knee Bolster . . . . None
Crash Avoidance:
  Collision Avoidance . . . . Optional CIB
  Blind Spot Detection . . . . Optional
  Lane Keeping Assist . . . . Optional
  Pedestrian Crash Avoidance . . . . None
General:
  Auto. Crash Notif. . . Op. Assist. & Crash Info-Fee
  Day Running Lamps . . . . Standard
Safety Belt/Restraint:
  Dynamic Head Restraints . . . . None
  Adjustable Belt . . . . . Optional Front & Rear

^Warning feature does not meet government standards.

Chevrolet Silverado

Specifications

Drive	4WD
Engine	5.3-liter V8
Transmission	8-sp. Automatic
Tow Rating (lbs.)	Very High-9,900
Head/Leg Room (in.)	Very Roomy-43/44.5
Interior Space (cu. ft.)	—
Cargo Space (cu. ft.)	Very Roomy-71.7
Wheelbase/Length (in.)	147.4/231.8

Ratings—10 Best, 1 Worst

Combo Crash Tests	7
Safety Features	3
Rollover	8
Preventive Maintenance	9
Repair Costs	9
Warranty	6
Fuel Economy	7
Complaints	6
Insurance Costs	3
OVERALL RATING	**7**

Chevrolet Sonic

Chevrolet Sonic

At-a-Glance

Status/Year Series Started	Unchanged/2012
Twins	—
Body Styles	Sedan, Hatchback
Seating	5
Anti-Theft Device	Std. Pass. Immobil. & Active Alarm
Parking Index Rating	Very Easy
Where Made	Orion Township, MI
Fuel Factor	
MPG Rating (city/hwy)	Good-25/34
Driving Range (mi.)	Very Short-346
Fuel Type	Regular
Annual Fuel Cost	Low-$1295
Gas Guzzler Tax	No
Greenhouse Gas Emissions (tons/yr.)	Average-6.5
Barrels of Oil Used per year	Average-11.8

How the Competition Rates

Competitors	Rating	Pg.
Ford Fiesta	2	130
Nissan Versa	1	207
Toyota Yaris Liftback	5	247

Price Range	Retail	Markup
LS Sedan MT	$15,295	4%
LT Sedan MT	$17,695	4%
LT Hatchback AT	$19,195	4%
Premier Hatchback AT	$21,295	4%

Safety Checklist

Crash Test:
  Frontal . . . . Very Good
  Side . . . . Very Poor
Airbags:
  Torso Std. Front & Rear Pelvis/Torso from Seat
  Roll Sensing . . . . Yes
  Knee Bolster . . . . Standard Front
Crash Avoidance:
  Collision Avoidance . Warning Only Optional
  Blind Spot Detection . . . . None
  Lane Keeping Assist . . Warn. Only Optional
  Pedestrian Crash Avoidance . . . . None
General:
  Auto. Crash Notif. . . Op. Assist. & Crash Info-Fee
  Day Running Lamps . . . . Standard
Safety Belt/Restraint:
  Dynamic Head Restraints . . . . None
  Adjustable Belt . . . . . Optional Front & Rear

^Warning feature does not meet government standards.

Chevrolet Sonic

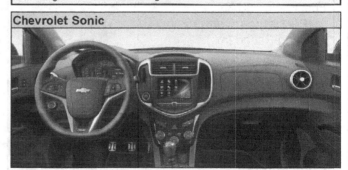

Specifications

Drive	FWD
Engine	1.8-liter I4
Transmission	6-sp. Automatic
Tow Rating (lbs.)	—
Head/Leg Room (in.)	Cramped-38.7/41.8
Interior Space (cu. ft.)	Cramped-90.6
Cargo Space (cu. ft.)	Average-19
Wheelbase/Length (in.)	99.4/159

Ratings—10 Best, 1 Worst

Combo Crash Tests	2
Safety Features	3
Rollover	3
Preventive Maintenance	9
Repair Costs	8
Warranty	6
Fuel Economy	9
Complaints	4
Insurance Costs	3
OVERALL RATING	**5**

Chevrolet Spark

Chevrolet Spark

At-a-Glance

Status/Year Series Started........ Unchanged/2016
Twins .... —
Body Styles .... Hatchback
Seating 4
Anti-Theft Device . Std. Pass. Immobil. & Active Alarm
Parking Index Rating ....Very Easy
Where Made.............. Changwon, South Korea
Fuel Factor
  MPG Rating (city/hwy) .... Very Good-29/38
  Driving Range (mi.) ....Very Short-292
  Fuel Type.............................Regular
  Annual Fuel Cost .... Very Low-$1132
  Gas Guzzler Tax ....No
  Greenhouse Gas Emissions (tons/yr.). Very Low-4.2
  Barrels of Oil Used per year Low-9.4

How the Competition Rates

Competitors	Rating	Pg.
Fiat 500	2	122
Honda Fit	9	146
Nissan Versa	1	207

Price Range	Retail	Markup
LS MT	$13,050	4%
1LT MT	$14,875	4%
1LT AT	$15,975	4%
2LT AT	$17,475	4%

Safety Checklist

Crash Test:
  Frontal...................... Very Poor
  Side............................ Poor
Airbags:
  Torso Std. Front & Rear Pelvis/Torso from Seat
  Roll Sensing......................Yes
  Knee Bolster .... Standard Front
Crash Avoidance:
  Collision Avoidance . Warning Only Optional
  Blind Spot Detection ....None
  Lane Keeping Assist . .Warn. Only Optional
  Pedestrian Crash Avoidance ....None
General:
  Auto. Crash Notif... Op. Assist. & Crash Info-Fee
  Day Running Lamps ....Standard
Safety Belt/Restraint:
  Dynamic Head Restraints ....None
  Adjustable Belt...........Optional Rear

^Warning feature does not meet government standards.

Chevrolet Spark

Specifications

Drive.................................FWD
Engine 1.4-liter I4
Transmission .... CVT
Tow Rating (lbs.) .... —
Head/Leg Room (in.) Cramped-39/41.7
Interior Space (cu. ft.)............. Very Cramped-83
Cargo Space (cu. ft.) .... Very Cramped-11.1
Wheelbase/Length (in.) 93.9/143.1

Ratings—10 Best, 1 Worst	Chevy Suburban	GMC Yukon XL
Combo Crash Tests	6	6
Safety Features	4	4
Rollover	2	2
Preventive Maintenance	1	5
Repair Costs	5	6
Warranty	6	5
Fuel Economy	1	1
Complaints	3	6
Insurance Costs	10	10
OVERALL RATING	**2**	**4**

Chevrolet Suburban

GMC Yukon XL

At-a-Glance

Status/Year Series Started Unchanged/2015
Twins . . . . . .Cadillac Escalade ESV, GMC Yukon XL
Body Styles . . . . SUV
Seating 6/9
Anti-Theft Device . Std. Pass. Immobil. & Active Alarm
Parking Index Rating . . . . Very Hard
Where Made. . . . . Arlington, TX
Fuel Factor
  MPG Rating (city/hwy) . . . . .Very Poor-15/22
  Driving Range (mi.) . . . . Very Long-543
  Fuel Type. . . . . .Regular
  Annual Fuel Cost . . . . Very High-$2099
  Gas Guzzler Tax . . . . .No
  Greenhouse Gas Emissions (tons/yr.)Very High-10.0
  Barrels of Oil Used per year . . . . Very High-18.3

How the Competition Rates

Competitors	Rating	Pg.
Buick Enclave	4	89
Ford Expedition		127
Volvo XC90	8	256

Price Range	Retail	Markup
1500 LS RWD	$50,150	6%
1500 LT RWD	$55,280	6%
1500 LT 4WD	$58,280	6%
1500 Premier 4WD	$67,830	6%

Safety Checklist

Crash Test:
  Frontal. . . . . Average
  Side. . . . . Average
Airbags:
  Torso . . . Std. Front Pelvis/Torso from Seat
  Roll Sensing. . . . . .Yes
  Knee Bolster . . . . .None
Crash Avoidance:
  Collision Avoidance . . . . .Optional CIB
  Blind Spot Detection . . . . Optional
  Lane Keeping Assist . . . . Optional
  Pedestrian Crash Avoidance . . . . .None
General:
  Auto. Crash Notif. . . Op. Assist. & Crash Info-Fee
  Day Running Lamps . . . . .Standard
Safety Belt/Restraint:
  Dynamic Head Restraints . . . . .None
  Adjustable Belt. . . . . Optional Front & Rear

^Warning feature does not meet government standards.

Chevrolet Suburban

Specifications

Drive. 4WD
Engine 5.3-liter V8
Transmission . . . . 6-sp. Automatic
Tow Rating (lbs.) High-8000
Head/Leg Room (in.) . . . . Very Roomy-42.8/45.3
Interior Space (cu. ft.). Roomy-120.8
Cargo Space (cu. ft.) . . . . Very Roomy-39.3
Wheelbase/Length (in.) 130/224.4

Ratings—10 Best, 1 Worst

Combo Crash Tests	8
Safety Features	4
Rollover	2
Preventive Maintenance	1
Repair Costs	3
Warranty	6
Fuel Economy	2
Complaints	5
Insurance Costs	10
OVERALL RATING	**4**

Chevrolet Tahoe

Chevrolet Tahoe

At-a-Glance

Status/Year Series Started. Unchanged/2015
Twins . . . . Cadillac Escalade, GMC Yukon
Body Styles . . . . SUV
Seating 6/9
Anti-Theft Device . Std. Pass. Immobil. & Active Alarm
Parking Index Rating . . . . Very Hard
Where Made. . . . . Arlington, TX
Fuel Factor
 MPG Rating (city/hwy) . . . . Very Poor-16/22
 Driving Range (mi.) . . . . Very Long-474
 Fuel Type. . . . . .Regular
 Annual Fuel Cost . . . . Very High-$2015
 Gas Guzzler Tax . . . . .No
 Greenhouse Gas Emissions (tons/yr.) High-8.2
 Barrels of Oil Used per year . . . . . . Very High-18.3

How the Competition Rates

Competitors	Rating	Pg.
Buick Enclave	4	89
Infiniti QX80		162
Volvo XC90	8	256

Price Range

Price Range	Retail	Markup
LS RWD	$47,450	6%
LT RWD	$52,580	6%
LT4WD	$55,580	6%
Premier 4WD	$65,130	6%

Safety Checklist

Crash Test:
 Frontal. . . . . .Good
 Side. . . . . Very Good
Airbags:
 Torso . . . Std. Front Pelvis/Torso from Seat
 Roll Sensing. .Yes
 Knee Bolster . . . . .None
Crash Avoidance:
 Collision Avoidance . . . . .Optional CIB
 Blind Spot Detection . . . . Optional
 Lane Keeping Assist . . . . Optional
 Pedestrian Crash Avoidance . . . . .None
General:
 Auto. Crash Notif. . . Op. Assist. & Crash Info-Fee
 Day Running Lamps . . . . .Standard
Safety Belt/Restraint:
 Dynamic Head Restraints . . . . .None
 Adjustable Belt. . . . . Optional Front & Rear

^Warning feature does not meet government standards.

Chevrolet Tahoe

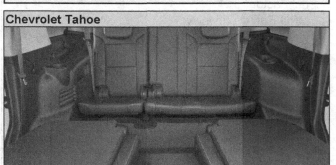

Specifications

Drive. 4WD
Engine 5.3-liter V8
Transmission . . . . 6-sp. Automatic
Tow Rating (lbs.) . . . . Very High-8400
Head/Leg Room (in.) . . . . Very Roomy-42.8/45.3
Interior Space (cu. ft.). Roomy-120.8
Cargo Space (cu. ft.) Cramped-15.3
Wheelbase/Length (in.) 116/204

Ratings—10 Best, 1 Worst

Combo Crash Tests	5
Safety Features	6
Rollover	4
Preventive Maintenance	2
Repair Costs	5
Warranty	6
Fuel Economy	3
Complaints	6
Insurance Costs	10
OVERALL RATING	**4**

Chevrolet Traverse

At-a-Glance

Status/Year Series Started	Unchanged/2018
Twins	Buick Enclave
Body Styles	SUV
Seating	7/8
Anti-Theft Device	Std. Pass. Immobil. & Active Alarm
Parking Index Rating	Very Hard
Where Made	Lansing, Michigan

Fuel Factor
MPG Rating (city/hwy)	Poor-18/27
Driving Range (mi.)	Average-411
Fuel Type	Regular
Annual Fuel Cost	High-$1735
Gas Guzzler Tax	No
Greenhouse Gas Emissions (tons/yr.)	Average-6.9
Barrels of Oil Used per year	High-15.7

How the Competition Rates

Competitors	Rating	Pg.
Buick Enclave	4	89
Ford Flex		131
Volvo XC90	8	256

Price Range

	Retail	Markup
LS FWD	$32,050	5%
LT FWD	$34,550	5%
Premier AWD	$47,350	5%
High Country AWD	$52,050	5%

Chevrolet Traverse

Safety Checklist

Crash Test:
Frontal	Average
Side	Poor

Airbags:
Torso	Std. Front Pelvis/Torso from Seat
Roll Sensing	Yes
Knee Bolster	None

Crash Avoidance:
Collision Avoidance	Optional CIB & DBS^
Blind Spot Detection	Optional
Lane Keeping Assist	Optional
Pedestrian Crash Avoidance	Optional

General:
Auto. Crash Notif.	Op. Assist. & Crash Info-Fee
Day Running Lamps	Standard

Safety Belt/Restraint:
Dynamic Head Restraints	None
Adjustable Belt	Optional Rear

^Warning feature does not meet government standards.

Chevrolet Traverse

Specifications

Drive	FWD
Engine	3.6-liter V6
Transmission	9-sp. Automatic
Tow Rating (lbs.)	Low-5000
Head/Leg Room (in.)	Average-41.3/41
Interior Space (cu. ft.)	Very Roomy-157.3
Cargo Space (cu. ft.)	Roomy-23
Wheelbase/Length (in.)	120.9/204.3

Chevrolet Trax

Ratings—10 Best, 1 Worst

Combo Crash Tests	8
Safety Features	7
Rollover	3
Preventive Maintenance	7
Repair Costs	5
Warranty	6
Fuel Economy	6
Complaints	10
Insurance Costs	10
OVERALL RATING	**10**

Chevrolet Trax

Chevrolet Trax

Safety Checklist

Crash Test:
  Frontal . . . . Very Good
  Side . . . . Average
Airbags:
  Torso Std. Front & Rear Pelvis/Torso from Seat
  Roll Sensing . . . . Yes
  Knee Bolster . . . . Standard Front
Crash Avoidance:
  Collision Avoidance . Warning Only Optional
  Blind Spot Detection . . . . Optional
  Lane Keeping Assist . . Warn. Only Optional
  Pedestrian Crash Avoidance . . . . None
General:
  Auto. Crash Notif . . . Op. Assist. & Crash Info-Fee
  Day Running Lamps . . . . Standard
Safety Belt/Restraint:
  Dynamic Head Restraints . . . . None
  Adjustable Belt . . . . . Optional Front & Rear

^Warning feature does not meet government standards.

At-a-Glance

Status/Year Series Started Unchanged/2015
Twins . . . . Buick Encore
Body Styles . . . . SUV
Seating 5
Anti-Theft Device . Std. Pass. Immobil. & Active Alarm
Parking Index Rating . . . . Easy
Where Made . . . . South Korea/Mexico
Fuel Factor
  MPG Rating (city/hwy) Average-24/30
  Driving Range (mi.) . . . . Very Short-369
  Fuel Type . . . . Regular
  Annual Fuel Cost . . . . Low-$1393
  Gas Guzzler Tax . . . . No
  Greenhouse Gas Emissions (tons/yr.) Low-5.5
  Barrels of Oil Used per year Average-12.2

How the Competition Rates

Competitors	Rating	Pg.
Ford Escape	5	126
Honda HR-V	5	147
Jeep Compass	4	164

Price Range	Retail	Markup
LS FWD	$21,000	4%
LT FWD	$22,900	4%
LT AWD	$24,400	4%
Premier AWD	$28,795	4%

Chevrolet Trax

Specifications

Drive . . . . AWD
Engine 1.4-liter I4
Transmission . . . . 6-sp. Automatic
Tow Rating (lbs.) . . . . —
Head/Leg Room (in.) Cramped-39.6/40.8
Interior Space (cu. ft.) Cramped-92.8
Cargo Space (cu. ft.) Average-18.7
Wheelbase/Length (in.) 100.6/168.5

Chevrolet Volt   Compact

Ratings—10 Best, 1 Worst

Combo Crash Tests	4
Safety Features	8
Rollover	9
Preventive Maintenance	3
Repair Costs	7
Warranty	6
Fuel Economy	10
Complaints	1
Insurance Costs	10
OVERALL RATING	**7**

Chevrolet Volt

Chevrolet Volt

At-a-Glance

Status/Year Series Started . . Apperance Change/2016
Twins . . . . —
Body Styles . . . . Sedan
Seating 5
Anti-Theft Device . Std. Pass. Immobil. & Active Alarm
Parking Index Rating . . . . Easy
Where Made. . . . . .Detroit, MI
Fuel Factor
  MPG Rating (city/hwy) . . . . Very Good-43/42
  Driving Range (mi.) Short-379
  Fuel Type . . . . .Regular
  Annual Fuel Cost . . . . Very Low-$864
  Gas Guzzler Tax . . . . .No
  Greenhouse Gas Emissions (tons/yr.). Very Low-0.8
  Barrels of Oil Used per year . . . . Very Low-2.0

How the Competition Rates

Competitors	Rating	Pg.
Audi A3	5	71
Ford Fusion Energi	8	133
Toyota Prius Prime		240

Price Range	Retail	Markup
LT	$33,220	4%
Premier	$37,570	4%

Safety Checklist

Crash Test:
  Frontal. . . . . Poor
  Side. . . . . .Good
Airbags:
  Torso Std. Fr. & Opt. Rr. Pelvis/Torso from Seat
  Roll Sensing. .Yes
  Knee Bolster . . . . Standard Front
Crash Avoidance:
  Collision Avoidance . . .Optional CIB & DBS
  Blind Spot Detection . . . . Optional
  Lane Keeping Assist . . . . Optional
  Pedestrian Crash Avoidance . . . . . . .None
General:
  Auto. Crash Notif. . . Op. Assist. & Crash Info-Fee
  Day Running Lamps . . . . Standard
Safety Belt/Restraint:
  Dynamic Head Restraints . . . . None
  Adjustable Belt. . . . . None

^Warning feature does not meet government standards.

Chevrolet Volt

Specifications

Drive. . . . . .FWD
Engine 1.5-liter I4
Transmission . . . . CVT
Tow Rating (lbs.) . . . . —
Head/Leg Room (in.) Cramped-37.8/42.1
Interior Space (cu. ft.). . . . . Very Cramped-90
Cargo Space (cu. ft.) . . . . Very Cramped-10.6
Wheelbase/Length (in.) 106.1/180.4

Chrysler 300

Large

Ratings—10 Best, 1 Worst	
Combo Crash Tests	2
Safety Features	5
Rollover	6
Preventive Maintenance	8
Repair Costs	2
Warranty	4
Fuel Economy	4
Complaints	3
Insurance Costs	1
OVERALL RATING	**1**

Chrysler 300

Chrysler 300

At-a-Glance

Status/Year Series Started	Unchanged/2011
Twins	Dodge Charger
Body Styles	Sedan
Seating	5
Anti-Theft Device	Std. Pass. Immobil. & Alarm
Parking Index Rating	Very Hard
Where Made	Brampton, Ontario

Fuel Factor
MPG Rating (city/hwy)	Poor-19/30
Driving Range (mi.)	Average-421
Fuel Type	Regular
Annual Fuel Cost	Average-$1615
Gas Guzzler Tax	No
Greenhouse Gas Emissions (tons/yr.)	High-7.8
Barrels of Oil Used per year	High-14.3

How the Competition Rates

Competitors	Rating	Pg.
Buick LaCrosse	5	92
Cadillac XT5	3	98
Toyota Avalon	8	23

Price Range	Retail	Markup
Touring RWD	$28,995	1%
Limited RWD	$36,595	3%
S V6 AWD	$38,295	4%
C V8	$40,995	4%

Safety Checklist

Crash Test:
  Frontal...................Very Poor
  Side....................Poor
Airbags:
  Torso ... Std. Front Pelvis/Torso from Seat
  Roll Sensing....................Yes
  Knee Bolster ....Standard Driver
Crash Avoidance:
  Collision Avoidance ...Optional CIB & DBS
  Blind Spot Detection ....Optional
  Lane Keeping Assist ....Optional^
  Pedestrian Crash Avoidance ....None
General:
  Auto. Crash Notification...........None
  Day Running Lamps ....Standard
Safety Belt/Restraint:
  Dynamic Head Restraints ....None
  Adjustable Belt..........Standard Front

^Warning feature does not meet government standards.

Chrysler 300

Specifications

Drive	RWD
Engine	3.6-liter V6
Transmission	8-sp. Automatic
Tow Rating (lbs.)	—
Head/Leg Room (in.)	Cramped-38.6/41.8
Interior Space (cu. ft.)	Roomy-106.3
Cargo Space (cu. ft.)	Cramped-16.3
Wheelbase/Length (in.)	120.2/198.6

Chrysler Pacifica

Ratings—10 Best, 1 Worst	
Combo Crash Tests	8
Safety Features	7
Rollover	6
Preventive Maintenance	10
Repair Costs	6
Warranty	4
Fuel Economy	3
Complaints	1
Insurance Costs	10
OVERALL RATING	**8**

Chrysler Pacifica

At-a-Glance

Status/Year Series Started.	Unchanged/2017
Twins	—
Body Styles	Minivan
Seating	7/8
Anti-Theft Device	Std. Pass. Immobil. & Alarm
Parking Index Rating	Very Hard
Where Made.	Windsor, Ontario
Fuel Factor	
MPG Rating (city/hwy)	Poor-18/28
Driving Range (mi.)	Average-407
Fuel Type.	Regular
Annual Fuel Cost	High-$1714
Gas Guzzler Tax	No
Greenhouse Gas Emissions (tons/yr.) . .	Average-6.9
Barrels of Oil Used per year	High-15.0

How the Competition Rates

Competitors	Rating	Pg.
Honda Odyssey	9	148
Kia Sedona		171
Toyota Sienna	2	243

Price Range	Retail	Markup
LX	$26,995	0%
Touring L	$35,495	3%
Touring L Plus	$38,695	4%
Limited	$43,695	4%

Safety Checklist

Crash Test:
  Frontal. Very Good
  Side. . . . . Poor
Airbags:
  Torso . . . Std. Front Pelvis/Torso from Seat
  Roll Sensing. . . . . Yes
  Knee Bolster . . . . Standard Front
Crash Avoidance:
  Collision Avoidance . . . Optional CIB & DBS
  Blind Spot Detection . . . . Optional
  Lane Keeping Assist . . . . Optional
  Pedestrian Crash Avoidance . . . . None
General:
  Auto. Crash Notification . . . . None
  Day Running Lamps . . . . Standard
Safety Belt/Restraint:
  Dynamic Head Restraints . . . . None
  Adjustable Belt. . . . . Standard Front & Rear

^Warning feature does not meet government standards.

Chrysler Pacifica

Specifications

Drive	FWD
Engine	3.6-liter V6
Transmission	9-sp. Automatic
Tow Rating (lbs.)	Low-3600
Head/Leg Room (in.)	Average-40.1/41.1
Interior Space (cu. ft.).	Very Roomy-165
Cargo Space (cu. ft.)	Very Roomy-32.3
Wheelbase/Length (in.)	121.6/203.8

Dodge Challenger

Ratings—10 Best, 1 Worst

Combo Crash Tests	7
Safety Features	2
Rollover	7
Preventive Maintenance	8
Repair Costs	3
Warranty	4
Fuel Economy	4
Complaints	9
Insurance Costs	1
OVERALL RATING	**4**

Dodge Challenger

Dodge Challenger

At-a-Glance

Status/Year Series Started	Unchanged/2015
Twins	—
Body Styles	Coupe
Seating	5
Anti-Theft Device	Std. Pass. Immobil. & Alarm
Parking Index Rating	Hard
Where Made	Brampton, Ontario
Fuel Factor	
MPG Rating (city/hwy)	Poor-19/30
Driving Range (mi.)	Average-421
Fuel Type	Regular
Annual Fuel Cost	Average-$1615
Gas Guzzler Tax	No
Greenhouse Gas Emissions (tons/yr.)	High-7.8
Barrels of Oil Used per year	High-14.3

How the Competition Rates

Competitors	Rating	Pg.
Chevrolet Camaro	4	101
Chevrolet Corvette		102
Ford Mustang	6	134

Price Range

	Retail	Markup
SXT	$26,995	1%
R/T	$33,495	2%
R/T 392	$38,995	4%
SRT Hellcat	$63,795	3%

Safety Checklist

Crash Test:
- Frontal ... Average
- Side ... Very Good

Airbags:
- Torso ... Std. Front Pelvis/Torso from Seat
- Roll Sensing ... Yes
- Knee Bolster ... None

Crash Avoidance:
- Collision Avoidance . Warning Only Optional
- Blind Spot Detection ... Optional
- Lane Keeping Assist ... None
- Pedestrian Crash Avoidance ... None

General:
- Auto. Crash Notification ... None
- Day Running Lamps ... Standard

Safety Belt/Restraint:
- Dynamic Head Restraints ... None
- Adjustable Belt ... None

^Warning feature does not meet government standards.

Dodge Challenger

Specifications

Drive	RWD
Engine	3.6-liter V6
Transmission	8-sp. Automatic
Tow Rating (lbs.)	Very Low-1000
Head/Leg Room (in.)	Average-39.3/42
Interior Space (cu. ft.)	Cramped-93.9
Cargo Space (cu. ft.)	Cramped-16.2
Wheelbase/Length (in.)	116.2/197.9

Dodge Charger

Ratings—10 Best, 1 Worst

Rating	
Combo Crash Tests	3
Safety Features	5
Rollover	8
Preventive Maintenance	8
Repair Costs	7
Warranty	4
Fuel Economy	4
Complaints	3
Insurance Costs	1
OVERALL RATING	**2**

Dodge Charger

Dodge Charger

At-a-Glance

Status/Year Series Started	Unchanged/2011
Twins	Chrysler 300
Body Styles	Sedan
Seating	5
Anti-Theft Device	Std. Pass. Immobil. & Alarm
Parking Index Rating	Hard
Where Made	Brampton, Ontario
Fuel Factor	
MPG Rating (city/hwy)	Poor-19/31
Driving Range (mi.)	Long-426
Fuel Type	Regular
Annual Fuel Cost	Average-$1597
Gas Guzzler Tax	No
Greenhouse Gas Emissions (tons/yr.)	High-7.8
Barrels of Oil Used per year	High-14.3

How the Competition Rates

Competitors	Rating	Pg.
Buick LaCrosse	5	92
Chevrolet Impala	4	106
Ford Taurus	3	136

Price Range

	Retail	Markup
SXT	$28,495	1%
AWD GT	$32,495	3%
R/T	$34,995	3%
SRT Hellcat	$66,295	4%

Safety Checklist

Crash Test:	
Frontal	Very Poor
Side	Average
Airbags:	
Torso	Std. Front Pelvis/Torso from Seat
Roll Sensing	Yes
Knee Bolster	Standard Driver
Crash Avoidance:	
Collision Avoidance	Optional CIB & DBS
Blind Spot Detection	Optional
Lane Keeping Assist	Optional
Pedestrian Crash Avoidance	None
General:	
Auto. Crash Notification	None
Day Running Lamps	Standard
Safety Belt/Restraint:	
Dynamic Head Restraints	None
Adjustable Belt	Standard Front

^Warning feature does not meet government standards.

Dodge Charger

Specifications

Drive	RWD
Engine	3.6-liter V6
Transmission	8-sp. Automatic
Tow Rating (lbs.)	Very Low-1000
Head/Leg Room (in.)	Cramped-38.6/41.8
Interior Space (cu. ft.)	Roomy-104.7
Cargo Space (cu. ft.)	Cramped-16.1
Wheelbase/Length (in.)	120.2/198.4

Ratings—10 Best, 1 Worst

Combo Crash Tests	3
Safety Features	7
Rollover	2
Preventive Maintenance	5
Repair Costs	6
Warranty	4
Fuel Economy	3
Complaints	1
Insurance Costs	10
OVERALL RATING	**2**

Dodge Durango

Dodge Durango

Safety Checklist

Crash Test:
Frontal . . . . Very Poor
Side . . . . Average
Airbags:
Torso . . . Std. Front Pelvis/Torso from Seat
Roll Sensing . . . . Yes
Knee Bolster . . . . Standard Driver
Crash Avoidance:
Collision Avoidance . . Optional CIB & DBS^
Blind Spot Detection . . . . Optional
Lane Keeping Assist . . . . Optional^
Pedestrian Crash Avoidance . . . . None
General:
Auto. Crash Notification . . . . None
Day Running Lamps . . . . Standard
Safety Belt/Restraint:
Dynamic Head Restraints . . Standard Front
Adjustable Belt . . . . Standard Front

^Warning feature does not meet government standards.

At-a-Glance

Status/Year Series Started Unchanged/2011
Twins . . . . —
Body Styles . . . . SUV
Seating 6/7
Anti-Theft Device Std. Pass. Immob. & Opt. Pass. Alarm
Parking Index Rating . . . . Hard
Where Made . . . . Detroit, MI
Fuel Factor
MPG Rating (city/hwy) Poor-18/25
Driving Range (mi.) . . . . Very Long-507
Fuel Type . . . . Regular
Annual Fuel Cost . . . . High-$1784
Gas Guzzler Tax . . . . No
Greenhouse Gas Emissions (tons/yr.) . . Average-7.1
Barrels of Oil Used per year High-15.7

How the Competition Rates

Competitors	Rating	Pg.
Ford Edge	9	125
GMC Acadia	2	138
Jeep Grand Cherokee	4	165

Dodge Durango

Price Range	Retail	Markup
SXT RWD	$29,995	0%
GT RWD	$37,795	3%
R/T AWD	$46,295	4%
SRT AWD	$62,995	3%

Specifications

Drive . . . . AWD
Engine 3.6-liter V6
Transmission . . . . 8-sp. Automatic
Tow Rating (lbs.) . . . . Very Low-1350
Head/Leg Room (in.) Cramped-39.9/40.3
Interior Space (cu. ft.) . . . . Very Roomy-133.9
Cargo Space (cu. ft.) Average-17.2
Wheelbase/Length (in.) 119.8/201.2

Ratings—10 Best, 1 Worst

Combo Crash Tests	2
Safety Features	3
Rollover	2
Preventive Maintenance	9
Repair Costs	4
Warranty	4
Fuel Economy	3
Complaints	1
Insurance Costs	8
OVERALL RATING	**1**

Dodge Journey

Dodge Journey

At-a-Glance

Status/Year Series Started	Unchanged/2009
Twins	—
Body Styles	SUV
Seating	5/7
Anti-Theft Device	Std. Pass. Immobil. & Alarm
Parking Index Rating	Hard
Where Made	Toluca, Mexico
Fuel Factor	
MPG Rating (city/hwy)	Poor-19/25
Driving Range (mi.)	Long-437
Fuel Type	Regular
Annual Fuel Cost	High-$1725
Gas Guzzler Tax	No
Greenhouse Gas Emissions (tons/yr.)	Very High-9.4
Barrels of Oil Used per year	Very High-17.3

How the Competition Rates

Competitors	Rating	Pg.
Chevrolet Equinox	4	105
Ford Edge	9	125
GMC Acadia	2	138

Price Range

	Retail	Markup
SE FWD	$22,495	1%
SXT FWD	$25,695	3%
Crossroad AWD	$31,395	4%
GT AWD	$34,395	4%

Safety Checklist

Crash Test:	
Frontal	Poor
Side	Very Poor
Airbags:	
Torso	Std. Front Pelvis/Torso from Seat
Roll Sensing	Yes
Knee Bolster	Standard Driver
Crash Avoidance:	
Collision Avoidance	None
Blind Spot Detection	None
Lane Keeping Assist	None
Pedestrian Crash Avoidance	None
General:	
Auto. Crash Notification	None
Day Running Lamps	Standard
Safety Belt/Restraint:	
Dynamic Head Restraints	Standard Front
Adjustable Belt	Standard Front

^Warning feature does not meet government standards.

Dodge Journey

Specifications

Drive	FWD
Engine	3.6-liter V6
Transmission	6-sp. Automatic
Tow Rating (lbs.)	Very Low-2500
Head/Leg Room (in.)	Average-40.8/40.8
Interior Space (cu. ft.)	Roomy-123.7
Cargo Space (cu. ft.)	Very Cramped-10.7
Wheelbase/Length (in.)	113.8/192.4

Ratings—10 Best, 1 Worst

Combo Crash Tests	1
Safety Features	1
Rollover	4
Preventive Maintenance	8
Repair Costs	9
Warranty	5
Fuel Economy	7
Complaints	2
Insurance Costs	5
OVERALL RATING	**2**

Fiat 500

Fiat 500

At-a-Glance

Status/Year Series Started Unchanged/2012
Twins . . . . —
Body Styles . . . . Hatchback
Seating 4
Anti-Theft Device . . . . . . Std. Pass. Immobil. & Alarm
Parking Index Rating . . . . Very Easy
Where Made . . . . Toluca, Mexico
Fuel Factor
  MPG Rating (city/hwy) Good-27/34
  Driving Range (mi.) . . . . Very Short-312
  Fuel Type . . . . Regular
  Annual Fuel Cost . . . . Low-$1235
  Gas Guzzler Tax . . . . No
  Greenhouse Gas Emissions (tons/yr.) . . Average-6.0
  Barrels of Oil Used per year Average-11.0

How the Competition Rates

Competitors	Rating	Pg.
Chevrolet Sonic	8	109
Mini Hardtop	6	205
Volkswagen Golf	4	249

Price Range

	Retail	Markup
Pop Hatchback	$14,995	0%
Lounge Hatchback	$18,395	1%
Abarth Cabriolet	$21,490	2%
Electric	$31,800	2%

Safety Checklist

Crash Test:
  Frontal . . . . Very Poor
  Side . . . . Poor
Airbags:
  Torso . . . Std. Front Pelvis/Torso from Seat
  Roll Sensing . . . . No
  Knee Bolster . . . . Standard Driver
Crash Avoidance:
  Collision Avoidance . . . . None
  Blind Spot Detection . . . . None
  Lane Keeping Assist . . . . None
  Pedestrian Crash Avoidance . . . . None
General:
  Auto. Crash Notification . . . . None
  Day Running Lamps . . . . Standard
Safety Belt/Restraint:
  Dynamic Head Restraints . . Standard Front
  Adjustable Belt . . . . None

^Warning feature does not meet government standards.

Fiat 500

Specifications

Drive . . . . FWD
Engine 1.4-liter I4
Transmission . . . . 6-sp. Automatic
Tow Rating (lbs.) . . . . Very Low-0
Head/Leg Room (in.) Cramped-38.9/40.7
Interior Space (cu. ft.) . . . . Very Cramped-75.5
Cargo Space (cu. ft.) . . . . Very Cramped-9.5
Wheelbase/Length (in.) 90.6/139.6

Ratings—10 Best, 1 Worst

Combo Crash Tests	—
Safety Features	4
Rollover	4
Preventive Maintenance	8
Repair Costs	9
Warranty	5
Fuel Economy	5
Complaints	3
Insurance Costs	5

OVERALL RATING —

Fiat 500X

At-a-Glance

Status/Year Series Started	Unchanged/2015
Twins	—
Body Styles	SUV
Seating	5
Anti-Theft Device	Std. Pass. Immobil. & Alarm
Parking Index Rating	Easy
Where Made	Melfi, Italy
Fuel Factor	
MPG Rating (city/hwy)	Average-22/31
Driving Range (mi.)	Very Short-321
Fuel Type	Regular
Annual Fuel Cost	Low-$1452
Gas Guzzler Tax	No
Greenhouse Gas Emissions (tons/yr.)	Low-5.8
Barrels of Oil Used per year	High-13.2

How the Competition Rates

Competitors	Rating	Pg.
Honda HR-V	5	147
Jeep Compass	4	164
Mazda CX-3	10	190

Price Range

Price Range	Retail	Markup
Pop FWD	$19,995	1%
Trekking FWD	$23,335	3%
Trekking AWD	$25,235	3%
Lounge AWD	$27,035	3%

Fiat 500X

Safety Checklist

Crash Test:
  Frontal . . . . —
  Side . . . . —
Airbags:
  Torso . . . Std. Front Pelvis/Torso from Seat
  Roll Sensing . . . . Yes
  Knee Bolster . . . . Standard Driver
Crash Avoidance:
  Collision Avoidance . . Optional CIB & DBS^
  Blind Spot Detection . . . . Optional
  Lane Keeping Assist . . . . Optional^
  Pedestrian Crash Avoidance . . . . None
General:
  Auto. Crash Notification . . . . None
  Day Running Lamps . . . . Standard
Safety Belt/Restraint:
  Dynamic Head Restraints . . . . None
  Adjustable Belt . . . . Standard Front

^Warning feature does not meet government standards.

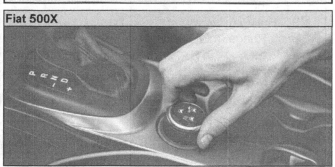

Fiat 500X

Specifications

Drive	FWD
Engine	2.4-liter I4
Transmission	9-sp. Automatic
Tow Rating (lbs.)	Very Low-1000
Head/Leg Room (in.)	Cramped-39.1/41.4
Interior Space (cu. ft.)	Cramped-91.7
Cargo Space (cu. ft.)	Very Cramped-12.2
Wheelbase/Length (in.)	101.2/167.2

Ford EcoSport | Small SUV

Ratings—10 Best, 1 Worst

Combo Crash Tests	—
Safety Features	4
Rollover	2
Preventive Maintenance	7
Repair Costs	7
Warranty	4
Fuel Economy	7
Complaints	8
Insurance Costs	8
OVERALL RATING	**—**

Ford EcoSport

Ford EcoSport

At-a-Glance

Status/Year Series Started	Unchanged/2018
Twins	—
Body Styles	SUV
Seating	5
Anti-Theft Device	Std. Pass. Immobil. & Alarm
Parking Index Rating	Very Easy
Where Made	Chennai, India
Fuel Factor	
MPG Rating (city/hwy)	Good-27/29
Driving Range (mi.)	Short-379
Fuel Type	Regular
Annual Fuel Cost	Low-$1319
Gas Guzzler Tax	No
Greenhouse Gas Emissions (tons/yr.)	Low-5.2
Barrels of Oil Used per year	Average-11.8

How the Competition Rates

Competitors	Rating	Pg.
Chevrolet Trax	10	114
Jeep Compass	4	164
Mazda CX-3	10	190

Price Range	Retail	Markup
S	$19,995	4%
SE	$22,905	4%
Titanium	$25,740	4%
SES	$26,740	4%

Safety Checklist

Crash Test:
- Frontal . . . . —
- Side . . . . —

Airbags:
- Torso Std. Front & Rear Pelvis/Torso from Seat
- Roll Sensing . . . . Yes
- Knee Bolster . . . . Standard Front

Crash Avoidance:
- Collision Avoidance . . . . None
- Blind Spot Detection . . . . Optional
- Lane Keeping Assist . . . . None
- Pedestrian Crash Avoidance . . . . None

General:
- Auto. Crash Notification . . . Dial Assist.-Free
- Day Running Lamps . . . . Standard

Safety Belt/Restraint:
- Dynamic Head Restraints . . . . None
- Adjustable Belt . . . . Standard Front

^Warning feature does not meet government standards.

Ford EcoSport

Specifications

Drive	FWD
Engine	2.0-liter I4
Transmission	6-sp. Automatic
Tow Rating (lbs.)	Very Low-2000
Head/Leg Room (in.)	Cramped-39.6/41.1
Interior Space (cu. ft.)	Cramped-91.1
Cargo Space (cu. ft.)	Average-20.9
Wheelbase/Length (in.)	99.2/161.3

Ratings—10 Best, 1 Worst

Combo Crash Tests	10
Safety Features	8
Rollover	4
Preventive Maintenance	6
Repair Costs	6
Warranty	4
Fuel Economy	4
Complaints	4
Insurance Costs	10
OVERALL RATING	**9**

Ford Edge

Ford Edge

At-a-Glance

Status/Year Series Started . . Apperance	Change/2015
Twins	—
Body Styles	SUV
Seating	5
Anti-Theft Device	Std. Pass. Immobil. & Alarm
Parking Index Rating	Very Easy
Where Made	Oakville, Ontario
Fuel Factor	
MPG Rating (city/hwy)	Poor-20/30
Driving Range (mi.)	Long-431
Fuel Type	Regular
Annual Fuel Cost	Average-$1562
Gas Guzzler Tax	No
Greenhouse Gas Emissions (tons/yr.)	Average-7.1
Barrels of Oil Used per year	High-15.7

How the Competition Rates

Competitors	Rating	Pg.
Chevrolet Equinox	4	105
Dodge Journey	1	121
Infiniti QX60	5	161

Price Range	Retail	Markup
SE FWD	$29,220	4%
SEL FWD	$31,955	5%
Titanium AWD	$37,925	5%
Sport AWD	$40,675	5%

Safety Checklist

Crash Test:
    Frontal . . . . Very Good
    Side . . . . .Good
Airbags:
    Torso . . . Std. Front Pelvis/Torso from Seat
    Roll Sensing . . . . Yes
    Knee Bolster . . . . Standard Front
Crash Avoidance:
    Collision Avoidance . . .Optional CIB & DBS
    Blind Spot Detection . . . . Optional
    Lane Keeping Assist . . . . Optional
    Pedestrian Crash Avoidance . . . . .None
General:
    Auto. Crash Notification . . . Dial Assist.-Free
    Day Running Lamps . . . . .Standard
Safety Belt/Restraint:
    Dynamic Head Restraints . . . . .None
    Adjustable Belt . . . . Standard Front

^Warning feature does not meet government standards.

Ford Edge

Specifications

Drive	FWD
Engine	3.5-liter V6
Transmission	6-sp. Automatic
Tow Rating (lbs.)	Very Low-1500
Head/Leg Room (in.)	Roomy-40.2/42.6
Interior Space (cu. ft.)	Roomy-113.9
Cargo Space (cu. ft.)	Very Roomy-39.2
Wheelbase/Length (in.)	112.2/188.1

Ratings—10 Best, 1 Worst	
Combo Crash Tests	9
Safety Features	5
Rollover	2
Preventive Maintenance	7
Repair Costs	3
Warranty	4
Fuel Economy	5
Complaints	6
Insurance Costs	5
OVERALL RATING	**6**

Ford Escape

Ford Escape

At-a-Glance

Status/Year Series Started	Unchanged/2013
Twins	Lincoln MKC
Body Styles	SUV
Seating	5
Anti-Theft Device	Std. Pass. Immobil. & Alarm
Parking Index Rating	Average
Where Made	Louisville, Kentucky
Fuel Factor	
MPG Rating (city/hwy)	Average-22/31
Driving Range (mi.)	Short-390
Fuel Type	Regular
Annual Fuel Cost	Low-$1452
Gas Guzzler Tax	No
Greenhouse Gas Emissions (tons/yr.)	Average-7.2
Barrels of Oil Used per year	High-13.2

How the Competition Rates

Competitors	Rating	Pg.
Honda HR-V	5	147
Jeep Cherokee	5	163
Kia Sportage	9	174

Price Range	Retail	Markup
S FWD	$23,850	4%
SE FWD	$26,955	5%
SEL 4WD	$29,335	5%
Titanium 4WD	$33,395	5%

Safety Checklist

Crash Test:
   Frontal . . . . Good
   Side . . . . Very Good
Airbags:
   Torso . . . Std. Front Pelvis/Torso from Seat
   Roll Sensing . . . . Yes
   Knee Bolster . . . . Standard Driver
Crash Avoidance:
   Collision Avoidance . Warning Only Optional
   Blind Spot Detection . . . . Optional
   Lane Keeping Assist . . . . Optional
   Pedestrian Crash Avoidance . . . . None
General:
   Auto. Crash Notification . . . Dial Assist.-Free
   Day Running Lamps . . . . Standard
Safety Belt/Restraint:
   Dynamic Head Restraints . . . . None
   Adjustable Belt . . . . Standard Front

^Warning feature does not meet government standards.

Ford Escape

Specifications

Drive	FWD
Engine	2.5-liter I4
Transmission	6-sp. Automatic
Tow Rating (lbs.)	Very Low-1500
Head/Leg Room (in.)	Roomy-39.9/43.1
Interior Space (cu. ft.)	Average-98.1
Cargo Space (cu. ft.)	Very Roomy-34.3
Wheelbase/Length (in.)	105.9/178.1

Ratings—10 Best, 1 Worst

Combo Crash Tests	—
Safety Features	7
Rollover	1
Preventive Maintenance	2
Repair Costs	9
Warranty	4
Fuel Economy	2
Complaints	7
Insurance Costs	10
OVERALL RATING	—

Ford Expedition

Ford Expedition

At-a-Glance

Status/Year Series Started	Unchanged/2003
Twins	Lincoln Navigator
Body Styles	SUV
Seating	7/8
Anti-Theft Device	Std. Pass. Immobil. & Alarm
Parking Index Rating	Very Hard
Where Made	Louisville, Kentucky
Fuel Factor	
MPG Rating (city/hwy)	Very Poor-17/22
Driving Range (mi.)	Very Long-530
Fuel Type	Regular
Annual Fuel Cost	High-$1941
Gas Guzzler Tax	No
Greenhouse Gas Emissions (tons/yr.)	High-7.7
Barrels of Oil Used per year	Very High-17.3

How the Competition Rates

Competitors	Rating	Pg.
Buick Enclave	4	89
Chevrolet Suburban	2	111
Toyota 4Runner	2	231

Price Range

	Retail	Markup
XL RWD	$48,095	5%
XLT RWD	$54,705	5%
Limited 4WD	$65,705	5%
Platinum 4WD	$75,855	5%

Ford Expedition

Safety Checklist

Crash Test:
Frontal . . . . —
Side. . . . . —
Airbags:
Torso . . . . Std. Front Torso from Seat
Roll Sensing. . . . . Yes
Knee Bolster . . . . None
Crash Avoidance:
Collision Avoidance . . . Optional CIB & DBS
Blind Spot Detection . . . . Optional
Lane Keeping Assist . . . . Optional
Pedestrian Crash Avoidance . . . . . Optional
General:
Auto. Crash Notification . . . Dial Assist.-Free
Day Running Lamps . . . . Standard
Safety Belt/Restraint:
Dynamic Head Restraints . . . . None
Adjustable Belt . . . . Standard Front

^Warning feature does not meet government standards.

Ford Expedition

Specifications

Drive	4WD
Engine	3.5-liter V6
Transmission	10-sp. Automatic
Tow Rating (lbs.)	Very High-9300
Head/Leg Room (in.)	Very Roomy-42/43.9
Interior Space (cu. ft.)	Very Roomy-171.9
Cargo Space (cu. ft.)	Average-20.9
Wheelbase/Length (in.)	122.5/210

Ratings—10 Best, 1 Worst

Combo Crash Tests	5
Safety Features	5
Rollover	3
Preventive Maintenance	5
Repair Costs	6
Warranty	4
Fuel Economy	2
Complaints	2
Insurance Costs	10
OVERALL RATING	**3**

Ford Explorer

At-a-Glance

Status/Year Series Started	Unchanged/2011
Twins	—
Body Styles	SUV
Seating	6/7
Anti-Theft Device	Std. Pass. Immobil. & Alarm
Parking Index Rating	Hard
Where Made	Chicago, IL
Fuel Factor	
MPG Rating (city/hwy)	Very Poor-17/23
Driving Range (mi.)	Very Short-358
Fuel Type	Regular
Annual Fuel Cost	High-$1908
Gas Guzzler Tax	No
Greenhouse Gas Emissions (tons/yr.)	Very High-9.5
Barrels of Oil Used per year	Very High-17.3

How the Competition Rates

Competitors	Rating	Pg.
Dodge Journey	1	121
Honda Pilot	8	149
Toyota Highlander	8	237

Price Range

	Retail	Markup
Base FWD	$31,660	4%
XLT FWD	$33,775	5%
Limited 4WD	$43,825	5%
Platinum 4WD	$53,235	5%

Ford Explorer

Safety Checklist

Crash Test:
  Frontal.........................Good
  Side........................Poor
Airbags:
  Torso . . . Std. Front Pelvis/Torso from Seat
  Roll Sensing.....................Yes
  Knee Bolster ....Std. Passenger
Crash Avoidance:
  Collision Avoidance . Warning Only Optional
  Blind Spot Detection .... Optional
  Lane Keeping Assist .... Optional
  Pedestrian Crash Avoidance ....None
General:
  Auto. Crash Notification . . . Dial Assist.-Free
  Day Running Lamps ....Standard
Safety Belt/Restraint:
  Dynamic Head Restraints ....None
  Adjustable Belt..........Standard Front

^Warning feature does not meet government standards.

Ford Explorer

Specifications

Drive	AWD
Engine	3.5-liter V6
Transmission	6-sp. Automatic
Tow Rating (lbs.)	Low-5000
Head/Leg Room (in.)	Very Roomy-41.4/42.9
Interior Space (cu. ft.)	Very Roomy-151.5
Cargo Space (cu. ft.)	Roomy-21
Wheelbase/Length (in.)	112.8/198.3

Ratings—10 Best, 1 Worst

Combo Crash Tests	10
Safety Features	6
Rollover	2
Preventive Maintenance	8
Repair Costs	8
Warranty	4
Fuel Economy	2
Complaints	5
Insurance Costs	8
OVERALL RATING	**8**

Ford F-150

At-a-Glance

Status/Year Series Started	Unchanged/2015
Twins	—
Body Styles	Pickup
Seating	5/6
Anti-Theft Device	Std. Pass. Immobil. & Alarm
Parking Index Rating	Very Hard
Where Made	Dearborn, MI
Fuel Factor	
MPG Rating (city/hwy)	Very Poor-17/23
Driving Range (mi.)	Very Long-693
Fuel Type	Regular
Annual Fuel Cost	High-$1908
Gas Guzzler Tax	No
Greenhouse Gas Emissions (tons/yr.)	Very High-9.5
Barrels of Oil Used per year	Very High-17.3

How the Competition Rates

Competitors	Rating	Pg.
Chevrolet Silverado		108
Nissan Titan	1	218
Ram 1500	5	221

Price Range

	Retail	Markup
XL Reg. Cab 2WD	$27,680	5%
XLT Supercab 2WD	$37,185	8%
Lariat Supercrew 4WD	$48,220	8%
Platinum Supercrew 4WD	$57,880	8%S

Ford F-150

Safety Checklist

Crash Test:
    Frontal . . . . Very Good
    Side . . . . Very Good
Airbags:
    Torso . . . Std. Front Pelvis/Torso from Seat
    Roll Sensing . . . . Yes
    Knee Bolster . . . . None
Crash Avoidance:
    Collision Avoidance . Warning Only Optional
    Blind Spot Detection . . . . Optional
    Lane Keeping Assist . . . . Optional
    Pedestrian Crash Avoidance . . . . None
General:
    Auto. Crash Notification . . . Dial Assist.-Free
    Day Running Lamps . . . . Standard
Safety Belt/Restraint:
    Dynamic Head Restraints . . . . None
    Adjustable Belt . . . . Standard Front

^Warning feature does not meet government standards.

Ford F-150

Specifications

Drive	4WD
Engine	3.5-liter V6
Transmission	6-sp. Automatic
Tow Rating (lbs.)	Very High-10700
Head/Leg Room (in.)	Very Roomy-40.8/43.9
Interior Space (cu. ft.)	Roomy-116
Cargo Space (cu. ft.)	Very Roomy-62.3
Wheelbase/Length (in.)	141.1/231.9

Ratings—10 Best, 1 Worst	
Combo Crash Tests	3
Safety Features	2
Rollover	4
Preventive Maintenance	6
Repair Costs	10
Warranty	4
Fuel Economy	8
Complaints	2
Insurance Costs	3
OVERALL RATING	**2**

Ford Fiesta

Ford Fiesta

At-a-Glance

Status/Year Series Started Unchanged/2011
Twins . . . . —
Body Styles . . . . Sedan, Hatchback
Seating 5
Anti-Theft Device . . . . . . Std. Pass. Immobil. & Alarm
Parking Index Rating . . . . .Very Easy
Where Made. . . . . Cuautitlán, Mexico
Fuel Factor
  MPG Rating (city/hwy) Good-27/37
  Driving Range (mi.) Short-381
  Fuel Type. . . . . .Regular
Annual Fuel Cost . . . . Low-$1196
  Gas Guzzler Tax . . . . .No
  Greenhouse Gas Emissions (tons/yr.) Low-5.8
  Barrels of Oil Used per year Average-10.6

How the Competition Rates

Competitors	Rating	Pg.
Chevrolet Sonic	8	109
Nissan Versa	1	219
Toyota Yaris Liftback	5	247

Price Range	Retail	Markup
Sedan	$14,130	2%
SE Hatchback	$15,660	2%
Titanium Sedan	$19,120	2%
ST Hatchback	$21,610	2%

Safety Checklist

Crash Test:
  Frontal. . . . . Average
  Side. .Very Poor
Airbags:
  Torso . . . Std. Front Pelvis/Torso from Seat
  Roll Sensing. .Yes
  Knee Bolster . . . . Standard Driver
Crash Avoidance:
  Collision Avoidance . . . . .None
  Blind Spot Detection . . . . .None
  Lane Keeping Assist . . . . .None
  Pedestrian Crash Avoidance . . . . .None
General:
  Auto. Crash Notification . . . Dial Assist.-Free
  Day Running Lamps . . . . .None
Safety Belt/Restraint:
  Dynamic Head Restraints . . . . .None
  Adjustable Belt . . . . Standard Front

^Warning feature does not meet government standards.

Ford Fiesta

Specifications

Drive. . . . . .FWD
Engine 1.6-liter I4
Transmission . . . . 6-sp. Automatic
Tow Rating (lbs.) . . . . .Very Low-0
Head/Leg Room (in.) Average-39.1/42.2
Interior Space (cu. ft.). . . . . Very Cramped-85.1
Cargo Space (cu. ft.) Cramped-14.9
Wheelbase/Length (in.) 98/159.7

Ratings—10 Best, 1 Worst

Combo Crash Tests	—
Safety Features	2
Rollover	3
Preventive Maintenance	6
Repair Costs	6
Warranty	4
Fuel Economy	2
Complaints	3
Insurance Costs	5
OVERALL RATING	—

Ford Flex

Ford Flex

At-a-Glance

Status/Year Series Started	Unchanged/2009
Twins	—
Body Styles	SUV
Seating	6/7
Anti-Theft Device	Std. Pass. Immobil. & Alarm
Parking Index Rating	Very Hard
Where Made	Oakville, Ontario
Fuel Factor	
MPG Rating (city/hwy)	Very Poor-16/23
Driving Range (mi.)	Very Short-345
Fuel Type	Regular
Annual Fuel Cost	Very High-$1982
Gas Guzzler Tax	No
Greenhouse Gas Emissions (tons/yr.)	High-7.7
Barrels of Oil Used per year	Very High-17.3

How the Competition Rates

Competitors	Rating	Pg.
Buick Enclave	4	89
Chevrolet Tahoe	4	112
Volvo XC90	8	256

Price Range

	Retail	Markup
SE FWD	$30,025	4%
SEL AWD	$34,680	5%
Limited FWD	$38,230	5%
Limited AWD	$40,180	5%

Safety Checklist

Crash Test:
- Frontal . . . . —
- Side . . . . —

Airbags:
- Torso . . . . Std. Front Torso from Seat
- Roll Sensing . . . . Yes
- Knee Bolster . . . . None

Crash Avoidance:
- Collision Avoidance . Warning Only Optional
- Blind Spot Detection . . . . Optional
- Lane Keeping Assist . . . . None
- Pedestrian Crash Avoidance . . . . None

General:
- Auto. Crash Notification . . . Dial Assist.-Free
- Day Running Lamps . . . . None

Safety Belt/Restraint:
- Dynamic Head Restraints . . . . None
- Adjustable Belt . . . . Standard Front

^Warning feature does not meet government standards.

Ford Flex

Specifications

Drive	FWD
Engine	3.5-liter V6
Transmission	6-sp. Automatic
Tow Rating (lbs.)	Low-4500
Head/Leg Room (in.)	Roomy-41.8/40.8
Interior Space (cu. ft.)	Very Roomy-155.8
Cargo Space (cu. ft.)	Average-20
Wheelbase/Length (in.)	117.9/201.8

Ratings—10 Best, 1 Worst

Combo Crash Tests	3
Safety Features	8
Rollover	7
Preventive Maintenance	8
Repair Costs	9
Warranty	4
Fuel Economy	5
Complaints	2
Insurance Costs	1
OVERALL RATING	**4**

Ford Fusion

Ford Fusion

At-a-Glance

Status/Year Series Started	Unchanged/2013
Twins	Lincoln MKZ
Body Styles	Sedan
Seating	5
Anti-Theft Device	Std. Pass. Immobil. & Alarm
Parking Index Rating	Average
Where Made	Hermosillo, Mexico

Fuel Factor

MPG Rating (city/hwy)	Average-21/32
Driving Range (mi.)	Average-410
Fuel Type	Regular
Annual Fuel Cost	Average-$1479
Gas Guzzler Tax	No
Greenhouse Gas Emissions (tons/yr.)	Average-6.9
Barrels of Oil Used per year	Average-12.7

How the Competition Rates

Competitors	Rating	Pg.
Chevrolet Malibu	9	107
Infiniti Q50	3	158
Toyota Camry	8	234

Price Range	Retail	Markup
S	$22,120	5%
SE AWD	$27,045	6%
Sport	$33,605	6%
Platimum	$36,750	6%

Safety Checklist

Crash Test:
- Frontal . . . . Very Poor
- Side . . . . Average

Airbags:
- Torso . . . . Std. Front Pelvis/Torso from Seat
- Roll Sensing . . . . Yes
- Knee Bolster . . . . Standard Front

Crash Avoidance:
- Collision Avoidance . . . Optional CIB & DBS
- Blind Spot Detection . . . . Optional
- Lane Keeping Assist . . . . Optional
- Pedestrian Crash Avoidance . . . . None

General:
- Auto. Crash Notification . . . Dial Assist.-Free
- Day Running Lamps . . . . Standard

Safety Belt/Restraint:
- Dynamic Head Restraints . . . . None
- Adjustable Belt . . . . Standard Front

^Warning feature does not meet government standards.

Ford Fusion

Specifications

Drive	FWD
Engine	2.5-liter I4
Transmission	6-sp. Automatic
Tow Rating (lbs.)	—
Head/Leg Room (in.)	Roomy-39.2/44.3
Interior Space (cu. ft.)	Roomy-118.8
Cargo Space (cu. ft.)	Cramped-16
Wheelbase/Length (in.)	112.2/191.8

Ratings—10 Best, 1 Worst

Combo Crash Tests	7
Safety Features	8
Rollover	7
Preventive Maintenance	6
Repair Costs	10
Warranty	4
Fuel Economy	9
Complaints	1
Insurance Costs	5
OVERALL RATING	**8**

Ford Fusion Energi

Ford Fusion Energi

At-a-Glance

Status/Year Series Started	Unchanged/2016
Twins	—
Body Styles	Sedan
Seating	5
Anti-Theft Device	Std. Pass. Immobil. & Alarm
Parking Index Rating	Average
Where Made	Hermosillo, Mexico
Fuel Factor	
MPG Rating (city/hwy)	Very Good-40/36
Driving Range (mi.)	Very Long-533
Fuel Type	Regular
Annual Fuel Cost	Very Low-$965
Gas Guzzler Tax	No
Greenhouse Gas Emissions (tons/yr.)	Very Low-2.1
Barrels of Oil Used per year	Very Low-4.9

How the Competition Rates

Competitors	Rating	Pg.
Hyundai Sonata	9	155
Mazda 6	6	191
Subaru Legacy	7	226

Price Range

	Retail	Markup
SE Luxury Energi	$33,120	6%
Titanium Energi	$34,120	6%
Platinum Energi	$41,120	6%
	—	

Safety Checklist

Crash Test:	
Frontal	Very Good
Side	Very Poor
Airbags:	
Torso	Std. Front Pelvis/Torso from Seat
Roll Sensing	Yes
Knee Bolster	Standard Front
Crash Avoidance:	
Collision Avoidance	Optional CIB & DBS
Blind Spot Detection	Optional
Lane Keeping Assist	Optional
Pedestrian Crash Avoidance	None
General:	
Auto. Crash Notification	Dial Assist.-Free
Day Running Lamps	Standard
Safety Belt/Restraint:	
Dynamic Head Restraints	None
Adjustable Belt	Standard Front

^Warning feature does not meet government standards.

Ford Fusion Energi

Specifications

Drive	FWD
Engine	2.0-liter I4
Transmission	CVT
Tow Rating (lbs.)	—
Head/Leg Room (in.)	Roomy-39.2/44.3
Interior Space (cu. ft.)	Average-102.8
Cargo Space (cu. ft.)	Very Cramped-8.2
Wheelbase/Length (in.)	112.2/191.8

Ratings—10 Best, 1 Worst

Combo Crash Tests	8
Safety Features	2
Rollover	10
Preventive Maintenance	8
Repair Costs	6
Warranty	4
Fuel Economy	3
Complaints	6
Insurance Costs	3
OVERALL RATING	**6**

Ford Mustang

Ford Mustang

At-a-Glance

Status/Year Series Started	Unchanged/2015
Twins	—
Body Styles	Coupe, Convertible
Seating	4
Anti-Theft Device	Std. Pass. Immobil. & Alarm
Parking Index Rating	Easy
Where Made	Flat Rock, MI
Fuel Factor	
MPG Rating (city/hwy)	Poor-19/28
Driving Range (mi.)	Very Short-355
Fuel Type	Regular
Annual Fuel Cost	Average-$1654
Gas Guzzler Tax	No
Greenhouse Gas Emissions (tons/yr.)	High-8.1
Barrels of Oil Used per year	High-15.0

How the Competition Rates

Competitors	Rating	Pg.
Chevrolet Camaro	4	101
Chevrolet Corvette		103
Dodge Challenger	4	118

Price Range

	Retail	Markup
Base Coupe	$24,645	4%
Eco Premium Coupe	$29,645	6%
GT Premium Convertible	$42,145	6%
Shelby GT350	$54,295	6%

Safety Checklist

Crash Test:
  Frontal . . . . Very Good
  Side . . . . Poor
Airbags:
  Torso . . . . .Std. Front Pelvis/Torso from Seat
  Roll Sensing . . . . No
  Knee Bolster . . . . Standard Front
Crash Avoidance:
  Collision Avoidance . Warning Only Optional
  Blind Spot Detection . . . . Optional
  Lane Keeping Assist . . . . None
  Pedestrian Crash Avoidance . . . . .None
General:
  Auto. Crash Notification . . . Dial Assist.-Free
  Day Running Lamps . . . . None
Safety Belt/Restraint:
  Dynamic Head Restraints . . . . None
  Adjustable Belt . . . . .None

^Warning feature does not meet government standards.

Ford Mustang

Specifications

Drive	RWD
Engine	3.7-liter V6
Transmission	6-sp. Automatic
Tow Rating (lbs.)	—
Head/Leg Room (in.)	Average-37.6/44.5
Interior Space (cu. ft.)	Very Cramped-84.5
Cargo Space (cu. ft.)	Very Cramped-13.5
Wheelbase/Length (in.)	107.1/188.5

Ratings—10 Best, 1 Worst

Combo Crash Tests	—
Safety Features	9
Rollover	2
Preventive Maintenance	2
Repair Costs	6
Warranty	4
Fuel Economy	4
Complaints	—
Insurance Costs	5
OVERALL RATING	**—**

Ford Ranger

Ford Ranger

At-a-Glance

Status/Year Series Started	All New/2019
Twins	—
Body Styles	Pickup
Seating	4/5
Anti-Theft Device	Std. Pass. Immobil. & Alarm
Parking Index Rating	Very Hard
Where Made	Wayne, Michigan
Fuel Factor	
MPG Rating (city/hwy)	Poor-21/28
Driving Range (mi.)	Long-432
Fuel Type	Regular
Annual Fuel Cost	Average-$1553
Gas Guzzler Tax	No
Greenhouse Gas Emissions (tons/yr.)	Average-6.2
Barrels of Oil Used per year	High-13.7

How the Competition Rates

Competitors	Rating	Pg.
Chevrolet Colorado	2	102
Nissan Frontier	1	211
Toyota Tacoma	1	244

Price Range

	Retail	Markup
XL 2WD	$25,495	6%
XLT 2WD	$27,940	6%
XLT 4WD	$31,940	6%
Lariat 4WD	$36,210	6%

Safety Checklist

Crash Test:
- Frontal .... —
- Side .... —

Airbags:
- Torso .... Std. Front Pelvis/Torso from Seat
- Roll Sensing .... Yes
- Knee Bolster .... Standard Front

Crash Avoidance:
- Collision Avoidance .. Standard CIB & DBS
- Blind Spot Detection .... Optional
- Lane Keeping Assist .... Optional
- Pedestrian Crash Avoidance ..... Standard

General:
- Auto. Crash Notification . . . Dial Assist.-Free
- Day Running Lamps .... Standard

Safety Belt/Restraint:
- Dynamic Head Restraints .... None
- Adjustable Belt .... Standard Front

^Warning feature does not meet government standards.

Ford Ranger

Specifications

Drive	RWD
Engine	2.3-liter I4
Transmission	10-sp. Automatic
Tow Rating (lbs.)	High-7500
Head/Leg Room (in.)	Average-39.8/43.1
Interior Space (cu. ft.)	Very Cramped-89.2
Cargo Space (cu. ft.)	Very Roomy-43.3
Wheelbase/Length (in.)	126.8/210.8

Ratings—10 Best, 1 Worst	
Combo Crash Tests	6
Safety Features	3
Rollover	6
Preventive Maintenance	5
Repair Costs	7
Warranty	4
Fuel Economy	3
Complaints	7
Insurance Costs	1
OVERALL RATING	**3**

Ford Taurus

At-a-Glance

Status/Year Series Started	Unchanged/2010
Twins	—
Body Styles	Sedan
Seating	5
Anti-Theft Device	Std. Pass. Immobil. & Alarm
Parking Index Rating	Very Hard
Where Made	Chicago, IL
Fuel Factor	
MPG Rating (city/hwy)	Poor-19/29
Driving Range (mi.)	Long-427
Fuel Type	Regular
Annual Fuel Cost	Average-$1634
Gas Guzzler Tax	No
Greenhouse Gas Emissions (tons/yr.)	High-7.8
Barrels of Oil Used per year	High-14.3

How the Competition Rates

Competitors	Rating	Pg.
Buick LaCrosse	5	92
Chevrolet Impala	4	106
Toyota Avalon	8	233

Price Range	Retail	Markup
SE	$27,595	6%
SEL	$30,025	6%
Limited AWD	$38,955	6%
SHO AWD	$42,270	5%

Ford Taurus

Safety Checklist

Crash Test:
   Frontal . . . . Very Good
   Side. . . . . Very Poor
Airbags:
   Torso . . . . Std. Front Torso from Seat
   Roll Sensing. . . . . .Yes
   Knee Bolster .None
Crash Avoidance:
   Collision Avoidance . Warning Only Optional
   Blind Spot Detection . . . . Optional
   Lane Keeping Assist . . . . Optional
   Pedestrian Crash Avoidance . . . . None
General:
   Auto. Crash Notification . . . Dial Assist.-Free
   Day Running Lamps . . . . None
Safety Belt/Restraint:
   Dynamic Head Restraints . . . . None
   Adjustable Belt. . . . . Standard Front

^Warning feature does not meet government standards.

Ford Taurus

Specifications

Drive	FWD
Engine	3.5-liter V6
Transmission	6-sp. Automatic
Tow Rating (lbs.)	Very Low-1000
Head/Leg Room (in.)	Cramped-39/41.9
Interior Space (cu. ft.)	Average-102.2
Cargo Space (cu. ft.)	Average-20.1
Wheelbase/Length (in.)	112.9/202.9

Ratings—10 Best, 1 Worst

Combo Crash Tests	—
Safety Features	10
Rollover	7
Preventive Maintenance	3
Repair Costs	4
Warranty	10
Fuel Economy	3
Complaints	10
Insurance Costs	—
OVERALL RATING	—

Genesis G80

Genesis G80

At-a-Glance

Status/Year Series Started. Unchanged/2017
Twins . . . . —
Body Styles . . . . .Sedan
Seating. 5
Anti-Theft Device . Std. Pass. Immobil. & Active Alarm
Parking Index Rating . . . . Average
Where Made. . . . . Ulsan, South Korea
Fuel Factor
  MPG Rating (city/hwy) Poor-19/27
  Driving Range (mi.) Long-445
  Fuel Type. . . . . .Regular
  Annual Fuel Cost . . . . .High-$1676
  Gas Guzzler Tax .No
  Greenhouse Gas Emissions (tons/yr.). . Average-6.8
  Barrels of Oil Used per year High-15.0

How the Competition Rates

Competitors	Rating	Pg.
Cadillac XTS	8	99
Lincon Continental	6	185
Tesla Model S	10	229

Price Range

	Retail	Markup
3.8L V6	$42,050	6%
3.8L V6 AWD	$44,550	6%
3.3L Turbo V6 Sport	$55,250	7%
5.0L V8 AWD	$59,500	7%

Safety Checklist

Crash Test:
  Frontal. . . . . —
  Side. . . . . —
Airbags:
  Torso Std. Fr. & Opt. Rr. Pelvis/Torso from Seat
  Roll Sensing. . . . . .Yes
  Knee Bolster . . . . .Standard Driver
Crash Avoidance:
  Collision Avoidance . . Standard CIB & DBS
  Blind Spot Detection . . . . Std.
  Lane Keeping Assist . . . . Standard
  Pedestrian Crash Avoidance . . . . .None
General:
  Auto. Crash Notification Operat. Assist.-Fee
  Day Running Lamps . . . . Standard
Safety Belt/Restraint:
  Dynamic Head Restraints . . . . .None
  Adjustable Belt. . . . . Standard Front

^Warning feature does not meet government standards.

Genesis G80

Specifications

Drive. . . . . .RWD
Engine 3.8-liter V6
Transmission . . . . 8-sp. Automatic
Tow Rating (lbs.) . . . . —
Head/Leg Room (in.) . . . . Very Roomy-41.1/45.7
Interior Space (cu. ft.). Roomy-107.7
Cargo Space (cu. ft.) Cramped-15.3
Wheelbase/Length (in.) 118.5/196.5

GMC Acadia

Medium SUV

GMC Acadia

Ratings—10 Best, 1 Worst

Combo Crash Tests	3
Safety Features	7
Rollover	4
Preventive Maintenance	2
Repair Costs	3
Warranty	5
Fuel Economy	3
Complaints	4
Insurance Costs	10
OVERALL RATING	**2**

GMC Acadia

At-a-Glance

Status/Year Series Started........Unchanged/2017
Twins.............................Cadillac XT5
Body Styles..............................SUV
Seating.................................5/6/7
Anti-Theft Device . Std. Pass. Immobil. & Active Alarm
Parking Index Rating.....................Hard
Where Made......................Lansing, MI
Fuel Factor
  MPG Rating (city/hwy)............Poor-18/25
  Driving Range (mi.)..............Short-391
  Fuel Type..........................Regular
  Annual Fuel Cost..............High-$1784
  Gas Guzzler Tax.........................No
  Greenhouse Gas Emissions (tons/yr.)..Average-7.0
  Barrels of Oil Used per year.........High-15.7

How the Competition Rates

Competitors	Rating	Pg.
Lincoln Nautilis	5	188
Mitsubishi Outlander	4	207
Nissan Rogue	3	216

Price Range

	Retail	Markup
SLE1 FWD	$32,800	5%
SLT1 FWD	$38,000	5%
SLT2 AWD	$43,900	5%
Denali AWD	$47,500	5%

Safety Checklist

Crash Test:
  Frontal..............................Poor
  Side...........................Very Poor
Airbags:
  Torso....Std. Front Pelvis/Torso from Seat
  Roll Sensing..........................Yes
  Knee Bolster...........Standard Driver
Crash Avoidance:
  Collision Avoidance...Optional CIB & DBS
  Blind Spot Detection...........Optional
  Lane Keeping Assist...........Optional
  Pedestrian Crash Avoidance.....Optional
General:
  Auto. Crash Notif...Op. Assist. & Crash Info-Fee
  Day Running Lamps...........Standard
Safety Belt/Restraint:
  Dynamic Head Restraints..........None
  Adjustable Belt...........Optional Rear

GMC Acadia

Specifications

Drive.................................FWD
Engine.......................3.6-liter V6
Transmission..........6-sp. Automatic
Tow Rating (lbs.)...............Low-4000
Head/Leg Room (in.).........Average-40.3/41
Interior Space (cu. ft.)......Very Roomy-143.8
Cargo Space (cu. ft.)....Very Cramped-12.8
Wheelbase/Length (in.)........112.5/193.6

Ratings—10 Best, 1 Worst

Combo Crash Tests	—
Safety Features	3
Rollover	2
Preventive Maintenance	2
Repair Costs	1
Warranty	8
Fuel Economy	5
Complaints	4
Insurance Costs	3

OVERALL RATING   —

GMC Canyon

GMC Canyon

At-a-Glance

Status/Year Series Started Unchanged/2015
Twins . . . . Chevrolet Colorado
Body Styles . . . . Pickup
Seating 5
Anti-Theft Device . Std. Pass. Immobil. & Active Alarm
Parking Index Rating . . . . Very Hard
Where Made. . . . . Wentzville, MO
Fuel Factor
  MPG Rating (city/hwy) Poor-20/27
  Driving Range (mi.) . . . . Very Long-475
  Fuel Type. Regular
  Annual Fuel Cost . . . . Average-$1623
  Gas Guzzler Tax . . . . No
  Greenhouse Gas Emissions (tons/yr.) High-8.2
  Barrels of Oil Used per year High-15.0

How the Competition Rates

Competitors	Rating	Pg.
Ford Ranger		135
Nissan Frontier	1	211
Toyota Tacoma	1	244

Price Range

	Retail	Markup
SL Ext. Cab 2WD	$21,400	3%
SLE Crew Cab 2WD	$35,900	4%
SLT Crew Cab 4WD	$36,400	4%
Denali Crew Cab 4WD	$44,100	5%

Safety Checklist

Crash Test:
  Frontal . . . . .Poor
   Side. . . . . Poor
Airbags:
  Torso . . . .Std. Front Pelvis/Torso from Seat
  Roll Sensing. .Yes
  Knee Bolster .None
Crash Avoidance:
  Collision Avoidance . Warning Only Optional
  Blind Spot Detection . . . . .None
  Lane Keeping Assist . .Warn. Only Optional
  Pedestrian Crash Avoidance . . . . .None
General:
  Auto. Crash Notif. . . Op. Assist. & Crash Info-Fee
  Day Running Lamps . . . . Standard
Safety Belt/Restraint:
  Dynamic Head Restraints . . . . .None
  Adjustable Belt. . . . . Optional Front & Rear

^Warning feature does not meet government standards.

GMC Canyon

Specifications

Drive. . . . . .RWD
Engine 2.5-liter I4
Transmission . . . . 6-sp. Automatic
Tow Rating (lbs.) Low-3500
Head/Leg Room (in.) . . . . Very Roomy-41.4/45
Interior Space (cu. ft.). . . . . —
Cargo Space (cu. ft.) . . . . Very Roomy-49.9
Wheelbase/Length (in.) 128.3/212.7

Ratings—10 Best, 1 Worst

Combo Crash Tests	—
Safety Features	3
Rollover	3
Preventive Maintenance	1
Repair Costs	5
Warranty	5
Fuel Economy	2
Complaints	—
Insurance Costs	10
OVERALL RATING	—

GMC Sierra

GMC Sierra

At-a-Glance

Status/Year Series Started . . . . All New/2019
Twins . . . . Chevrolet Silverado
Body Styles . . . . Pickup
Seating 5/6
Anti-Theft Device . Std. Pass. Immobil. & Active Alarm
Parking Index Rating . . . . Very Hard
Where Made . . . . Fort Wayne, IN
Fuel Factor
  MPG Rating (city/hwy) . . . . Very Poor-16/22
  Driving Range (mi.) Long-432
  Fuel Type . . . . Regular
  Annual Fuel Cost . . . . Very High-$2015
  Gas Guzzler Tax . . . . No
  Greenhouse Gas Emissions (tons/yr.) High-8.1
  Barrels of Oil Used per year . . . . . . Very High-18.3

How the Competition Rates

Competitors	Rating	Pg.
Chevrolet Silverado		108
Ford F-150	8	129
Ram 1500	5	221

Price Range

	Retail	Markup
Base Reg. Cab 2WD	$29,600	5%
SLE Dbl. Cab 2WD	$37,800	7%
SLT Dbl. Cab 4WD	$47,600	7%
Denali Crew Cab 4WD	$58,300	7%

Safety Checklist

Crash Test:
  Frontal . . . . —
  Side . . . . —
Airbags:
  Torso . . . . .Std. Front Pelvis/Torso from Seat
  Roll Sensing . . . . Yes
  Knee Bolster . . . . None
Crash Avoidance:
  Collision Avoidance . . . . Optional CIB
  Blind Spot Detection . . . . None
  Lane Keeping Assist . . . . Optional
  Pedestrian Crash Avoidance . . . . None
General:
  Auto. Crash Notif . . . Op. Assist. & Crash Info-Fee
  Day Running Lamps . . . . Standard
Safety Belt/Restraint:
  Dynamic Head Restraints . . . . None
  Adjustable Belt . . . . . Optional Front & Rear

^Warning feature does not meet government standards.

GMC Sierra

Specifications

Drive 4WD
Engine 5.3-liter V8
Transmission . . . . 8-sp. Automatic
Tow Rating (lbs.) . . . . Very High-9900
Head/Leg Room (in.) . . . . Very Roomy-43/44.5
Interior Space (cu. ft.) . . . . —
Cargo Space (cu. ft.) . . . . Very Roomy-71.7
Wheelbase/Length (in.) 147.4/231.8

Ratings—10 Best, 1 Worst

Combo Crash Tests	6
Safety Features	4
Rollover	4
Preventive Maintenance	1
Repair Costs	3
Warranty	5
Fuel Economy	7
Complaints	8
Insurance Costs	10
OVERALL RATING	**5**

GMC Terrain

GMC Terrain

Safety Checklist

Crash Test:
  Frontal . . . . Very Good
  Side . . . . Very Poor
Airbags:
  Torso . . . . .Std. Front Pelvis/Torso from Seat
  Roll Sensing . . . . Yes
  Knee Bolster .None
Crash Avoidance:
  Collision Avoidance . . . . .Optional CIB
  Blind Spot Detection . . . . Optional
  Lane Keeping Assist . . . . Optional
  Pedestrian Crash Avoidance . . . . .None
General:
  Auto. Crash Notif. . . Op. Assist. & Crash Info-Fee
  Day Running Lamps . . . . Standard
Safety Belt/Restraint:
  Dynamic Head Restraints . . . . .None
  Adjustable Belt . . . . .Std. Rear

^Warning feature does not meet government standards.

At-a-Glance

Status/Year Series Started Unchanged/2010
Twins . . . . Chevrolet Equinox
Body Styles . . . . SUV
Seating 5
Anti-Theft Device . Std. Pass. Immobil. & Active Alarm
Parking Index Rating . . . . Average
Where Made . . . . Ingersoll, Ontario
Fuel Factor
  MPG Rating (city/hwy) Good-26/30
  Driving Range (mi.) Average-412
  Fuel Type . . . . .Regular
  Annual Fuel Cost . . . . Low-$1329
  Gas Guzzler Tax . . . . .No
  Greenhouse Gas Emissions (tons/yr.) Low-5.2
  Barrels of Oil Used per year Average-11.8

GMC Terrain

Specifications

Drive . . . . FWD
Engine 1.5-liter I4
Transmission . . . . 6-sp. Automatic
Tow Rating (lbs.) . . . . Very Low-1500
Head/Leg Room (in.) Cramped-40/40.9
Interior Space (cu. ft.) Average-103.2
Cargo Space (cu. ft.) Roomy-29.6
Wheelbase/Length (in.) 107.3/182.3

How the Competition Rates

Competitors	Rating	Pg.
Ford Escape	5	126
Honda CR-V	10	145
Hyundai Tucson	8	156

Price Range

	Retail	Markup
SL FWD	$24,995	1%
SLE FWD	$27,820	5%
SLT AWD	$33,070	5%
Denali AWD	$39,270	5%

Ratings—10 Best, 1 Worst

Combo Crash Tests	—
Safety Features	6
Rollover	4
Preventive Maintenance	2
Repair Costs	5
Warranty	6
Fuel Economy	5
Complaints	1
Insurance Costs	6
OVERALL RATING	**5**

GMC Yukon

GMC Yukon

At-a-Glance

Status/Year Series Started. Unchanged/2015
Twins . . . . .Chevrolet Tahoe, GMC Yukon
Body Styles . . . . SUV
Seating 6/9
Anti-Theft Device . Std. Pass. Immobil. & Active Alarm
Parking Index Rating . . . . Very Hard
Where Made. Arlington, TX
Fuel Factor
  MPG Rating (city/hwy) . . . . .Very Poor-16/22
  Driving Range (mi.) . . . . Very Long-474
  Fuel Type. . . . . .Regular
  Annual Fuel Cost . . . . Very High-$2015
  Gas Guzzler Tax . . . . .No
  Greenhouse Gas Emissions (tons/yr.) High-8.2
  Barrels of Oil Used per year . . . . . . .Very High-18.3

How the Competition Rates

Competitors	Rating	Pg.
Buick Enclave	5	89
Infiniti QX80		162
Volvo XC90	8	256

Price Range

	Retail	Markup
SLE RWD	$49,500	6%
Standard Edition RWD	$54,700	6%
SLT AWD	$60,500	6%
Denali AWD	$66,600	7%

Safety Checklist

Crash Test:
  Frontal . . . . .Good
   Side. . . . . Very Good
Airbags:
  Torso . . . .Std. Front Pelvis/Torso from Seat
  Roll Sensing. . . . . .Yes
  Knee Bolster . . . . .None
Crash Avoidance:
  Collision Avoidance . . . . .Optional CIB
  Blind Spot Detection . . . . Optional
  Lane Keeping Assist . . . . Optional
  Pedestrian Crash Avoidance . . . . . . .None
General:
  Auto. Crash Notif.. . . Op. Assist. & Crash Info-Fee
  Day Running Lamps . . . . Standard
Safety Belt/Restraint:
  Dynamic Head Restraints . . . . .None
  Adjustable Belt. . . . . Optional Front & Rear

^Warning feature does not meet government standards.

GMC Yukon

Specifications

Drive. 4WD
Engine 5.3-liter V8
Transmission . . . . 6-sp. Automatic
Tow Rating (lbs.) . . . . Very High-8400
Head/Leg Room (in.) . . . . Very Roomy-42.8/45.3
Interior Space (cu. ft.). Roomy-120.8
Cargo Space (cu. ft.) Cramped-15.3
Wheelbase/Length (in.) 116/204

Ratings—10 Best, 1 Worst

Combo Crash Tests	—
Safety Features	9
Rollover	7
Preventive Maintenance	10
Repair Costs	6
Warranty	2
Fuel Economy	6
Complaints	4
Insurance Costs	8
OVERALL RATING	**—**

Honda Accord

At-a-Glance

Status/Year Series Started	Unchanged/2018
Twins	—
Body Styles	Sedan
Seating	5
Anti-Theft Device	Std. Pass. Immobil. & Alarm
Parking Index Rating	Hard
Where Made	Marysville, OH
Fuel Factor	
MPG Rating (city/hwy)	Average-23/34
Driving Range (mi.)	Short-398
Fuel Type	Regular
Annual Fuel Cost	Low-$1365
Gas Guzzler Tax	No
Greenhouse Gas Emissions (tons/yr.)	Low-5.5
Barrels of Oil Used per year	Average-12.2

How the Competition Rates

Competitors	Rating	Pg.
Ford Fusion	4	132
Hyundai Sonata	9	155
Toyota Camry	8	234

Price Range

	Retail	Markup
LX Sedan MT	$22,335	9%
EX Sedan AT	$26,530	9%
EX-L Coupe V6 AT	$31,175	9%
Touring Sedan V6 AT	$34,830	9%

Honda Accord

Safety Checklist

Crash Test:	
Frontal	—
Side	—
Airbags:	
Torso	Std. Front Pelvis/Torso from Seat
Roll Sensing	Yes
Knee Bolster	Standard Front
Crash Avoidance:	
Collision Avoidance	Optional CIB & DBS^
Blind Spot Detection	Optional
Lane Keeping Assist	Optional
Pedestrian Crash Avoidance	Standard
General:	
Auto. Crash Notification	Dial Assist.-Free
Day Running Lamps	Standard
Safety Belt/Restraint:	
Dynamic Head Restraints	None
Adjustable Belt	Standard Front

^Warning feature does not meet government standards.

Honda Accord

Specifications

Drive	FWD
Engine	2.0-liter I4
Transmission	CVT
Tow Rating (lbs.)	—
Head/Leg Room (in.)	Average-39.5/42.3
Interior Space (cu. ft.)	Roomy-105.6
Cargo Space (cu. ft.)	Cramped-16.7
Wheelbase/Length (in.)	111.4/192.2

143

Ratings—10 Best, 1 Worst

Combo Crash Tests	5
Safety Features	6
Rollover	9
Preventive Maintenance	10
Repair Costs	8
Warranty	2
Fuel Economy	9
Complaints	8
Insurance Costs	10
OVERALL RATING	**10**

Honda Civic

At-a-Glance

Status/Year Series Started. . Apperance Change/2016
Twins . . . . —
Body Styles . . . . .Coupe
Seating 5
Anti-Theft Device . . . . . . Std. Pass. Immobil. & Alarm
Parking Index Rating . . . . Easy
Where Made. . . . . . Greensburg, IN / Alliston, Ontario
Fuel Factor
  MPG Rating (city/hwy) . . . . Very Good-31/41
  Driving Range (mi.) Long-432
  Fuel Type . . . . .Regular
  Annual Fuel Cost . . . . Very Low-$1055
  Gas Guzzler Tax . . . . .No
  Greenhouse Gas Emissions (tons/yr.) . Very Low-4.2
  Barrels of Oil Used per year Low-9.4

How the Competition Rates

Competitors	Rating	Pg.
Nissan Sentra	5	205
Toyota Corolla	7	235
Volkswagen Golf	4	249

Price Range

Price Range	Retail	Markup
LX Coupe MT	$19,150	8%
EX Sedan AT	$21,140	8%
EX-L Sedan w/Sensing	$24,800	8%
Touring Sedan	$26,600	8%

Honda Civic

Safety Checklist

Crash Test:
  Frontal . . . . .Average
   Side. . . . . Poor
Airbags:
  Torso . . . . .Std. Front Pelvis/Torso from Seat
  Roll Sensing. . . . . .Yes
  Knee Bolster . . . . .None
Crash Avoidance:
  Collision Avoidance . . .Optional CIB & DBS
  Blind Spot Detection . . . . .None
  Lane Keeping Assist . . . . Optional
  Pedestrian Crash Avoidance . . . . . Optional
General:
  Auto. Crash Notification. . . Dial Assist.-Free
  Day Running Lamps . . . . Standard
Safety Belt/Restraint:
  Dynamic Head Restraints . . . . .None
  Adjustable Belt. . . . . Standard Front

^Warning feature does not meet government standards.

Honda Civic

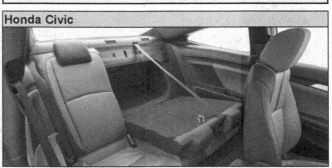

Specifications

Drive. . . . . .FWD
Engine 1.8-liter I4
Transmission . . . . CVT
Tow Rating (lbs.) . . . . —
Head/Leg Room (in.) Average-39.3/42.3
Interior Space (cu. ft.). Cramped-94.8
Cargo Space (cu. ft.) Cramped-15.1
Wheelbase/Length (in.) 106.3/179.4

Honda CR-V

Honda CR-V

Ratings—10 Best, 1 Worst

Combo Crash Tests	9
Safety Features	7
Rollover	4
Preventive Maintenance	10
Repair Costs	8
Warranty	2
Fuel Economy	7
Complaints	7
Insurance Costs	10
OVERALL RATING	**10**

Honda CR-V

At-a-Glance

Year Series Started	Unchanged/2017
Twins	—
Body Styles	SUV
Seating	5
Anti-Theft Device	Std. Pass. Immobil. & Alarm
Parking Index Rating	Easy
Where Made	East Liberty, OH
Fuel Factor	
MPG Rating (city/hwy)	Good-26/32
Driving Range (mi.)	Short-398
Fuel Type	Regular
Annual Fuel Cost	Low-$1294
Gas Guzzler Tax	No
Greenhouse Gas Emissions (tons/yr.)	Low-5.2
Barrels of Oil Used per year	Average-11.8

How the Competition Rates

Competitors	Rating	Pg.
Ford Escape	5	126
Jeep Cherokee	5	163
Kia Sportage	9	174

Price Range

	Retail	Markup
LX 2WD	$24,045	6%
EX 2WD	$26,695	7%
EX-L AWD	$30,495	7%
Touring AWD	$33,695	7%

Safety Checklist

Crash Test:
- Frontal . . . . Very Good
- Side . . . . Good

Airbags:
- Torso . . . . Std. Front Pelvis/Torso from Seat
- Roll Sensing . . . . Yes
- Knee Bolster . . . . None

Crash Avoidance:
- Collision Avoidance . . . Optional CIB & DBS
- Blind Spot Detection . . . . Optional
- Lane Keeping Assist . . . . Optional
- Pedestrian Crash Avoidance . . . . . Optional

General:
- Auto. Crash Notification . . . Dial Assist.-Free
- Day Running Lamps . . . . Standard

Safety Belt/Restraint:
- Dynamic Head Restraints . . . . None
- Adjustable Belt . . . . Standard Front

^Warning feature does not meet government standards.

Honda CR-V

Specifications

Drive	FWD
Engine	2.4-liter I4
Transmission	CVT
Tow Rating (lbs.)	Very Low-1500
Head/Leg Room (in.)	Very Cramped-38/41.3
Interior Space (cu. ft.)	Average-102.9
Cargo Space (cu. ft.)	Very Roomy-39.2
Wheelbase/Length (in.)	104.7/180.6

Ratings—10 Best, 1 Worst

Combo Crash Tests	9
Safety Features	4
Rollover	4
Preventive Maintenance	10
Repair Costs	9
Warranty	2
Fuel Economy	9
Complaints	8
Insurance Costs	5
OVERALL RATING	**9**

Honda Fit

Honda Fit

At-a-Glance

Status/Year Series Started. Unchanged/2015
Twins . . . . —
Body Styles . . . . Sedan, Hatchback
Seating. 5
Anti-Theft Device . . . . . . Std. Pass. Immobil. & Alarm
Parking Index Rating . . . . .Very Easy
Where Made. . . . . .Celaya, Mexico
Fuel Factor
  MPG Rating (city/hwy) . . . . Very Good-33/41
  Driving Range (mi.) Short-383
  Fuel Type . . . . .Regular
  Annual Fuel Cost . . . . Very Low-$1016
  Gas Guzzler Tax . . . . .No
  Greenhouse Gas Emissions (tons/yr.) Low-5.0
  Barrels of Oil Used per year Low-9.1

How the Competition Rates

Competitors	Rating	Pg.
Chevrolet Spark	5	110
Nissan Versa	1	207
Kia Sportage	9	174

Price Range

	Retail	Markup
LX MT	$16,190	3%
EX MT	$18,160	3%
EX AT	$18,960	3%
EX-L AT w/Nav	$21,520	3%

Safety Checklist

Crash Test:
  Frontal . . . . .Good
   Side. . . . . .Good
Airbags:
  Torso . . . . .Std. Front Pelvis/Torso from Seat
  Roll Sensing. . . . . .Yes
  Knee Bolster .None
Crash Avoidance:
  Collision Avoidance . . . . .Optional CIB
  Blind Spot Detection . . . . .None
  Lane Keeping Assist . . . . .Optional
  Pedestrian Crash Avoidance . . . . .None
General:
  Auto. Crash Notification . . .Dial Assist.-Free
  Day Running Lamps . . . . .None
Safety Belt/Restraint:
  Dynamic Head Restraints . . . . .None
  Adjustable Belt. . . . . Standard Front

^Warning feature does not meet government standards.

Honda Fit

Specifications

Drive. . . . . .FWD
Engine 1.5-liter I4
Transmission . . . . CVT
Tow Rating (lbs.) . . . . —
Head/Leg Room (in.) Cramped-39.5/41.4
Interior Space (cu. ft.). Cramped-95.7
Cargo Space (cu. ft.) Cramped-16.6
Wheelbase/Length (in.) 99.6/160

Ratings—10 Best, 1 Worst

Combo Crash Tests	3
Safety Features	2
Rollover	4
Preventive Maintenance	7
Repair Costs	8
Warranty	2
Fuel Economy	8
Complaints	6
Insurance Costs	10
OVERALL RATING	**5**

Honda HR-V

Honda HR-V

At-a-Glance

Status/Year Series Started	Unchanged/2016
Twins	—
Body Styles	SUV
Seating	5
Anti-Theft Device	Std. Pass. Immobil. & Alarm
Parking Index Rating	Easy
Where Made	Celaya, Mexico
Fuel Factor	
MPG Rating (city/hwy)	Good-28/34
Driving Range (mi.)	Average-401
Fuel Type	Regular
Annual Fuel Cost	Low-$1208
Gas Guzzler Tax	No
Greenhouse Gas Emissions (tons/yr.)	Low-4.7
Barrels of Oil Used per year	Average-10.6

How the Competition Rates

Competitors	Rating	Pg.
Chevrolet Trax	10	114
Jeep Renegade	1	166
Mazda CX-5	4	191

Price Range

	Retail	Markup
LX FWD MT	$19,570	3%
LX AWD AT	$21,670	3%
EX FWD AT	$22,420	3%
EX-L AWD w/Nav	$26,340	3%

Safety Checklist

Crash Test:
    Frontal . . . . Poor
    Side . . . . Average
Airbags:
    Torso . . . . Std. Front Pelvis/Torso from Seat
    Roll Sensing . . . . Yes
    Knee Bolster . . . . None
Crash Avoidance:
    Collision Avoidance . . . . None
    Blind Spot Detection . . . . None
    Lane Keeping Assist . . . . None
    Pedestrian Crash Avoidance . . . . None
General:
    Auto. Crash Notification . . . Dial Assist.-Free
    Day Running Lamps . . . . Standard
Safety Belt/Restraint:
    Dynamic Head Restraints . . . . None
    Adjustable Belt . . . . Standard Front

^Warning feature does not meet government standards.

Honda HR-V

Specifications

Drive	FWD
Engine	1.8-liter I4
Transmission	CVT
Tow Rating (lbs.)	—
Head/Leg Room (in.)	Cramped-39.5/41.2
Interior Space (cu. ft.)	Average-100.1
Cargo Space (cu. ft.)	Roomy-24.3
Wheelbase/Length (in.)	102.8/169.1

Ratings—10 Best, 1 Worst

Combo Crash Tests	7
Safety Features	10
Rollover	5
Preventive Maintenance	9
Repair Costs	8
Warranty	2
Fuel Economy	3
Complaints	3
Insurance Costs	10
OVERALL RATING	**9**

Honda Odyssey

Honda Odyssey

At-a-Glance

Status/Year Series Started	Unchanged/2018
Twins	—
Body Styles	Minivan
Seating	7
Anti-Theft Device	Std. Pass. Immobil. & Alarm
Parking Index Rating	Very Hard
Where Made	"Lincoln, Alabama"
Fuel Factor	
MPG Rating (city/hwy)	Poor-19/28
Driving Range (mi.)	Long-433
Fuel Type	Regular
Annual Fuel Cost	Average-$1654
Gas Guzzler Tax	No
Greenhouse Gas Emissions (tons/yr.)	Average-6.7
Barrels of Oil Used per year	High-15.0

How the Competition Rates

Competitors	Rating	Pg.
Chrysler Pacifica	8	117
Kia Sedona		171
Toyota Sienna	2	243

Price Range

	Retail	Markup
LX	$29,990	9%
EX	$33,860	9%
EX-L w/Nav	$39,360	9%
Touring	$44,510	9%

Safety Checklist

Crash Test:
  Frontal . . . . Good
  Side . . . . Good
Airbags:
  Torso . . . . .Std. Front Pelvis/Torso from Seat
  Roll Sensing . . . . Yes
  Knee Bolster . . . . Standard Front
Crash Avoidance:
  Collision Avoidance . . Standard CIB & DBS
  Blind Spot Detection . . . . Optional
  Lane Keeping Assist . . . . Optional
  Pedestrian Crash Avoidance . . . . . Optional
General:
  Auto. Crash Notification . . .Dial Assist.-Free
  Day Running Lamps . . . . Standard
Safety Belt/Restraint:
  Dynamic Head Restraints . . . . . . Std. Front
  Adjustable Belt . . . . Standard Front

^Warning feature does not meet government standards.

Honda Odyssey

Specifications

Drive	FWD
Engine	3.5-liter V6
Transmission	9-sp. Automatic
Tow Rating (lbs.)	—
Head/Leg Room (in.)	Average-40.7/40.9
Interior Space (cu. ft.)	Very Roomy-163.6
Cargo Space (cu. ft.)	Very Roomy-32.8
Wheelbase/Length (in.)	118.1/203.2

Honda Pilot Medium SUV

Ratings—10 Best, 1 Worst

Combo Crash Tests	8
Safety Features	6
Rollover	4
Preventive Maintenance	10
Repair Costs	7
Warranty	2
Fuel Economy	3
Complaints	4
Insurance Costs	10
OVERALL RATING	**8**

Honda Pilot

At-a-Glance

Status/Year Series Started   Apperance Change/2016
Twins . . . . .Acura MDX
Body Styles . . . . SUV
Seating 8
Anti-Theft Device . . . . . . Std. Pass. Immobil. & Alarm
Parking Index Rating . . . . Hard
Where Made. . . . . Lincoln, AL
Fuel Factor
  MPG Rating (city/hwy) Poor-19/27
  Driving Range (mi.) Long-428
  Fuel Type. . . . . .Regular
  Annual Fuel Cost . . . . .High-$1676
  Gas Guzzler Tax . . . . .No
  Greenhouse Gas Emissions (tons/yr.). . Average-6.4
  Barrels of Oil Used per year High-14.3

How the Competition Rates

Competitors	Rating	Pg.
Ford Edge	9	125
Mitsubishi Outlander	4	207
Subaru Outback	8	227

Price Range

	Retail	Markup
LX 2WD	$30,595	9%
EX AWD	$34,830	9%
EX-L AWD	$38,255	9%
Touring AWD	$43,470	9%

Honda Pilot

Safety Checklist

Crash Test:
  Frontal . . . . .Good
  Side. Very Good
Airbags:
  Torso . . . .Std. Front Pelvis/Torso from Seat
  Roll Sensing. . . . . .Yes
  Knee Bolster . . . . .None
Crash Avoidance:
  Collision Avoidance . . .Optional CIB & DBS
  Blind Spot Detection . . . . Optional
  Lane Keeping Assist . . . . Optional
  Pedestrian Crash Avoidance . . . . . Optional
General:
  Auto. Crash Notification . . .Dial Assist.-Free
  Day Running Lamps . . . . Standard
Safety Belt/Restraint:
  Dynamic Head Restraints . . . . .None
  Adjustable Belt. . . . . Standard Front

^Warning feature does not meet government standards.

Honda Pilot

Specifications

Drive. . . . . .AWD
Engine 3.5-liter V6
Transmission . . . . 6-sp. Automatic
Tow Rating (lbs.) Low-3500
Head/Leg Room (in.) Average-40.1/40.9
Interior Space (cu. ft.). . . . . Very Roomy-152.9
Cargo Space (cu. ft.) Cramped-16.5
Wheelbase/Length (in.) 111/194.5

149

Hyundai Accent | Subcompact

Hyundai Accent

Ratings—10 Best, 1 Worst

Combo Crash Tests	—
Safety Features	2
Rollover	—
Preventive Maintenance	6
Repair Costs	10
Warranty	10
Fuel Economy	8
Complaints	8
Insurance Costs	1
OVERALL RATING	**—**

Hyundai Accent

At-a-Glance

Status/Year Series Started	Unchanged/2018
Twins	Kia Rio
Body Styles	Sedan, Hatchback
Seating	5
Anti-Theft Device	Std. Pass. Immobil. & Active Alarm
Parking Index Rating	Very Easy
Where Made	Ulsan, South Korea
Fuel Factor	
MPG Rating (city/hwy)	Good-28/38
Driving Range (mi.)	Very Short-362
Fuel Type	Regular
Annual Fuel Cost	Very Low-$1157
Gas Guzzler Tax	No
Greenhouse Gas Emissions (tons/yr.)	Very Low-4.6
Barrels of Oil Used per year	Low-10.3

How the Competition Rates

Competitors	Rating	Pg.
Ford Fiesta	2	130
Nissan Versa	1	207
Toyota Yaris Liftback	5	247

Price Range

	Retail	Markup
SE Sedan MT	$14,745	3%
SE Hatchback AT	$16,195	3%
Value Edition AT	$16,450	3%
Sport Hatchback AT	$17,495	3%

Safety Checklist

Crash Test:
  Frontal . . . . —
  Side . . . . —
Airbags:
  Torso . . . . Std. Front Pelvis/Torso from Seat
  Roll Sensing . . . . Yes
  Knee Bolster . . . . None
Crash Avoidance:
  Collision Avoidance . . . Optional CIB & DBS
  Blind Spot Detection . . . . None
  Lane Keeping Assist . . . . None
  Pedestrian Crash Avoidance . . . . None
General:
  Auto. Crash Notification Operat. Assist.-Fee
  Day Running Lamps . . . . Optional
Safety Belt/Restraint:
  Dynamic Head Restraints . . . . None
  Adjustable Belt . . . . Standard Front

^Warning feature does not meet government standards.

Hyundai Accent

Specifications

Drive	FWD
Engine	1.6-liter I4
Transmission	6-sp. Automatic
Tow Rating (lbs.)	—
Head/Leg Room (in.)	Average-39.2/41.8
Interior Space (cu. ft.)	Very Cramped-89.7
Cargo Space (cu. ft.)	Cramped-13.7
Wheelbase/Length (in.)	101.6/172

Hyundai Elantra — Compact

Ratings—10 Best, 1 Worst

Combo Crash Tests	—
Safety Features	7
Rollover	3.5
Preventive Maintenance	4
Repair Costs	10
Warranty	10
Fuel Economy	8
Complaints	6
Insurance Costs	1

OVERALL RATING — —

Hyundai Elantra

At-a-Glance

Status/Year Series Started Unchanged/2017
Twins . . . . Kia Forte
Body Styles . . . . Sedan, Coupe, Hatchback
Seating 5
Anti-Theft Device . Std. Pass. Immobil. & Active Alarm
Parking Index Rating . . . . Easy
Where Made. . . . . Montgomery, AL
Fuel Factor
  MPG Rating (city/hwy) Good-28/37
  Driving Range (mi.) Long-440
  Fuel Type . . . . Regular
  Annual Fuel Cost . . . . Very Low-$1169
  Gas Guzzler Tax . . . . No
  Greenhouse Gas Emissions (tons/yr.) Low-4.7
  Barrels of Oil Used per year Low-10.3

How the Competition Rates

Competitors	Rating	Pg.
Honda Civic	10	144
Nissan Sentra	5	205
Toyota Corolla	7	235

Price Range

	Retail	Markup
SE MT	$16,950	3%
SEL AT	$18,850	3%
Eco AT	$20,550	4%
Limited AT	$22,100	5%

Hyundai Elantra

Safety Checklist

Crash Test:
  Frontal. . . . . —
  Side. . . . . —
Airbags:
  Torso . . . .Std. Front Pelvis/Torso from Seat
  Roll Sensing. . . . . .Yes
  Knee Bolster . . . . .Standard Driver
Crash Avoidance:
  Collision Avoidance . . .Optional CIB & DBS
  Blind Spot Detection . . . . Optional
  Lane Keeping Assist . . . . Optional
  Pedestrian Crash Avoidance . . . . . Optional
General:
  Auto. Crash Notification Operat. Assist.-Fee
  Day Running Lamps . . . . Standard
Safety Belt/Restraint:
  Dynamic Head Restraints . . . . .None
  Adjustable Belt. . . . . Standard Front

^Warning feature does not meet government standards.

Hyundai Elantra

Specifications

Drive. . . . . .FWD
Engine 2.0-liter I4
Transmission . . . . 6-sp. Automatic
Tow Rating (lbs.) . . . . —
Head/Leg Room (in.) Average-30.0/42.2
Interior Space (cu. ft.). Cramped-95.8
Cargo Space (cu. ft.) Cramped-14.4
Wheelbase/Length (in.) 106.3/179.9

Ratings—10 Best, 1 Worst

Combo Crash Tests	—
Safety Features	7
Rollover	—
Preventive Maintenance	6
Repair Costs	9
Warranty	10
Fuel Economy	—
Complaints	9
Insurance Costs	8
OVERALL RATING	**—**

Hyundai Kona

Hyundai Kona

At-a-Glance

Status/Year Series Started	Unchanged/2018
Twins	—
Body Styles	SUV
Seating	5
Anti-Theft Device	Std. Pass. Immobil. & Active Alarm
Parking Index Rating	Very Easy
Where Made	Ulsan, South Korea
Fuel Factor	
MPG Rating (city/hwy)	Good-28/32
Driving Range (mi.)	Short-396
Fuel Type	Regular
Annual Fuel Cost	Low-$1224
Gas Guzzler Tax	No
Greenhouse Gas Emissions (tons/yr.)	Low-5.0
Barrels of Oil Used per year	Low-11.0

How the Competition Rates

Competitors	Rating	Pg.
Buick Encore	10	90
Chevrolet Trax	10	114
Honda HR-V	5	147

Price Range

	Retail	Markup
SE 2.0L FWD	$19,990	3%
SEL 2.0L FWD	$21,800	4%
Limited 2.6L AWD	$26,950	4%
Ultimate 2.6L AWD	$28,900	5%

Safety Checklist

Crash Test:
Frontal	—
Side	—

Airbags:
Torso	Std. Front Pelvis/Torso from Seat
Roll Sensing	Yes
Knee Bolster	None

Crash Avoidance:
Collision Avoidance	Optional CIB & DBS^
Blind Spot Detection	Optional
Lane Keeping Assist	Optional^
Pedestrian Crash Avoidance	Optional

General:
Auto. Crash Notification	Operat. Assist.-Fee
Day Running Lamps	Standard

Safety Belt/Restraint:
Dynamic Head Restraints	None
Adjustable Belt	Standard Front

^Warning feature does not meet government standards.

Hyundai Kona

Specifications

Drive	FWD
Engine	1.6-liter I4
Transmission	7-sp. Automatic
Tow Rating (lbs.)	Very Low-2755
Head/Leg Room (in.)	Average-39.6/41.5
Interior Space (cu. ft.)	Cramped-94
Cargo Space (cu. ft.)	Cramped-14.2
Wheelbase/Length (in.)	102.4/164

Hyundai Santa Fe | Medium SUV

Ratings—10 Best, 1 Worst

Combo Crash Tests	—
Safety Features	9
Rollover	4
Preventive Maintenance	4
Repair Costs	7
Warranty	10
Fuel Economy	4
Complaints	—
Insurance Costs	5
OVERALL RATING	—

Hyundai Santa Fe

Hyundai Santa Fe

At-a-Glance

Status/Year Series Started . . . . All New/2019
Twins . . . . —
Body Styles . . . . SUV
Seating 5
Anti-Theft Device . Std. Pass. Immobil. & Active Alarm
Parking Index Rating . . . . Average
Where Made. . . . . West Point, GA
Fuel Factor
  MPG Rating (city/hwy) Average-22/29
  Driving Range (mi.) . . . . Very Long-470
  Fuel Type . . . . Regular
  Annual Fuel Cost . . . . Average-$1458
  Gas Guzzler Tax . . . . No
  Greenhouse Gas Emissions (tons/yr.) . . Average-6.0
  Barrels of Oil Used per year High-13.2

How the Competition Rates

Competitors	Rating	Pg.
Kia Sorento	6	172
Mazda CX-5	4	191
Mitsubishi Outlander Sport	3	208

Price Range

	Retail	Markup
SE FWD	$25,500	5%
SEL Plus FWD	$39,800	5%
Limited 2.0T AWD	$35,900	5%
Ultimate 2.0T Turbo AWD	$38,800	5%

Safety Checklist

Crash Test:
  Frontal. . . . . —
  Side. . . . . —
Airbags:
  Torso . . . . .Std. Front Pelvis/Torso from Seat
  Roll Sensing. . . . . Yes
  Knee Bolster . . . . .Standard Driver
Crash Avoidance:
  Collision Avoidance . . Standard CIB & DBS
  Blind Spot Detection . . . . Optional
  Lane Keeping Assist . . . . Standard
  Pedestrian Crash Avoidance . . . . . Standard
General:
  Auto. Crash Notif.. . . . Operator Assist.-Fee
  Day Running Lamps . . . . Standard
Safety Belt/Restraint:
  Dynamic Head Restraints . . . . None
  Adjustable Belt. . . . . Standard Front

^Warning feature does not meet government standards.

Hyundai Santa Fe

Specifications

Drive. . . . . FWD
Engine 2.4-liter I4
Transmission . . . . 8-sp. Automatic
Tow Rating (lbs.) . . . . Very Low-2000
Head/Leg Room (in.) . . . . Very Roomy-41.2/44.1
Interior Space (cu. ft.). Roomy-110.7
Cargo Space (cu. ft.) . . . . Very Roomy-35.9
Wheelbase/Length (in.) 108.9/187.8

Ratings—10 Best, 1 Worst

Combo Crash Tests	—
Safety Features	7
Rollover	4
Preventive Maintenance	4
Repair Costs	5
Warranty	10
Fuel Economy	3
Complaints	2
Insurance Costs	8
OVERALL RATING	**—**

Hyundai Santa Fe XL

At-a-Glance

Status/Year Series Started	Unchanged/2013
Twins	—
Body Styles	SUV
Seating	6/7
Anti-Theft Device	Std. Pass. Immobil. & Active Alarm
Parking Index Rating	Average
Where Made	West Point, GA

Fuel Factor

MPG Rating (city/hwy)	Poor-18/25
Driving Range (mi.)	Short-387
Fuel Type	Regular
Annual Fuel Cost	High-$1784
Gas Guzzler Tax	No
Greenhouse Gas Emissions (tons/yr.)	High-8.5
Barrels of Oil Used per year	High-15.7

How the Competition Rates

Competitors	Rating	Pg.
Acura MDX	7	67
Kia Sorento	6	173
Mitsubishi Outlander	4	207

Price Range

	Retail	Markup
SE FWD	$30,850	5%
SE AWD	$32,600	6%
Limited Ultimate FWD	$39,550	5%
Limited Ultimate AWD	$41,300	6%

Hyundai Santa Fe XL

Safety Checklist

Crash Test:
  Frontal......................... —
  Side........................... —
Airbags:
  Torso ....Std. Front Pelvis/Torso from Seat
  Roll Sensing......................Yes
  Knee Bolster ....Standard Driver
Crash Avoidance:
  Collision Avoidance . . .Optional CIB & DBS
  Blind Spot Detection .... Optional
  Lane Keeping Assist ..Warn. Only Optional
  Pedestrian Crash Avoidance..... Optional
General:
  Auto. Crash Notification Operat. Assist.-Fee
  Day Running Lamps .... Standard
Safety Belt/Restraint:
  Dynamic Head Restraints ....None
  Adjustable Belt........... Standard Front

^Warning feature does not meet government standards.

Hyundai Santa Fe XL

Specifications

Drive	FWD
Engine	3.3-liter V6
Transmission	6-sp. Automatic
Tow Rating (lbs.)	Low-5000
Head/Leg Room (in.)	Cramped-39.6/41.3
Interior Space (cu. ft.)	Very Roomy-146.6
Cargo Space (cu. ft.)	Very Cramped-13.5
Wheelbase/Length (in.)	110.2/193.1

Ratings—10 Best, 1 Worst

Combo Crash Tests	9
Safety Features	6
Rollover	7
Preventive Maintenance	5
Repair Costs	8
Warranty	10
Fuel Economy	7
Complaints	5
Insurance Costs	5
OVERALL RATING	**9**

Hyundai Sonata

Hyundai Sonata

At-a-Glance

Status/Year Series Started	Unchanged/2015
Twins	—
Body Styles	Sedan
Seating	5
Anti-Theft Device	Std. Pass. Immobil. & Active Alarm
Parking Index Rating	Easy
Where Made	Montgomery, AL
Fuel Factor	
MPG Rating (city/hwy)	Good-25/35
Driving Range (mi.)	Very Long-531
Fuel Type	Regular
Annual Fuel Cost	Low-$1281
Gas Guzzler Tax	No
Greenhouse Gas Emissions (tons/yr.)	Low-5.2
Barrels of Oil Used per year	Average-11.8

How the Competition Rates

Competitors	Rating	Pg.
Mazda 6	5	194
Toyota Camry	8	234
Volkswagen Passat	4	251

Price Range	Retail	Markup
SE 2.4L	$22,050	4%
SEL 2.4L	$23,700	6%
Sport 2.0L Turbo	$26,600	2%
Limited 2.0L Turbo	$32,450	6%

Safety Checklist

Crash Test:
- Frontal . . . . Very Good
- Side. . . . . Average

Airbags:
- Torso . . . . Std. Front Pelvis/Torso from Seat
- Roll Sensing. . . . . Yes
- Knee Bolster . . . . Standard Driver

Crash Avoidance:
- Collision Avoidance . . . Optional CIB & DBS
- Blind Spot Detection . . . . Optional
- Lane Keeping Assist . . Warn. Only Optional
- Pedestrian Crash Avoidance . . . . . Optional

General:
- Auto. Crash Notification Operat. Assist.-Fee
- Day Running Lamps . . . . Standard

Safety Belt/Restraint:
- Dynamic Head Restraints . . . . None
- Adjustable Belt. . . . . Standard Front

^Warning feature does not meet government standards.

Hyundai Sonata

Specifications

Drive	FWD
Engine	2.4-liter I4
Transmission	6-sp. Automatic
Tow Rating (lbs.)	Very Low-0
Head/Leg Room (in.)	Very Roomy-40.4/45.5
Interior Space (cu. ft.)	Roomy-106.1
Cargo Space (cu. ft.)	Cramped-16.3
Wheelbase/Length (in.)	110.4/191.1

Hyundai Tucson

Ratings—10 Best, 1 Worst

Combo Crash Tests	4
Safety Features	8
Rollover	4
Preventive Maintenance	4
Repair Costs	10
Warranty	10
Fuel Economy	6
Complaints	1
Insurance Costs	10
OVERALL RATING	**8**

Hyundai Tucson

At-a-Glance

Status/Year Series Started	Unchanged/2016
Twins	—
Body Styles	SUV
Seating	5
Anti-Theft Device	Std. Pass. Immobil. & Active Alarm
Parking Index Rating	Very Easy
Where Made	Ulsan, South Korea

Fuel Factor
MPG Rating (city/hwy)	Average-24/28
Driving Range (mi.)	Average-421
Fuel Type	Regular
Annual Fuel Cost	Low-$1433
Gas Guzzler Tax	No
Greenhouse Gas Emissions (tons/yr.)	Low-5.8
Barrels of Oil Used per year	Average-12.7

How the Competition Rates

Competitors	Rating	Pg.
Ford Escape	5	126
Honda HR-V	5	147
Kia Sportage	9	174

Price Range

	Retail	Markup
SE FWD	$22,700	4%
Eco AWD	$25,550	5%
Sport AWD	$27,300	5%
Limited AWD	$31,175	5%

Safety Checklist

Crash Test:
Frontal	Poor
Side	Average

Airbags:
Torso	Std. Front Pelvis/Torso from Seat
Roll Sensing	Yes
Knee Bolster	None

Crash Avoidance:
Collision Avoidance	Optional CIB & DBS
Blind Spot Detection	Optional
Lane Keeping Assist	Warn. Only Optional
Pedestrian Crash Avoidance	Optional

General:
Auto. Crash Notification	Operat. Assist.-Fee
Day Running Lamps	Optional

Safety Belt/Restraint:
Dynamic Head Restraints	Std. Front
Adjustable Belt	Standard Front

^Warning feature does not meet government standards.

Hyundai Tucson

Specifications

Drive	FWD
Engine	2.0-liter I4
Transmission	6-sp. Automatic
Tow Rating (lbs.)	—
Head/Leg Room (in.)	Average-39.6/41.5
Interior Space (cu. ft.)	Average-102.2
Cargo Space (cu. ft.)	Very Roomy-31
Wheelbase/Length (in.)	105.1/176.2

Hyundai Veloster

Ratings—10 Best, 1 Worst

Combo Crash Tests	—
Safety Features	3
Rollover	7
Preventive Maintenance	5
Repair Costs	9
Warranty	10
Fuel Economy	8
Complaints	—
Insurance Costs	3
OVERALL RATING	**6**

Hyundai Veloster

At-a-Glance

Status/Year Series Started	All New/2019
Twins	—
Body Styles	Coupe
Seating	5
Anti-Theft Device	Std. Pass. Immobil. & Active Alarm
Parking Index Rating	Very Easy
Where Made	Ulsan, South Korea
Fuel Factor	
MPG Rating (city/hwy)	Good-27/34
Driving Range (mi.)	Short-396
Fuel Type	Regular
Annual Fuel Cost	Low-$1242
Gas Guzzler Tax	No
Greenhouse Gas Emissions (tons/yr.)	Low-4.9
Barrels of Oil Used per year	Average-11.0

How the Competition Rates

Competitors	Rating	Pg.
Chevrolet Sonic	8	109
Mini Hardtop	6	205
Toyota Yaris Liftback	5	247

Price Range

	Retail	Markup
Base MT	$18,500	4%
Premium AT	$22,750	4%
Turbo AT	$25,400	5%
Turbo Ultimate AT	$28,150	5%

Hyundai Veloster

Safety Checklist

Crash Test:
- Frontal . . . . —
- Side . . . . —

Airbags:
- Torso . . . . Std. Front Pelvis/Torso from Seat
- Roll Sensing . . . . Yes
- Knee Bolster . . . . None

Crash Avoidance:
- Collision Avoidance . . Standard CIB & DBS
- Blind Spot Detection . . . . Optional
- Lane Keeping Assist . . . . Standard
- Pedestrian Crash Avoidance . . . . None

General:
- Auto. Crash Notification Operat. Assist.-Fee
- Day Running Lamps . . . . Standard

Safety Belt/Restraint:
- Dynamic Head Restraints . . . . . . Std. Front
- Adjustable Belt . . . . Standard Front

^Warning feature does not meet government standards.

Hyundai Veloster

Specifications

Drive	FWD
Engine	2.0 liter I4
Transmission	6-sp. Automatic
Tow Rating (lbs.)	—
Head/Leg Room (in.)	Cramped-38.1/42.6
Interior Space (cu. ft.)	Very Cramped-89.9
Cargo Space (cu. ft.)	Average-19.9
Wheelbase/Length (in.)	104.3/166.9

Ratings—10 Best, 1 Worst

Combo Crash Tests	4
Safety Features	5
Rollover	8
Preventive Maintenance	5
Repair Costs	3
Warranty	9
Fuel Economy	4
Complaints	8
Insurance Costs	1
OVERALL RATING	**3**

Infiniti Q50

Infiniti Q50

At-a-Glance

Status/Year Series Started	Unchanged/2014
Twins	—
Body Styles	Sedan
Seating	5
Anti-Theft Device	Std. Pass. Immobil. & Alarm
Parking Index Rating	Average
Where Made	Tochigi, Japan
Fuel Factor	
MPG Rating (city/hwy)	Poor-20/29
Driving Range (mi.)	Very Long-465
Fuel Type	Premium
Annual Fuel Cost	High-$1916
Gas Guzzler Tax	No
Greenhouse Gas Emissions (tons/yr.)	High-7.8
Barrels of Oil Used per year	High-14.3

How the Competition Rates

Competitors	Rating	Pg.
Audi A3	5	71
Lexus IS	8	181
Lincoln MKZ	4	187

Price Range	Retail	Markup
Base RWD 2.0T	$34,200	8%
Luxe RWD 3.0T	$38,950	8%
Sport AWD 3.0T	$42,650	8%
Hybrid Luxe AWD	$52,600	8%

Safety Checklist

Crash Test:
  Frontal . . . . Very Poor
   Side . . . . Very Good
Airbags:
  Torso Std. Fr. & Opt. Rr. Pelvis/Torso from Seat
  Roll Sensing . . . . Yes
  Knee Bolster . . . . None
Crash Avoidance:
  Collision Avoidance . . . Optional CIB & DBS
  Blind Spot Detection . . . . Optional
  Lane Keeping Assist . . Warn. Only Optional
  Pedestrian Crash Avoidance . . . . None
General:
  Auto. Crash Notification Operat. Assist.-Fee
  Day Running Lamps . . . . Standard
Safety Belt/Restraint:
  Dynamic Head Restraints . . . . None
  Adjustable Belt . . . . Standard Front

^Warning feature does not meet government standards.

Infiniti Q50

Specifications

Drive	RWD
Engine	3.0-liter V6
Transmission	7-sp. Automatic
Tow Rating (lbs.)	—
Head/Leg Room (in.)	Very Roomy-39.5/44.5
Interior Space (cu. ft.)	Average-100
Cargo Space (cu. ft.)	Very Cramped-13.5
Wheelbase/Length (in.)	112.2/189.6

Ratings—10 Best, 1 Worst

Combo Crash Tests	—
Safety Features	7
Rollover	6
Preventive Maintenance	7
Repair Costs	2
Warranty	9
Fuel Economy	6
Complaints	2
Insurance Costs	5
OVERALL RATING	**—**

Infiniti QX30

Infiniti QX30

At-a-Glance

Status/Year Series Started	Unchanged/2017
Twins	—
Body Styles	SUV
Seating	5
Anti-Theft Device	Standard Pass. Immobil.
Parking Index Rating	Easy
Where Made	"Sunderland, England"

Fuel Factor
MPG Rating (city/hwy)	Average-24/33
Driving Range (mi.)	Very Short-361
Fuel Type	Premium
Annual Fuel Cost	Average-$1628
Gas Guzzler Tax	No
Greenhouse Gas Emissions (tons/yr.)	Low-5.4
Barrels of Oil Used per year	Average-12.2

How the Competition Rates

Competitors	Rating	Pg.
Acura RDX	9	68
Buick Encore	10	90
Lexus NX	5	182

Price Range

	Retail	Markup
Base FWD	$29,950	7%
Luxury FWD	$32,600	8%
Premium AWD	$37,700	8%
Sport FWD	$38,500	8%

Safety Checklist

Crash Test:
Frontal	—
Side	—

Airbags:
Torso	Std. Front Pelvis/Torso from Seat
Roll Sensing	Yes
Knee Bolster	Standard Front

Crash Avoidance:
Collision Avoidance	Optional CIB & DBS
Blind Spot Detection	Optional
Lane Keeping Assist	Warn. Only Optional
Pedestrian Crash Avoidance	None

General:
Auto. Crash Notification	Operat. Assist.-Fee
Day Running Lamps	Standard

Safety Belt/Restraint:
Dynamic Head Restraints	None
Adjustable Belt	Standard Front

^Warning feature does not meet government standards.

Infiniti QX30

Specifications

Drive	FWD
Engine	2.0-liter I4
Transmission	7-sp. Automatic
Tow Rating (lbs.)	—
Head/Leg Room (in.)	Cramped-38.4/41.3
Interior Space (cu. ft.)	Very Cramped-88.8
Cargo Space (cu. ft.)	Average-19.2
Wheelbase/Length (in.)	106.3/174.2

Infiniti QX50

Ratings—10 Best, 1 Worst

Combo Crash Tests	—
Safety Features	3
Rollover	4
Preventive Maintenance	9
Repair Costs	2
Warranty	9
Fuel Economy	2
Complaints	—
Insurance Costs	10
OVERALL RATING	—

Infiniti QX50

At-a-Glance

Status/Year Series Started	All New/2019
Twins	—
Body Styles	SUV
Seating	5
Anti-Theft Device	Std. Pass. Immobil. & Alarm
Parking Index Rating	Average
Where Made	Tochigi, Japan
Fuel Factor	
MPG Rating (city/hwy)	Average-24/31
Driving Range (mi.)	Long-432
Fuel Type	Premium
Annual Fuel Cost	Average-$1689
Gas Guzzler Tax	No
Greenhouse Gas Emissions (tons/yr.)	Average-6.2
Barrels of Oil Used per year	Average-12.2

How the Competition Rates

Competitors	Rating	Pg.
Buick Encore	10	90
Mazda CX-5	4	191
Subaru Crosstrek	5	223

Price Range

	Retail	Markup
Pure FWD	$36,550	8%
Luxe FWD	$39,400	8%
Luxe AWD	$41,200	8%
Essential AWD	$45,150	8%

Safety Checklist

Crash Test:
- Frontal . . . . —
- Side . . . . —

Airbags:
- Torso . . . . Std. Front Pelvis/Torso from Seat
- Roll Sensing . . . . Yes
- Knee Bolster . . . . None

Crash Avoidance:
- Collision Avoidance . . Standard CIB & DBS
- Blind Spot Detection . . . . Optional
- Lane Keeping Assist . . . . Optional
- Pedestrian Crash Avoidance . . . . None

General:
- Auto. Crash Notification Operat. Assist.-Fee
- Day Running Lamps . . . . Standard

Safety Belt/Restraint:
- Dynamic Head Restraints . . . . . . Std. Front
- Adjustable Belt . . . . Standard Front

^Warning feature does not meet government standards.

Infiniti QX50

Specifications

Drive	FWD
Engine	2.0-liter I4
Transmission	8-sp. Automatic
Tow Rating (lbs.)	—
Head/Leg Room (in.)	Cramped-41.0/39.6
Interior Space (cu. ft.)	—
Cargo Space (cu. ft.)	Roomy-31.4
Wheelbase/Length (in.)	110.2/184.7

Ratings—10 Best, 1 Worst

Combo Crash Tests	6
Safety Features	5
Rollover	3
Preventive Maintenance	3
Repair Costs	3
Warranty	9
Fuel Economy	3
Complaints	5
Insurance Costs	8
OVERALL RATING	**5**

Infiniti QX60

Infiniti QX60

At-a-Glance

Status/Year Series Started	Unchanged/2013
Twins	Nissan Pathfinder
Body Styles	SUV
Seating	7
Anti-Theft Device	Std. Pass. Immobil. & Alarm
Parking Index Rating	Hard
Where Made	Smyrna, TN
Fuel Factor	
MPG Rating (city/hwy)	Poor-19/26
Driving Range (mi.)	Average-422
Fuel Type	Premium
Annual Fuel Cost	Very High-$2061
Gas Guzzler Tax	No
Greenhouse Gas Emissions (tons/yr.)	High-8.2
Barrels of Oil Used per year	High-15.0

How the Competition Rates

Competitors	Rating	Pg.
Acura MDX	7	67
Audi Q7	3	78
Volkswagen Atlas	6	248

Price Range

	Retail	Markup
RWD	$43,100	8%
AWD	$44,900	8%

Safety Checklist

Crash Test:
- Frontal .... Average
- Side .... Average

Airbags:
- Torso .... Std. Front Pelvis/Torso from Seat
- Roll Sensing .... Yes
- Knee Bolster .... None

Crash Avoidance:
- Collision Avoidance . . . Optional CIB & DBS
- Blind Spot Detection .... Optional
- Lane Keeping Assist . . Warn. Only Optional
- Pedestrian Crash Avoidance ..... Optional

General:
- Auto. Crash Notification Operat. Assist.-Fee
- Day Running Lamps .... Standard

Safety Belt/Restraint:
- Dynamic Head Restraints .... None
- Adjustable Belt . . . Standard Front and Rear

^Warning feature does not meet government standards.

Infiniti QX60

Specifications

Drive	AWD
Engine	3.5-liter V6
Transmission	7-sp. Automatic
Tow Rating (lbs.)	Low-5000
Head/Leg Room (in.)	Roomy-40.7/42.3
Interior Space (cu. ft.)	Very Roomy-149.8
Cargo Space (cu. ft.)	Cramped-15.8
Wheelbase/Length (in.)	114.2/196.4

Ratings—10 Best, 1 Worst

Combo Crash Tests	—
Safety Features	7
Rollover	2
Preventive Maintenance	3
Repair Costs	4
Warranty	9
Fuel Economy	1
Complaints	7
Insurance Costs	5
OVERALL RATING	**—**

Infiniti QX80

Infiniti QX80

At-a-Glance

Status/Year Series Started. Unchanged/2011
Twins . . . . —
Body Styles . . . . SUV
Seating 7/8
Anti-Theft Device . . . . . . Std. Pass. Immobil. & Alarm
Parking Index Rating . . . . Very Hard
Where Made. . . . . Kyushu, Japan
Fuel Factor
  MPG Rating (city/hwy) . . . . .Very Poor-14/20
  Driving Range (mi.) Average-421
  Fuel Type. . . . . .Premium
  Annual Fuel Cost . . . . Very High-$2753
  Gas Guzzler Tax . . . . .No
  Greenhouse Gas Emissions (tons/yr.)Very High-11.2
  Barrels of Oil Used per year . . . . . . .Very High-20.6

How the Competition Rates

Competitors	Rating	Pg.
Buick Enclave	4	89
Chevrolet Tahoe	4	112
Volvo XC90	8	256

Price Range

	Retail	Markup
Base RWD	$63,850	8%
Base AWD	$66,950	8%
Signature AWD	$70,435	8%
Limited AWD	$89,450	8%

Safety Checklist

Crash Test:
  Frontal. . . . . —
  Side. . . . . —
Airbags:
  Torso . . . .Std. Front Pelvis/Torso from Seat
  Roll Sensing. . . . . .Yes
  Knee Bolster .None
Crash Avoidance:
  Collision Avoidance . . .Optional CIB & DBS
  Blind Spot Detection . . . . Optional
  Lane Keeping Assist . .Warn. Only Optional
  Pedestrian Crash Avoidance . . . . . Optional
General:
  Auto. Crash Notification Operat. Assist.-Fee
  Day Running Lamps . . . . Standard
Safety Belt/Restraint:
  Dynamic Head Restraints . . . . . . Std. Front
  Adjustable Belt. . . . . Standard Front & Rear

^Warning feature does not meet government standards.

Infiniti QX80

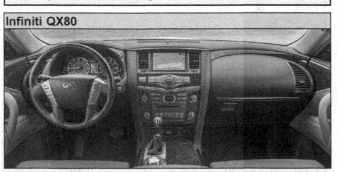

Specifications

Drive. . . . . .AWD
Engine 5.6-liter V8
Transmission . . . . 7-sp. Automatic
Tow Rating (lbs.) . . . . Very High-8500
Head/Leg Room (in.) . . . . Very Cramped-39.9/39.6
Interior Space (cu. ft.). . . . . .Very Roomy-151.3
Cargo Space (cu. ft.) Cramped-16.6
Wheelbase/Length (in.) 121.1/208.9

Ratings—10 Best, 1 Worst

Combo Crash Tests	5
Safety Features	7
Rollover	3
Preventive Maintenance	10
Repair Costs	5
Warranty	3
Fuel Economy	4
Complaints	1
Insurance Costs	10
OVERALL RATING	**5**

Jeep Cherokee

Jeep Cherokee

At-a-Glance

Status/Year Series Started Unchanged/2014
Twins . . . . —
Body Styles . . . . SUV
Seating 5
Anti-Theft Device Std. Pass. Immobil. & Opt. Pass. Alarm
Parking Index Rating . . . . Average
Where Made. Toldeo, OH
Fuel Factor
 MPG Rating (city/hwy) Poor-21/28
 Driving Range (mi.) Short-376
 Fuel Type . . . . Regular
 Annual Fuel Cost . . . . .Average-$1553
 Gas Guzzler Tax .No
 Greenhouse Gas Emissions (tons/yr.). . Average-6.3
 Barrels of Oil Used per year High-14.3

How the Competition Rates

Competitors	Rating	Pg.
Ford Escape	5	126
Kia Sportage	9	174
Mazda CX-5	4	191

Price Range

	Retail	Markup
Latitude FWD	$24,395	1%
Trailhawk 4WD	$30,995	2%
Limited 4WD	$31,295	2%
Overland 4WD	$37,340	3%

Safety Checklist

Crash Test:
 Frontal . . . . Very Poor
 Side. . . . . Very Good
Airbags:
 Torso Std. Fr. & Opt. Rr. Pelvis/Torso from Seat
 Roll Sensing. . . . . .Yes
 Knee Bolster . . . . Standard Front
Crash Avoidance:
 Collision Avoidance . . .Optional CIB & DBS
 Blind Spot Detection . . . . Optional
 Lane Keeping Assist . . . . Optional^
 Pedestrian Crash Avoidance . . . . . . .None
General:
 Auto. Crash Notification . . . . .None
 Day Running Lamps . . . . Standard
Safety Belt/Restraint:
 Dynamic Head Restraints . . . . .None
 Adjustable Belt . . . . Standard Front

^Warning feature does not meet government standards.

Jeep Cherokee

Specifications

Drive. . . . . .AWD
Engine 2.4-liter I4
Transmission . . . . 9-sp. Automatic
Tow Rating (lbs.) . . . . Very Low-2000
Head/Leg Room (in.) Cramped-39.4/41.1
Interior Space (cu. ft.) Average-103.4
Cargo Space (cu. ft.) Roomy-24.6
Wheelbase/Length (in.) 106.2/182

Jeep Compass

Small SUV

Ratings—10 Best, 1 Worst

Combo Crash Tests	2
Safety Features	2
Rollover	2
Preventive Maintenance	10
Repair Costs	10
Warranty	3
Fuel Economy	5
Complaints	3
Insurance Costs	10
OVERALL RATING	**4**

Jeep Compass

Jeep Compass

At-a-Glance

Status/Year Series Started	Unchanged/2007
Twins	—
Body Styles	SUV
Seating	5
Anti-Theft Device	Std. Pass. Immobil. & Opt. Pass. Alarm
Parking Index Rating	Easy
Where Made	Toluca, Mexico

Fuel Factor

MPG Rating (city/hwy)	Average-22/30
Driving Range (mi.)	Very Short-338
Fuel Type	Regular
Annual Fuel Cost	Average-$1470
Gas Guzzler Tax	No
Greenhouse Gas Emissions (tons/yr.)	Average-5.9
Barrels of Oil Used per year	High-13.2

How the Competition Rates

Competitors	Rating	Pg.
Acura RDX	9	68
GMC Terrain	5	141
Honda HR-V	5	147

Price Range	Retail	Markup
Sport FWD	$20,995	1%
Latitude FWD	$24,295	2%
Trailhawk 4WD	$28,695	2%
Limited 4WD	$29,095	3%

Safety Checklist

Crash Test:
- Frontal . . . . Poor
- Side . . . . Very Poor

Airbags:
- Torso . . . . Std. Front Pelvis/Torso from Seat
- Roll Sensing . . . . Yes
- Knee Bolster . . . . None

Crash Avoidance:
- Collision Avoidance . . Optional CIB & DBS^
- Blind Spot Detection . . . . Optional
- Lane Keeping Assist . . . . Optional
- Pedestrian Crash Avoidance . . . . None

General:
- Auto. Crash Notification . . . . None
- Day Running Lamps . . . . Standard

Safety Belt/Restraint:
- Dynamic Head Restraints . . . . . . Std. Front
- Adjustable Belt . . . . Standard Front

^Warning feature does not meet government standards.

Jeep Compass

Specifications

Drive	AWD
Engine	2.4-liter I4
Transmission	6-sp. Automatic
Tow Rating (lbs.)	Very Low-2000
Head/Leg Room (in.)	Average-39.2/41.8
Interior Space (cu. ft.)	Roomy-126.7
Cargo Space (cu. ft.)	Roomy-27.2
Wheelbase/Length (in.)	103.8/173

Jeep Grand Cherokee

Medium SUV

Ratings—10 Best, 1 Worst	
Combo Crash Tests	6
Safety Features	7
Rollover	3
Preventive Maintenance	8
Repair Costs	6
Warranty	3
Fuel Economy	1
Complaints	2
Insurance Costs	8
OVERALL RATING	**4**

Jeep Grand Cherokee

Jeep Grand Cherokee

At-a-Glance

Status/Year Series Started	Unchanged/2011
Twins	—
Body Styles	SUV
Seating	5
Anti-Theft Device	Std. Pass. Immobil. & Opt. Pass. Alarm
Parking Index Rating	Average
Where Made	Detroit, MI
Fuel Factor	
MPG Rating (city/hwy)	Very Poor-14/22
Driving Range (mi.)	Average-412
Fuel Type	Regular
Annual Fuel Cost	Very High-$2195
Gas Guzzler Tax	No
Greenhouse Gas Emissions (tons/yr.)	Very High-8.8
Barrels of Oil Used per year	Very High-19.4

How the Competition Rates

Competitors	Rating	Pg.
Chevrolet Equinox	4	105
Honda CR-V	10	145
Lexus NX	5	182

Price Range

	Retail	Markup
Laredo RWD	$30,595	0%
Limited RWD	$38,195	3%
Trailhawk 4WD	$43,295	4%
Overland 4WD	$47,995	4%

Safety Checklist

Crash Test:
- Frontal .... Good
- Side .... Poor

Airbags:
- Torso .... Std. Front Pelvis/Torso from Seat
- Roll Sensing .... Yes
- Knee Bolster .... Standard Driver

Crash Avoidance:
- Collision Avoidance . . . Optional CIB & DBS
- Blind Spot Detection .... Optional
- Lane Keeping Assist .... Optional^
- Pedestrian Crash Avoidance .... None

General:
- Auto. Crash Notification .... None
- Day Running Lamps .... Standard

Safety Belt/Restraint:
- Dynamic Head Restraints ...... Std. Front
- Adjustable Belt .... Standard Front

^Warning feature does not meet government standards.

Jeep Grand Cherokee

Specifications

Drive	4WD
Engine	5.7-liter V8
Transmission	8-sp. Automatic
Tow Rating (lbs.)	High-7200
Head/Leg Room (in.)	Cramped-39.9/40.3
Interior Space (cu. ft.)	Average-103.9
Cargo Space (cu. ft.)	Very Roomy-36.3
Wheelbase/Length (in.)	114.8/189.8

Ratings—10 Best, 1 Worst

Combo Crash Tests	2
Safety Features	4
Rollover	3
Preventive Maintenance	4
Repair Costs	7
Warranty	3
Fuel Economy	5
Complaints	2
Insurance Costs	5
OVERALL RATING	**1**

Jeep Renegade

At-a-Glance

Status/Year Series Started . . Apperance Change/2015
Twins . . . . —
Body Styles . . . . SUV
Seating 5
Anti-Theft Device .Std. Pass. Immobil. & Opt. Pass. Alarm
Parking Index Rating . . . . Easy
Where Made. . . . . Melfi, Italy
Fuel Factor
  MPG Rating (city/hwy) Average-22/31
  Driving Range (mi.) . . . . Very Short-321
  Fuel Type. . . . . Premium
  Annual Fuel Cost . . . . .High-$1760
  Gas Guzzler Tax . . . . .No
  Greenhouse Gas Emissions (tons/yr.) . . Average-6.1
  Barrels of Oil Used per year Average-12.9

How the Competition Rates

Competitors	Rating	Pg.
Chevrolet Equinox	4	105
Ford Edge	9	125
Hyundai Tucson	8	156

Price Range

	Retail	Markup
Sport FWD	$17,995	1%
Latitude FWD	$21,495	2%
Trailhawk 4WD	$26,645	2%
Limited 4WD	$27,195	2%

Jeep Renegade

Safety Checklist

Crash Test:
  Frontal . . . . .Poor
   Side. . . . . Very Poor
Airbags:
  Torso . . . .Std. Front Pelvis/Torso from Seat
  Roll Sensing. . . . . .Yes
  Knee Bolster . . . . .Standard Driver
Crash Avoidance:
  Collision Avoidance . . Optional CIB & DBS^
  Blind Spot Detection . . . . Optional
  Lane Keeping Assist . . . . Optional^
  Pedestrian Crash Avoidance . . . . . . .None
General:
  Auto. Crash Notification. . . . . .None
  Day Running Lamps . . . . Optional
Safety Belt/Restraint:
  Dynamic Head Restraints . . . . .None
  Adjustable Belt. . . . . Standard Front

^Warning feature does not meet government standards.

Jeep Renegade

Specifications

Drive. . . . . .FWD
Engine 1.4-liter I4
Transmission . . . . 9-sp. Automatic
Tow Rating (lbs.) . . . . Very Low-2000
Head/Leg Room (in.) Average-41.1/41.2
Interior Space (cu. ft.). Average-100.1
Cargo Space (cu. ft.) Average-18.5
Wheelbase/Length (in.) 101.2/166.6

Ratings—10 Best, 1 Worst

Combo Crash Tests	—
Safety Features	1
Rollover	1
Preventive Maintenance	10
Repair Costs	9
Warranty	3
Fuel Economy	2
Complaints	1
Insurance Costs	3
OVERALL RATING	**—**

Jeep Wrangler

Jeep Wrangler

At-a-Glance

Status/Year Series Started. Unchanged/2018
Twins . . . . —
Body Styles . . . . SUV
Seating. 5
Anti-Theft Device .Std. Pass. Immobil. & Opt. Pass. Alarm
Parking Index Rating . . . . Hard
Where Made. .Toledo, Ohio
Fuel Factor
  MPG Rating (city/hwy) . . . . Very Poor-17/21
  Driving Range (mi.) Average-418
  Fuel Type. . . . . .Regular
  Annual Fuel Cost . . . . Very High-$1976
  Gas Guzzler Tax . . . . .No
  Greenhouse Gas Emissions (tons/yr.). High-8.0
  Barrels of Oil Used per year . . . . Very High-18.3

How the Competition Rates

Competitors	Rating	Pg.
Mazda CX-5	4	191
Mitsubishi Outlander Sport	3	208
Subaru Crosstrek	5	223

Price Range	Retail	Markup
Sport	$23,995	1%
Rubicon	$33,645	5%
Unlimited Sahara	$34,245	5%
Unlimited Rubicon	$37,445	5%

Safety Checklist

Crash Test:
  Frontal. . . . . —
  Side. . . . . —
Airbags:
  Torso . . . . .None
  Roll Sensing. . . . . .No
  Knee Bolster .None
Crash Avoidance:
  Collision Avoidance . . . . .None
  Blind Spot Detection . . . . .None
  Lane Keeping Assist . . . . .None
  Pedestrian Crash Avoidance . . . . .None
General:
  Auto. Crash Notification. . . . . .None
  Day Running Lamps . . . . Standard
Safety Belt/Restraint:
  Dynamic Head Restraints . . . . .None
  Adjustable Belt. . . . . Standard Front

^Warning feature does not meet government standards.

Jeep Wrangler

Specifications

Drive. 4WD
Engine 3.6-liter V6
Transmission . . . . 6-sp. Automatic
Tow Rating (lbs.) . . . . Very Low-1000
Head/Leg Room (in.) Average-41.3/41
Interior Space (cu. ft.). Average-104
Cargo Space (cu. ft.) . . . . Very Roomy-31.5
Wheelbase/Length (in.) 95.4/184.9

Ratings—10 Best, 1 Worst

Combo Crash Tests	—
Safety Features	2
Rollover	7
Preventive Maintenance	9
Repair Costs	10
Warranty	9
Fuel Economy	8
Complaints	—
Insurance Costs	3

OVERALL RATING   —

Kia Forte

At-a-Glance

Status/Year Series Started	All New/2019
Twins	—
Body Styles	Sedan, Hatchback
Seating	5
Anti-Theft Device	Std. Pass. Immobil. & Active Alarm
Parking Index Rating	Easy
Where Made	Pesquería, Mexico

Fuel Factor
MPG Rating (city/hwy)	Very Good-30/40
Driving Range (mi.)	Very Long-476
Fuel Type	Regular
Annual Fuel Cost	Very Low-$1025
Gas Guzzler Tax	No
Greenhouse Gas Emissions (tons/yr.)	Very Low-4.4
Barrels of Oil Used per year	Low-9.7

How the Competition Rates

Competitors	Rating	Pg.
Honda Civic	10	144
Toyota Corolla	7	235
Volkswagen Golf	4	249

Price Range

	Retail	Markup
FE MT	$17,690	3%
LXS AT	$19,090	4%
S AT	$20,190	5%
EX AT	$21,990	5%

Kia Forte

Safety Checklist

Crash Test:
Frontal	—
Side	—

Airbags:
Torso	Std. Front Pelvis/Torso from Seat
Roll Sensing	Yes
Knee Bolster	None

Crash Avoidance:
Collision Avoidance	Standard CIB & DBS
Blind Spot Detection	Optional
Lane Keeping Assist	Standard^
Pedestrian Crash Avoidance	Optional

General:
Auto. Crash Notification	Dial Assist.-Free
Day Running Lamps	Optional

Safety Belt/Restraint:
Dynamic Head Restraints	None
Adjustable Belt	Standard Front

^Warning feature does not meet government standards.

Kia Forte

Specifications

Drive	FWD
Engine	2.0-liter I4
Transmission	6-sp. Automatic
Tow Rating (lbs.)	—
Head/Leg Room (in.)	Cramped-38.8/42.2
Interior Space (cu. ft.)	Cramped-96
Cargo Space (cu. ft.)	Cramped-15.3
Wheelbase/Length (in.)	106.3/182.7

Ratings—10 Best, 1 Worst	
Combo Crash Tests	7
Safety Features	7
Rollover	8
Preventive Maintenance	6
Repair Costs	10
Warranty	9
Fuel Economy	7
Complaints	6
Insurance Costs	1
OVERALL RATING	**9**

Kia Optima

Kia Optima

At-a-Glance

Status/Year Series Started	Unchanged/2011
Twins	—
Body Styles	Sedan
Seating	5
Anti-Theft Device	Std. Pass. Immobil. & Active Alarm
Parking Index Rating	Easy
Where Made	West Point, GA
Fuel Factor	
MPG Rating (city/hwy)	Good-24/34
Driving Range (mi.)	Very Long-512
Fuel Type	Regular
Annual Fuel Cost	Low-$1329
Gas Guzzler Tax	No
Greenhouse Gas Emissions (tons/yr.)	Low-5.3
Barrels of Oil Used per year	Average-11.8

How the Competition Rates

Competitors	Rating	Pg.
Hyundai Sonata	9	155
Mazda 6	5	194
Toyota Camry	8	234

Price Range	Retail	Markup
LX	$22,500	4%
S	$23,500	4%
LX Turbo	$24,300	6%
SX Turbo	$30,500	7%

Safety Checklist

Crash Test:
- Frontal . . . . Good
- Side . . . . Poor

Airbags:
- Torso . . . . Std. Front Pelvis/Torso from Seat
- Roll Sensing . . . . Yes
- Knee Bolster . . . . Standard Driver

Crash Avoidance:
- Collision Avoidance . . . Optional CIB & DBS
- Blind Spot Detection . . . . Optional
- Lane Keeping Assist . . Warn. Only Optional
- Pedestrian Crash Avoidance . . . . . Optional

General:
- Auto. Crash Notification . . . Dial Assist.-Free
- Day Running Lamps . . . . Optional

Safety Belt/Restraint:
- Dynamic Head Restraints . . . . None
- Adjustable Belt . . . . Standard Front

^Warning feature does not meet government standards.

Kia Optima

Specifications

Drive	FWD
Engine	2.4-liter I4
Transmission	6-sp. Automatic
Tow Rating (lbs.)	—
Head/Leg Room (in.)	Very Roomy-40/45.5
Interior Space (cu. ft.)	Roomy-117.6
Cargo Space (cu. ft.)	Cramped-15.4
Wheelbase/Length (in.)	110/190.7

Kia Rio

Kia Rio

Ratings—10 Best, 1 Worst

Combo Crash Tests	—
Safety Features	3
Rollover	6
Preventive Maintenance	7
Repair Costs	10
Warranty	9
Fuel Economy	8
Complaints	10
Insurance Costs	1
OVERALL RATING	**—**

Kia Rio

At-a-Glance

Status/Year Series Started........ Unchanged/2018
Twins . . . . Hyundai Accent
Body Styles . . . . Sedan, Hatchback
Seating 5
Anti-Theft Device . Std. Pass. Immobil. & Active Alarm
Parking Index Rating . . . . .Very Easy
Where Made. . . . . .Gwanmyeong, South Korea
Fuel Factor
  MPG Rating (city/hwy). Good-28/37
  Driving Range (mi.) . . . . .Very Short-374
  Fuel Type. . . . . .Regular
  Annual Fuel Cost . . . . .Very Low-$1169
  Gas Guzzler Tax . . . . .No
  Greenhouse Gas Emissions (tons/yr.). Very Low-4.6
  Barrels of Oil Used per year Low-10.3

How the Competition Rates

Competitors	Rating	Pg.
Chevrolet Sonic	8	109
Nissan Versa	1	207
Toyota Yaris Liftback	5	247

Price Range	Retail	Markup
LX Sedan MT	$14,165	2%
LX Hatchback AT	$15,495	3%
EX Sedan AT	$17,755	5%
SX Hatchback AT	$20,905	6%

Safety Checklist

Crash Test:
  Frontal. . . . . —
  Side. . . . . —
Airbags:
  Torso . . . .Std. Front Pelvis/Torso from Seat
  Roll Sensing. . . . . .Yes
  Knee Bolster .None
Crash Avoidance:
  Collision Avoidance . . .Optional CIB & DBS
  Blind Spot Detection . . . . .None
  Lane Keeping Assist . . . . .None
  Pedestrian Crash Avoidance . . . . .None
General:
  Auto. Crash Notification. . .Dial Assist.-Free
  Day Running Lamps . . . . Optional
Safety Belt/Restraint:
  Dynamic Head Restraints . . . . .None
  Adjustable Belt. . . . . Standard Front

^Warning feature does not meet government standards.

Kia Rio

Specifications

Drive. . . . . .FWD
Engine 1.6-liter I4
Transmission . . . . 6-sp. Automatic
Tow Rating (lbs.) . . . . —
Head/Leg Room (in.) Average-38.9/42.1
Interior Space (cu. ft.). . . . . Very Cramped-89.9
Cargo Space (cu. ft.) Cramped-13.7
Wheelbase/Length (in.) 101.6/172.6

Kia Sedona Minivan

Ratings—10 Best, 1 Worst

Combo Crash Tests	—
Safety Features	4
Rollover	5
Preventive Maintenance	4
Repair Costs	9
Warranty	9
Fuel Economy	3
Complaints	7
Insurance Costs	5

OVERALL RATING — —

Kia Sedona

Kia Sedona

At-a-Glance

Status/Year Series Started Unchanged/2015
Twins . . . . —
Body Styles . . . . Minivan
Seating 7/8
Anti-Theft Device . Std. Pass. Immobil. & Active Alarm
Parking Index Rating . . . . Hard
Where Made . . . . West Point, GA
Fuel Factor
  MPG Rating (city/hwy) Poor-18/25
  Driving Range (mi.) Long-435
  Fuel Type . . . . Regular
  Annual Fuel Cost . . . . High-$1784
  Gas Guzzler Tax . . . . No
  Greenhouse Gas Emissions (tons/yr.) . . Average-7.2
  Barrels of Oil Used per year High-15.7

How the Competition Rates

Competitors	Rating	Pg.
Chrysler Pacifica	8	117
Honda Odyssey	9	148
Toyota Sienna	2	243

Price Range

	Retail	Markup
L	$26,900	3%
EX	$33,600	6%
SX	$36,900	7%
SXL	$41,900	7%

Safety Checklist

Crash Test:
  Frontal . . . . —
  Side . . . . —
Airbags:
  Torso . . . .Std. Front Pelvis/Torso from Seat
  Roll Sensing . . . . Yes
  Knee Bolster . . . . None
Crash Avoidance:
  Collision Avoidance . . . Optional CIB & DBS
  Blind Spot Detection . . . . Optional
  Lane Keeping Assist . . Warn. Only Optional
  Pedestrian Crash Avoidance . . . . . Optional
General:
  Auto. Crash Notification . . . Dial Assist.-Free
  Day Running Lamps . . . . None
Safety Belt/Restraint:
  Dynamic Head Restraints . . . . None
  Adjustable Belt . . . . . Standard Front & Rear

^Warning feature does not meet government standards.

Kia Sedona

Specifications

Drive . . . . FWD
Engine 3.3-liter V6
Transmission . . . . 6-sp. Automatic
Tow Rating (lbs.) Low-3500
Head/Leg Room (in.) Roomy-39.8/43.1
Interior Space (cu. ft.) . . . . Very Roomy-172.3
Cargo Space (cu. ft.) . . . . Very Roomy-33.9
Wheelbase/Length (in.) 120.5/201.4

Kia Sorento

Ratings—10 Best, 1 Worst

Combo Crash Tests	7
Safety Features	4
Rollover	4
Preventive Maintenance	5
Repair Costs	8
Warranty	9
Fuel Economy	4
Complaints	4
Insurance Costs	5
OVERALL RATING	**6**

Kia Sorento

Kia Sorento

At-a-Glance

Status/Year Series Started . . Apperance Change/2016
Twins . . . . —
Body Styles . . . . SUV
Seating 5
Anti-Theft Device . Std. Pass. Immobil. & Active Alarm
Parking Index Rating . . . . .Very Easy
Where Made . . . . West Point, GA
Fuel Factor
  MPG Rating (city/hwy) Poor-21/28
  Driving Range (mi.) Long-445
  Fuel Type . . . . .Regular
  Annual Fuel Cost . . . . .Average-$1553
  Gas Guzzler Tax .No
  Greenhouse Gas Emissions (tons/yr.) . . Average-6.2
  Barrels of Oil Used per year High-13.7

How the Competition Rates

Competitors	Rating	Pg.
Dodge Durango	2	120
Ford Edge	9	125
Nissan Rogue	3	216

Price Range

	Retail	Markup
L FWD	$25,800	4%
LX AWD V6	$31,300	4%
SX AWD	$40,400	5%
SXL AWD	$45,700	7%

Safety Checklist

Crash Test:
  Frontal . . . . .Good
    Side . . . . Poor
Airbags:
  Torso . . . . .Std. Front Pelvis/Torso from Seat
  Roll Sensing . . . . .Yes
  Knee Bolster .None
Crash Avoidance:
  Collision Avoidance . . . Optional CIB & DBS
  Blind Spot Detection . . . . Optional
  Lane Keeping Assist . . Warn. Only Optional
  Pedestrian Crash Avoidance . . . . . Optional
General:
  Auto. Crash Notification . . . Dial Assist.-Free
  Day Running Lamps . . . . .None
Safety Belt/Restraint:
  Dynamic Head Restraints . . . . .None
  Adjustable Belt . . . . Standard Front

^Warning feature does not meet government standards.

Kia Sorento

Specifications

Drive . . . . .FWD
Engine 2.4-liter I4
Transmission . . . . 6-sp. Automatic
Tow Rating (lbs.) . . . . .Very Low-2000
Head/Leg Room (in.) Roomy-39.5/44.1
Interior Space (cu. ft.) . . . . Very Roomy-146.4
Cargo Space (cu. ft.) . . . . Very Roomy-38.8
Wheelbase/Length (in.) 109.4/187.4

Ratings—10 Best, 1 Worst

Combo Crash Tests	8
Safety Features	5
Rollover	4
Preventive Maintenance	4
Repair Costs	8
Warranty	9
Fuel Economy	6
Complaints	6
Insurance Costs	1
OVERALL RATING	**7**

Kia Soul

Kia Soul

At-a-Glance

Status/Year Series Started	Unchanged/2014
Twins	—
Body Styles	Wagon
Seating	5
Anti-Theft Device	Std. Pass. Immobil
Parking Index Rating	Very Easy
Where Made	Gwangju, South Korea
Fuel Factor	
MPG Rating (city/hwy)	Average-25/30
Driving Range (mi.)	Short-384
Fuel Type	Regular
Annual Fuel Cost	Low-$1360
Gas Guzzler Tax	No
Greenhouse Gas Emissions (tons/yr.)	Low-5.5
Barrels of Oil Used per year	Average-12.2

How the Competition Rates

Competitors	Rating	Pg.
Chevrolet Spark	5	110
Mini Hardtop	6	205
Toyota Yaris	6	246

Price Range

	Retail	Markup
Base MT	$16,100	2%
!	$22,800	6%
EV e	$32,250	7%
EV +	$35,950	8%

Safety Checklist

Crash Test:
  Frontal . . . . Good
  Side . . . . Good
Airbags:
  Torso . . . . Std. Front Pelvis/Torso from Seat
  Roll Sensing . . . . Yes
  Knee Bolster . . . . None
Crash Avoidance:
  Collision Avoidance . . . Optional CIB & DBS
  Blind Spot Detection . . . . Optional
  Lane Keeping Assist . . . . None
  Pedestrian Crash Avoidance . . . . . Optional
General:
  Auto. Crash Notification . . . Dial Assist.-Free
  Day Running Lamps . . . . Optional
Safety Belt/Restraint:
  Dynamic Head Restraints . . . . None
  Adjustable Belt . . . . Standard Front

^Warning feature does not meet government standards.

Kia Soul

Specifications

Drive	FWD
Engine	2.0-liter I4
Transmission	6-sp. Automatic
Tow Rating (lbs.)	—
Head/Leg Room (in.)	Cramped-39.6/40.9
Interior Space (cu. ft.)	Average-101
Cargo Space (cu. ft.)	Roomy-24.2
Wheelbase/Length (in.)	101.2/163

Ratings—10 Best, 1 Worst

Combo Crash Tests	7
Safety Features	6
Rollover	4
Preventive Maintenance	5
Repair Costs	7
Warranty	9
Fuel Economy	5
Complaints	8
Insurance Costs	8
OVERALL RATING	**9**

Kia Sportage

Kia Sportage

Kia Sportage

At-a-Glance

Status/Year Series Started Unchanged/2011
Twins . . . . —
Body Styles . . . . SUV
Seating 5
Anti-Theft Device . Std. Pass. Immobil. & Active Alarm
Parking Index Rating . . . . .Very Easy
Where Made . . . . .Gwangju, South Korea
Fuel Factor
  MPG Rating (city/hwy) Average-22/29
  Driving Range (mi.) . . . . .Very Short-358
  Fuel Type .Regular
  Annual Fuel Cost . . . . .Average-$1489
  Gas Guzzler Tax .No
  Greenhouse Gas Emissions (tons/yr.) . . Average-5.9
  Barrels of Oil Used per year High-13.2

How the Competition Rates

Competitors	Rating	Pg.
Ford Escape	5	126
Honda HR-V	5	147
Kia Sportage	9	174

Price Range	Retail	Markup
LX FWD	$23,500	4%
EX FWD	$26,300	5%
EX AWD	$27,800	5%
SX AWD	$34,300	6%

Safety Checklist

Crash Test:
  Frontal . . . . .Average
  Side . . . . .Good
Airbags:
  Torso . . . .Std. Front Pelvis/Torso from Seat
  Roll Sensing . . . . .Yes
  Knee Bolster . . . . .None
Crash Avoidance:
  Collision Avoidance . . .Optional CIB & DBS
  Blind Spot Detection . . . . Optional
  Lane Keeping Assist . .Warn. Only Optional
  Pedestrian Crash Avoidance . . . . . Optional
General:
  Auto. Crash Notification . . .Dial Assist.-Free
  Day Running Lamps . . . . Standard
Safety Belt/Restraint:
  Dynamic Head Restraints . . . . .None
  Adjustable Belt . . . . Standard Front

^Warning feature does not meet government standards.

Kia Sportage

Specifications

Drive . . . . .FWD
Engine 2.4-liter I4
Transmission . . . . 6-sp. Automaitc
Tow Rating (lbs.) . . . . .Very Low-2000
Head/Leg Room (in.) Cramped-39.1/41.4
Interior Space (cu. ft.) Average-100
Cargo Space (cu. ft.) Roomy-26.1
Wheelbase/Length (in.) 103.9/174.8

Land Rover Range Rover

Ratings—10 Best, 1 Worst

Combo Crash Tests	—
Safety Features	5
Rollover	2
Preventive Maintenance	6
Repair Costs	4
Warranty	7
Fuel Economy	1
Complaints	7
Insurance Costs	5
OVERALL RATING	**—**

Land Rover Range Rover

944 CBS

At-a-Glance

Status/Year Series Started	Unchanged/2013
Twins	—
Body Styles	SUV
Seating	5
Anti-Theft Device	Std. Pass. Immobil. & Alarm
Parking Index Rating	Very Hard
Where Made	Solihull, England
Fuel Factor	
MPG Rating (city/hwy)	Very Poor-14/19
Driving Range (mi.)	Long-440
Fuel Type	Premium
Annual Fuel Cost	Very High-$2805
Gas Guzzler Tax	No
Greenhouse Gas Emissions (tons/yr.)	Very High-11.3
Barrels of Oil Used per year	Very High-20.6

How the Competition Rates

Competitors	Rating	Pg.
Buick Enclave	4	89
Chevrolet Suburban	2	111
Toyota 4Runner	2	231

Price Range

	Retail	Markup
Base	$85,650	6%
HSE	$92,650	6%
Supercharged	$103,895	6%
Autobiography	$140,995	6%

Safety Checklist

Crash Test:
  Frontal . . . . —
  Side . . . . —
Airbags:
  Torso . . . . Std. Front Pelvis/Torso from Seat
  Roll Sensing . . . . Yes
  Knee Bolster . . . . None
Crash Avoidance:
  Collision Avoidance . Std. CIB & Opt. DBS^
  Blind Spot Detection . . . . Optional
  Lane Keeping Assist . . . . Optional^
  Pedestrian Crash Avoidance . . . . None
General:
  Auto. Crash Notification Operat. Assist.-Fee
  Day Running Lamps . . . . Standard
Safety Belt/Restraint:
  Dynamic Head Restraints . . . . None
  Adjustable Belt . . . . Standard Front

^Warning feature does not meet government standards.

Land Rover Range Rover

Specifications

Drive	4WD
Engine	5.0-liter V8
Transmission	6-sp. Automatic
Tow Rating (lbs.)	High-7716
Head/Leg Room (in.)	Average-42.5/39.1
Interior Space (cu. ft.)	—
Cargo Space (cu. ft.)	Very Roomy-32.1
Wheelbase/Length (in.)	115/196.8

Ratings—10 Best, 1 Worst

Combo Crash Tests	—
Safety Features	6
Rollover	4
Preventive Maintenance	6
Repair Costs	5
Warranty	7
Fuel Economy	5
Complaints	6
Insurance Costs	3
OVERALL RATING	**—**

Land Rover Range Rover Evoque

At-a-Glance

Status/Year Series Started	Unchanged/2012
Twins	—
Body Styles	SUV
Seating	5
Anti-Theft Device	Std. Pass. Immobil. & Alarm
Parking Index Rating	Easy
Where Made	Halewood, England
Fuel Factor	
MPG Rating (city/hwy)	Average-21/30
Driving Range (mi.)	Long-449
Fuel Type	Premium
Annual Fuel Cost	High-$1835
Gas Guzzler Tax	No
Greenhouse Gas Emissions (tons/yr.)	High-7.5
Barrels of Oil Used per year	High-13.7

How the Competition Rates

Competitors	Rating	Pg.
Lexus NX	5	182
Mazda CX-5	4	191
Subaru Crosstrek	5	223

Price Range

	Retail	Markup
SE	$41,800	6%
SE Premium	$45,700	6%
HSE	$51,000	6%
HSE Dynamic	$54,200	6%

Land Rover Range Rover Evoque

Safety Checklist

Crash Test:
  Frontal .... —
  Side .... —
Airbags:
  Torso .....Std. Front Pelvis/Torso from Seat
  Roll Sensing .... Yes
  Knee Bolster .... Standard Driver
Crash Avoidance:
  Collision Avoidance . Std. CIB & Opt. DBS^
  Blind Spot Detection .... Optional
  Lane Keeping Assist .... Optional^
  Pedestrian Crash Avoidance ....None
General:
  Auto. Crash Notification Operat. Assist.-Fee
  Day Running Lamps .... Standard
Safety Belt/Restraint:
  Dynamic Head Restraints ....None
  Adjustable Belt .... Standard Front

^Warning feature does not meet government standards.

Land Rover Range Rover Evoque

Specifications

Drive	4WD
Engine	2.0-liter I4
Transmission	9-sp. Automatic
Tow Rating (lbs.)	—
Head/Leg Room (in.)	Cramped-40.3/40.1
Interior Space (cu. ft.)	—
Cargo Space (cu. ft.)	Average-20.3
Wheelbase/Length (in.)	104.8/171.5

Land Rover Range Rover Sport

Medium SUV

Ratings—10 Best, 1 Worst

Combo Crash Tests	—
Safety Features	5
Rollover	3
Preventive Maintenance	1
Repair Costs	4
Warranty	7
Fuel Economy	1
Complaints	9
Insurance Costs	1

OVERALL RATING — —

Land Rover Range Rover Sport

At-a-Glance

Status/Year Series Started	Unchanged/2014
Twins	—
Body Styles	SUV
Seating	5
Anti-Theft Device	Std. Pass. Immobil. & Alarm
Parking Index Rating	Hard
Where Made	Solihull, England
Fuel Factor	
MPG Rating (city/hwy)	Very Poor-14/19
Driving Range (mi.)	Long-440
Fuel Type	Premium
Annual Fuel Cost	Very High-$2805
Gas Guzzler Tax	No
Greenhouse Gas Emissions (tons/yr.)	Very High-11.2
Barrels of Oil Used per year	Very High-20.6

How the Competition Rates

Competitors	Rating	Pg.
Acura MDX	7	67
Audi Q7	3	77
BMW X5		86

Price Range

	Retail	Markup
SE	$65,650	6%
HSE	$70,650	6%
Supercharged	$80,650	6%
Autobiography	$94,450	6%

Land Rover Range Rover Sport

Safety Checklist

Crash Test:
Frontal . . . . —
Side . . . . —
Airbags:
Torso . . . .Std. Front Pelvis/Torso from Seat
Roll Sensing . . . . .Yes
Knee Bolster .None
Crash Avoidance:
Collision Avoidance . Std. CIB & Opt. DBS^
Blind Spot Detection . . . . Optional
Lane Keeping Assist . . . . Optional^
Pedestrian Crash Avoidance . . . . .None
General:
Auto. Crash Notification Operat. Assist.-Fee
Day Running Lamps . . . . Standard
Safety Belt/Restraint:
Dynamic Head Restraints . . . . .None
Adjustable Belt . . . . Standard Front

^Warning feature does not meet government standards.

Land Rover Range Rover Sport

Specifications

Drive	4WD
Engine	5.0-liter V8
Transmission	8-sp. Automatic
Tow Rating (lbs.)	High-7716
Head/Leg Room (in.)	Average-39.4/42.2
Interior Space (cu. ft.)	—
Cargo Space (cu. ft.)	Roomy-27.7
Wheelbase/Length (in.)	115.1/191.8

Ratings—10 Best, 1 Worst

Combo Crash Tests	—
Safety Features	9
Rollover	7
Preventive Maintenance	6
Repair Costs	2
Warranty	7
Fuel Economy	5
Complaints	—
Insurance Costs	1
OVERALL RATING	**—**

Lexus ES

Lexus ES

At-a-Glance

Status/Year Series Started. . . . . All New/2019
Twins . . . . —
Body Styles . . . . Sedan
Seating 5
Anti-Theft Device . . . . . . Std. Pass. Immobil. & Alarm
Parking Index Rating . . . . Very Easy
Where Made. . . . . Kyushu, Japan
Fuel Factor
  MPG Rating (city/hwy) Average-22/33
  Driving Range (mi.) Average-413
  Fuel Type. . . . . Regular
  Annual Fuel Cost . . . . Average-$1369
  Gas Guzzler Tax . . . . No
  Greenhouse Gas Emissions (tons/yr.) Low-5.7
  Barrels of Oil Used per year Average-12.7

How the Competition Rates

Competitors	Rating	Pg.
Acura TLX	9	70
Lincoln MKZ	4	187
Volkswagen Passat	4	251

Price Range	Retail	Markup
Sedan	$39,500	7%
Luxury	$42,155	7%
Ultra Luxury	$43,150	7%
F Sport	$44,035	7%

Safety Checklist

Crash Test:
  Frontal. . . . . —
  Side. . . . . —
Airbags:
  Torso Std. Front & Rear Pelvis/Torso from Seat
  Roll Sensing. . . . . Yes
  Knee Bolster . . . . Standard Front
Crash Avoidance:
  Collision Avoidance . . Standard CIB & DBS
  Blind Spot Detection . . . . Optional
  Lane Keeping Assist . . . . Standard
  Pedestrian Crash Avoidance . . . . None
General:
  Auto. Crash Notification Operat. Assist.-Fee
  Day Running Lamps . . . . Standard
Safety Belt/Restraint:
  Dynamic Head Restraints . . . . None
  Adjustable Belt. . . . . Standard Front

^Warning feature does not meet government standards.

Lexus ES

Specifications

Drive. . . . . FWD
Engine 3.5-liter V6
Transmission . . . . 8-sp. Automatic
Tow Rating (lbs.) . . . . —
Head/Leg Room (in.) Cramped-37.5/42.4
Interior Space (cu. ft.). Average-99.9
Cargo Space (cu. ft.) Cramped-16.7
Wheelbase/Length (in.) 113.0/195.9

Ratings—10 Best, 1 Worst

Combo Crash Tests	—
Safety Features	9
Rollover	7
Preventive Maintenance	8
Repair Costs	1
Warranty	7
Fuel Economy	3
Complaints	4
Insurance Costs	1

OVERALL RATING —

Lexus GS

Lexus GS

At-a-Glance

Status/Year Series Started	Unchanged/2012
Twins	—
Body Styles	Sedan
Seating	5
Anti-Theft Device	Std. Pass. Immobil. & Alarm
Parking Index Rating	Average
Where Made	Tahara, Japan
Fuel Factor	
MPG Rating (city/hwy)	Poor-19/29
Driving Range (mi.)	Short-391
Fuel Type	Premium
Annual Fuel Cost	Very High-$1981
Gas Guzzler Tax	No
Greenhouse Gas Emissions (tons/yr.)	High-7.8
Barrels of Oil Used per year	High-14.3

How the Competition Rates

Competitors	Rating	Pg.
Cadillac XTS	8	99
Lincoln MKZ	4	187
Volkswagen Passat	4	251

Price Range

	Retail	Markup
200t	$46,310	8%
350	$50,695	8%
200t F Sport	$53,980	8%
350 F Sport AWD	$56,555	8%

Safety Checklist

Crash Test:
  Frontal . . . . —
  Side . . . . —
Airbags:
  Torso Std. Front & Rear Pelvis/Torso from Seat
  Roll Sensing . . . . Yes
  Knee Bolster . . . . Standard Front
Crash Avoidance:
  Collision Avoidance . . . Optional CIB & DBS
  Blind Spot Detection . . . . Optional
  Lane Keeping Assist . . . . Optional
  Pedestrian Crash Avoidance . . . . None
General:
  Auto. Crash Notification Operat. Assist.-Fee
  Day Running Lamps . . . . Standard
Safety Belt/Restraint:
  Dynamic Head Restraints . . . . None
  Adjustable Belt . . . . Standard Front

^Warning feature does not meet government standards.

Specifications

Drive	RWD
Engine	3.5-liter V6
Transmission	8-sp. Automatic
Tow Rating (lbs.)	—
Head/Leg Room (in.)	Cramped-38/42.3
Interior Space (cu. ft.)	Average-99
Cargo Space (cu. ft.)	Cramped-14.1
Wheelbase/Length (in.)	112.2/190.7

Ratings—10 Best, 1 Worst

Combo Crash Tests	—
Safety Features	9
Rollover	1
Preventive Maintenance	6
Repair Costs	2
Warranty	7
Fuel Economy	1
Complaints	9
Insurance Costs	10

OVERALL RATING —

Lexus GX

Lexus GX

At-a-Glance

Status/Year Series Started....... Unchanged/2010
Twins Lexus RX, Toyota 4Runner, Toyota Highlander
Body Styles .... SUV
Seating 7
Anti-Theft Device ...... Std. Pass. Immobil. & Alarm
Parking Index Rating ....Very Hard
Where Made.................... Tahara, Japan
Fuel Factor
  MPG Rating (city/hwy) ....Very Poor-15/20
  Driving Range (mi.) Short-389
  Fuel Type....................Premium
  Annual Fuel Cost .... Very High-$2636
  Gas Guzzler Tax ....No
  Greenhouse Gas Emissions (tons/yr.)Very High-10.6
  Barrels of Oil Used per year .... Very High-19.4

How the Competition Rates

Competitors	Rating	Pg.
Buick Enclave	4	89
Chevrolet Suburban	2	111
Volvo XC90	8	256

Price Range

	Retail	Markup
460	$51,680	9%
460 Luxury	$63,380	9%
		—

Lexus GX

Safety Checklist

Crash Test:
  Frontal............................... —
  Side................................. —
Airbags:
  Torso Std. Fr. & Opt. Rr. Pelvis/Torso from Seat
  Roll Sensing.....................Yes
  Knee Bolster .... Standard Front
Crash Avoidance:
  Collision Avoidance . . .Optional CIB & DBS
  Blind Spot Detection .... Optional
  Lane Keeping Assist . .Warn. Only Optional
  Pedestrian Crash Avoidance ....None
General:
  Auto. Crash Notification Operat. Assist.-Fee
  Day Running Lamps .... Standard
Safety Belt/Restraint:
  Dynamic Head Restraints ...... Std. Front
  Adjustable Belt ..... Standard Front & Rear

^Warning feature does not meet government standards.

Lexus GX

Specifications

Drive..4WD
Engine 4.6-liter V8
Transmission .... 6-sp. Automatic
Tow Rating (lbs.) Average-6500
Head/Leg Room (in.) Cramped-38/41.7
Interior Space (cu. ft.). .... Very Roomy-129.7
Cargo Space (cu. ft.) .... Very Cramped-11.6
Wheelbase/Length (in.) 109.8/192.1

Lexus IS

Ratings—10 Best, 1 Worst

Combo Crash Tests	5
Safety Features	9
Rollover	9
Preventive Maintenance	7
Repair Costs	1
Warranty	7
Fuel Economy	5
Complaints	10
Insurance Costs	5
OVERALL RATING	**8**

Lexus IS

At-a-Glance

Status/Year Series Started. Unchanged/2014
Twins . . . . —
Body Styles . . . . .Sedan, Convertible
Seating. 5
Anti-Theft Device . . . . . . Std. Pass. Immobil. & Alarm
Parking Index Rating . . . . Easy
Where Made. . . . . Kyushu, Japan / Tahara, Japan
Fuel Factor
  MPG Rating (city/hwy) Average-21/30
  Driving Range (mi.) Average-422
  Fuel Type . . . . .Premium
  Annual Fuel Cost . . . . .High-$1835
  Gas Guzzler Tax . . . . .No
  Greenhouse Gas Emissions (tons/yr.). High-7.5
  Barrels of Oil Used per year High-13.7

How the Competition Rates

Competitors	Rating	Pg.
Audi A3	5	71
Audi A3	5	71
Infiniti Q50	3	158

Price Range	Retail	Markup
200t	$37,825	8%
300 AWD	$40,200	8%
350	$41,370	8%
350 AWD	$43,535	8%

Safety Checklist

Crash Test:
  Frontal . . . . .Poor
  Side. . . . . .Good
Airbags:
  Torso Std. Front & Rear Pelvis/Torso from Seat
  Roll Sensing. . . . . .Yes
  Knee Bolster . . . . Standard Front
Crash Avoidance:
  Collision Avoidance . . Optional CIB & DBS^
  Blind Spot Detection . . . . Optional
  Lane Keeping Assist . . . . Standard
  Pedestrian Crash Avoidance . . . . .None
General:
  Auto. Crash Notification Operat. Assist.-Fee
  Day Running Lamps . . . . Standard
Safety Belt/Restraint:
  Dynamic Head Restraints . . . . .None
  Adjustable Belt. . . . . Standard Front

^Warning feature does not meet government standards.

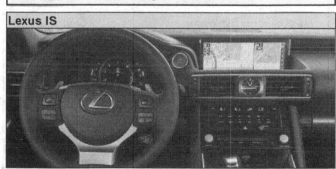
Lexus IS

Specifications

Drive . . . . .RWD
Engine 2.5-liter V6
Transmission . . . . 6-sp. Automatic
Tow Rating (lbs.) . . . . —
Head/Leg Room (in.) Roomy-38.2/44.8
Interior Space (cu. ft.). . . . . Very Cramped-90.2
Cargo Space (cu. ft.) Cramped-13.8
Wheelbase/Length (in.) 110.2/183.7

Ratings—10 Best, 1 Worst

Combo Crash Tests	7
Safety Features	8
Rollover	4
Preventive Maintenance	1
Repair Costs	3
Warranty	7
Fuel Economy	5
Complaints	7
Insurance Costs	5
OVERALL RATING	**5**

Lexus NX

At-a-Glance

Status/Year Series Started	Unchanged/2015
Twins	—
Body Styles	SUV
Seating	5
Anti-Theft Device	Std. Pass. Immobil. & Alarm
Parking Index Rating	Very Easy
Where Made	Kyushu, Japan

Fuel Factor

MPG Rating (city/hwy)	Average-22/28
Driving Range (mi.)	Short-387
Fuel Type	Premium
Annual Fuel Cost	High-$1830
Gas Guzzler Tax	No
Greenhouse Gas Emissions (tons/yr.)	Very Low-3.5
Barrels of Oil Used per year	High-13

How the Competition Rates

Competitors	Rating	Pg.
Buick Enclave	4	89
Lincoln MKC	6	186
Mazda CX-5	4	191

Price Range

	Retail	Markup
200t FWD	$35,285	7%
200t AWD	$36,685	7%
200t F Sport AWD	$38,785	7%
300h	$39,720	6%

Lexus NX

Safety Checklist

Crash Test:
  Frontal . . . . Very Good
  Side . . . . Very Poor
Airbags:
  Torso . . . . Std. Front Pelvis/Torso from Seat
  Roll Sensing . . . . Yes
  Knee Bolster . . . . Standard Front
Crash Avoidance:
  Collision Avoidance . . . Optional CIB & DBS
  Blind Spot Detection . . . . Optional
  Lane Keeping Assist . . . . Optional
  Pedestrian Crash Avoidance . . . . None
General:
  Auto. Crash Notif. . . . . Operator Assist.-Fee
  Day Running Lamps . . . . Standard
Safety Belt/Restraint:
  Dynamic Head Restraints . . . . None
  Adjustable Belt . . . . Standard Front

^Warning feature does not meet government standards.

Lexus NX

Specifications

Drive	AWD
Engine	2.0-liter I4
Transmission	6-sp. Automatic
Tow Rating (lbs.)	Very Low-2000
Head/Leg Room (in.)	Average-38.2/42.8
Interior Space (cu. ft.)	Very Cramped-71.6
Cargo Space (cu. ft.)	Average-17.7
Wheelbase/Length (in.)	104.7/182.3

Ratings—10 Best, 1 Worst

Combo Crash Tests	—
Safety Features	8
Rollover	8
Preventive Maintenance	6
Repair Costs	1
Warranty	7
Fuel Economy	6
Complaints	10
Insurance Costs	3
OVERALL RATING	**—**

Lexus RC

Lexus RC

At-a-Glance

Status/Year Series Started	Unchanged/2016
Twins	—
Body Styles	Coupe
Seating	4
Anti-Theft Device	Std. Pass. Immobil. & Alarm
Parking Index Rating	Easy
Where Made	Tahara, Japan
Fuel Factor	
MPG Rating (city/hwy)	Average-22/32
Driving Range (mi.)	Long-445
Fuel Type	Premium
Annual Fuel Cost	High-$1740
Gas Guzzler Tax	No
Greenhouse Gas Emissions (tons/yr.)	Low-5.7
Barrels of Oil Used per year	Average-12.7

How the Competition Rates

Competitors	Rating	Pg.
Audi A3	5	71
Cadillac ATS	4	94
Mercedes-Benz C-Class	1	196

Price Range

	Retail	Markup
200T	$40,155	8%
300 AWD	$42,770	8%
350	$43,010	8%
350 AWD	$45,175	8%

Safety Checklist

Crash Test:
- Frontal . . . . —
- Side . . . . —

Airbags:
- Torso . . . . Std. Front Pelvis/Torso from Seat
- Roll Sensing . . . . Yes
- Knee Bolster . . . . Standard Front

Crash Avoidance:
- Collision Avoidance . . . Optional CIB & DBS
- Blind Spot Detection . . . . Std.
- Lane Keeping Assist . . Warn. Only Optional
- Pedestrian Crash Avoidance . . . . None

General:
- Auto. Crash Notif . . . . . Operator Assist.-Fee
- Day Running Lamps . . . . Standard

Safety Belt/Restraint:
- Dynamic Head Restraints . . . . None
- Adjustable Belt . . . . None

^Warning feature does not meet government standards.

Lexus RC

Specifications

Drive	RWD
Engine	2.0-liter I4
Transmission	8-sp. Automatic
Tow Rating (lbs.)	—
Head/Leg Room (in.)	Roomy-37.8/45.4
Interior Space (cu. ft.)	Very Cramped-82
Cargo Space (cu. ft.)	Very Cramped-10.4
Wheelbase/Length (in.)	107.5/184.8

Ratings—10 Best, 1 Worst	
Combo Crash Tests	3
Safety Features	8
Rollover	4
Preventive Maintenance	5
Repair Costs	1
Warranty	7
Fuel Economy	4
Complaints	10
Insurance Costs	5
OVERALL RATING	**4**

Lexus RX

Lexus RX

At-a-Glance

```
Status/Year Series Started........ Unchanged/2016
Twins  Lexus GX, Toyota 4Runner, Toyota Highlander
Body Styles .................................. SUV
Seating................................... 5
Anti-Theft Device ...... Std. Pass. Immobil. & Alarm
Parking Index Rating ....................... Hard
Where Made.... Kyushu, Japan / Cambridge, Ontario
Fuel Factor
  MPG Rating (city/hwy)............. Poor-20/28
  Driving Range (mi.) .............. Long-441
  Fuel Type.........................Regular
  Annual Fuel Cost ..............Average-$1601
  Gas Guzzler Tax .........................No
  Greenhouse Gas Emissions (tons/yr.). . Average-6.4
  Barrels of Oil Used per year .......... High-14.3
```

How the Competition Rates

Competitors	Rating	Pg.
Audi Q7	3	77
Infiniti QX60	5	161
Lincoln MKC	6	186

Price Range	Retail	Markup
350 Base FWD	$43,120	7%
350 Base AWD	$44,520	7%
350 F Sport	$50,420	7%
450 Hybrid AWD	$53,035	6%

Safety Checklist

```
Crash Test:
  Frontal ......................... Very Poor
   Side.............................Good
Airbags:
  Torso  Std. Fr. & Opt. Rr. Pelvis/Torso from Seat
  Roll Sensing......................Yes
  Knee Bolster ............ Standard Driver
Crash Avoidance:
  Collision Avoidance . . . Optional CIB & DBS
  Blind Spot Detection .............. Std.
  Lane Keeping Assist .......... Optional
  Pedestrian Crash Avoidance ....... None
General:
  Auto. Crash Notif..... Operator Assist.-Fee
  Day Running Lamps .......... Standard
Safety Belt/Restraint:
  Dynamic Head Restraints ......... None
  Adjustable Belt.......... Standard Front
```

^Warning feature does not meet government standards.

Lexus RX

Specifications

```
Drive.......................................FWD
Engine ......................... 3.5-liter V6
Transmission ............... 8-sp. Automatic
Tow Rating (lbs.) ............................. —
Head/Leg Room (in.) .......... Roomy-39.4/44.4
Interior Space (cu. ft.)....... Very Roomy-139.7
Cargo Space (cu. ft.) .......... Average-18.4
Wheelbase/Length (in.) ......... 109.8/192.5
```

Ratings—10 Best, 1 Worst

Combo Crash Tests	10
Safety Features	8
Rollover	7
Preventive Maintenance	5
Repair Costs	2
Warranty	9
Fuel Economy	2
Complaints	4
Insurance Costs	3
OVERALL RATING	**6**

Lincoln Continental

At-a-Glance

Status/Year Series Started	Unchanged/2017
Twins	—
Body Styles	Sedan
Seating	5
Anti-Theft Device	Std. Pass. Immobil. & Alarm
Parking Index Rating	Very Hard
Where Made	Chicago, IL
Fuel Factor	
MPG Rating (city/hwy)	Very Poor-17/26
Driving Range (mi.)	Very Short-362
Fuel Type	Regular
Annual Fuel Cost	High-$1825
Gas Guzzler Tax	No
Greenhouse Gas Emissions (tons/yr.)	High-7.3
Barrels of Oil Used per year	High-16.5

How the Competition Rates

Competitors	Rating	Pg.
Buick LaCrosse	5	92
Cadillac XTS	8	99
Mercedes-Benz E-Class	3	198

Price Range

	Retail	Markup
Premiere FWD	$44,560	5%
Select FWD	$47,515	5%
Reserve AWD	$55,915	6%
Black Label AWD	$64,915	6%

Lincoln Continental

Safety Checklist

Crash Test:
Frontal . . . . Very Good
Side . . . . Very Good
Airbags:
Torso . . . . .Std. Front Pelvis/Torso from Seat
Roll Sensing . . . . Yes
Knee Bolster . . . . Standard Front
Crash Avoidance:
Collision Avoidance . . .Optional CIB & DBS
Blind Spot Detection . . . . Optional
Lane Keeping Assist . . . . Optional
Pedestrian Crash Avoidance . . . . .None
General:
Auto. Crash Notification . . .Dial Assist.-Free
Day Running Lamps . . . . Standard
Safety Belt/Restraint:
Dynamic Head Restraints . . . . .None
Adjustable Belt . . . . Standard Front

^Warning feature does not meet government standards.

Lincoln Continental

Specifications

Drive	FWD
Engine	3.7-liter V6
Transmission	6-sp. Automatic
Tow Rating (lbs.)	—
Head/Leg Room (in.)	Roomy-39.3/44.4
Interior Space (cu. ft.)	Roomy-106.4
Cargo Space (cu. ft.)	Cramped-16.7
Wheelbase/Length (in.)	117.9/201.4

Lincoln MKC   Small SUV

Ratings—10 Best, 1 Worst

Combo Crash Tests	3
Safety Features	5
Rollover	3
Preventive Maintenance	6
Repair Costs	4
Warranty	9
Fuel Economy	3
Complaints	8
Insurance Costs	10
OVERALL RATING	**6**

Lincoln MKC

Lincoln MKC

At-a-Glance

Status/Year Series Started Unchanged/2015
Twins . . . . Ford Escape
Body Styles . . . . SUV
Seating 5
Anti-Theft Device . . . . . Std. Pass. Immobil. & Alarm
Parking Index Rating . . . . Average
Where Made . . . . Louisville, Kentucky
Fuel Factor
 MPG Rating (city/hwy) Poor-19/26
 Driving Range (mi.) . . . . Very Short-335
 Fuel Type . . . . Regular
 Annual Fuel Cost . . . . High-$1700
 Gas Guzzler Tax . . . . No
 Greenhouse Gas Emissions (tons/yr.) High-8.2
 Barrels of Oil Used per year High-15.0

How the Competition Rates

Competitors	Rating	Pg.
Buick Encore	10	90
Lexus NX	5	182
Mitsubishi Outlander Sport	3	208

Price Range	Retail	Markup
Premiere FWD	$33,355	5%
Select FWD	$36,110	6%
Reserve AWD	$42,395	6%
Black Label AWD	$48,380	7%

Safety Checklist

Crash Test:
 Frontal . . . . Poor
 Side . . . . Poor
Airbags:
 Torso . . . . Std. Front Pelvis/Torso from Seat
 Roll Sensing . . . . Yes
 Knee Bolster . . . . Standard Driver
Crash Avoidance:
 Collision Avoidance . Warning Only Optional
 Blind Spot Detection . . . . Optional
 Lane Keeping Assist . . . . Optional
 Pedestrian Crash Avoidance . . . . None
General:
 Auto. Crash Notification . . . Dial Assist.-Free
 Day Running Lamps . . . . Optional
Safety Belt/Restraint:
 Dynamic Head Restraints . . . . None
 Adjustable Belt . . . . Standard Front

^Warning feature does not meet government standards.

Lincoln MKC

Specifications

Drive . . . . AWD
Engine 2.0-liter I5
Transmission . . . . 6-sp. Automatic
Tow Rating (lbs.) . . . . Very Low-2000
Head/Leg Room (in.) Average-39.6/42.8
Interior Space (cu. ft.) Average-97.9
Cargo Space (cu. ft.) Roomy-25.2
Wheelbase/Length (in.) 105.9/179.2

Lincoln MKZ   Intermediate

Ratings—10 Best, 1 Worst

Combo Crash Tests	3
Safety Features	6
Rollover	7
Preventive Maintenance	8
Repair Costs	2
Warranty	9
Fuel Economy	3
Complaints	4
Insurance Costs	5
OVERALL RATING	**4**

Lincoln MKZ

At-a-Glance

Status/Year Series Started	Unchanged/2013
Twins	Ford Fusion
Body Styles	Sedan
Seating	5
Anti-Theft Device	Std. Pass. Immobil. & Alarm
Parking Index Rating	Hard
Where Made	Hermosillo, Mexico
Fuel Factor	
MPG Rating (city/hwy)	Poor-18/27
Driving Range (mi.)	Very Short-349
Fuel Type	Regular
Annual Fuel Cost	High-$1735
Gas Guzzler Tax	No
Greenhouse Gas Emissions (tons/yr.)	High-8.1
Barrels of Oil Used per year	High-15.0

How the Competition Rates

Competitors	Rating	Pg.
Acura TLX	9	70
BMW 5 Series	6	81
Infiniti Q50	3	158

Price Range

	Retail	Markup
Base FWD	$35,010	5%
Hybrid Select	$36,760	5%
Select AWD	$38,650	5%
Black Label Hybrid FWD	$47,670	6%

Lincoln MKZ

Safety Checklist

Crash Test:
    Frontal .... Very Poor
    Side .... Average
Airbags:
    Torso .... Std. Front Pelvis/Torso from Seat
    Roll Sensing .... Yes
    Knee Bolster .... None
Crash Avoidance:
    Collision Avoidance . . . Optional CIB & DBS
    Blind Spot Detection .... Optional
    Lane Keeping Assist .... Optional
    Pedestrian Crash Avoidance .... None
General:
    Auto. Crash Notification . . . Dial Assist.-Free
    Day Running Lamps .... Standard
Safety Belt/Restraint:
    Dynamic Head Restraints .... None
    Adjustable Belt .... Standard Front

^Warning feature does not meet government standards.

Lincoln MKZ

Specifications

Drive	FWD
Engine	3.7-liter V6
Transmission	6-sp. Automatic
Tow Rating (lbs.)	Very Low-1000
Head/Leg Room (in.)	Average-37.9/44.3
Interior Space (cu. ft.)	Cramped-96.5
Cargo Space (cu. ft.)	Cramped-15.4
Wheelbase/Length (in.)	112.2/194.1

Ratings—10 Best, 1 Worst

Combo Crash Tests	2
Safety Features	6
Rollover	5
Preventive Maintenance	7
Repair Costs	6
Warranty	9
Fuel Economy	2
Complaints	3
Insurance Costs	10
OVERALL RATING	**5**

Linoln Nautilis

At-a-Glance

Status/Year Series Started	Apperance Change/2016
Twins	—
Body Styles	SUV
Seating	5
Anti-Theft Device	Std. Pass. Immobil. & Alarm
Parking Index Rating	Hard
Where Made	"Oakville, Ontario"
Fuel Factor	
MPG Rating (city/hwy)	Very Poor-18/25
Driving Range (mi.)	Very Short-357
Fuel Type	Regular
Annual Fuel Cost	High-$1850
Gas Guzzler Tax	No
Greenhouse Gas Emissions (tons/yr.)	High-7.5
Barrels of Oil Used per year	High-16.5

Linoln Nautilis

How the Competition Rates

Competitors	Rating	Pg.
Acura MDX	7	67
Audi Q7	3	77
Lexus RX	4	184

Price Range

	Retail	Markup
Premiere FWD	$39,035	5%
Select FWD	$42,550	6%
Reserve AWD	$49,055	6%
Black Label AWD	$56,725	7%

Safety Checklist

Crash Test:
  Frontal . . . . Very Poor
  Side . . . . Poor
Airbags:
  Torso . . . . .Std. Front Pelvis/Torso from Seat
  Roll Sensing . . . . Yes
  Knee Bolster . . . . Standard Front
Crash Avoidance:
  Collision Avoidance . . . . Optional CIB
  Blind Spot Detection . . . . Optional
  Lane Keeping Assist . . Warn. Only Optional
  Pedestrian Crash Avoidance . . . . . Optional
General:
  Auto. Crash Notification . . . Dial Assist.-Free
  Day Running Lamps . . . . Optional
Safety Belt/Restraint:
  Dynamic Head Restraints . . . . None
  Adjustable Belt . . . . Standard Front

^Warning feature does not meet government standards.

Linoln Nautilis

Specifications

Drive	FWD
Engine	2.0-liter I4
Transmission	8-sp. Automatic
Tow Rating (lbs.)	—
Head/Leg Room (in.)	Roomy-39.9/42.8
Interior Space (cu. ft.)	—
Cargo Space (cu. ft.)	Very Roomy-37.2
Wheelbase/Length (in.)	112.2/190

Ratings—10 Best, 1 Worst

Combo Crash Tests	—
Safety Features	5
Rollover	1
Preventive Maintenance	2
Repair Costs	6
Warranty	9
Fuel Economy	1
Complaints	9
Insurance Costs10	10

OVERALL RATING —

Linoln Navigator

At-a-Glance

Status/Year Series Started	Unchanged/2018
Twins	Ford Expedition
Body Styles	SUV
Seating	7/8
Anti-Theft Device	Std. Pass. Immobil. & Alarm
Parking Index Rating	Very Hard
Where Made	Louisville, Kentucky
Fuel Factor	
MPG Rating (city/hwy)	Very Poor-16/21
Driving Range (mi.)	Average-412
Fuel Type	Regular
Annual Fuel Cost	Very High-$2051
Gas Guzzler Tax	No
Greenhouse Gas Emissions (tons/yr.)	High-8.3
Barrels of Oil Used per year	Very High-18.3

How the Competition Rates

Competitors	Rating	Pg.
Buick Enclave	4	89
Chevrolet Suburban	2	111
Volvo XC90	8	256

Price Range

	Retail	Markup
Premier RWD	$72,055	5%
Select 4WD	$78,710	6%
Select L 4WD	$83,905	6%
Black Label 4WD	$93,205	6%

Linoln Navigator

Safety Checklist

Crash Test:
Frontal . . . . —
Side . . . . —
Airbags:
Torso . . . . Std. Front Torso from Seat
Roll Sensing . . . . Yes
Knee Bolster .None
Crash Avoidance:
Collision Avoidance . . .Optional CIB & DBS
Blind Spot Detection . . . . Std.
Lane Keeping Assist . . . . Optional
Pedestrian Crash Avoidance . . . . . Optional
General:
Auto. Crash Notification . . . Dial Assist.-Free
Day Running Lamps . . . . Standard
Safety Belt/Restraint:
Dynamic Head Restraints . . . . None
Adjustable Belt . . . . Standard Front

^Warning feature does not meet government standards.

Linoln Navigator

Specifications

Drive	4WD
Engine	3.5-liter V6
Transmission	10-sp. Automatic
Tow Rating (lbs.)	Very High-8400
Head/Leg Room (in.)	Very Roomy-41.8/43.9
Interior Space (cu. ft.)	Very Roomy-172
Cargo Space (cu. ft.)	Average-19.3
Wheelbase/Length (in.)	122.5/210

Ratings—10 Best, 1 Worst	
Combo Crash Tests	9
Safety Features	5
Rollover	5
Preventive Maintenance	7
Repair Costs	9
Warranty	1
Fuel Economy	8
Complaints	9
Insurance Costs	8
OVERALL RATING	**10**

Mazda CX-3

Mazda CX-3

At-a-Glance

Status/Year Series Started	Unchanged/2016
Twins	—
Body Styles	SUV
Seating	5
Anti-Theft Device	Std. Passive Immobil. Only
Parking Index Rating	Very Easy
Where Made	Hiroshima, Japan / Hofu, Japan
Fuel Factor	
MPG Rating (city/hwy)	Good-29/34
Driving Range (mi.)	Short-394
Fuel Type	Regular
Annual Fuel Cost	Low-$1183
Gas Guzzler Tax	No
Greenhouse Gas Emissions (tons/yr.)	Low-4.8
Barrels of Oil Used per year	Average-10.6

How the Competition Rates

Competitors	Rating	Pg.
Buick Encore	10	90
Chevrolet Trax	10	114
Honda HR-V	5	147

Price Range	Retail	Markup
Sport FWD	$19,960	3%
Sport AWD	$21,210	3%
Touring AWD	$23,210	3%
Grand Touring AWD	$26,240	3%

Safety Checklist

Crash Test:
  Frontal . . . . Very Good
   Side . . . . Good
Airbags:
  Torso . . . . Std. Front Pelvis/Torso from Seat
  Roll Sensing . . . . Yes
  Knee Bolster . . . . None
Crash Avoidance:
  Collision Avoidance . . Optional CIB & DBS^
  Blind Spot Detection . . . . Optional
  Lane Keeping Assist . . . . Optional^
  Pedestrian Crash Avoidance . . . . None
General:
  Auto. Crash Notification . . . Dial Assist.-Free
  Day Running Lamps . . . . Standard
Safety Belt/Restraint:
  Dynamic Head Restraints . . . . None
  Adjustable Belt . . . . Standard Front

^Warning feature does not meet government standards.

Mazda CX-3

Specifications

Drive	FWD
Engine	2.0-liter I4
Transmission	6-sp. Automatic
Tow Rating (lbs.)	—
Head/Leg Room (in.)	Cramped-38.4/41.7
Interior Space (cu. ft.)	Very Cramped-87.6
Cargo Space (cu. ft.)	Very Cramped-12.4
Wheelbase/Length (in.)	101.2/168.3

Ratings—10 Best, 1 Worst

Combo Crash Tests	6
Safety Features	4
Rollover	3
Preventive Maintenance	7
Repair Costs	10
Warranty	1
Fuel Economy	7
Complaints	8
Insurance Costs	1
OVERALL RATING	**4**

Mazda CX-5

At-a-Glance

Status/Year Series Started	Unchanged/2013
Twins	—
Body Styles	SUV
Seating	5
Anti-Theft Device	Std. Passive Immobil. Only
Parking Index Rating	Average
Where Made	Hiroshima, Japan
Fuel Factor	
MPG Rating (city/hwy)	Good-26/32
Driving Range (mi.)	Average-420
Fuel Type	Regular
Annual Fuel Cost	Low-$1294
Gas Guzzler Tax	No
Greenhouse Gas Emissions (tons/yr.)	Average-6.2
Barrels of Oil Used per year	Average-11.4

How the Competition Rates

Competitors	Rating	Pg.
Buick Enclave	4	89
Honda CR-V	10	145
Mitsubishi Outlander Sport	3	208

Price Range

	Retail	Markup
Sport FWD	$24,045	3%
Touring FWD	$25,915	3%
Grand Select AWD	$30,195	3%
Grand Touring AWD	$30,695	3%

Mazda CX-5

Safety Checklist

Crash Test:
    Frontal . . . . Good
    Side . . . . Very Poor
Airbags:
    Torso . . . . .Std. Front Pelvis/Torso from Seat
    Roll Sensing . . . . Yes
    Knee Bolster . . . . None
Crash Avoidance:
    Collision Avoidance . . Optional CIB & DBS^
    Blind Spot Detection . . . . Optional
    Lane Keeping Assist . . . . Optional^
    Pedestrian Crash Avoidance . . . . None
General:
    Auto. Crash Notification . . . Dial Assist.-Free
    Day Running Lamps . . . . Standard
Safety Belt/Restraint:
    Dynamic Head Restraints . . . . None
    Adjustable Belt . . . . Standard Front

^Warning feature does not meet government standards.

Mazda CX-5

Specifications

Drive	FWD
Engine	2.0-liter I4
Transmission	6-sp. Automatic
Tow Rating (lbs.)	Very Low-2000
Head/Leg Room (in.)	Average-40.1/41
Interior Space (cu. ft.)	Average-103.8
Cargo Space (cu. ft.)	Very Roomy-34.1
Wheelbase/Length (in.)	106.3/178.7

Ratings—10 Best, 1 Worst

Combo Crash Tests	—
Safety Features	5
Rollover	3
Preventive Maintenance	7
Repair Costs	3
Warranty	1
Fuel Economy	3
Complaints	9
Insurance Costs	10
OVERALL RATING	**—**

Mazda CX-9

Mazda CX-9

At-a-Glance

Status/Year Series Started. Unchanged/2016
Twins . . . . —
Body Styles . . . . SUV
Seating 7
Anti-Theft Device . . . . Std. Passive Immobil. Only
Parking Index Rating . . . . Hard
Where Made. . . . . Hiroshima, Japan
Fuel Factor
  MPG Rating (city/hwy) Poor-20/26
  Driving Range (mi.) Long-424
  Fuel Type . . . . .Regular
  Annual Fuel Cost . . . . Average-$1647
  Gas Guzzler Tax . . . . .No
  Greenhouse Gas Emissions (tons/yr.)Very High-10.0
  Barrels of Oil Used per year . . . . . . Very High-18.3

How the Competition Rates

Competitors	Rating	Pg.
Infiniti QX60	5	161
Kia Sorento	6	172
Lexus RX	4	184

Price Range

Price Range	Retail	Markup
Sport FWD	$31,520	6%
Touring FWD	$35,970	6%
Grand Touring AWD	$42,270	6%
Signature AWD	$44,315	6%

Safety Checklist

Crash Test:
  Frontal. . . . . —
  Side. . . . . —
Airbags:
  Torso . . . .Std. Front Pelvis/Torso from Seat
  Roll Sensing. .Yes
  Knee Bolster . . . . .None
Crash Avoidance:
  Collision Avoidance . . Optional CIB & DBS^
  Blind Spot Detection . . . . Optional
  Lane Keeping Assist . . . . Optional^
  Pedestrian Crash Avoidance . . . . .None
General:
  Auto. Crash Notification . . .Dial Assist.-Free
  Day Running Lamps . . . . Standard
Safety Belt/Restraint:
  Dynamic Head Restraints . . . . .None
  Adjustable Belt . . . . Standard Front

^Warning feature does not meet government standards.

Mazda CX-9

Specifications

Drive. . . . . .AWD
Engine 3.7-liter I4
Transmission . . . . 6-sp. Automatic
Tow Rating (lbs.) Low-3500
Head/Leg Room (in.) Cramped-39.3/40.9
Interior Space (cu. ft.). . . . . .Very Roomy-135.1
Cargo Space (cu. ft.) Cramped-14.4
Wheelbase/Length (in.) 115.3/199.4

Ratings—10 Best, 1 Worst

Combo Crash Tests	4
Safety Features	5
Rollover	7
Preventive Maintenance	7
Repair Costs	9
Warranty	1
Fuel Economy	8
Complaints	10
Insurance Costs	3
OVERALL RATING	**6**

Mazda Mazda3

At-a-Glance

/Year Series Started	All New/2019
Twins	—
Body Styles	Sedan, Hatchback
Seating	5
Anti-Theft Device	Std. Passive Immobil. Only
Parking Index Rating	Easy
Where Made	Hofu, Japan
Fuel Factor	
MPG Rating (city/hwy)	Good-28/37
Driving Range (mi.)	Average-415
Fuel Type	Regular
Annual Fuel Cost	Very Low-$1169
Gas Guzzler Tax	No
Greenhouse Gas Emissions (tons/yr.)	Low-4.7
Barrels of Oil Used per year	Average-10.6

How the Competition Rates

Competitors	Rating	Pg.
Chevrolet Cruze	8	104
Nissan Sentra	5	205
Volkswagen Golf	4	249

Price Range

	Retail	Markup
Sport Sedan MT	$18,095	4%
Touring Sedan AT	$21,140	4%
Touring Hatchback AT	$21,890	5%
Grand Touring Hatchback AT	$24,945	5%

Mazda Mazda3

Safety Checklist

Crash Test:
- Frontal .... Poor
- Side .... Poor

Airbags:
- Torso .... Std. Front Pelvis/Torso from Seat
- Roll Sensing .... Yes
- Knee Bolster .... None

Crash Avoidance:
- Collision Avoidance .. Optional CIB & DBS^
- Blind Spot Detection .... Optional
- Lane Keeping Assist .... Optional
- Pedestrian Crash Avoidance .... None

General:
- Auto. Crash Notification ... Dial Assist.-Free
- Day Running Lamps .... Standard

Safety Belt/Restraint:
- Dynamic Head Restraints .... None
- Adjustable Belt .... Standard Front

^Warning feature does not meet government standards.

Mazda Mazda3

Specifications

Drive	FWD
Engine	2.0-liter I4
Transmission	6-sp. Automatic
Tow Rating (lbs.)	—
Head/Leg Room (in.)	Cramped-38.6/42.2
Interior Space (cu. ft.)	Cramped-96.3
Cargo Space (cu. ft.)	Very Cramped-12.4
Wheelbase/Length (in.)	106.3/180.3

Ratings—10 Best, 1 Worst

Combo Crash Tests	7
Safety Features	5
Rollover	8
Preventive Maintenance	6
Repair Costs	8
Warranty	1
Fuel Economy	8
Complaints	7
Insurance Costs	1
OVERALL RATING	**6**

Mazda Mazda6

At-a-Glance

Status/Year Series Started	Unchanged/2014
Twins	—
Body Styles	Sedan
Seating	5
Anti-Theft Device	Std. Passive Immobil. Only
Parking Index Rating	Average
Where Made	Flat Rock, MI
Fuel Factor	
MPG Rating (city/hwy)	Good-26/38
Driving Range (mi.)	Very Long-497
Fuel Type	Regular
Annual Fuel Cost	Low-$1213
Gas Guzzler Tax	No
Greenhouse Gas Emissions (tons/yr.)	Average-6.0
Barrels of Oil Used per year	Average-11.0

How the Competition Rates

Competitors	Rating	Pg.
Kia Optima	9	169
Hyundai Sonata	9	155
Toyota Camry	8	234

Price Range

	Retail	Markup
Sport MT	$21,945	5%
Sport AT	$22,995	5%
Touring AT	$25,245	6%
Grand Touring AT	$30,695	6%

Mazda Mazda6

Safety Checklist

Crash Test:
    Frontal . . . . Good
    Side . . . . Good
Airbags:
    Torso . . . . Std. Front Pelvis/Torso from Seat
    Roll Sensing . . . . Yes
    Knee Bolster . . . . None
Crash Avoidance:
    Collision Avoidance . . . Optional CIB & DBS
    Blind Spot Detection . . . . Optional
    Lane Keeping Assist . . Warn. Only Optional
    Pedestrian Crash Avoidance . . . . None
General:
    Auto. Crash Notification . . . Dial Assist.-Free
    Day Running Lamps . . . . Standard
Safety Belt/Restraint:
    Dynamic Head Restraints . . . . None
    Adjustable Belt . . . . Standard Front

^Warning feature does not meet government standards.

Mazda Mazda6

Specifications

Drive	FWD
Engine	2.5-liter I4
Transmission	6-sp. Automatic
Tow Rating (lbs.)	—
Head/Leg Room (in.)	Cramped-38.4/42.2
Interior Space (cu. ft.)	Average-99.7
Cargo Space (cu. ft.)	Cramped-14.8
Wheelbase/Length (in.)	111.4/191.5

Ratings—10 Best, 1 Worst

Combo Crash Tests	—
Safety Features	1
Rollover	10
Preventive Maintenance	6
Repair Costs	6
Warranty	1
Fuel Economy	8
Complaints	5
Insurance Costs	10
OVERALL RATING	**—**

Mazda MX-5 Miata

At-a-Glance

Status/Year Series Started	Unchanged/2016
Twins	—
Body Styles	Coupe, Convertible
Seating	2
Anti-Theft Device	Std. Passive Immobil. Only
Parking Index Rating	Very Easy
Where Made	Hiroshima, Japan
Fuel Factor	
MPG Rating (city/hwy)	Good-27/36
Driving Range (mi.)	Very Short-362
Fuel Type	Premium
Annual Fuel Cost	Average-$1464
Gas Guzzler Tax	No
Greenhouse Gas Emissions (tons/yr.)	Low-4.9
Barrels of Oil Used per year	Average-11.0

How the Competition Rates

Competitors	Rating	Pg.
Buick Cascada		88
Toyota 86		232

Price Range

	Retail	Markup
Sport MT	$24,915	6%
Club AT	$29,530	6%
Grand Touring AT	$31,270	6%
Launch Edition AT	$34,925	6%

Mazda MX-5 Miata

Safety Checklist

Crash Test:
- Frontal . . . . —
- Side . . . . —

Airbags:
- Torso . . . . Std. Front Pelvis/Torso from Seat
- Roll Sensing . . . . No
- Knee Bolster . . . . None

Crash Avoidance:
- Collision Avoidance . . . . None
- Blind Spot Detection . . . . Optional
- Lane Keeping Assist . . Warn. Only Optional
- Pedestrian Crash Avoidance . . . . None

General:
- Auto. Crash Notification . . . . None
- Day Running Lamps . . . . Standard

Safety Belt/Restraint:
- Dynamic Head Restraints . . . . None
- Adjustable Belt . . . . None

^Warning feature does not meet government standards.

Mazda MX-5 Miata

Specifications

Drive	RWD
Engine	2.0-liter I4
Transmission	6-sp. Manual
Tow Rating (lbs.)	—
Head/Leg Room (in.)	Cramped-37.4/43.1
Interior Space (cu. ft.)	—
Cargo Space (cu. ft.)	Very Cramped-4.6
Wheelbase/Length (in.)	90.9/154.1

Ratings—10 Best, 1 Worst	
Combo Crash Tests	3
Safety Features	9
Rollover	7
Preventive Maintenance	1
Repair Costs	3
Warranty	3
Fuel Economy	5
Complaints	5
Insurance Costs	3
OVERALL RATING	**1**

Mercedes-Benz C-Class

Mercedes-Benz C-Class

At-a-Glance

Status/Year Series Started. . Apperance Change/2015
Twins . . . . —
Body Styles . . . . .Sedan, Coupe, Wagon
Seating 5
Anti-Theft Device . Std. Active Immobil. & Pass. Alarm
Parking Index Rating . . . . Average
Where Made. Tuscaloosa, AL
Fuel Factor
  MPG Rating (city/hwy) Average-22/30
  Driving Range (mi.) Long-450
  Fuel Type . . . . Premium
  Annual Fuel Cost . . . . High-$1782
  Gas Guzzler Tax . . . . .No
  Greenhouse Gas Emissions (tons/yr.) . . Average-7.2
  Barrels of Oil Used per year High-13.2

How the Competition Rates

Competitors	Rating	Pg.
Audi A3	5	72
Cadillac ATS	4	94
Lexus IS	8	181

Price Range

	Retail	Markup
C300 Sedan	$39,500	8%
C300 Coupe	$42,650	8%
C300 Coupe 4Matic	$44,650	8%
AMG C63 Coupe	$67,000	8%

Safety Checklist

Crash Test:
  Frontal . . . . .Average
  Side. . . . . Very Poor
Airbags:
  Torso Std. Fr. & Opt. Rr. Pelvis/Torso from Seat
  Roll Sensing. . . . . .No
  Knee Bolster . . . . .Standard Driver
Crash Avoidance:
  Collision Avoidance . . Standard CIB & DBS
  Blind Spot Detection . . . . Optional
  Lane Keeping Assist . . . . Optional
  Pedestrian Crash Avoidance . . . . . Optional
General:
  Auto. Crash Notif. . . Op. Assist. & Crash Info-Fee
  Day Running Lamps . . . . .None
Safety Belt/Restraint:
  Dynamic Head Restraints . . . . . . Std. Front
  Adjustable Belt. . . . . Standard Front

^Warning feature does not meet government standards.

Mercedes-Benz C-Class

Specifications

Drive. . . . . .RWD
Engine 2.0-liter I4
Transmission . . . . 9-sp. Automatic
Tow Rating (lbs.) . . . . —
Head/Leg Room (in.) . . . . Very Cramped-37.1/41.7
Interior Space (cu. ft.). . . . . .Very Cramped-81
Cargo Space (cu. ft.) . . . . Very Cramped-12.8
Wheelbase/Length (in.) 111.8/184.5

Mercedes-Benz CLA

Compact

Mercedes-Benz CLA-Class

Ratings—10 Best, 1 Worst

Combo Crash Tests	—
Safety Features	8
Rollover	6
Preventive Maintenance	1
Repair Costs	3
Warranty	3
Fuel Economy	7
Complaints	1
Insurance Costs	1
OVERALL RATING	**—**

Mercedes-Benz CLA-Class

At-a-Glance

Status/Year Series Started Unchanged/2014
Twins . . . . —
Body Styles . . . . .Coupe
Seating 5
Anti-Theft Device . Std. Active Immobil. & Pass. Alarm
Parking Index Rating . . . . Easy
Where Made. . . . . Kecskemet, Hungary
Fuel Factor
  MPG Rating (city/hwy) Good-24/37
  Driving Range (mi.) Short-376
  Fuel Type. . . . . .Premium
  Annual Fuel Cost . . . . .Average-$1563
  Gas Guzzler Tax . . . . .No
  Greenhouse Gas Emissions (tons/yr.). Low-5.1
  Barrels of Oil Used per year Average-11.4

How the Competition Rates

Competitors	Rating	Pg.
Audi A4	2	72
Cadillac ATS	4	97
Infiniti Q50	3	158

Price Range

	Retail	Markup
Coupe 4Matic	$3,440	—89%
Coupe	$32,400	8%
AMG 4Matic	$49,950	8%
		—

Safety Checklist

Crash Test:
  Frontal. . . . . —
  Side. . . . . —
Airbags:
  Torso Std. Fr. & Opt. Rr. Pelvis/Torso from Seat
  Roll Sensing. . . . . .Yes
  Knee Bolster . . . . Standard Front
Crash Avoidance:
  Collision Avoidance . . Standard CIB & DBS
  Blind Spot Detection . . . . Optional
  Lane Keeping Assist . .Warn. Only Optional
  Pedestrian Crash Avoidance . . . . .None
General:
  Auto. Crash Notif.. . Op. Assist. & Crash Info-Fee
  Day Running Lamps . . . . .None
Safety Belt/Restraint:
  Dynamic Head Restraints . . . . None
  Adjustable Belt. . . . . Standard Front

^Warning feature does not meet government standards.

Mercedes-Benz CLA-Class

Specifications

Drive. . . . . .FWD
Engine 2.0-liter I4
Transmission . . . . 7-sp. Automatic
Tow Rating (lbs.) . . . . —
Head/Leg Room (in.) . . . . Very Cramped-38.2/40.2
Interior Space (cu. ft.). . . . . .Very Cramped-88
Cargo Space (cu. ft.) . . . . .Very Cramped-13
Wheelbase/Length (in.) 106.3/182.3

Ratings—10 Best, 1 Worst

Combo Crash Tests	5
Safety Features	10
Rollover	8
Preventive Maintenance	3
Repair Costs	1
Warranty	3
Fuel Economy	5
Complaints	5
Insurance Costs	5
OVERALL RATING	**3**

Mercedes-Benz E-Class

Mercedes-Benz E-Class

At-a-Glance

Status/Year Series Started Unchanged/2017
Twins . . . . —
Body Styles . . . . Sedan
Seating 5
Anti-Theft Device . Std. Active Immobil. & Pass. Alarm
Parking Index Rating . . . . Average
Where Made . . . . Sindelfingen, Germany
Fuel Factor
  MPG Rating (city/hwy) Average-22/30
  Driving Range (mi.) Long-435
  Fuel Type . . . . Premium
  Annual Fuel Cost . . . . High-$1782
  Gas Guzzler Tax . . . . No
  Greenhouse Gas Emissions (tons/yr.) Low-5.8
  Barrels of Oil Used per year High-13.2

How the Competition Rates

Competitors	Rating	Pg.
Buick LaCrosse	5	92
Lincoln Continental	6	185
Tesla Model S	10	229

Price Range

	Retail	Markup
E300 Sedan	$52,150	8%
E400 Coupe	$54,550	8%
E400 Cabriolet	$62,600	8%
E550 Cabriolet	$69,100	8%

Safety Checklist

Crash Test:
  Frontal . . . . Poor
  Side . . . . Good
Airbags:
  Torso Std. Fr. & Opt. Rr. Pelvis/Torso from Seat
  Roll Sensing . . . . Yes
  Knee Bolster . . . . Standard Driver
Crash Avoidance:
  Collision Avoidance . . Standard CIB & DBS
  Blind Spot Detection . . . . Optional
  Lane Keeping Assist . . . . Optional
  Pedestrian Crash Avoidance . . . . . Optional
General:
  Auto. Crash Notif. . . Op. Assist. & Crash Info-Fee
  Day Running Lamps . . . . None
Safety Belt/Restraint:
  Dynamic Head Restraints . . . . . . Std. Front
  Adjustable Belt . . . . Standard Front

^Warning feature does not meet government standards.

Mercedes-Benz E-Class

Specifications

Drive . . . . RWD
Engine 2.0-liter V6
Transmission . . . . 9-sp. Automatic
Tow Rating (lbs.) . . . . —
Head/Leg Room (in.) . . . . Very Cramped-37.9/41.3
Interior Space (cu. ft.) Average-98
Cargo Space (cu. ft.) . . . . Very Cramped-13.1
Wheelbase/Length (in.) 115.7/193.8

Ratings—10 Best, 1 Worst

Combo Crash Tests	—
Safety Features	8
Rollover	5
Preventive Maintenance	10
Repair Costs	2
Warranty	3
Fuel Economy	6
Complaints	6
Insurance Costs	10
OVERALL RATING	**—**

Mercedes-Benz GLA-Class

Mercedes-Benz GLA-Class

At-a-Glance

Status/Year Series Started Unchanged/2015
Twins . . . . —
Body Styles . . . . SUV
Seating 5
Anti-Theft Device . Std. Active Immobil. & Pass. Alarm
Parking Index Rating . . . . Average
Where Made . . . . Rastatt, Germany
Fuel Factor
  MPG Rating (city/hwy) Average-23/31
  Driving Range (mi.) Short-385
  Fuel Type . . . . Premium
  Annual Fuel Cost . . . . High-$1712
  Gas Guzzler Tax . . . . No
  Greenhouse Gas Emissions (tons/yr.) Low-5.6
  Barrels of Oil Used per year Average-12.7

How the Competition Rates

Competitors	Rating	Pg.
Acura RDX	9	68
Lexus NX	5	182
Lincoln MKC	6	186

Price Range

	Retail	Markup
GLA250	$32,850	8%
GLA250 4Matic	$34,850	8%
AMG GLA45 4Matic	$49,900	8%
		—

Safety Checklist

Crash Test:
  Frontal . . . . —
  Side . . . . —
Airbags:
  Torso Std. Fr. & Opt. Rr. Pelvis/Torso from Seat
  Roll Sensing . . . . Yes
  Knee Bolster . . . . Standard Front
Crash Avoidance:
  Collision Avoidance . . Standard CIB & DBS
  Blind Spot Detection . . . . Optional
  Lane Keeping Assist . . Warn. Only Optional
  Pedestrian Crash Avoidance . . . . None
General:
  Auto. Crash Notif . . . Op. Assist. & Crash Info-Fee
  Day Running Lamps . . . . None
Safety Belt/Restraint:
  Dynamic Head Restraints . . . . None
  Adjustable Belt . . . . None

^Warning feature does not meet government standards.

Mercedes-Benz GLA-Class

Specifications

Drive . . . . AWD
Engine 2.0-liter I4
Transmission . . . . 7-sp. Automatic
Tow Rating (lbs.) . . . . —
Head/Leg Room (in.) Cramped-38.3/41.9
Interior Space (cu. ft.) Cramped-91
Cargo Space (cu. ft.) Average-17.2
Wheelbase/Length (in.) 106.3/173.9

Ratings—10 Best, 1 Worst

Combo Crash Tests	—
Safety Features	10
Rollover	—
Preventive Maintenance	3
Repair Costs	2
Warranty	3
Fuel Economy	4
Complaints	1
Insurance Costs	10
OVERALL RATING	**—**

Mercedes-Benz GLC-Class

Mercedes-Benz GLC-Class

At-a-Glance

Status/Year Series Started	Unchanged/2016
Twins	—
Body Styles	SUV
Seating	5
Anti-Theft Device	Std. Active Immobil. & Pass. Alarm
Parking Index Rating	Average
Where Made	Tuscaloosa, AL
Fuel Factor	
MPG Rating (city/hwy)	Poor-21/28
Driving Range (mi.)	Average-412
Fuel Type	Premium
Annual Fuel Cost	High-$1883
Gas Guzzler Tax	No
Greenhouse Gas Emissions (tons/yr.)	High-8.6
Barrels of Oil Used per year	High-13.7

How the Competition Rates

Competitors	Rating	Pg.
Acura RDX	9	69
Audi Q7	3	77
Volkswagen Atlas	6	248

Price Range	Retail	Markup
GLC300	$39,150	8%
GLC300 4Matic	$41,150	8%
AMG GLC43	$54,900	8%
		—

Safety Checklist

Crash Test:
- Frontal . . . . —
- Side . . . . —

Airbags:
- Torso Std. Fr. & Opt. Rr. Pelvis/Torso from Seat
- Roll Sensing . . . . Yes
- Knee Bolster . . . . Standard Driver

Crash Avoidance:
- Collision Avoidance . . Standard CIB & DBS
- Blind Spot Detection . . . . Optional
- Lane Keeping Assist . . . . Optional
- Pedestrian Crash Avoidance . . . . . Optional

General:
- Auto. Crash Notif . . . Op. Assist. & Crash Info-Fee
- Day Running Lamps . . . . None

Safety Belt/Restraint:
- Dynamic Head Restraints . . . . . . Std. Front
- Adjustable Belt . . . . Standard Front

^Warning feature does not meet government standards.

Mercedes-Benz GLC-Class

Specifications

Drive	4WD
Engine	2.0-liter I4
Transmission	9-sp. Automatic
Tow Rating (lbs.)	Low-3500
Head/Leg Room (in.)	Very Cramped-37.8/40.8
Interior Space (cu. ft.)	Very Cramped-79.5
Cargo Space (cu. ft.)	Cramped-16.5
Wheelbase/Length (in.)	113.1/183.3

Ratings—10 Best, 1 Worst

Combo Crash Tests	—
Safety Features	9
Rollover	2
Preventive Maintenance	3
Repair Costs	2
Warranty	3
Fuel Economy	2
Complaints	6
Insurance Costs	8
OVERALL RATING	**—**

Mercedes-Benz GLE-Class

Mercedes-Benz GLE-Class

At-a-Glance

Status/Year Series Started	Unchanged/2012
Twins	—
Body Styles	SUV
Seating	5
Anti-Theft Device	Std. Active Immobil. & Pass. Alarm
Parking Index Rating	Hard
Where Made	Bremen, Germany

Fuel Factor

MPG Rating (city/hwy)	Very Poor-18/23
Driving Range (mi.)	Very Long-491
Fuel Type	Premium
Annual Fuel Cost	Very High-$2233
Gas Guzzler Tax	No
Greenhouse Gas Emissions (tons/yr.)	High-7.3
Barrels of Oil Used per year	High-16.5

How the Competition Rates

Competitors	Rating	Pg.
Buick Encore	10	90
Lexus NX	5	182
Lincoln MKC	6	186

Price Range	Retail	Markup
GLS350	$67,050	8%
GLS450	$68,700	8%
GLS550	$93,850	8%
GLS63 AMG	$124,100	8%

Safety Checklist

Crash Test:
- Frontal . . . . —
- Side . . . . —

Airbags:
- Torso Std. Fr. & Opt. Rr. Pelvis/Torso from Seat
- Roll Sensing . . . . Yes
- Knee Bolster . . . . Standard Driver

Crash Avoidance:
- Collision Avoidance . . Std. CIB & Opt. DBS
- Blind Spot Detection . . . . Optional
- Lane Keeping Assist . . . . Optional
- Pedestrian Crash Avoidance . . . . . Optional

General:
- Auto. Crash Notif. . . Op. Assist. & Crash Info-Fee
- Day Running Lamps . . . . None

Safety Belt/Restraint:
- Dynamic Head Restraints . . . . None
- Adjustable Belt . . . . Standard Front

^Warning feature does not meet government standards.

Mercedes-Benz GLE-Class

Specifications

Drive	RWD
Engine	3.5-liter V6
Transmission	7-sp. Automatic
Tow Rating (lbs.)	Average-6600
Head/Leg Room (in.)	Very Cramped-38.9/40.3
Interior Space (cu. ft.)	—
Cargo Space (cu. ft.)	Very Roomy-38.2
Wheelbase/Length (in.)	114.8/189.1

Ratings—10 Best, 1 Worst

Combo Crash Tests	—
Safety Features	9
Rollover	2
Preventive Maintenance	3
Repair Costs	2
Warranty	3
Fuel Economy	2
Complaints	7
Insurance Costs	10

OVERALL RATING — —

Mercedes-Benz GLS-Class

Mercedes-Benz GLS-Class

At-a-Glance

Status/Year Series Started........ Unchanged/2016
Twins . . . . —
Body Styles . . . . SUV
Seating 5
Anti-Theft Device . Std. Active Immobil. & Pass. Alarm
Parking Index Rating . . . . Very Hard
Where Made. Tuscaloosa, AL
Fuel Factor
  MPG Rating (city/hwy) . . . . Very Poor-17/22
  Driving Range (mi.) . . . . Very Long-500
  Fuel Type . . . . Premium
  Annual Fuel Cost . . . . Very High-$2353
  Gas Guzzler Tax . . . . No
  Greenhouse Gas Emissions (tons/yr.) Low-5.1
  Barrels of Oil Used per year . . . . Very Low-0.0

How the Competition Rates

Competitors	Rating	Pg.
Buick Enclave	4	89
Chevrolet Suburban	2	111
Volvo XC90	8	256

Price Range	Retail	Markup
GLE300d 4Matic	$53,400	8%
GLE350 4Matic	$54,500	8%
GLE550e 4Matic	$66,300	8%
GLE63 AMG 4Matic	$101,690	8%

Safety Checklist

Crash Test:
  Frontal . . . . —
  Side. . . . . —
Airbags:
  Torso Std. Fr. & Opt. Rr. Pelvis/Torso from Seat
  Roll Sensing. . . . . Yes
  Knee Bolster . . . . Standard Driver
Crash Avoidance:
  Collision Avoidance . . Standard CIB & DBS
  Blind Spot Detection . . . . Optional
  Lane Keeping Assist . . . . Optional
  Pedestrian Crash Avoidance . . . . . Optional
General:
  Auto. Crash Notif. . . Op. Assist. & Crash Info-Fee
  Day Running Lamps . . . . .None
Safety Belt/Restraint:
  Dynamic Head Restraints . . . . .None
  Adjustable Belt . . . . Standard Front

^Warning feature does not meet government standards.

Mercedes-Benz GLS-Class

Specifications

Drive. 4WD
Engine 3.0-liter V6
Transmission . . . . 9-sp. Automatic
Tow Rating (lbs.) High-7500
Head/Leg Room (in.) Average-41.2/40.3
Interior Space (cu. ft.). . . . . —
Cargo Space (cu. ft.) Cramped-16
Wheelbase/Length (in.) 121.1/201.6

Mercedes-Benz S   Large

Mercedes-Benz S-Class

Ratings—10 Best, 1 Worst

Combo Crash Tests	—
Safety Features	10
Rollover	7
Preventive Maintenance	3
Repair Costs	1
Warranty	3
Fuel Economy	3
Complaints	7
Insurance Costs	1
OVERALL RATING	**—**

Mercedes-Benz S-Class

At-a-Glance

Status/Year Series Started. Unchanged/2014
Twins . . . . —
Body Styles . . . . Sedan, Coupe
Seating 5
Anti-Theft Device . Std. Active Immobil. & Pass. Alarm
Parking Index Rating . . . . .Very Hard
Where Made. . . . . .Sindelfingen, Germany
Fuel Factor
  MPG Rating (city/hwy). Poor-19/28
  Driving Range (mi.) . . . . Very Long-511
  Fuel Type. . . . . .Premium
  Annual Fuel Cost . . . . Very High-$2006
  Gas Guzzler Tax . . . . .No
  Greenhouse Gas Emissions (tons/yr.) Low-5.7
  Barrels of Oil Used per year High-15.0

How the Competition Rates

Competitors	Rating	Pg.
Cadillac XTS	8	99
Lincoln Continental	6	185
Tesla Model S	10	229

Price Range

	Retail	Markup
S450	$89,900	8%
S560	$99,900	8%
S560 4Matic	$102,900	8%
S63 AMG	$147,500	8%

Safety Checklist

Crash Test:
  Frontal . . . . —
  Side. . . . . —
Airbags:
  Torso Std. Fr. & Opt. Rr. Pelvis/Torso from Seat
  Roll Sensing. . . . . .Yes
  Knee Bolster . . . . .Standard Front
Crash Avoidance:
  Collision Avoidance . . Standard CIB & DBS
  Blind Spot Detection . . . . Optional
  Lane Keeping Assist . . . . Optional
  Pedestrian Crash Avoidance . . . . . Optional
General:
  Auto. Crash Notif. . . Op. Assist. & Crash Info-Fee
  Day Running Lamps . . . . .None
Safety Belt/Restraint:
  Dynamic Head Restraints . . . . . . Std. Front
  Adjustable Belt. . . . . .Standard Front

^Warning feature does not meet government standards.

Mercedes-Benz S-Class

Specifications

Drive. . . . . .RWD
Engine 3.0-liter V6
Transmission . . . . 9-sp. Automatic
Tow Rating (lbs.) . . . . —
Head/Leg Room (in.) Average-39.7/41.4
Interior Space (cu. ft.). Roomy-112
Cargo Space (cu. ft.) Cramped-16.3
Wheelbase/Length (in.) 124.6/206.5

Ratings—10 Best, 1 Worst

Combo Crash Tests	—
Safety Features	4
Rollover	7
Preventive Maintenance	5
Repair Costs	6
Warranty	9
Fuel Economy	6
Complaints	9
Insurance Costs	5
OVERALL RATING	**—**

Mini Countryman

Mini Countryman

At-a-Glance

```
Status/Year Series Started. . . . . . . . Unchanged/2017
Twins . . . . . . . . . . . . . . . . . . . . . . . . . . . . . . . . —
Body Styles . . . . . . . . . . . . . . . . . . . . . . . Hatchback
Seating . . . . . . . . . . . . . . . . . . . . . . . . . . . . . . . . 5
Anti-Theft Device . Std. Pass. Immobil. & Active Alarm
Parking Index Rating . . . . . . . . . . . . . . . . .Very Easy
Where Made. . . . . . . . . . . . . . . . . . . Oxford, England
Fuel Factor
  MPG Rating (city/hwy) . . . . . . . . . . . Average-24/32
  Driving Range (mi.) . . . . . . . . . . . . . . . . Long-435
  Fuel Type. . . . . . . . . . . . . . . . . . . . . . . . . Premium
  Annual Fuel Cost . . . . . . . . . . . . . . . Average-$1647
  Gas Guzzler Tax . . . . . . . . . . . . . . . . . . . . . . . . No
  Greenhouse Gas Emissions (tons/yr.) . . . . . Low-5.3
  Barrels of Oil Used per year . . . . . . . Average-12.2
```

How the Competition Rates

Competitors	Rating	Pg.
Chevrolet Cruze	8	104
Kia Soul	7	173
Toyota Yaris	6	246

Price Range	Retail	Markup
Base	$26,100	8%
ALL4	$28,100	8%
S	$29,100	8%
S ALL4	$31,100	8%

Safety Checklist

```
Crash Test:
  Frontal . . . . . . . . . . . . . . . . . . . . . . . . . . —
  Side. . . . . . . . . . . . . . . . . . . . . . . . . . . . . —
Airbags:
  Torso . . . . . . . . Std. Front Torso from Seat
  Roll Sensing. . . . . . . . . . . . . . . . . . . . . .Yes
  Knee Bolster . . . . . . . . . . . Standard Front
Crash Avoidance:
  Collision Avoidance . . Optional CIB & DBS^
  Blind Spot Detection . . . . . . . . . . . . .None
  Lane Keeping Assist . . . . . . . . . . . . .None
  Pedestrian Crash Avoidance . . . . . . . .None
General:
  Auto. Crash Notif. . . Op. Assist. & Crash Info-Fee
  Day Running Lamps . . . . . . . . . . .Standard
Safety Belt/Restraint:
  Dynamic Head Restraints . . . . . . . . . .None
  Adjustable Belt. . . . . . . . . . . . . . . . . .None
```

^Warning feature does not meet government standards.

Mini Countryman

Specifications

```
Drive. . . . . . . . . . . . . . . . . . . . . . . . . . . . . . . . .FWD
Engine . . . . . . . . . . . . . . . . . . . . . . . . . 1.5-liter I3
Transmission . . . . . . . . . . . . . . . . 6-sp. Automatic
Tow Rating (lbs.) . . . . . . . . . . . . . . . . . . . . . . . . —
Head/Leg Room (in.) . . . . . . . . . . Cramped-39.9/40.4
Interior Space (cu. ft.). . . . . . . . . . . . . . .Average-97
Cargo Space (cu. ft.) . . . . . . . . . . . . . Average-17.6
Wheelbase/Length (in.) . . . . . . . . . . . 105.1/169.8
```

Ratings—10 Best, 1 Worst

Combo Crash Tests	4
Safety Features	4
Rollover	7
Preventive Maintenance	5
Repair Costs	4
Warranty	9
Fuel Economy	8
Complaints	7
Insurance Costs	5
OVERALL RATING	**6**

Mini Hardtop

Mini Hardtop

At-a-Glance

Status/Year Series Started. . Apperance Change/2016
Twins . . . . —
Body Styles . . . . .Sedan
Seating 4
Anti-Theft Device . Std. Pass. Immobil. & Active Alarm
Parking Index Rating . . . . .Very Easy
Where Made. . . . . Oxford, England
Fuel Factor
  MPG Rating (city/hwy) Good-27/35
  Driving Range (mi.) . . . . Very Short-349
  Fuel Type. . . . . .Premium
  Annual Fuel Cost . . . . .Average-$1480
  Gas Guzzler Tax . . . . .No
  Greenhouse Gas Emissions (tons/yr.) Low-4.9
  Barrels of Oil Used per year Average-11.0

How the Competition Rates

Competitors	Rating	Pg.
Chevrolet Sonic	8	109
Honda Fit	9	146
Toyota Yaris Liftback	5	247

Price Range

	Retail	Markup
Base Hatchback	$20,950	5%
S Hatchback	$25,400	9%
S Convertible	$29,600	9%
John Cooper Works Hatchback	$30,900	12%

Safety Checklist

Crash Test:
  Frontal. . . . . Average
  Side. . . . . Very Poor
Airbags:
  Torso . . . . Std. Front Torso from Seat
  Roll Sensing. .Yes
  Knee Bolster . . . . Standard Front
Crash Avoidance:
  Collision Avoidance . . Optional CIB & DBS^
  Blind Spot Detection . . . . .None
  Lane Keeping Assist . . . . .None
  Pedestrian Crash Avoidance . . . . . . .None
General:
  Auto. Crash Notif. . . Op. Assist. & Crash Info-Fee
  Day Running Lamps . . . . .Standard
Safety Belt/Restraint:
  Dynamic Head Restraints . . . . .None
  Adjustable Belt. . . . . .None

^Warning feature does not meet government standards.

Mini Hardtop

Specifications

Drive. . . . . .FWD
Engine 1.5-liter I3
Transmission . . . . 6-sp. Automatic
Tow Rating (lbs.) . . . . —
Head/Leg Room (in.) Average-39.9/41.4
Interior Space (cu. ft.). . . . . .Very Cramped-84
Cargo Space (cu. ft.) . . . . Very Cramped-9
Wheelbase/Length (in.) 101.1/157.4

Mitsubishi Mirage   Subcompact

Ratings—10 Best, 1 Worst

Combo Crash Tests	2
Safety Features	1
Rollover	4
Preventive Maintenance	8
Repair Costs	7
Warranty	10
Fuel Economy	9
Complaints	4
Insurance Costs	1
OVERALL RATING	**3**

Mitsubishi Mirage

Mitsubishi Mirage

At-a-Glance

Status/Year Series Started........ Unchanged/2014
Twins .... —
Body Styles .... Hatchback
Seating 5
Anti-Theft Device . Std. Pass. Immobil. & Active Alarm
Parking Index Rating .... Very Easy
Where Made............... Laem Chabang, Thailand
Fuel Factor
  MPG Rating (city/hwy) .... Very Good-37/43
  Driving Range (mi.) .... Very Short-363
  Fuel Type........................... Regular
  Annual Fuel Cost .... Very Low-$931
  Gas Guzzler Tax .... No
  Greenhouse Gas Emissions (tons/yr.). Very Low-3.7
  Barrels of Oil Used per year Low-8.5

How the Competition Rates

Competitors	Rating	Pg.
Ford Fiesta	2	130
Nissan Versa	1	207
Toyota Yaris Liftback	5	247

Price Range	Retail	Markup
ES MT	$13,395	2%
ES AT	$14,595	2%
SE AT	$16,095	2%
GT AT	$16,595	2%

Safety Checklist

Crash Test:
  Frontal......................... Poor
  Side......................... Very Poor
Airbags:
  Torso . . . Std. Front Pelvis/Torso from Seat
  Roll Sensing....................... Yes
  Knee Bolster .... Standard Driver
Crash Avoidance:
  Collision Avoidance .... None
  Blind Spot Detection .... None
  Lane Keeping Assist .... None
  Pedestrian Crash Avoidance .... None
General:
  Auto. Crash Notification........... None
  Day Running Lamps .... None
Safety Belt/Restraint:
  Dynamic Head Restraints .... None
  Adjustable Belt.......... Standard Front

^Warning feature does not meet government standards.

Mitsubishi Mirage

Specifications

Drive....................................... FWD
Engine 1.2-liter I3
Transmission .... CVT
Tow Rating (lbs.) .... —
Head/Leg Room (in.) Cramped-39.1/41.7
Interior Space (cu. ft.)....... Very Cramped-86.1
Cargo Space (cu. ft.) Average-17.2
Wheelbase/Length (in.) 96.5/148.8

Ratings—10 Best, 1 Worst

Combo Crash Tests	5
Safety Features	5
Rollover	4
Preventive Maintenance	4
Repair Costs	8
Warranty	10
Fuel Economy	6
Complaints	3
Insurance Costs	1
OVERALL RATING	**4**

Mitsubishi Outlander

Mitsubishi Outlander

At-a-Glance

Status/Year Series Started	Unchanged/2014
Twins	—
Body Styles	SUV
Seating	7
Anti-Theft Device	Std. Pass. Immobil. & Active Alarm
Parking Index Rating	Easy
Where Made	Okazaki, Japan
Fuel Factor	
MPG Rating (city/hwy)	Average-24/29
Driving Range (mi.)	Average-411
Fuel Type	Regular
Annual Fuel Cost	Low-$1412
Gas Guzzler Tax	No
Greenhouse Gas Emissions (tons/yr.)	Low-5.6
Barrels of Oil Used per year	Average-12.7

How the Competition Rates

Competitors	Rating	Pg.
Ford Edge	9	125
Kia Sorento	6	172
Nissan Rogue	3	216

Price Range

	Retail	Markup
ES FWD	$23,495	3%
SE FWD	$24,495	3%
SEL AWD	$27,495	3%
GT AWD	$31,695	3%

Safety Checklist

Crash Test:
- Frontal . . . . Average
- Side . . . . Poor

Airbags:
- Torso . . . Std. Front Pelvis/Torso from Seat
- Roll Sensing . . . . Yes
- Knee Bolster . . . . Standard Driver

Crash Avoidance:
- Collision Avoidance . . . Optional CIB & DBS
- Blind Spot Detection . . . . Optional
- Lane Keeping Assist . . Warn. Only Optional
- Pedestrian Crash Avoidance . . . . . Optional

General:
- Auto. Crash Notification . . . . None
- Day Running Lamps . . . . Standard

Safety Belt/Restraint:
- Dynamic Head Restraints . . . . None
- Adjustable Belt . . . . Standard Front

^Warning feature does not meet government standards.

Mitsubishi Outlander

Specifications

Drive	4WD
Engine	2.4-liter I4
Transmission	CVT
Tow Rating (lbs.)	Very Low-1500
Head/Leg Room (in.)	Average-40.6/40.9
Interior Space (cu. ft.)	Very Roomy-128.2
Cargo Space (cu. ft.)	Very Cramped-10.3
Wheelbase/Length (in.)	105.1/183.3

Ratings—10 Best, 1 Worst

Combo Crash Tests	4
Safety Features	2
Rollover	2
Preventive Maintenance	7
Repair Costs	5
Warranty	10
Fuel Economy	5
Complaints	7
Insurance Costs	1
OVERALL RATING	**3**

Mitsubishi Outlander Sport

Mitsubishi Outlander Sport

At-a-Glance

Status/Year Series Started Unchanged/2013
Twins . . . . —
Body Styles . . . . SUV
Seating 5
Anti-Theft Device . Std. Pass. Immobil. & Active Alarm
Parking Index Rating . . . . Very Easy
Where Made. . . . . Okazaki, Japan
Fuel Factor
  MPG Rating (city/hwy) Average-23/29
  Driving Range (mi.) Short-388
  Fuel Type . . . . .Regular
  Annual Fuel Cost . . . . Low-$1449
  Gas Guzzler Tax . . . . .No
  Greenhouse Gas Emissions (tons/yr.) Low-5.8
  Barrels of Oil Used per year High-13.2

How the Competition Rates

Competitors	Rating	Pg.
Acura RDX	9	68
GMC Terrain	5	141
Jeep Cherokee	5	163

Price Range	Retail	Markup
ES 2.0L FWD MT	$19,795	3%
ES 2.0L AWD AT	$22,495	3%
SEL 2.4L FWD AT	$24,195	3%
GT 2.4L 4WD	$27,695	3%

Safety Checklist

Crash Test:
  Frontal. . . . . Average
  Side. . . . . Poor
Airbags:
  Torso . . . Std. Front Pelvis/Torso from Seat
  Roll Sensing. .Yes
  Knee Bolster . . . . Standard Driver
Crash Avoidance:
  Collision Avoidance . . . . .None
  Blind Spot Detection . . . . .None
  Lane Keeping Assist . . . . .None
  Pedestrian Crash Avoidance . . . . . Optional
General:
  Auto. Crash Notification . . . . .None
  Day Running Lamps . . . . Optional
Safety Belt/Restraint:
  Dynamic Head Restraints . . . . .None
  Adjustable Belt . . . . Standard Front

^Warning feature does not meet government standards.

Mitsubishi Outlander Sport

Specifications

Drive. . . . . .FWD
Engine 2.0-liter I4
Transmission . . . . CVT
Tow Rating (lbs.) . . . . —
Head/Leg Room (in.) Average-39.4/41.6
Interior Space (cu. ft.). Average-97.5
Cargo Space (cu. ft.) Roomy-21.7
Wheelbase/Length (in.) 105.1/169.1

Ratings—10 Best, 1 Worst	
Combo Crash Tests	—
Safety Features	3
Rollover	8
Preventive Maintenance	4
Repair Costs	9
Warranty	1
Fuel Economy	8
Complaints	—
Insurance Costs	1
OVERALL RATING	**—**

Nissan Altima

Nissan Altima

At-a-Glance

Status/Year Series Started	All New/2019
Twins	—
Body Styles	Sedan, Coupe
Seating	5
Anti-Theft Device	Std. Pass. Immobil. & Alarm
Parking Index Rating	Average
Where Made	Smyrna, TN / Canton, MS
Fuel Factor	
MPG Rating (city/hwy)	Good-28/39
Driving Range (mi.)	Very Long-518
Fuel Type	Regular
Annual Fuel Cost	Very Low-$1146
Gas Guzzler Tax	No
Greenhouse Gas Emissions (tons/yr.)	Very Low-4.6
Barrels of Oil Used per year	Low-10.3

How the Competition Rates

Competitors	Rating	Pg.
Chevrolet Malibu	9	107
Ford Fusion	4	132
Kia Optima	9	169

Price Range	Retail	Markup
S 2.5L	$23,750	7%
SV 2.5L	$27,930	7%
SR 2.5L	$26,450	7%
Platinum 2.0L AWD	$33,130	7%

Safety Checklist

Crash Test:
  Frontal .... —
  Side .... —
Airbags:
  Torso ... Std. Front Pelvis/Torso from Seat
  Roll Sensing .... Yes
  Knee Bolster .... None
Crash Avoidance:
  Collision Avoidance .. Standard CIB & DBS
  Blind Spot Detection .... Optional
  Lane Keeping Assist .... Optional
  Pedestrian Crash Avoidance .... None
General:
  Auto. Crash Notification Operat. Assist.-Fee
  Day Running Lamps .... Optional
Safety Belt/Restraint:
  Dynamic Head Restraints .... None
  Adjustable Belt .... Standard Front

^Warning feature does not meet government standards.

Nissan Altima

Specifications

Drive	FWD
Engine	2.5-liter I4
Transmission	CVT
Tow Rating (lbs.)	—
Head/Leg Room (in.)	Very Roomy-39.2/43.8
Interior Space (cu. ft.)	Average-100.8
Cargo Space (cu. ft.)	Cramped-15.4
Wheelbase/Length (in.)	111.2/192.9

Nissan Armada

Ratings—10 Best, 1 Worst

Combo Crash Tests	—
Safety Features	7
Rollover	2
Preventive Maintenance	3
Repair Costs	5
Warranty	1
Fuel Economy	1
Complaints	7
Insurance Costs	10

OVERALL RATING   —

Nissan Armada

At-a-Glance

```
Status/Year Series Started........ Unchanged/2017
Twins .......................................... —
Body Styles ............................... SUV
Seating.................................... 7/8
Anti-Theft Device ...... Std. Pass. Immobil. & Alarm
Parking Index Rating ................ Very Hard
Where Made....................... Canton, MS
Fuel Factor
  MPG Rating (city/hwy) .......... Very Poor-14/19
  Driving Range (mi.) .............. Average-413
  Fuel Type...................... Regular
  Annual Fuel Cost ............. Very High-$2314
  Gas Guzzler Tax ...................... No
  Greenhouse Gas Emissions (tons/yr.)  Very High-9.2
  Barrels of Oil Used per year ...... Very High-20.6
```

How the Competition Rates

Competitors	Rating	Pg.
Buick Enclave	4	89
Chevrolet Suburban	2	111
Volvo XC90	8	256

Price Range

	Retail	Markup
SV 2WD	$44,900	8%
SL 2WD	$49,650	8%
SL 4WD	$52,550	8%
Platinum 4WD	$60,490	8%

Nissan Armada

Safety Checklist

```
Crash Test:
  Frontal . . . . . . . . . . . . . . . . . . . . . . . . —
  Side. . . . . . . . . . . . . . . . . . . . . . . . . . —
Airbags:
  Torso . . . Std. Front Pelvis/Torso from Seat
  Roll Sensing. . . . . . . . . . . . . . . . . . . . . Yes
  Knee Bolster . . . . . . . . . . . . . . . . . . . None
Crash Avoidance:
  Collision Avoidance . . . Optional CIB & DBS
  Blind Spot Detection . . . . . . . . . . Optional
  Lane Keeping Assist . . Warn. Only Optional
  Pedestrian Crash Avoidance . . . . . . . None
General:
  Auto. Crash Notification Operat. Assist.-Fee
  Day Running Lamps . . . . . . . . . . Standard
Safety Belt/Restraint:
  Dynamic Head Restraints . . . . . . Std. Front
  Adjustable Belt. . . Standard Front and Rear
```

^Warning feature does not meet government standards.

Nissan Armada

Specifications

```
Drive. . . . . . . . . . . . . . . . . . . . . . . . . . . . . RWD
Engine . . . . . . . . . . . . . . . . . . . . . 5.6-liter V8
Transmission . . . . . . . . . . . . . . . . . 7-sp. Automatic
Tow Rating (lbs.) . . . . . . . . . . . . . . . . . Very High-8500
Head/Leg Room (in.) . . . . . . . . . . . Roomy-40.9/41.9
Interior Space (cu. ft.). . . . . . . . . . . Very Roomy-154.5
Cargo Space (cu. ft.) . . . . . . . . . . . Cramped-16.2
Wheelbase/Length (in.) . . . . . . . . . . 121.1/208.9
```

Nissan Frontier

Ratings—10 Best, 1 Worst

Rating	
Combo Crash Tests	4
Safety Features	2
Rollover	2
Preventive Maintenance	3
Repair Costs	7
Warranty	1
Fuel Economy	1
Complaints	6
Insurance Costs	5
OVERALL RATING	**1**

Nissan Frontier

At-a-Glance

Status/Year Series Started	Unchanged/2005
Twins	—
Body Styles	Pickup
Seating	5
Anti-Theft Device	Std. Pass. Immobil. & Alarm
Parking Index Rating	Very Hard
Where Made	Canton, MS
Fuel Factor	
MPG Rating (city/hwy)	Very Poor-15/21
Driving Range (mi.)	Very Short-363
Fuel Type	Regular
Annual Fuel Cost	Very High-$2135
Gas Guzzler Tax	No
Greenhouse Gas Emissions (tons/yr.)	Very High-10.5
Barrels of Oil Used per year	Very High-19.4

How the Competition Rates

Competitors	Rating	Pg.
Chevrolet Colorado	2	102
Ford Ranger		135
Toyota Tacoma	1	244

Price Range

	Retail	Markup
S King Cab I4 2WD MT	$18,390	3%
SV Crew Cab V6 2WD AT	$25,950	4%
PRO-4X Crew Cab 4WD AT	$33,390	6%
SL Crew Cab 4WD AT	$35,550	7%

Safety Checklist

Crash Test:
Frontal . . . . Very Poor
Side . . . . Very Good
Airbags:
Torso . . . Std. Front Pelvis/Torso from Seat
Roll Sensing . . . . Yes
Knee Bolster . . . . None
Crash Avoidance:
Collision Avoidance . . . . None
Blind Spot Detection . . . . None
Lane Keeping Assist . . . . None
Pedestrian Crash Avoidance . . . . None
General:
Auto. Crash Notification . . . . None
Day Running Lamps . . . . None
Safety Belt/Restraint:
Dynamic Head Restraints . . . . . . Std. Front
Adjustable Belt . . . . Standard Front

^Warning feature does not meet government standards.

Nissan Frontier

Specifications

Drive	4WD
Engine	4.0-liter V6
Transmission	5-sp. Automatic
Tow Rating (lbs.)	Average-6300
Head/Leg Room (in.)	Average-39.7/42.4
Interior Space (cu. ft.)	Very Cramped-87.7
Cargo Space (cu. ft.)	Very Roomy-33.5
Wheelbase/Length (in.)	125.9/205.5

Ratings—10 Best, 1 Worst

Combo Crash Tests	—
Safety Features	7
Rollover	—
Preventive Maintenance	8
Repair Costs	10
Warranty	1
Fuel Economy	10
Complaints	9
Insurance Costs	10
OVERALL RATING	**—**

Nissan Leaf

At-a-Glance

Status/Year Series Started	Unchanged/2018
Twins	—
Body Styles	Hatchback
Seating	5
Anti-Theft Device	Std. Pass. Immobil. & Alarm
Parking Index Rating	Very Easy
Where Made	Smyrna, TN
Fuel Factor	
MPG Rating (city/hwy)	Very Good-126/101
Driving Range (mi.)	—
Fuel Type	Electricity
Annual Fuel Cost	—
Gas Guzzler Tax	No
Greenhouse Gas Emissions (tons/yr.)	Very Low-0.0
Barrels of Oil Used per year	Very Low-0.0

How the Competition Rates

Competitors	Rating	Pg.
BMW i3		83
Chevrolet Bolt		100
Tesla Model 3		228

Price Range

Price Range	Retail	Markup
S	$29,990	6%
SV	$32,490	6%
SL	$36,200	6%

Nissan Leaf

Safety Checklist

Crash Test:
  Frontal . . . . —
  Side . . . . —
Airbags:
  Torso . . . Std. Front Pelvis/Torso from Seat
  Roll Sensing . . . . No
  Knee Bolster . . . . None
Crash Avoidance:
  Collision Avoidance . . Standard CIB & DBS
  Blind Spot Detection . . . . Optional
  Lane Keeping Assist . . . . Optional
  Pedestrian Crash Avoidance . . . . . Optional
General:
  Auto. Crash Notification Operat. Assist.-Fee
  Day Running Lamps . . . . None
Safety Belt/Restraint:
  Dynamic Head Restraints . . . . None
  Adjustable Belt . . . . Standard Front

^Warning feature does not meet government standards.

Nissan Leaf

Specifications

Drive	FWD
Engine	Electric
Transmission	1-sp. Automatic
Tow Rating (lbs.)	—
Head/Leg Room (in.)	Roomy-41.2/42.1
Interior Space (cu. ft.)	Cramped-92.4
Cargo Space (cu. ft.)	Roomy-24
Wheelbase/Length (in.)	106.3/176.4

Ratings—10 Best, 1 Worst	
Combo Crash Tests	7
Safety Features	3
Rollover	9
Preventive Maintenance	6
Repair Costs	6
Warranty	1
Fuel Economy	5
Complaints	8
Insurance Costs	1
OVERALL RATING	**4**

Nissan Maxima

Nissan Maxima

At-a-Glance

Status/Year Series Started	Unchanged/2016
Twins	—
Body Styles	Sedan
Seating	5
Anti-Theft Device	Std. Pass. Immobil. & Alarm
Parking Index Rating	Hard
Where Made	Smyrna, TN
Fuel Factor	
MPG Rating (city/hwy)	Average-22/30
Driving Range (mi.)	Long-450
Fuel Type	Premium
Annual Fuel Cost	High-$1782
Gas Guzzler Tax	No
Greenhouse Gas Emissions (tons/yr.)	Average-6.0
Barrels of Oil Used per year	High-13.2

How the Competition Rates

Competitors	Rating	Pg.
Hyundai Sonata	9	155
Mazda 6	5	194
Toyota Camry	8	234

Price Range	Retail	Markup
S	$32,910	7%
SV	$34,890	7%
SR	$38,030	7%
Platinum	$40,340	7%

Nissan Maxima

Safety Checklist

Crash Test:	
Frontal	Good
Side	Average
Airbags:	
Torso	Std. Front Pelvis/Torso from Seat
Roll Sensing	Yes
Knee Bolster	None
Crash Avoidance:	
Collision Avoidance	Optional CIB & DBS
Blind Spot Detection	Optional
Lane Keeping Assist	None
Pedestrian Crash Avoidance	None
General:	
Auto. Crash Notification	Operat. Assist.-Fee
Day Running Lamps	Standard
Safety Belt/Restraint:	
Dynamic Head Restraints	None
Adjustable Belt	Standard Front

^Warning feature does not meet government standards.

Nissan Maxima

Specifications

Drive	FWD
Engine	3.5-liter V6
Transmission	CVT
Tow Rating (lbs.)	—
Head/Leg Room (in.)	Very Roomy-39.4/45
Interior Space (cu. ft.)	Average-98.6
Cargo Space (cu. ft.)	Cramped-14.3
Wheelbase/Length (in.)	109.3/192.8

Ratings—10 Best, 1 Worst

Combo Crash Tests	—
Safety Features	4
Rollover	4
Preventive Maintenance	8
Repair Costs	3
Warranty	1
Fuel Economy	4
Complaints	8
Insurance Costs	10
OVERALL RATING	**—**

Nissan Murano

Nissan Murano

At-a-Glance

Status/Year Series Started	Unchanged/2015
Twins	—
Body Styles	SUV
Seating	5
Anti-Theft Device	Std. Pass. Immobil. & Alarm
Parking Index Rating	Hard
Where Made	Canton, MS
Fuel Factor	
MPG Rating (city/hwy)	Poor-21/28
Driving Range (mi.)	Long-450
Fuel Type	Regular
Annual Fuel Cost	Average-$1553
Gas Guzzler Tax	No
Greenhouse Gas Emissions (tons/yr.)	High-7.5
Barrels of Oil Used per year	High-13.7

How the Competition Rates

Competitors	Rating	Pg.
Cadillac XT5	3	98
Ford Edge	9	125
Jeep Grand Cherokee	4	165

Price Range

	Retail	Markup
S FWD	$29,740	6%
SV FWD	$32,800	7%
SL AWD	$38,730	7%
Platinum AWD	$40,780	7%

Safety Checklist

Crash Test:
- Frontal . . . . —
- Side . . . . —

Airbags:
- Torso . . . Std. Front Pelvis/Torso from Seat
- Roll Sensing . . . . Yes
- Knee Bolster . . . . Standard Driver

Crash Avoidance:
- Collision Avoidance . . . Optional CIB & DBS
- Blind Spot Detection . . . . Optional
- Lane Keeping Assist . . . . None
- Pedestrian Crash Avoidance . . . . None

General:
- Auto. Crash Notification Operat. Assist.-Fee
- Day Running Lamps . . . . Standard

Safety Belt/Restraint:
- Dynamic Head Restraints . . . . None
- Adjustable Belt . . . . Standard Front

^Warning feature does not meet government standards.

Nissan Murano

Specifications

Drive	AWD
Engine	3.5-liter V6
Transmission	CVT
Tow Rating (lbs.)	Very Low-1500
Head/Leg Room (in.)	Cramped-39.9/40.5
Interior Space (cu. ft.)	Roomy-108.1
Cargo Space (cu. ft.)	Very Roomy-39.6
Wheelbase/Length (in.)	111.2/192.4

Ratings—10 Best, 1 Worst

Combo Crash Tests	—
Safety Features	3
Rollover	3
Preventive Maintenance	1
Repair Costs	4
Warranty	1
Fuel Economy	3
Complaints	3
Insurance Costs	10
OVERALL RATING	**—**

Nissan Pathfinder

Nissan Pathfinder

At-a-Glance

Status/Year Series Started	Unchanged/2013
Twins	Infiniti QX60
Body Styles	SUV
Seating	7
Anti-Theft Device	Std. Pass. Immobil. & Alarm
Parking Index Rating	Hard
Where Made	Smyrna, TN
Fuel Factor	
MPG Rating (city/hwy)	Poor-19/26
Driving Range (mi.)	Average-422
Fuel Type	Regular
Annual Fuel Cost	High-$1700
Gas Guzzler Tax	No
Greenhouse Gas Emissions (tons/yr.)	High-8.2
Barrels of Oil Used per year	High-15.0

How the Competition Rates

Competitors	Rating	Pg.
Dodge Durango	2	120
Ford Explorer	3	128
GMC Acadia	2	138

Price Range

	Retail	Markup
S FWD	$29,990	8%
SV FWD	$32,680	8%
SL 4WD	$37,390	8%
Platinum 4WD	$43,560	8%

Safety Checklist

Crash Test:
- Frontal .... —
- Side .... —

Airbags:
- Torso . . . Std. Front Pelvis/Torso from Seat
- Roll Sensing .... Yes
- Knee Bolster .... None

Crash Avoidance:
- Collision Avoidance . . . Optional CIB & DBS
- Blind Spot Detection .... Optional
- Lane Keeping Assist .... None
- Pedestrian Crash Avoidance .... None

General:
- Auto. Crash Notification Operat. Assist.-Fee
- Day Running Lamps .... Standard

Safety Belt/Restraint:
- Dynamic Head Restraints .... None
- Adjustable Belt ..... Standard Front & Rear

^Warning feature does not meet government standards.

Nissan Pathfinder

Specifications

Drive	4WD
Engine	3.5-liter V6
Transmission	CVT
Tow Rating (lbs.)	Low-5000
Head/Leg Room (in.)	Roomy-41.1/42.3
Interior Space (cu. ft.)	Very Roomy-157.8
Cargo Space (cu. ft.)	Cramped-16
Wheelbase/Length (in.)	114.2/197.2

Ratings—10 Best, 1 Worst

Combo Crash Tests	1
Safety Features	5
Rollover	4
Preventive Maintenance	3
Repair Costs	4
Warranty	1
Fuel Economy	7
Complaints	10
Insurance Costs	10
OVERALL RATING	**3**

Nissan Rogue

Nissan Rogue

At-a-Glance

Status/Year Series Started	Unchanged/2014
Twins	—
Body Styles	SUV
Seating	5/7
Anti-Theft Device	Std. Pass. Immobil. & Alarm
Parking Index Rating	Average
Where Made	Smyrna, TN
Fuel Factor	
MPG Rating (city/hwy)	Good-25/32
Driving Range (mi.)	Average-402
Fuel Type	Regular
Annual Fuel Cost	Low-$1325
Gas Guzzler Tax	No
Greenhouse Gas Emissions (tons/yr.)	Average-6.4
Barrels of Oil Used per year	Average-11.8

How the Competition Rates

Competitors	Rating	Pg.
Kia Sorento	6	172
Mazda CX-5	4	191
Subaru Outback	8	227

Price Range

	Retail	Markup
S FWD	$23,820	6%
SV FWD	$25,240	6%
SV AWD	$26,590	6%
SL AWD	$31,310	6%

Safety Checklist

Crash Test:
- Frontal . . . . Very Poor
- Side . . . . Very Poor

Airbags:
- Torso . . . Std. Front Pelvis/Torso from Seat
- Roll Sensing . . . . Yes
- Knee Bolster . . . . None

Crash Avoidance:
- Collision Avoidance . . . Optional CIB & DBS
- Blind Spot Detection . . . . Optional
- Lane Keeping Assist . . Warn. Only Optional
- Pedestrian Crash Avoidance . . . . . Optional

General:
- Auto. Crash Notification Operat. Assist.-Fee
- Day Running Lamps . . . . Standard

Safety Belt/Restraint:
- Dynamic Head Restraints . . . . None
- Adjustable Belt . . . . Standard Front

^Warning feature does not meet government standards.

Nissan Rogue

Specifications

Drive	AWD
Engine	2.5-liter I4
Transmission	CVT
Tow Rating (lbs.)	Very Low-1000
Head/Leg Room (in.)	Very Roomy-41.6/43
Interior Space (cu. ft.)	Roomy-105.8
Cargo Space (cu. ft.)	Very Cramped-9.4
Wheelbase/Length (in.)	106.5/182.3

Ratings—10 Best, 1 Worst

Combo Crash Tests	2
Safety Features	2
Rollover	6
Preventive Maintenance	8
Repair Costs	9
Warranty	1
Fuel Economy	9
Complaints	9
Insurance Costs	5
OVERALL RATING	**5**

Nissan Sentra

Nissan Sentra

At-a-Glance

Status/Year Series Started	Unchanged/2013
Twins	—
Body Styles	Sedan
Sealing	5
Anti-Theft Device	Std. Pass. Immobil. & Alarm
Parking Index Rating	Easy
Where Made	Aguascalientes, Mexico / Kyushu, Japan

Fuel Factor

MPG Rating (city/hwy)	Very Good-30/39
Driving Range (mi.)	Long-442
Fuel Type	Regular
Annual Fuel Cost	Very Low-$1098
Gas Guzzler Tax	No
Greenhouse Gas Emissions (tons/yr.)	Low-5.3
Barrels of Oil Used per year	Low-9.7

How the Competition Rates

Competitors	Rating	Pg.
Chevrolet Cruze	8	104
Honda Civic	10	144
Toyota Corolla	7	235

Price Range

	Retail	Markup
S MT	$16,990	3%
SV	$18,840	5%
SR	$19,990	5%
SL	$21,500	5%

Safety Checklist

Crash Test:
- Frontal . . . . Very Poor
- Side . . . . Average

Airbags:
- Torso . . . Std. Front Pelvis/Torso from Seat
- Roll Sensing . . . . Yes
- Knee Bolster . . . . None

Crash Avoidance:
- Collision Avoidance . . . Optional CIB & DBS
- Blind Spot Detection . . . . Optional
- Lane Keeping Assist . . . . None
- Pedestrian Crash Avoidance . . . . None

General:
- Auto. Crash Notification Operat. Assist.-Fee
- Day Running Lamps . . . . None

Safety Belt/Restraint:
- Dynamic Head Restraints . . . . None
- Adjustable Belt . . . . Standard Front

^Warning feature does not meet government standards.

Nissan Sentra

Specifications

Drive	FWD
Engine	2.0-liter I4
Transmission	CVT
Tow Rating (lbs.)	—
Head/Leg Room (in.)	Average-39.4/42.5
Interior Space (cu. ft.)	Cramped-95.9
Cargo Space (cu. ft.)	Cramped-15.1
Wheelbase/Length (in.)	106.3/182.1

Ratings—10 Best, 1 Worst

Combo Crash Tests	7
Safety Features	2
Rollover	2
Preventive Maintenance	2
Repair Costs	5
Warranty	1
Fuel Economy	1
Complaints	2
Insurance Costs	8
OVERALL RATING	**1**

Nissan Titan

Nissan Titan

At-a-Glance

Status/Year Series Started	Unchanged/2016
Twins	—
Body Styles	Pickup
Seating	6
Anti-Theft Device	Std. Pass. Immobil. & Alarm
Parking Index Rating	Very Hard
Where Made	Canton, MS
Fuel Factor	
MPG Rating (city/hwy)	Very Poor-15/21
Driving Range (mi.)	Long-448
Fuel Type	Regular
Annual Fuel Cost	Very High-$2135
Gas Guzzler Tax	No
Greenhouse Gas Emissions (tons/yr.)	High-8.4
Barrels of Oil Used per year	Very High-18.3

How the Competition Rates

Competitors	Rating	Pg.
Chevrolet Silverado		108
Ford F-150	8	129
Ram 1500	5	221

Price Range

	Retail	Markup
S Crew Cab 2WD	$35,230	4%
SV Crew Cab 4WD	$41,400	6%
SL Crew Cab 4WD	$49,910	6%
Platinum Crew Cab 4WD	$55,850	6%

Safety Checklist

Crash Test:
  Frontal . . . . Average
  Side . . . . Very Good
Airbags:
  Torso . . . Std. Front Pelvis/Torso from Seat
  Roll Sensing . . . . Yes
  Knee Bolster . . . . None
Crash Avoidance:
  Collision Avoidance . . . . None
  Blind Spot Detection . . . . Optional
  Lane Keeping Assist . . . . None
  Pedestrian Crash Avoidance . . . . None
General:
  Auto. Crash Notification Operat. Assist.-Fee
  Day Running Lamps . . . . Optional
Safety Belt/Restraint:
  Dynamic Head Restraints . . . . None
  Adjustable Belt . . . . Standard Front

^Warning feature does not meet government standards.

Nissan Titan

Specifications

Drive	4WD
Engine	5.0-liter V8
Transmission	6-sp. Automatic
Tow Rating (lbs.)	Very High-12038
Head/Leg Room (in.)	Roomy-41/41.8
Interior Space (cu. ft.)	—
Cargo Space (cu. ft.)	Very Roomy-58.1
Wheelbase/Length (in.)	151.6/242.7

Ratings—10 Best, 1 Worst

Combo Crash Tests	1
Safety Features	1
Rollover	4
Preventive Maintenance	9
Repair Costs	9
Warranty	1
Fuel Economy	9
Complaints	5
Insurance Costs	1
OVERALL RATING	**1**

Nissan Versa

At-a-Glance

Status/Year Series Started	Unchanged/2006
Twins	—
Body Styles	Sedan, Hatchback
Seating	4
Anti-Theft Device	Std. Pass. Immobil.
Parking Index Rating	Very Easy
Where Made	Aguascalientes, Mexico / Kyushu, Japan

Fuel Factor

MPG Rating (city/hwy)	Very Good-31/40
Driving Range (mi.)	Very Short-373
Fuel Type	Regular
Annual Fuel Cost	Very Low-$1065
Gas Guzzler Tax	No
Greenhouse Gas Emissions (tons/yr.)	Low-5.1
Barrels of Oil Used per year	Low-9.4

How the Competition Rates

Competitors	Rating	Pg.
Chevrolet Sonic	8	109
Ford Fiesta	2	130
Toyota Yaris Liftback	5	247

Price Range

	Retail	Markup
S MT	$11,900	2%
S Plus	$14,130	3%
SV	$15,720	3%
		—

Nissan Versa

Safety Checklist

Crash Test:
  Frontal . . . . Very Poor
  Side . . . . Very Poor
Airbags:
  Torso . . . Std. Front Pelvis/Torso from Seat
  Roll Sensing . . . . Yes
  Knee Bolster . . . . None
Crash Avoidance:
  Collision Avoidance . . . . None
  Blind Spot Detection . . . . None
  Lane Keeping Assist . . . . None
  Pedestrian Crash Avoidance . . . . None
General:
  Auto. Crash Notification . . . . None
  Day Running Lamps . . . . None
Safety Belt/Restraint:
  Dynamic Head Restraints . . . . None
  Adjustable Belt . . . . Standard Front

^Warning feature does not meet government standards.

Specifications

Drive	FWD
Engine	1.6-liter I4
Transmission	CVT
Tow Rating (lbs.)	—
Head/Leg Room (in.)	Average-39.8/41.8
Interior Space (cu. ft.)	Very Cramped-90.2
Cargo Space (cu. ft.)	Cramped-14.9
Wheelbase/Length (in.)	102.4/175.4

Porsche Macan

Ratings—10 Best, 1 Worst

Combo Crash Tests	—
Safety Features	6
Rollover	—
Preventive Maintenance	3
Repair Costs	1
Warranty	7
Fuel Economy	2
Complaints	10
Insurance Costs	5
OVERALL RATING	**—**

Porsche Macan

Porsche Macan

At-a-Glance

Status/Year Series Started	All New/2019
Twins	—
Body Styles	SUV
Seating	5
Anti-Theft Device	Std. Pass. Immobil. & Active Alarm
Parking Index Rating	Hard
Where Made	Leipzig, Germany
Fuel Factor	
MPG Rating (city/hwy)	Very Poor-17/23
Driving Range (mi.)	Short-381
Fuel Type	Premium
Annual Fuel Cost	Very High-$2313
Gas Guzzler Tax	No
Greenhouse Gas Emissions (tons/yr.)	Average-6.6
Barrels of Oil Used per year	High-15.0

How the Competition Rates

Competitors	Rating	Pg.
BMW X5		86
Cadillac XT5	3	98
Lexus RX	4	184

Price Range

	Retail	Markup
Base	$47,800	11%
S	$55,400	11%
GTS	$68,900	11%
Turbo	$77,200	11%

Safety Checklist

Crash Test:
  Frontal . . . . —
  Side. . . . . —
Airbags:
  Torso . . Std. Front & Rear Torso from Seat
  Roll Sensing. Yes
  Knee Bolster . . . . Standard Front
Crash Avoidance:
  Collision Avoidance . . Optional CIB & DBS^
  Blind Spot Detection . . . . Optional
  Lane Keeping Assist . . . . Optional^
  Pedestrian Crash Avoidance . . . . None
General:
  Auto. Crash Notification . . . . None
  Day Running Lamps . . . . Standard
Safety Belt/Restraint:
  Dynamic Head Restraints . . . . None
  Adjustable Belt. . . . . Standard Front & Rear

^Warning feature does not meet government standards.

Porsche Macan

Specifications

Drive	AWD
Engine	3.0-liter V6
Transmission	7-sp. Automatic
Tow Rating (lbs.)	Low-4400
Head/Leg Room (in.)	—
Interior Space (cu. ft.)	—
Cargo Space (cu. ft.)	Average-17.7
Wheelbase/Length (in.)	110.5/184.9

Ratings—10 Best, 1 Worst	
Combo Crash Tests	5
Safety Features	6
Rollover	2
Preventive Maintenance	8
Repair Costs	10
Warranty	2
Fuel Economy	2
Complaints	5
Insurance Costs	10
OVERALL RATING	**5**

Ram 1500

Ram 1500

At-a-Glance

Status/Year Series Started	All New/2019
Twins	—
Body Styles	Pickup
Seating	6
Anti-Theft Device	Std. Pass. Immobil. & Opt. Pass. Alarm
Parking Index Rating	Very Hard
Where Made	Warren, MI / Saltillo, Mexico
Fuel Factor	
MPG Rating (city/hwy)	Very Poor-17/22
Driving Range (mi.)	Short-494
Fuel Type	Regular
Annual Fuel Cost	High-$1941
Gas Guzzler Tax	No
Greenhouse Gas Emissions (tons/yr.)	High-7.8
Barrels of Oil Used per year	Very High-17.3

How the Competition Rates

Competitors	Rating	Pg.
Chevrolet Silverado		108
Ford F-150	8	129
Nissan Titan	1	218

Price Range

	Retail	Markup
Tradesman Reg. Cab 2WD	$31,795	4%
Big Horn Quad Cab 2WD	$35,895	6%
Laramie Crew Cab 4WD	$46,295	9%
Limited Crew Cab 4WD	$56,895	10%

Safety Checklist

Crash Test:	
Frontal	Very Poor
Side	Poor
Airbags:	
Torso	Std. Front Pelvis/Torso from Seat
Roll Sensing	Yes
Knee Bolster	None
Crash Avoidance:	
Collision Avoidance	Optional CIB & DBS
Blind Spot Detection	Optional
Lane Keeping Assist	Optional
Pedestrian Crash Avoidance	Optional
General:	
Auto. Crash Notification	None
Day Running Lamps	Standard
Safety Belt/Restraint:	
Dynamic Head Restraints	None
Adjustable Belt	Standard Front

^Warning feature does not meet government standards.

Ram 1500

Specifications

Drive	4WD
Engine	5.7-liter V8
Transmission	8-sp. Automatic
Tow Rating (lbs.)	Very High-7520
Head/Leg Room (in.)	Average-40.9/40.9
Interior Space (cu. ft.)	—
Cargo Space (cu. ft.)	Very Roomy-61.5
Wheelbase/Length (in.)	140.5/228.9

Mercedes-Benz CLA — Compact

Ratings—10 Best, 1 Worst

Combo Crash Tests	—
Safety Features	8
Rollover	6
Preventive Maintenance	1
Repair Costs	3
Warranty	3
Fuel Economy	7
Complaints	1
Insurance Costs	1
OVERALL RATING	**—**

Mercedes-Benz CLA-Class

Mercedes-Benz CLA-Class

At-a-Glance

Status/Year Series Started. Unchanged/2014
Twins . . . . —
Body Styles . . . . .Coupe
Seating. 5
Anti-Theft Device . Std. Active Immobil. & Pass. Alarm
Parking Index Rating . . . . Easy
Where Made. . . . . Kecskemet, Hungary
Fuel Factor
  MPG Rating (city/hwy) Good-24/37
  Driving Range (mi.) Short-376
  Fuel Type. . . . . .Premium
  Annual Fuel Cost . . . . .Average-$1563
  Gas Guzzler Tax . . . . .No
  Greenhouse Gas Emissions (tons/yr.) Low-5.1
  Barrels of Oil Used per year Average-11.4

How the Competition Rates

Competitors	Rating	Pg.
Audi A4	2	72
Cadillac ATS	4	97
Infiniti Q50	3	158

Price Range

Price Range	Retail	Markup
Coupe 4Matic	$3,440	89%
Coupe	$32,400	8%
AMG 4Matic	$49,950	8%

Safety Checklist

Crash Test:
  Frontal. . . . . —
  Side. . . . . —
Airbags:
  Torso Std. Fr. & Opt. Rr. Pelvis/Torso from Seat
  Roll Sensing. . . . . .Yes
  Knee Bolster . . . . Standard Front
Crash Avoidance:
  Collision Avoidance . . Standard CIB & DBS
  Blind Spot Detection . . . . Optional
  Lane Keeping Assist . .Warn. Only Optional
  Pedestrian Crash Avoidance . . . . . . .None
General:
  Auto. Crash Notif. . . Op. Assist. & Crash Info-Fee
  Day Running Lamps . . . . .None
Safety Belt/Restraint:
  Dynamic Head Restraints . . . . .None
  Adjustable Belt. . . . . Standard Front

^Warning feature does not meet government standards.

Mercedes-Benz CLA-Class

Specifications

Drive. . . . . .FWD
Engine 2.0-liter I4
Transmission . . . . 7-sp. Automatic
Tow Rating (lbs.) . . . . —
Head/Leg Room (in.) . . . . Very Cramped-38.2/40.2
Interior Space (cu. ft.). . . . . .Very Cramped-88
Cargo Space (cu. ft.) . . . . .Very Cramped-13
Wheelbase/Length (in.) 106.3/182.3

Subaru Crosstrek

Small SUV

Ratings—10 Best, 1 Worst

Combo Crash Tests	5
Safety Features	8
Rollover	4
Preventive Maintenance	4
Repair Costs	8
Warranty	3
Fuel Economy	7
Complaints	6
Insurance Costs	5
OVERALL RATING	**5**

Subaru Crosstrek

Subaru Crosstrek

At-a-Glance

Status/Year Series Started.......	Unchanged/2018
Twins	
Body Styles	SUV
Seating................................	5
Anti-Theft Device . Std. Pass. Immobil. & Active Alarm	
Parking Index Rating	Easy
Where Made..........................	Gunma, Japan
Fuel Factor	
MPG Rating (city/hwy)	Good-27/33
Driving Range (mi.)	Very Long-488
Fuel Type.........................	Regular
Annual Fuel Cost	Low-$1250
Gas Guzzler Tax	No
Greenhouse Gas Emissions (tons/yr.).....	Low-5.0
Barrels of Oil Used per year	Average-11.4

How the Competition Rates

Competitors	Rating	Pg.
Buick Encore	10	90
Jeep Renegade	1	166
Kia Sportage	9	174

Price Range	Retail	Markup
Base MT	$21,795	5%
Premium MT	$22,595	5%
Premium AT	$23,595	6%
Limited	$26,295	6%

Safety Checklist

Crash Test:
  Frontal....................... Average
  Side........................... Average
Airbags:
  Torso . . . Std. Front Pelvis/Torso from Seat
  Roll Sensing......................Yes
  Knee Bolster .... Standard Driver
Crash Avoidance:
  Collision Avoidance . . .Optional CIB & DBS
  Blind Spot Detection .... Optional
  Lane Keeping Assist .... Optional
  Pedestrian Crash Avoidance..... Optional
General:
  Auto. Crash Notif...... Operator Assist.-Fee
  Day Running Lamps ....Standard
Safety Belt/Restraint:
  Dynamic Head Restraints ....None
  Adjustable Belt........... Standard Front

^Warning feature does not meet government standards.

Subaru Crosstrek

Specifications

Drive...	AWD
Engine	2.0-liter I4
Transmission	CVT
Tow Rating (lbs.)	
Head/Leg Room (in.)	Average-39/43.1
Interior Space (cu. ft.)...............	Average-100.9
Cargo Space (cu. ft.)	Average-20.8
Wheelbase/Length (in.)	104.9/175.8

Ratings—10 Best, 1 Worst

Combo Crash Tests	—
Safety Features	8
Rollover	3
Preventive Maintenance	3
Repair Costs	7
Warranty	3
Fuel Economy	6
Complaints	—
Insurance Costs	1

OVERALL RATING   —

Subaru Forester

Subaru Forester

At-a-Glance

Status/Year Series Started	All New/2019
Twins	—
Body Styles	SUV
Seating	5
Anti-Theft Device	Std. Pass. Immobil. & Active Alarm
Parking Index Rating	Easy
Where Made	Lafayette, IN

Fuel Factor
MPG Rating (city/hwy)	Good-26/33
Driving Range (mi.)	Very Long-481
Fuel Type	Regular
Annual Fuel Cost	Low-$1263
Gas Guzzler Tax	No
Greenhouse Gas Emissions (tons/yr.)	Low-5.1
Barrels of Oil Used per year	Average-11.

How the Competition Rates

Competitors	Rating	Pg.
Chevrolet Trax	10	114
Mazda CX-3	10	190
Mitsubishi Outlander Sport	3	208

Price Range	Retail	Markup
2.5i	$24,295	6%
2.5i Premium	$26,695	6%
2.5i Limited	$30,795	7%
2.5i XT Touring	$34,295	7%

Safety Checklist

Crash Test:
Frontal	—
Side	—

Airbags:
Torso	Std. Front Pelvis/Torso from Seat
Roll Sensing	Yes
Knee Bolster	Standard Driver

Crash Avoidance:
Collision Avoidance	Standard CIB & DBS
Blind Spot Detection	Optional
Lane Keeping Assist	Optional
Pedestrian Crash Avoidance	Optional

General:
Auto. Crash Notif.	Operator Assist.-Fee
Day Running Lamps	Standard

Safety Belt/Restraint:
Dynamic Head Restraints	None
Adjustable Belt	Standard Front

^Warning feature does not meet government standards.

Subaru Forester

Specifications

Drive	AWD
Engine	2.5-liter I4
Transmission	CVT
Tow Rating (lbs.)	Very Low-1500
Head/Leg Room (in.)	Very Roomy-41.2/43.3
Interior Space (cu. ft.)	Roomy-111.9
Cargo Space (cu. ft.)	Very Roomy-35.4
Wheelbase/Length (in.)	105.1/182.1

Subaru Impreza | Compact

Ratings—10 Best, 1 Worst

Combo Crash Tests	6
Safety Features	8
Rollover	9
Preventive Maintenance	4
Repair Costs	8
Warranty	3
Fuel Economy	4
Complaints	6
Insurance Costs	1
OVERALL RATING	**5**

Subaru Impreza

At-a-Glance

Status/Year Series Started. Unchanged/2017
Twins . . . . —
Body Styles . . . . Sedan, Hatchback
Seating. 5
Anti-Theft Device . Std. Pass. Immobil. & Active Alarm
Parking Index Rating . . . . Easy
Where Made. . . . . Gunma, Japan
Fuel Factor
  MPG Rating (city/hwy) Poor-20/27
  Driving Range (mi.) Average-419
  Fuel Type . . . . .Regular
  Annual Fuel Cost . . . . .Average-$1623
  Gas Guzzler Tax . . . . .No
  Greenhouse Gas Emissions (tons/yr.) . . Average-6.5
  Barrels of Oil Used per year High-15.0

How the Competition Rates

Competitors	Rating	Pg.
Chevrolet Cruze	8	104
Mazda 3	6	193
Toyota Corolla	7	235

Price Range

	Retail	Markup
Base Sedan MT	$18,495	5%
Premium Wagon	$21,795	5%
Sport Sedan AT	$22,895	5%
Limited Wagon	$24,695	6%

Subaru Impreza

Safety Checklist

Crash Test:
  Frontal. . . . . .Good
  Side. . . . . Poor
Airbags:
  Torso . . . Std. Front Pelvis/Torso from Seat
  Roll Sensing. . . . . .Yes
  Knee Bolster . . . . Standard Driver
Crash Avoidance:
  Collision Avoidance . . .Optional CIB & DBS
  Blind Spot Detection . . . . Optional
  Lane Keeping Assist . . . . Optional
  Pedestrian Crash Avoidance . . . . . Optional
General:
  Auto. Crash Notif.. . . . Operator Assist.-Fee
  Day Running Lamps . . . . .Standard
Safety Belt/Restraint:
  Dynamic Head Restraints . . . . .None
  Adjustable Belt. . . . . Standard Front

^Warning feature does not meet government standards.

Subaru Impreza

Specifications

Drive. . . . . .AWD
Engine 2.0-liter I4
Transmission . . . . CVT
Tow Rating (lbs.) . . . . —
Head/Leg Room (in.) Roomy-39.8/43.1
Interior Space (cu. ft.). Average-100
Cargo Space (cu. ft.) . . . . Very Cramped-12.3
Wheelbase/Length (in.) 105.1/182.1

225

Ratings—10 Best, 1 Worst	
Combo Crash Tests	9
Safety Features	7
Rollover	8
Preventive Maintenance	2
Repair Costs	9
Warranty	3
Fuel Economy	7
Complaints	5
Insurance Costs	1
OVERALL RATING	**7**

Subaru Legacy

Subaru Legacy

At-a-Glance

Status/Year Series Started Unchanged/2015	
Twins . . . . —	
Body Styles . . . . Sedan	
Seating 5	
Anti-Theft Device . Std. Pass. Immobil. & Active Alarm	
Parking Index Rating . . . . Average	
Where Made . . . . Lafayette, IN	
Fuel Factor	
MPG Rating (city/hwy) Good-26/36	
Driving Range (mi.) . . . . Very Long-550	
Fuel Type . . . . Regular	
Annual Fuel Cost . . . . Low-$1237	
Gas Guzzler Tax . . . . No	
Greenhouse Gas Emissions (tons/yr.) . . Average-6.0	
Barrels of Oil Used per year Average-11.0	

How the Competition Rates

Competitors	Rating	Pg.
Ford Fusion	4	132
Nissan Maxima	4	213
Toyota Camry	8	234

Price Range	Retail	Markup
Base	$22,195	6%
Premium	$24,295	6%
Limited	$29,095	7%
3.6R Limited	$31,945	7%

Safety Checklist

Crash Test:	
Frontal . . . . Very Good	
Side . . . . Good	
Airbags:	
Torso . . . Std. Front Pelvis/Torso from Seat	
Roll Sensing . . . . Yes	
Knee Bolster . . . . None	
Crash Avoidance:	
Collision Avoidance . . . Optional CIB & DBS	
Blind Spot Detection . . . . Optional	
Lane Keeping Assist . . . . Optional	
Pedestrian Crash Avoidance . . . . . Optional	
General:	
Auto. Crash Notif. . . . . Operator Assist.-Fee	
Day Running Lamps . . . . Standard	
Safety Belt/Restraint:	
Dynamic Head Restraints . . . . None	
Adjustable Belt . . . . Standard Front	

^Warning feature does not meet government standards.

Subaru Legacy

Specifications

Drive . . . . AWD	
Engine 2.5-liter I4	
Transmission . . . . 6-sp. Automatic	
Tow Rating (lbs.) . . . . —	
Head/Leg Room (in.) Roomy-40/42.9	
Interior Space (cu. ft.) Roomy-104.6	
Cargo Space (cu. ft.) Cramped-15	
Wheelbase/Length (in.) 108.3/188.8	

Ratings—10 Best, 1 Worst

Combo Crash Tests	10
Safety Features	7
Rollover	3
Preventive Maintenance	2
Repair Costs	9
Warranty	3
Fuel Economy	7
Complaints	4
Insurance Costs	5
OVERALL RATING	**8**

Subaru Outback

At-a-Glance

Status/Year Series Started	Unchanged/2015
Twins	—
Body Styles	Wagon
Seating	5
Anti-Theft Device	Std. Pass. Immobil. & Active Alarm
Parking Index Rating	Easy
Where Made	Lafayette, IN
Fuel Factor	
MPG Rating (city/hwy)	Good-25/33
Driving Range (mi.)	Very Long-519
Fuel Type	Regular
Annual Fuel Cost	Low-$1310
Gas Guzzler Tax	No
Greenhouse Gas Emissions (tons/yr.)	Average-6.4
Barrels of Oil Used per year	Average-11.8

How the Competition Rates

Competitors	Rating	Pg.
Kia Sorento	6	172
Toyota Highlander	8	237
Volkswagen Atlas	6	248

Price Range

	Retail	Markup
Base	$25,895	6%
Premium	$27,995	6%
Limited	$32,695	7%
3.6R Limited	$35,395	7%

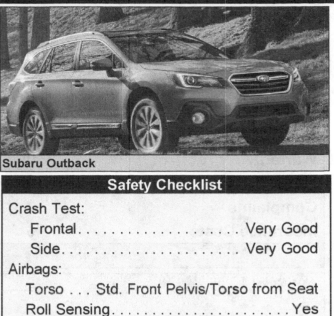

Subaru Outback

Safety Checklist

Crash Test:
  Frontal . . . . Very Good
  Side . . . . Very Good
Airbags:
  Torso . . . Std. Front Pelvis/Torso from Seat
  Roll Sensing . . . . Yes
  Knee Bolster . . . . None
Crash Avoidance:
  Collision Avoidance . . . Optional CIB & DBS
  Blind Spot Detection . . . . Optional
  Lane Keeping Assist . . . . Optional
  Pedestrian Crash Avoidance . . . . . Optional
General:
  Auto. Crash Notif. . . . . Operator Assist.-Fee
  Day Running Lamps . . . . Standard
Safety Belt/Restraint:
  Dynamic Head Restraints . . . . None
  Adjustable Belt . . . . Standard Front

^Warning feature does not meet government standards.

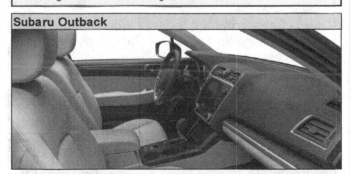

Subaru Outback

Specifications

Drive	AWD
Engine	2.5-liter I4
Transmission	6-sp. Automatic
Tow Rating (lbs.)	Very Low-2700
Head/Leg Room (in.)	Roomy-40.0/42.9
Interior Space (cu. ft.)	Roomy-108.1
Cargo Space (cu. ft.)	Very Roomy-35.5
Wheelbase/Length (in.)	108.1/189.6

Ratings—10 Best, 1 Worst

Combo Crash Tests	—
Safety Features	7
Rollover	7
Preventive Maintenance	8
Repair Costs	10
Warranty	10
Fuel Economy	10
Complaints	7
Insurance Costs	5
OVERALL RATING	**—**

Tesla Model 3

Tesla Model 3

At-a-Glance

Status/Year Series Started	Unchanged/2018
Twins	—
Body Styles	Sedan
Seating	5
Anti-Theft Device	Std. Passive Alarm Only
Parking Index Rating	Very Easy
Where Made	Fremont, CA
Fuel Factor	
MPG Rating (city/hwy)	Very Good-131/120
Driving Range (mi.)	Very Short-310
Fuel Type	Electricity
Annual Fuel Cost	Very Low-$500
Gas Guzzler Tax	No
Greenhouse Gas Emissions (tons/yr.)	Very Low-0.0
Barrels of Oil Used per year	Very Low-0.0

How the Competition Rates

Competitors	Rating	Pg.
BMW i3		83
Chevrolet Bolt		100
Nissan Leaf		212

Price Range	Retail	Markup
Base	$35,000	6%
Premium	$40,000	6%
Prem. w/Enhanced Autopilot	$45,000	6%
		—

Safety Checklist

Crash Test:
  Frontal . . . . —
  Side. . . . . —

Airbags:
  Torso . . . Std. Front Pelvis/Torso from Seat
  Roll Sensing. Yes
  Knee Bolster . . . . Standard Front

Crash Avoidance:
  Collision Avoidance . . Optional CIB & DBS^
  Blind Spot Detection . . . . Optional
  Lane Keeping Assist . . . . Optional
  Pedestrian Crash Avoidance . . . . None

General:
  Auto. Crash Notification . . . . None
  Day Running Lamps . . . . Standard

Safety Belt/Restraint:
  Dynamic Head Restraints . . . . None
  Adjustable Belt. . . . . None

^Warning feature does not meet government standards.

Tesla Model 3

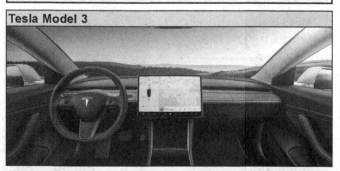

Specifications

Drive	RWD
Engine	Electric
Transmission	CVT
Tow Rating (lbs.)	—
Head/Leg Room (in.)	—
Interior Space (cu. ft.)	—
Cargo Space (cu. ft.)	Cramped-15
Wheelbase/Length (in.)	113.2/184.8

Ratings—10 Best, 1 Worst

Combo Crash Tests	9
Safety Features	9
Rollover	10
Preventive Maintenance	8
Repair Costs	10
Warranty	10
Fuel Economy	10
Complaints	1
Insurance Costs	1
OVERALL RATING	**10**

Tesla Model S

At-a-Glance

Status/Year Series Started	Unchanged/2015
Twins	—
Body Styles	Sedan
Seating	5
Anti-Theft Device	Std. Passive Alarm Only
Parking Index Rating	Hard
Where Made	Fremont, CA
Fuel Factor	
MPG Rating (city/hwy)	Very Good-88/90
Driving Range (mi.)	Very Short-335
Fuel Type	Electricity
Annual Fuel Cost	Very Low-$650
Gas Guzzler Tax	No
Greenhouse Gas Emissions (tons/yr.)	Very Low-0.0
Barrels of Oil Used per year	Very Low-0.0

How the Competition Rates

Competitors	Rating	Pg.
Buick LaCrosse	5	92
Cadillac XTS	8	99
Mercedes-Benz E-Class	3	198

Price Range

	Retail	Markup
75 kWh	$69,500	6%
75D kWh	$74,500	6%
90D kWh	$87,500	6%
P100D kWh	$135,000	6%

Tesla Model S

Safety Checklist

Crash Test:
  Frontal . . . . Good
  Side . . . . Very Good
Airbags:
  Torso . . . Std. Front Pelvis/Torso from Seat
  Roll Sensing . . . . Yes
  Knee Bolster . . . . Standard Front
Crash Avoidance:
  Collision Avoidance . . Standard CIB & DBS
  Blind Spot Detection . . . . Std.
  Lane Keeping Assist . . . . Optional
  Pedestrian Crash Avoidance . . . . None
General:
  Auto. Crash Notification . . . . None
  Day Running Lamps . . . . Standard
Safety Belt/Restraint:
  Dynamic Head Restraints . . . . None
  Adjustable Belt . . . . None

^Warning feature does not meet government standards.

Tesla Model S

Specifications

Drive	RWD
Engine	Electric
Transmission	CVT
Tow Rating (lbs.)	—
Head/Leg Room (in.)	Average-38.8/42.7
Interior Space (cu. ft.)	Cramped-94
Cargo Space (cu. ft.)	Very Roomy-31.6
Wheelbase/Length (in.)	116.5/196

Ratings—10 Best, 1 Worst

Combo Crash Tests	10
Safety Features	9
Rollover	9
Preventive Maintenance	8
Repair Costs	10
Warranty	10
Fuel Economy	10
Complaints	2
Insurance Costs	8
OVERALL RATING	**10**

Tesla Model X

Tesla Model X

At-a-Glance

```
Status/Year Series Started. . . . . . . Unchanged/2017
Twins . . . . . . . . . . . . . . . . . . . . . . . . . . . . . . . —
Body Styles . . . . . . . . . . . . . . . . . . . . . . . . . SUV
Seating . . . . . . . . . . . . . . . . . . . . . . . . . . . . . . 7
Anti-Theft Device . . . . . . . . Std. Passive Alarm Only
Parking Index Rating . . . . . . . . . . . . . . . Very Hard
Where Made. . . . . . . . . . . . . . . . . . . Fremont, CA
Fuel Factor
  MPG Rating (city/hwy) . . . . . . . . . Very Good-89/90
  Driving Range (mi.) . . . . . . . . . . . . Very Short-295
  Fuel Type. . . . . . . . . . . . . . . . . . . . . . Electricity
  Annual Fuel Cost . . . . . . . . . . . . . . Very Low-$700
  Gas Guzzler Tax . . . . . . . . . . . . . . . . . . . . . . No
  Greenhouse Gas Emissions (tons/yr.) . Very Low-0.0
  Barrels of Oil Used per year . . . . . . . Very Low-0.0
```

Safety Checklist

```
Crash Test:
  Frontal. . . . . . . . . . . . . . . . . . . . Very Good
  Side. . . . . . . . . . . . . . . . . . . . . . Very Good
Airbags:
  Torso . . . Std. Front Pelvis/Torso from Seat
  Roll Sensing. . . . . . . . . . . . . . . . . . . . . Yes
  Knee Bolster . . . . . . . . . . . Standard Front
Crash Avoidance:
  Collision Avoidance . . Standard CIB & DBS
  Blind Spot Detection . . . . . . . . . . . . . Std.
  Lane Keeping Assist . . . . . . . . . . Optional
  Pedestrian Crash Avoidance . . . . . . . None
General:
  Auto. Crash Notification . . . . . . . . . . None
  Day Running Lamps . . . . . . . . . Standard
Safety Belt/Restraint:
  Dynamic Head Restraints . . . . . . . . None
  Adjustable Belt. . . . . . . . . . . . . . . . . None
```

^Warning feature does not meet government standards.

Tesla Model X

How the Competition Rates

Competitors	Rating	Pg.
Audi Q7	3	77
BMW X5		86
Buick Enclave	4	89

Specifications

```
Drive. . . . . . . . . . . . . . . . . . . . . . . . . . . . . . AWD
Engine . . . . . . . . . . . . . . . . . . . . . . . . . . . Electric
Transmission . . . . . . . . . . . . . . . . . . . . . . . . CVT
Tow Rating (lbs.) . . . . . . . . . . . . . . . . . . . . . . . —
Head/Leg Room (in.) . . . . . . . . . . . Roomy-41.7/41.2
Interior Space (cu. ft.). . . . . . . . . . . . . . Roomy-120
Cargo Space (cu. ft.) . . . . . . . . . . . . . . . Roomy-26
Wheelbase/Length (in.) . . . . . . . . . . 116.7/198.3
```

Price Range

	Retail	Markup
75D kWh	$79,500	6%
90D kWh	$93,500	6%
100D kWh	$96,000	6%
P100D kWh	$140,000	6%

Ratings—10 Best, 1 Worst

Combo Crash Tests	—
Safety Features	2
Rollover	9
Preventive Maintenance	4
Repair Costs	3
Warranty	2
Fuel Economy	7
Complaints	9
Insurance Costs	1
OVERALL RATING	**—**

Toyota 86

Toyota 86

Toyota 86

Safety Checklist

Crash Test:
    Frontal . . . . —
    Side. . . . . —
Airbags:
    Torso . . . Std. Front Pelvis/Torso from Seat
    Roll Sensing. .Yes
    Knee Bolster . . . . Standard Front
Crash Avoidance:
    Collision Avoidance . . . . .None
    Blind Spot Detection . . . . .None
    Lane Keeping Assist . . . . .None
    Pedestrian Crash Avoidance . . . . .None
General:
    Auto. Crash Notif.. . . . . Operator Assist.-Fee
    Day Running Lamps . . . . .Standard
Safety Belt/Restraint:
    Dynamic Head Restraints . . . . None
    Adjustable Belt. . . . . .None

^Warning feature does not meet government standards.

At-a-Glance

Status/Year Series Started. Unchanged/2017
Twins . . . . —
Body Styles . . . . .Coupe
Seating 4
Anti-Theft Device . Std. Pass. Immobil. & Active Alarm
Parking Index Rating . . . . .Very Easy
Where Made. . . . . Gunma, Japan
Fuel Factor
    MPG Rating (city/hwy) Good-25/34
    Driving Range (mi.) . . . . .Very Short-375
    Fuel Type. . . . . .Premium
    Annual Fuel Cost . . . . .Average-$1570
    Gas Guzzler Tax . . . . .No
    Greenhouse Gas Emissions (tons/yr.) . . Average-6.4
    Barrels of Oil Used per year Average-11.8

How the Competition Rates

Competitors	Rating	Pg.
Buick Cascada		88
Mazda MX-5		195

Toyota 86

Specifications

Drive. . . . . .RWD
Engine 2.0-liter I4
Transmission . . . . 6-sp. Automatic
Tow Rating (lbs.) . . . . —
Head/Leg Room (in.) . . . . Very Cramped-37.1/41.9
Interior Space (cu. ft.). . . . . Very Cramped-76.5
Cargo Space (cu. ft.) . . . . Very Cramped-6.9
Wheelbase/Length (in.) 101.2/166.7

Price Range

	Retail	Markup
Base MT	$26,255	5%
Base AT	$26,975	5%
Special Edition MT	$29,155	5%
Special Edition AT	$29,875	5%

Ratings—10 Best, 1 Worst

Combo Crash Tests	1
Safety Features	4
Rollover	1
Preventive Maintenance	9
Repair Costs	4
Warranty	2
Fuel Economy	2
Complaints	9
Insurance Costs	10
OVERALL RATING	**2**

Toyota 4Runner

Toyota 4Runner

At-a-Glance

Status/Year Series Started	Unchanged/2006
Twins	Lexus GX, Lexus RX, Toyota Highlander
Body Styles	SUV
Seating	5/7
Anti-Theft Device	Std. Pass. Immobil. & Alarm
Parking Index Rating	Average
Where Made	Tahara, Japan

Fuel Factor

MPG Rating (city/hwy)	Very Poor-17/21
Driving Range (mi.)	Long-428
Fuel Type	Regular
Annual Fuel Cost	Very High-$1976
Gas Guzzler Tax	No
Greenhouse Gas Emissions (tons/yr.)	Very High-10.0
Barrels of Oil Used per year	Very High-18.3

How the Competition Rates

Competitors	Rating	Pg.
Buick Enclave	4	89
Chevrolet Tahoe	4	112
Volvo XC90	8	256

Price Range

	Retail	Markup
SR5 2WD	$34,410	9%
SR5 Premium 4WD	$38,115	9%
TRD Pro	$42,675	9%
Limited 4WD	$44,760	9%

Safety Checklist

Crash Test:
Frontal	Very Poor
Side	Poor

Airbags:
Torso	Std. Front Pelvis/Torso from Seat
Roll Sensing	Yes
Knee Bolster	Standard Front

Crash Avoidance:
Collision Avoidance	None
Blind Spot Detection	None
Lane Keeping Assist	None
Pedestrian Crash Avoidance	None

General:
Auto. Crash Notif	Operator Assist.-Fee
Day Running Lamps	Standard

Safety Belt/Restraint:
Dynamic Head Restraints	Std. Front
Adjustable Belt	Standard Front

^Warning feature does not meet government standards.

Toyota 4Runner

Specifications

Drive	4WD
Engine	4.0-liter V6
Transmission	5-sp. Automatic
Tow Rating (lbs.)	Low-4700
Head/Leg Room (in.)	Average-39.3/41.7
Interior Space (cu. ft.)	Very Roomy-128
Cargo Space (cu. ft.)	Very Cramped-9
Wheelbase/Length (in.)	109.8/190.2

Ratings—10 Best, 1 Worst

Combo Crash Tests	8
Safety Features	10
Rollover	7
Preventive Maintenance	6
Repair Costs	4
Warranty	2
Fuel Economy	5
Complaints	8
Insurance Costs	5
OVERALL RATING	**8**

Toyota Avalon

Toyota Avalon

At-a-Glance

Status/Year Series Started Unchanged/2013
Twins . . . . Lexus ES
Body Styles . . . . .Sedan
Seating. 5
Anti-Theft Device . . . . . . Std. Pass. Immobil. & Alarm
Parking Index Rating . . . . Average
Where Made. . . . . .Georgetown, KY
Fuel Factor
  MPG Rating (city/hwy) Average-21/31
  Driving Range (mi.) Average-418
  Fuel Type. . . . . .Regular
  Annual Fuel Cost . . . . .Average-$1496
  Gas Guzzler Tax . . . . .No
  Greenhouse Gas Emissions (tons/yr.) High-7.5
  Barrels of Oil Used per year High-13.7

How the Competition Rates

Competitors	Rating	Pg.
Chevrolet Impala	4	106
Ford Taurus	3	136
Hyundai Sonata	9	155

Price Range

	Retail	Markup
XLE	$33,500	11%
XLE Premium	$36,700	11%
Touring	$37,900	11%
Hybrid Limited	$42,800	11%

Safety Checklist

Crash Test:
  Frontal. . . . . Average
  Side. . . . . Very Good
Airbags:
  Torso Std. Front & Rear Pelvis/Torso from Seat
  Roll Sensing. .Yes
  Knee Bolster . . . . Standard Front
Crash Avoidance:
  Collision Avoidance . . .Optional CIB & DBS
  Blind Spot Detection . . . . Optional
  Lane Keeping Assist . . . . Optional
  Pedestrian Crash Avoidance . . . . . Optional
General:
  Auto. Crash Notif.. . . . . Operator Assist.-Fee
  Day Running Lamps . . . . .Standard
Safety Belt/Restraint:
  Dynamic Head Restraints . . . . .None
  Adjustable Belt. . . . . Standard Front

^Warning feature does not meet government standards.

Toyota Avalon

Specifications

Drive. . . . . .FWD
Engine 3.5-liter V6
Transmission . . . . 6-sp. Automatic
Tow Rating (lbs.) . . . . .Very Low-1000
Head/Leg Room (in.) Cramped-37.6/42.1
Interior Space (cu. ft.). Average-103.63
Cargo Space (cu. ft.) Cramped-16
Wheelbase/Length (in.) 111/195.3

Toyota Camry Intermediate

Ratings—10 Best, 1 Worst

Rating	
Combo Crash Tests	9
Safety Features	10
Rollover	8
Preventive Maintenance	6
Repair Costs	3
Warranty	2
Fuel Economy	8
Complaints	8
Insurance Costs	5
OVERALL RATING	**8**

Toyota Camry

Toyota Camry

Safety Checklist

Crash Test:
  Frontal . . . . Very Good
  Side . . . . Good
Airbags:
  Torso Std. Front & Rear Pelvis/Torso from Seat
  Roll Sensing . . . . Yes
  Knee Bolster . . . . Standard Front
Crash Avoidance:
  Collision Avoidance . . Optional CIB & DBS^
  Blind Spot Detection . . . . Optional
  Lane Keeping Assist . . . . Optional
  Pedestrian Crash Avoidance . . . . Std.
General:
  Auto. Crash Notif. . . . . Operator Assist.-Fee
  Day Running Lamps . . . . Standard
Safety Belt/Restraint:
  Dynamic Head Restraints . . . . None
  Adjustable Belt . . . . Standard Front

^Warning feature does not meet government standards.

At-a-Glance

Status/Year Series Started Unchanged/2018
Twins . . . . —
Body Styles . . . . Sedan
Seating 5
Anti-Theft Device . . . . . . Std. Pass. Immobil. & Alarm
Parking Index Rating . . . . Average
Where Made . . . . Georgetown, KY
Fuel Factor
  MPG Rating (city/hwy) Good-28/39
  Driving Range (mi.) . . . . Very Long-513
  Fuel Type . . . . Regular
  Annual Fuel Cost . . . . Very Low-$1146
  Gas Guzzler Tax . . . . No
  Greenhouse Gas Emissions (tons/yr.) . Very Low-4.6
  Barrels of Oil Used per year Low-10.3

Toyota Camry

How the Competition Rates

Competitors	Rating	Pg.
Ford Fusion	4	132
Nissan Altima		209
Subaru Legacy	7	226

Price Range

	Retail	Markup
LE	$24,000	9%
XSE	$29,000	10%
XLE Hybrid	$32,250	9%
XSE V6	$34,950	10%

Specifications

Drive . . . . FWD
Engine 2.5-liter I4
Transmission . . . . 8-sp. Automatic
Tow Rating (lbs.) . . . . —
Head/Leg Room (in.) Cramped-38.3/42.1
Interior Space (cu. ft.) Average-100.4
Cargo Space (cu. ft.) Cramped-15.1
Wheelbase/Length (in.) 111.2/192.1

Ratings—10 Best, 1 Worst

Combo Crash Tests	4
Safety Features	7
Rollover	6
Preventive Maintenance	9
Repair Costs	7
Warranty	2
Fuel Economy	8
Complaints	10
Insurance Costs	3
OVERALL RATING	**7**

Toyota Corolla

Toyota Corolla

At-a-Glance

Status/Year Series Started Unchanged/2014
Twins . . . . —
Body Styles . . . . Sedan
Seating 5
Anti-Theft Device . . . . Std. Passive Immobil. Only
Parking Index Rating . . . . Easy
Where Made . . . . Princeton, IN
Fuel Factor
  MPG Rating (city/hwy) Good-27/36
  Driving Range (mi.) Average-402
  Fuel Type . . . . .Regular
  Annual Fuel Cost . . . . Low-$1208
  Gas Guzzler Tax . . . . .No
  Greenhouse Gas Emissions (tons/yr.) Low-5.8
  Barrels of Oil Used per year Average-10.6

How the Competition Rates

Competitors	Rating	Pg.
Honda Civic	10	144
Nissan Sentra	5	205
Subaru Impreza	5	225

Price Range

	Retail	Markup
L	$18,500	6%
LE	$18,935	8%
SE AT	$20,445	8%
XSE	$22,680	8%

Safety Checklist

Crash Test:
  Frontal . . . . Poor
  Side . . . . Average
Airbags:
  Torso . . . Std. Front Pelvis/Torso from Seat
  Roll Sensing . . . . Yes
  Knee Bolster . . . . Standard Driver
Crash Avoidance:
  Collision Avoidance . . Optional CIB & DBS^
  Blind Spot Detection . . . . .None
  Lane Keeping Assist . . . . .Standard
  Pedestrian Crash Avoidance . . . . . Optional
General:
  Auto. Crash Notification . . . . .None
  Day Running Lamps . . . . .Standard
Safety Belt/Restraint:
  Dynamic Head Restraints . . . . .None
  Adjustable Belt . . . . Standard Front

^Warning feature does not meet government standards.

Toyota Corolla

Specifications

Drive . . . . .FWD
Engine 1.8-liter I4
Transmission . . . . 4-sp. Automatic
Tow Rating (lbs.) . . . . Very Low-0
Head/Leg Room (in.) Cramped-38.3/42.3
Interior Space (cu. ft.) Average-97.5
Cargo Space (cu. ft.) . . . . .Very Cramped-13
Wheelbase/Length (in.) 106.3/182.6

Toyota Corolla Hatchback   Compact

Ratings—10 Best, 1 Worst

Combo Crash Tests	—
Safety Features	4
Rollover	6
Preventive Maintenance	10
Repair Costs	9
Warranty	2
Fuel Economy	8
Complaints	—
Insurance Costs	8
OVERALL RATING	—

Toyota Corolla Hatchback

Toyota Corolla Hatchback

At-a-Glance

Status/Year Series Started. . . . . All New/2019
Twins . . . . —
Body Styles . . . . Hatchback
Seating 5
Anti-Theft Device . . . . . . Std. Passive Immobil. Only
Parking Index Rating . . . . .Very Easy
Where Made. . . . . .Tsutsumi, Japan
Fuel Factor
MPG Rating (city/hwy) . . . . Very Good-32/42
Driving Range (mi.) . . . . Very Long-475
Fuel Type. . . . . .Regular
Annual Fuel Cost . . . . Very Low-$1181
Gas Guzzler Tax . . . . .No
Greenhouse Gas Emissions (tons/yr.). Very Low-4.1
Barrels of Oil Used per year Low-9.2

How the Competition Rates

Competitors	Rating	Pg.
Honda Civic	10	144
Mazda 3	6	193
Volkswagen Golf	4	249

Price Range

Price Range	Retail	Markup
SE MT	19990	6%
SE AT	21090	8%
XSE MT	23385	8%
XSE AT	24090	8%

Safety Checklist

Crash Test:
  Frontal . . . . —
  Side. . . . . —
Airbags:
  Torso . . . Std. Front Pelvis/Torso from Seat
  Roll Sensing. .Yes
  Knee Bolster . . . . Standard Driver
Crash Avoidance:
  Collision Avoidance . . Standard CIB & DBS
  Blind Spot Detection . . . . .None
  Lane Keeping Assist . . . . .None
  Pedestrian Crash Avoidance . . . . . . .None
General:
  Auto. Crash Notification . . . . .None
  Day Running Lamps . . . . .Standard
Safety Belt/Restraint:
  Dynamic Head Restraints . . . . .None
  Adjustable Belt. . . . . Standard Front

^Warning feature does not meet government standards.

Toyota Corolla Hatchback

Specifications

Drive. . . . . .FWD
Engine 2.0-liter I4
Transmission . . . . CVT
Tow Rating (lbs.) . . . . —
Head/Leg Room (in.) . . . . —
Interior Space (cu. ft.). . . . . .Very Cramped-85
Cargo Space (cu. ft.) Average-18
Wheelbase/Length (in.) 103.9/169.9

236

Ratings—10 Best, 1 Worst	
Combo Crash Tests	8
Safety Features	9
Rollover	3
Preventive Maintenance	7
Repair Costs	6
Warranty	2
Fuel Economy	2
Complaints	10
Insurance Costs	8
OVERALL RATING	**8**

Toyota Highlander

Toyota Highlander

At-a-Glance

Status/Year Series Started. Unchanged/2014
Twins . . . . Lexus GX, Lexus RX, Toyota 4Runner
Body Styles . . . . SUV
Seating. 7/8
Anti-Theft Device . . . . . . Std. Pass. Immobil. & Alarm
Parking Index Rating . . . . Hard
Where Made. Princeton, IN
Fuel Factor
  MPG Rating (city/hwy) . . . . Very Poor-18/24
  Driving Range (mi.) Short-389
  Fuel Type. . . . . Regular
  Annual Fuel Cost . . . . High-$1812
  Gas Guzzler Tax . . . . No
  Greenhouse Gas Emissions (tons/yr.) Very High-9.0
  Barrels of Oil Used per year High-16.5

How the Competition Rates

Competitors	Rating	Pg.
Dodge Durango	2	120
Ford Explorer	3	128
Volkswagen Atlas	6	248

Price Range	Retail	Markup
LE I4 FWD	$30,630	10%
LE Plus AWD	$36,520	10%
Limited AWD	$43,140	10%
Hybrid LTD Platinum	$47,880	10%

Safety Checklist

Crash Test:
  Frontal. . . . . Average
  Side. . . . . Very Good
Airbags:
  Torso . . . Std. Front Pelvis/Torso from Seat
  Roll Sensing. . . . . Yes
  Knee Bolster . . . . Standard Driver
Crash Avoidance:
  Collision Avoidance . . . Optional CIB & DBS
  Blind Spot Detection . . . . Optional
  Lane Keeping Assist . . . . Standard
  Pedestrian Crash Avoidance . . . . . Optional
General:
  Auto. Crash Notif.. . . . . Operator Assist.-Fee
  Day Running Lamps . . . . Standard
Safety Belt/Restraint:
  Dynamic Head Restraints . . . . None
  Adjustable Belt. . . . . Standard Front

^Warning feature does not meet government standards.

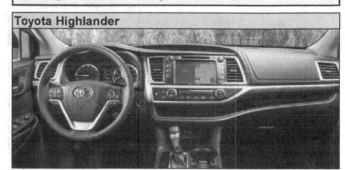
Toyota Highlander

Specifications

Drive. . . . . AWD
Engine 3.5-liter V6
Transmission . . . . 6-sp. Automatic
Tow Rating (lbs.) . . . . Very Low-2000
Head/Leg Room (in.) . . . . Very Roomy-40.7/44.2
Interior Space (cu. ft.). . . . . Very Roomy-144.9
Cargo Space (cu. ft.) . . . . Cramped 13.8
Wheelbase/Length (in.) 109.8/191.1

Ratings—10 Best, 1 Worst

Combo Crash Tests	5
Safety Features	7
Rollover	7
Preventive Maintenance	9
Repair Costs	5
Warranty	2
Fuel Economy	10
Complaints	4
Insurance Costs	5
OVERALL RATING	**7**

Toyota Prius

Toyota Prius

At-a-Glance

Status/Year Series Started. Unchanged/2016
Twins . . . . —
Body Styles . . . . Hatchback
Seating 5
Anti-Theft Device . . . . . . Std. Passive Immobil. Only
Parking Index Rating . . . . Very Easy
Where Made. . . . . .Tsutsumi, Japan
Fuel Factor
  MPG Rating (city/hwy) . . . . Very Good-54/50
  Driving Range (mi.) . . . . Very Long-589
  Fuel Type . . . . .Regular
  Annual Fuel Cost . . . . .Very Low-$705
  Gas Guzzler Tax . . . . .No
  Greenhouse Gas Emissions (tons/yr.) . Very Low-2.8
  Barrels of Oil Used per year . . . . Very Low-6.3

How the Competition Rates

Competitors	Rating	Pg.
Chevrolet Volt	7	115
Honda Civic	10	144
Volkswagen Golf	4	249

Price Range

	Retail	Markup
One	$23,475	6%
Three	$26,735	7%
Four	$29,135	7%
Four Touring	$30,015	7%

Safety Checklist

Crash Test:
  Frontal. . . . . Average
  Side. . . . . Average
Airbags:
  Torso . . . Std. Front Pelvis/Torso from Seat
  Roll Sensing. . . . . .Yes
  Knee Bolster . . . . Standard Driver
Crash Avoidance:
  Collision Avoidance . . .Optional CIB & DBS
  Blind Spot Detection . . . . Optional
  Lane Keeping Assist . . . . Optional
  Pedestrian Crash Avoidance. . . . . Optional
General:
  Auto. Crash Notif.. . . . Operator Assist.-Fee
  Day Running Lamps . . . . Optional
Safety Belt/Restraint:
  Dynamic Head Restraints . . . . .None
  Adjustable Belt. . . . . Standard Front

^Warning feature does not meet government standards.

Toyota Prius

Specifications

Drive. . . . . .FWD
Engine 1.8-liter I4
Transmission . . . . CVT
Tow Rating (lbs.) . . . . —
Head/Leg Room (in.) . . . . Very Cramped-34.4/42.3
Interior Space (cu. ft.). Cramped-93.1
Cargo Space (cu. ft.) Roomy-24.6
Wheelbase/Length (in.) 106.3/178.7

Ratings—10 Best, 1 Worst

Combo Crash Tests	2
Safety Features	2
Rollover	6
Preventive Maintenance	9
Repair Costs	5
Warranty	2
Fuel Economy	10
Complaints	9
Insurance Costs	5
OVERALL RATING	**4**

Toyota Prius C

Toyota Prius C

Toyota Prius C

At-a-Glance

Status/Year Series Started	Unchanged/2013
Twins	—
Body Styles	Hatchback
Seating	5
Anti-Theft Device	Std. Passive Immobil. Only
Parking Index Rating	Very Easy
Where Made	Iwata, Japan
Fuel Factor	
MPG Rating (city/hwy)	Very Good-53/46
Driving Range (mi.)	Very Long-471
Fuel Type	Regular
Annual Fuel Cost	Very Low-$741
Gas Guzzler Tax	No
Greenhouse Gas Emissions (tons/yr.)	Very Low-3.6
Barrels of Oil Used per year	Very Low-6.6

Safety Checklist

Crash Test:
Frontal . . . . Poor
Side . . . . Very Poor
Airbags:
Torso . . . Std. Front Pelvis/Torso from Seat
Roll Sensing . . . . No
Knee Bolster . . . . Standard Driver
Crash Avoidance:
Collision Avoidance . . . Optional CIB & DBS
Blind Spot Detection . . . . None
Lane Keeping Assist . . Warn. Only Optional
Pedestrian Crash Avoidance . . . . None
General:
Auto. Crash Notif. . . . . Operator Assist.-Fee
Day Running Lamps . . . . Standard
Safety Belt/Restraint:
Dynamic Head Restraints . . . . None
Adjustable Belt . . . . None

^Warning feature does not meet government standards.

How the Competition Rates

Competitors	Rating	Pg.
Chevrolet Sonic	8	109
Fiat 500	2	122
Mitsubishi Mirage	3	206

Price Range

	Retail	Markup
One	$20,630	5%
Two	$21,430	6%
Three	$22,855	7%
Four	$24,965	7%

Specifications

Drive	FWD
Engine	1.5-liter I4
Transmission	CVT
Tow Rating (lbs.)	—
Head/Leg Room (in.)	Cramped-38.6/41.7
Interior Space (cu. ft.)	Very Cramped-87.4
Cargo Space (cu. ft.)	Average-17.1
Wheelbase/Length (in.)	100.4/157.3

Toyota Prius Prime | Compact

Ratings—10 Best, 1 Worst

Combo Crash Tests	—
Safety Features	9
Rollover	6
Preventive Maintenance	9
Repair Costs	7
Warranty	2
Fuel Economy	10
Complaints	5
Insurance Costs	5
OVERALL RATING	**—**

Toyota Prius Prime

At-a-Glance

Status/Year Series Started	Unchanged/2017
Twins	—
Body Styles	Sedan
Seating	4
Anti-Theft Device	Std. Passive Immobil. Only
Parking Index Rating	Very Easy
Where Made	Tsutsumi, Japan
Fuel Factor	
MPG Rating (city/hwy)	Very Good-55/53
Driving Range (mi.)	Very Long-611
Fuel Type	Regular
Annual Fuel Cost	Very Low-$680
Gas Guzzler Tax	No
Greenhouse Gas Emissions (tons/yr.)	Very Low-1.3
Barrels of Oil Used per year	Very Low-3.0

How the Competition Rates

Competitors	Rating	Pg.
Audi A4	2	72
Chevrolet Volt	7	115
Nissan Leaf		212

Price Range

	Retail	Markup
Plus	$27,100	4%
Premium	$28,800	4%
Advanced	$33,100	4%

Toyota Prius Prime

Safety Checklist

Crash Test:
  Frontal . . . . —
  Side . . . . —
Airbags:
  Torso . . . Std. Front Pelvis/Torso from Seat
  Roll Sensing . . . . Yes
  Knee Bolster . . . . Standard Front
Crash Avoidance:
  Collision Avoidance . . . Optional CIB & DBS
  Blind Spot Detection . . . . Optional
  Lane Keeping Assist . . . . Optional
  Pedestrian Crash Avoidance . . . . . Standard
General:
  Auto. Crash Notification . . . . None
  Day Running Lamps . . . . Standard
Safety Belt/Restraint:
  Dynamic Head Restraints . . . . None
  Adjustable Belt . . . . Standard Front

^Warning feature does not meet government standards.

Toyota Prius Prime

Specifications

Drive	FWD
Engine	1.8-liter I4
Transmission	CVT
Tow Rating (lbs.)	—
Head/Leg Room (in.)	Roomy-39.4/43.2
Interior Space (cu. ft.)	Cramped-91.5
Cargo Space (cu. ft.)	Average-19.8
Wheelbase/Length (in.)	106.3/182.9

Ratings—10 Best, 1 Worst

Combo Crash Tests	—
Safety Features	7
Rollover	3
Preventive Maintenance	4
Repair Costs	7
Warranty	2
Fuel Economy	5
Complaints	—
Insurance Costs	10
OVERALL RATING	**—**

Toyota RAV4

Toyota RAV4

At-a-Glance

Status/Year Series Started	All New/2019
Twins	—
Body Styles	SUV
Seating	5
Anti-Theft Device	Std. Passive Immobil. Only
Parking Index Rating	Easy
Where Made	Woodstock, Ontario / Tahara, Japan

Fuel Factor

MPG Rating (city/hwy)	Good-27/34
Driving Range (mi.)	Long-435
Fuel Type	Regular
Annual Fuel Cost	Low-$1235
Gas Guzzler Tax	No
Greenhouse Gas Emissions (tons/yr.)	Low-4.9
Barrels of Oil Used per year	Average-11.0

How the Competition Rates

Competitors	Rating	Pg.
Ford Escape	5	126
Honda HR-V	5	147
Hyundai Tucson	8	156

Price Range

	Retail	Markup
LE FWD	$25,895	7%
XLE FWD	$27,695	7%
Adventure AWD	$32,900	7%
Limited AWD	$34,900	7%

Safety Checklist

Crash Test:
- Frontal . . . . Average
- Side . . . . Very Good

Airbags:
- Torso . . . Std. Front Pelvis/Torso from Seat
- Roll Sensing . . . . Yes
- Knee Bolster . . . . Standard Driver

Crash Avoidance:
- Collision Avoidance . . Standard CIB & DBS
- Blind Spot Detection . . . . Optional
- Lane Keeping Assist . . . . Standard
- Pedestrian Crash Avoidance . . . . . Optional

General:
- Auto. Crash Notif.. . . . Operator Assist.-Fee
- Day Running Lamps . . . . .Standard

Safety Belt/Restraint:
- Dynamic Head Restraints . . . . .None
- Adjustable Belt . . . . Standard Front

^Warning feature does not meet government standards.

Toyota RAV4

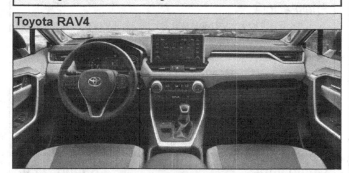

Specifications

Drive	AWD
Engine	2.5-liter I4
Transmission	8-sp. Automatic
Tow Rating (lbs.)	Very Low-1500
Head/Leg Room (in.)	Cramped-39.5/41.0
Interior Space (cu. ft.)	Average-98.9
Cargo Space (cu. ft.)	Very Roomy-37.0
Wheelbase/Length (in.)	105.9/180.9

Ratings—10 Best, 1 Worst

Combo Crash Tests	—
Safety Features	4
Rollover	2
Preventive Maintenance	6
Repair Costs	4
Warranty	2
Fuel Economy	1
Complaints	9
Insurance Costs	10
OVERALL RATING	**—**

Toyota Sequoia

Toyota Sequoia

At-a-Glance

Status/Year Series Started Unchanged/2008
Twins . . . . —
Body Styles . . . . SUV
Seating 8
Anti-Theft Device . . . . . . Std. Pass. Immobil. & Alarm
Parking Index Rating . . . . Very Hard
Where Made. Princeton, IN
Fuel Factor
  MPG Rating (city/hwy) . . . . .Very Poor-13/17
  Driving Range (mi.) Short-384
  Fuel Type. . . . . .Regular
  Annual Fuel Cost . . . . Very High-$2528
  Gas Guzzler Tax . . . . .No
  Greenhouse Gas Emissions (tons/yr.)Very High-12.8
  Barrels of Oil Used per year . . . . . . Very High-23.5

How the Competition Rates

Competitors	Rating	Pg.
Buick Enclave	4	89
Chevrolet Suburban	2	111
Volvo XC90	8	256

Price Range	Retail	Markup
SR5 2WD	$48,300	10%
Sport 2WD	$51,015	10%
Limited 4WD	$60,020	10%
Platinum 4WD	$67,235	10%

Safety Checklist

Crash Test:
  Frontal . . . . —
  Side. . . . . —
Airbags:
  Torso . . . Std. Front Pelvis/Torso from Seat
  Roll Sensing. . . . . .Yes
  Knee Bolster . . . . Standard Front
Crash Avoidance:
  Collision Avoidance . . . . .None
  Blind Spot Detection . . . . Optional
  Lane Keeping Assist . . . . .None
  Pedestrian Crash Avoidance . . . . . . .None
General:
  Auto. Crash Notification . . . . .None
  Day Running Lamps . . . . Optional
Safety Belt/Restraint:
  Dynamic Head Restraints . . . . .None
  Adjustable Belt. . . . .Standard Front & Rear

^Warning feature does not meet government standards.

Toyota Sequoia

Specifications

Drive. 4WD
Engine 5.7-liter V8
Transmission . . . . 6-sp. Automatic
Tow Rating (lbs.) Average-7100
Head/Leg Room (in.) . . . . Very Cramped-34.8/42.5
Interior Space (cu. ft.). . . . . —
Cargo Space (cu. ft.) Average-18.9
Wheelbase/Length (in.) 122/205.1

Toyota Sienna

Ratings—10 Best, 1 Worst

Combo Crash Tests	6
Safety Features	7
Rollover	5
Preventive Maintenance	2
Repair Costs	4
Warranty	2
Fuel Economy	3
Complaints	3
Insurance Costs	5
OVERALL RATING	**2**

Toyota Sienna

At-a-Glance

Status/Year Series Started	Unchanged/2004
Twins	—
Body Styles	Minivan
Seating	7/8
Anti-Theft Device	Std. Pass. Immobil. & Alarm
Parking Index Rating	Hard
Where Made	Princeton, IN

Fuel Factor

MPG Rating (city/hwy)	Poor-18/25
Driving Range (mi.)	Average-412
Fuel Type	Regular
Annual Fuel Cost	High-$1784
Gas Guzzler Tax	No
Greenhouse Gas Emissions (tons/yr.)	High-8.6
Barrels of Oil Used per year	High-15.7

How the Competition Rates

Competitors	Rating	Pg.
Chrysler Pacifica	8	117
Honda Odyssey	9	148
Kia Sedona		171

Price Range

	Retail	Markup
L FWD	$29,750	8%
SE FWD	$36,110	8%
XLE Premium FWD	$39,505	9%
LTD Premium AWD	$47,310	9%

Safety Checklist

Crash Test:

Frontal	Average
Side	Average

Airbags:

Torso	Std. Front Pelvis/Torso from Seat
Roll Sensing	Yes
Knee Bolster	Standard Driver

Crash Avoidance:

Collision Avoidance	Optional CIB & DBS
Blind Spot Detection	Optional
Lane Keeping Assist	None
Pedestrian Crash Avoidance	None

General:

Auto. Crash Notif.	Operator Assist.-Fee
Day Running Lamps	Optional

Safety Belt/Restraint:

Dynamic Head Restraints	Std. Front
Adjustable Belt	Standard Front & Rear

^Warning feature does not meet government standards.

Toyota Sienna

Specifications

Drive	FWD
Engine	3.5-liter V6
Transmission	6-sp. Automatic
Tow Rating (lbs.)	Low-3500
Head/Leg Room (in.)	Average-41/40.5
Interior Space (cu. ft.)	Very Roomy-164.4
Cargo Space (cu. ft.)	Very Roomy-39.1
Wheelbase/Length (in.)	119.3/200.2

Ratings—10 Best, 1 Worst

Combo Crash Tests	1
Safety Features	4
Rollover	2
Preventive Maintenance	9
Repair Costs	4
Warranty	2
Fuel Economy	3
Complaints	4
Insurance Costs	8
OVERALL RATING	**1**

Toyota Tacoma

Toyota Tacoma

At-a-Glance

Status/Year Series Started Unchanged/2016
Twins . . . . —
Body Styles . . . . Pickup
Seating 4
Anti-Theft Device . . . . . Std. Pass. Immobil. & Alarm
Parking Index Rating . . . . Very Hard
Where Made . . . . . San Antonio, TX / Tijuana, Mexico
Fuel Factor
   MPG Rating (city/hwy) Poor-19/23
   Driving Range (mi.) Long-435
   Fuel Type . . . . Regular
   Annual Fuel Cost . . . . High-$1783
   Gas Guzzler Tax . . . . No
   Greenhouse Gas Emissions (tons/yr.) High-7.3
   Barrels of Oil Used per year High-16.5

How the Competition Rates

Competitors	Rating	Pg.
Chevrolet Colorado	2	102
Ford Ranger		135
Nissan Frontier	1	211

Price Range

	Retail	Markup
SR Access Cab 2WD	$24,575	7%
SR5 Access Cab 2WD	$26,660	7%
SR5 Dbl Cab 4WD V6	$33,220	8%
Limited Sport Dbl. Cab 4WD V6	$39,250	8%

Safety Checklist

Crash Test:
   Frontal . . . . Very Poor
   Side . . . . Very Poor
Airbags:
   Torso . . . Std. Front Pelvis/Torso from Seat
   Roll Sensing . . . . Yes
   Knee Bolster . . . . Standard Front
Crash Avoidance:
   Collision Avoidance . . . . None
   Blind Spot Detection . . . . Optional
   Lane Keeping Assist . . . . None
   Pedestrian Crash Avoidance . . . . None
General:
   Auto. Crash Notification . . . . None
   Day Running Lamps . . . . Standard
Safety Belt/Restraint:
   Dynamic Head Restraints . . . . None
   Adjustable Belt . . . . Standard Front

^Warning feature does not meet government standards.

Toyota Tacoma

Specifications

Drive 4WD
Engine 2.7-liter I4
Transmission . . . . 6-sp. Automatic
Tow Rating (lbs.) Low-3500
Head/Leg Room (in.) Roomy-39.7/42.9
Interior Space (cu. ft.) . . . . Very Cramped-57.5
Cargo Space (cu. ft.) . . . . Very Roomy-33.5
Wheelbase/Length (in.) 127.4/212.3

Ratings—10 Best, 1 Worst

Combo Crash Tests	—
Safety Features	6
Rollover	2
Preventive Maintenance	6
Repair Costs	5
Warranty	2
Fuel Economy	1
Complaints	9
Insurance Costs	10
OVERALL RATING	—

Toyota Tundra

Toyota Tundra

At-a-Glance

Status/Year Series Started	Unchanged/2007
Twins	
Body Styles	Pickup
Seating	5/6
Anti-Theft Device	Std. Pass. Immobil. & Alarm
Parking Index Rating	Very Hard
Where Made	San Antonio, TX
Fuel Factor	
MPG Rating (city/hwy)	Very Poor-13/18
Driving Range (mi.)	Short-392
Fuel Type	Regular
Annual Fuel Cost	Very High-$2474
Gas Guzzler Tax	No
Greenhouse Gas Emissions (tons/yr.)	Very High-8.9
Barrels of Oil Used per year	Very High-20.6

How the Competition Rates

Competitors	Rating	Pg.
Ford F-150	8	129
Nissan Titan	1	206
Ram 1500	5	221

Price Range

	Retail	Markup
SR Reg. Cab 2WD 5.7 V8	$32,390	8%
SR5 Dbl. Cab 4WD 5.7 V8	$37,150	8%
Limited Crew Max 4WD 5.7 V8	$45,300	8%
1794 Edition Crew Max 5.7 V8	$50,130	8%

Safety Checklist

Crash Test:
 Frontal........................ Very Poor
 Side............................. —
Airbags:
 Torso . . . Std. Front Pelvis/Torso from Seat
 Roll Sensing...................... Yes
 Knee Bolster .... Standard Front
Crash Avoidance:
 Collision Avoidance .... None
 Blind Spot Detection .... Optional
 Lane Keeping Assist .... None
 Pedestrian Crash Avoidance .... None
General:
 Auto. Crash Notification........... None
 Day Running Lamps .... Standard
Safety Belt/Restraint:
 Dynamic Head Restraints ...... Std. Front
 Adjustable Belt..... Standard Front & Rear

^Warning feature does not meet government standards.

Toyota Tundra

Specifications

Drive	4WD
Engine	5.7-liter V8
Transmission	6-sp. Automatic
Tow Rating (lbs.)	Very High-10000
Head/Leg Room (in.)	Average-39.7/42.5
Interior Space (cu. ft.)	—
Cargo Space (cu. ft.)	Very Roomy-67.1
Wheelbase/Length (in.)	145.7/228.9

Ratings—10 Best, 1 Worst

Ratings—10 Best, 1 Worst	
Combo Crash Tests	5
Safety Features	2
Rollover	5
Preventive Maintenance	9
Repair Costs	10
Warranty	2
Fuel Economy	9
Complaints	3
Insurance Costs	5
OVERALL RATING	**6**

Toyota Yaris

Toyota Yaris

Safety Checklist

Crash Test:
    Frontal . . . . Poor
    Side . . . . Average
Airbags:
    Torso . . . Std. Front Pelvis/Torso from Seat
    Roll Sensing . . . . Yes
    Knee Bolster . . . . None
Crash Avoidance:
    Collision Avoidance . . . . None
    Blind Spot Detection . . . . None
    Lane Keeping Assist . . . . None
    Pedestrian Crash Avoidance . . . . None
General:
    Auto. Crash Notif . . . . Operator Assist.-Fee
    Day Running Lamps . . . . Standard
Safety Belt/Restraint:
    Dynamic Head Restraints . . . . None
    Adjustable Belt . . . . Standard Front

^Warning feature does not meet government standards.

At-a-Glance

Status/Year Series Started Unchanged/2017
Twins . . . . —
Body Styles . . . . Sedan
Seating 5
Anti-Theft Device . . . . Std. Passive Immobil. Only
Parking Index Rating . . . . Very Easy
Where Made . . . . Salamanca, Mexico
Fuel Factor
    MPG Rating (city/hwy) . . . . Very Good-32/40
    Driving Range (mi.) Average-408
    Fuel Type . . . . .Regular
    Annual Fuel Cost . . . . Very Low-$1045
    Gas Guzzler Tax . . . . .No
    Greenhouse Gas Emissions (tons/yr.) . Very Low-4.1
    Barrels of Oil Used per year Low-9.4

How the Competition Rates

Competitors	Rating	Pg.
Chevrolet Cruze	8	104
Kia Soul	7	173
Mazda 3	6	190

Price Range

Price Range	Retail	Markup
Sedan MT	$15,950	4%
Sedan AT	$17,050	4%

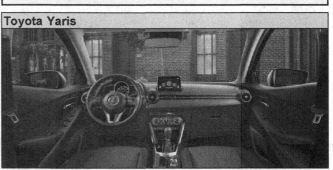

Toyota Yaris

Specifications

Drive . . . . .FWD
Engine 1.5-liter I4
Transmission . . . . 4-sp. Automatic
Tow Rating (lbs.) . . . . —
Head/Leg Room (in.) Cramped-39.3/40.6
Interior Space (cu. ft.) . . . . Very Cramped-85.1
Cargo Space (cu. ft.) Cramped-15.6
Wheelbase/Length (in.) 98.8/155.5

Ratings—10 Best, 1 Worst

Combo Crash Tests	2
Safety Features	1
Rollover	5
Preventive Maintenance	10
Repair Costs	10
Warranty	2
Fuel Economy	9
Complaints	9
Insurance Costs	3
OVERALL RATING	**5**

Toyota Yaris Liftback

Toyota Yaris Liftback

At-a-Glance

Status/Year Series Started Unchanged/2012
Twins . . . . —
Body Styles . . . . Hatchback
Seating 5
Anti-Theft Device . . . . . . Std. Passive Immobil. Only
Parking Index Rating . . . . .Very Easy
Where Made. . . . . .Iwata, Japan
Fuel Factor
  MPG Rating (city/hwy) . . . . Very Good-30/36
  Driving Range (mi.) . . . . Very Short-360
  Fuel Type. . . . . .Regular
  Annual Fuel Cost . . . . Very Low-$1133
  Gas Guzzler Tax . . . . .No
  Greenhouse Gas Emissions (tons/yr.) Low-5.6
  Barrels of Oil Used per year Low-10.3

How the Competition Rates

Competitors	Rating	Pg.
Chevrolet Sonic	8	109
Fiat 500	2	122
Mitsubishi Mirage	3	206

Price Range	Retail	Markup
L 2 Door MT	$15,635	4%
L 4 Door AT	$16,760	4%
LE 4 Door	$17,660	4%
SE 4 Door	$19,060	4%

Safety Checklist

Crash Test:
  Frontal. . . . . Poor
  Side. . . . . Very Poor
Airbags:
  Torso . . . Std. Front Pelvis/Torso from Seat
  Roll Sensing. . . . . .No
  Knee Bolster . . . . Standard Driver
Crash Avoidance:
  Collision Avoidance . . .Optional CIB & DBS
  Blind Spot Detection . . . . .None
  Lane Keeping Assist . Warn. Only Optional^
  Pedestrian Crash Avoidance . . . . .None
General:
  Auto. Crash Notif.. . . . . Operator Assist.-Fee
  Day Running Lamps . . . . Optional
Safety Belt/Restraint:
  Dynamic Head Restraints . . . . .None
  Adjustable Belt. . . . . .None

^Warning feature does not meet government standards.

Toyota Yaris Liftback

Specifications

Drive. . . . . .FWD
Engine 1.5-liter I4
Transmission . . . . 6-sp. Automatic
Tow Rating (lbs.) . . . . —
Head/Leg Room (in.) Cramped-38.2/41.9
Interior Space (cu. ft.). . . . . Very Cramped-85.9
Cargo Space (cu. ft.) . . . . Very Cramped-13.5
Wheelbase/Length (in.) 101.2/171.7

Volkswagen Atlas Medium SUV

Volkswagen Atlas

Ratings—10 Best, 1 Worst

Combo Crash Tests	9
Safety Features	7
Rollover	4
Preventive Maintenance	3
Repair Costs	1
Warranty	10
Fuel Economy	3
Complaints	4
Insurance Costs	5
OVERALL RATING	**6**

Volkswagen Atlas

At-a-Glance

Status/Year Series Started	Unchanged/2018
Twins	—
Body Styles	SUV
Seating	7
Anti-Theft Device	Std. Pass. Immobil. & Alarm
Parking Index Rating	Hard
Where Made	Chattanooga, Tennessee
Fuel Factor	
MPG Rating (city/hwy)	Poor-18/25
Driving Range (mi.)	Short-383
Fuel Type	Regular
Annual Fuel Cost	High-$1784
Gas Guzzler Tax	No
Greenhouse Gas Emissions (tons/yr.)	Average-7.2
Barrels of Oil Used per year	High-16.5

How the Competition Rates

Competitors	Rating	Pg.
Acura MDX	7	67
GMC Acadia	2	138
Toyota Highlander	8	237

Price Range

	Retail	Markup
S FWD	$30,500	4%
SE FWD V6	$34,990	4%
SEL 4Motion V6	$42,690	4%
SEL Premium 4Motion V6	$48,490	4%

Safety Checklist

Crash Test:
  Frontal.........................Good
  Side......................Very Good
Airbags:
  Torso........Std. Front Torso from Seat
  Roll Sensing.......................Yes
  Knee Bolster ....None
Crash Avoidance:
  Collision Avoidance ...Optional CIB & DBS
  Blind Spot Detection ....Optional
  Lane Keeping Assist ....Optional
  Pedestrian Crash Avoidance .....Optional
General:
  Auto. Crash Notif..... Operator Assist.-Fee
  Day Running Lamps ....Standard
Safety Belt/Restraint:
  Dynamic Head Restraints ....None
  Adjustable Belt...........Standard Front

^Warning feature does not meet government standards.

Volkswagen Atlas

Specifications

Drive	FWD
Engine	3.6-liter V6
Transmission	8-sp. Automatic
Tow Rating (lbs.)	Low-5000
Head/Leg Room (in.)	Roomy-41.3/41.5
Interior Space (cu. ft.)	Very Roomy-153.7
Cargo Space (cu. ft.)	Average-20.6
Wheelbase/Length (in.)	117.3/198.3

Ratings—10 Best, 1 Worst

Combo Crash Tests	5
Safety Features	5
Rollover	5
Preventive Maintenance	3
Repair Costs	7
Warranty	10
Fuel Economy	7
Complaints	3
Insurance Costs	1
OVERALL RATING	**4**

Volkswagen Golf

Volkswagen Golf

At-a-Glance

Status/Year Series Started	Unchanged/2015
Twins	Audi A3
Body Styles	Hatchback
Seating	5
Anti-Theft Device	Std. Pass. Immobil. & Alarm
Parking Index Rating	Very Easy
Where Made	Puebla, Mexico / Wolfsburg, Germany

Fuel Factor

MPG Rating (city/hwy)	Good-25/36
Driving Range (mi.)	Short-383
Fuel Type	Regular
Annual Fuel Cost	Low-$1268
Gas Guzzler Tax	No
Greenhouse Gas Emissions (tons/yr.)	Average-6.2
Barrels of Oil Used per year	Average-11.4

How the Competition Rates

Competitors	Rating	Pg.
Kia Soul	7	173
Mazda 3	6	193
Nissan Sentra	5	205

Price Range

	Retail	Markup
S Hatchback AT	$19,895	4%
S Sportswagon AT	$22,680	4%
SE Sportswagon AT	$27,030	4%
SEL Sportwagon AT	$29,970	4%

Safety Checklist

Crash Test:
- Frontal . . . . Average
- Side . . . . Average

Airbags:
- Torso . . . Std. Front Pelvis/Torso from Seat
- Roll Sensing . . . . Yes
- Knee Bolster . . . . None

Crash Avoidance:
- Collision Avoidance . . . . Optional CIB
- Blind Spot Detection . . . . Optional
- Lane Keeping Assist . . . . Optional
- Pedestrian Crash Avoidance . . . . None

General:
- Auto. Crash Notif. . . . . . Operator Assist.-Fee
- Day Running Lamps . . . . Standard

Safety Belt/Restraint:
- Dynamic Head Restraints . . . . None
- Adjustable Belt . . . . Standard Front

^Warning feature does not meet government standards.

Volkswagen Golf

Specifications

Drive	FWD
Engine	1.8-liter I4
Transmission	6-sp. Automatic
Tow Rating (lbs.)	—
Head/Leg Room (in.)	Cramped-38.4/41.2
Interior Space (cu. ft.)	Cramped-93.5
Cargo Space (cu. ft.)	Roomy-22.8
Wheelbase/Length (in.)	103.8/167.5

Volkswagen Jetta   Compact

Ratings—10 Best, 1 Worst

Combo Crash Tests	—
Safety Features	2
Rollover	7
Preventive Maintenance	5
Repair Costs	4
Warranty	10
Fuel Economy	8
Complaints	—
Insurance Costs	3
OVERALL RATING	**—**

Volkswagen Jetta

Volkswagen Jetta

Safety Checklist

Crash Test:
  Frontal . . . . —
  Side. . . . . —
Airbags:
  Torso . . . Std. Front Pelvis/Torso from Seat
  Roll Sensing. No
  Knee Bolster . . . . None
Crash Avoidance:
  Collision Avoidance . . Optional CIB & DBS^
  Blind Spot Detection . . . . Optional
  Lane Keeping Assist . . . . Optional
  Pedestrian Crash Avoidance . . . . .None
General:
  Auto. Crash Notif.. . . . Operator Assist.-Fee
  Day Running Lamps . . . . .Standard
Safety Belt/Restraint:
  Dynamic Head Restraints . . . . .None
  Adjustable Belt . . . . Standard Front

^Warning feature does not meet government standards.

At-a-Glance

Status/Year Series Started. . . . . All New/2019
Twins . . . . —
Body Styles . . . . .Sedan
Seating 5
Anti-Theft Device . . . . . . Std. Pass. Immobil. & Alarm
Parking Index Rating . . . . Easy
Where Made. . . . . .Puebla, Mexico
Fuel Factor
  MPG Rating (city/hwy) Good-30/39
  Driving Range (mi.) Long-435
  Fuel Type. . . . . .Regular
  Annual Fuel Cost . . . . Very Low-$1098
  Gas Guzzler Tax . . . . .No
  Greenhouse Gas Emissions (tons/yr.) . Very Low-4.3
  Barrels of Oil Used per year Low-9.7

How the Competition Rates

Competitors	Rating	Pg.
Chevrolet Cruze	8	104
Nissan Sentra	5	205
Toyota Corolla	7	235

Price Range

	Retail	Markup
S MT	$18,545	4%
SE AT	$22,155	4%
SEL AT	$24,415	4%
SEL Premium AT	$26,945	4%

Specifications

Drive. . . . . .FWD
Engine 1.4-liter I4
Transmission . . . . 8-sp. Automatic
Tow Rating (lbs.) . . . . —
Head/Leg Room (in.) . . . . Very Cramped-38.5/41.1
Interior Space (cu. ft.). Cramped-94.7
Cargo Space (cu. ft.) Cramped-14.1
Wheelbase/Length (in.) 105.7/185.1

Volkswagen Jetta

Ratings—10 Best, 1 Worst

Combo Crash Tests	5
Safety Features	2
Rollover	7
Preventive Maintenance	5
Repair Costs	5
Warranty	10
Fuel Economy	7
Complaints	3
Insurance Costs	1
OVERALL RATING	**4**

Volkswagen Passat

Volkswagen Passat

At-a-Glance

Status/Year Series Started	Unchanged/2012
Twins	—
Body Styles	Sedan
Seating	5
Anti-Theft Device	Std Pass. Immobil. & Alarm
Parking Index Rating	Average
Where Made	Chattanooga, TN
Fuel Factor	
MPG Rating (city/hwy)	Good-25/36
Driving Range (mi.)	Very Long-536
Fuel Type	Regular
Annual Fuel Cost	Low-$1268
Gas Guzzler Tax	No
Greenhouse Gas Emissions (tons/yr.)	Low-5.0
Barrels of Oil Used per year	Average-11.4

How the Competition Rates

Competitors	Rating	Pg.
Acura TLX	9	70
Ford Fusion	4	132
Subaru Legacy	7	226

Price Range	Retail	Markup
S 1.8T	$22,440	4%
R-Line 1.8T	$23,975	4%
SE 1.8T	$25,495	4%
SEL Premium V6	$33,995	4%

Safety Checklist

Crash Test:
Frontal . . . . Very Poor
Side . . . . Very Good
Airbags:
Torso . . . Std. Front Pelvis/Torso from Seat
Roll Sensing . . . . Yes
Knee Bolster . . . . None
Crash Avoidance:
Collision Avoidance . . . . None
Blind Spot Detection . . . . Optional
Lane Keeping Assist . . . . None
Pedestrian Crash Avoidance . . . . None
General:
Auto. Crash Notif.. . . . Operator Assist.-Fee
Day Running Lamps . . . . Standard
Safety Belt/Restraint:
Dynamic Head Restraints . . . . None
Adjustable Belt . . . . Standard Front

^Warning feature does not meet government standards.

Volkswagen Passat

Specifications

Drive	FWD
Engine	1.8-liter I4
Transmission	6-SP. Automatic
Tow Rating (lbs.)	—
Head/Leg Room (in.)	Cramped-38.3/42.4
Interior Space (cu. ft.)	Average-102
Cargo Space (cu. ft.)	Cramped-15.9
Wheelbase/Length (in.)	110.4/191.9

Ratings—10 Best, 1 Worst

Combo Crash Tests	—
Safety Features	3
Rollover	3
Preventive Maintenance	3
Repair Costs	4
Warranty	10
Fuel Economy	4
Complaints	4
Insurance Costs	10
OVERALL RATING	**—**

Volkswagen Tiguan

Volkswagen Tiguan

At-a-Glance

Status/Year Series Started	Unchanged/2018
Twins	—
Body Styles	SUV
Seating	7
Anti-Theft Device	Std. Pass. Immobil. & Alarm
Parking Index Rating	Average
Where Made	Puebla, Mexico
Fuel Factor	
MPG Rating (city/hwy)	Poor-22/27
Driving Range (mi.)	Very Short-367
Fuel Type	Regular
Annual Fuel Cost	Average-$1531
Gas Guzzler Tax	No
Greenhouse Gas Emissions (tons/yr.)	Average-6.1
Barrels of Oil Used per year	High-13.7

How the Competition Rates

Competitors	Rating	Pg.
Ford Escape	5	126
Lexus NX	5	182
Kia Sportage	9	174

Price Range

	Retail	Markup
S FWD	$25,195	4%
SE FWD	$28,930	4%
SEL 4Motion	$33,850	4%
SEL Premium 4Motion	$37,550	4%

Safety Checklist

Crash Test:
 Frontal . . . . —
 Side . . . . —
Airbags:
 Torso . . . Std. Front Pelvis/Torso from Seat
 Roll Sensing . . . . Yes
 Knee Bolster . . . . None
Crash Avoidance:
 Collision Avoidance . . Optional CIB & DBS^
 Blind Spot Detection . . . . None
 Lane Keeping Assist . . . . Optional^
 Pedestrian Crash Avoidance . . . . None
General:
 Auto. Crash Notif. . . . . Operator Assist.-Fee
 Day Running Lamps . . . . Standard
Safety Belt/Restraint:
 Dynamic Head Restraints . . . . None
 Adjustable Belt . . . . Standard Front

^Warning feature does not meet government standards.

Specifications

Drive	FWD
Engine	2.0-liter I4
Transmission	8-sp. Automatic
Tow Rating (lbs.)	Very Low-1500
Head/Leg Room (in.)	Cramped-39.6/40.2
Interior Space (cu. ft.)	Roomy-123.9
Cargo Space (cu. ft.)	Very Cramped-12
Wheelbase/Length (in.)	109.8/185.1

Volvo S60 ································· Intermediate

Ratings—10 Best, 1 Worst

Combo Crash Tests	—
Safety Features	6
Rollover	8
Preventive Maintenance	5
Repair Costs	6
Warranty	8
Fuel Economy	7
Complaints	—
Insurance Costs	5

OVERALL RATING —

Volvo S60

Volvo S60

At-a-Glance

Status/Year Series Started . . . . All New/2019
Twins . . . . —
Body Styles . . . . Sedan
Seating 5
Anti-Theft Device . Std. Pass. Immobil. & Active Alarm
Parking Index Rating . . . . Average
Where Made . . . . Torslanda, Sweden
Fuel Factor
  MPG Rating (city/hwy) Good-24/36
  Driving Range (mi.) Average-406
  Fuel Type . . . . Premium
  Annual Fuel Cost . . . . Average-$1628
  Gas Guzzler Tax . . . . No
  Greenhouse Gas Emissions (tons/yr.) Low-5.2
  Barrels of Oil Used per year Average-11.8

How the Competition Rates

Competitors	Rating	Pg.
Acura TLX	9	70
Nissan Maxima	4	213
Subaru Legacy	7	226

Price Range

	Retail	Markup
T5 Momentum FWD	$35,800	6%
T5 Inscription FWD	$42,900	6%
T6 Inscription AWD	$47,400	6%
T8 Inscription Plug-in Hyb	$55,400	6%

Safety Checklist

Crash Test:
  Frontal . . . . —
  Side . . . . —
Airbags:
  Torso . . . Std. Front Pelvis/Torso from Seat
  Roll Sensing . . . . Yes
  Knee Bolster . . . . None
Crash Avoidance:
  Collision Avoidance . . Std. CIB & Opt. DBS
  Blind Spot Detection . . . . Optional
  Lane Keeping Assist . . . . Optional
  Pedestrian Crash Avoidance . . . . Std.
General:
  Auto. Crash Notif. . . . . Operator Assist.-Fee
  Day Running Lamps . . . . Standard
Safety Belt/Restraint:
  Dynamic Head Restraints . . . . None
  Adjustable Belt . . . . Standard Front

^Warning feature does not meet government standards.

Volvo S60

Specifications

Drive . . . . FWD
Engine 2.0-liter I4
Transmission . . . . 8-sp. Automatic
Tow Rating (lbs.) . . . . —
Head/Leg Room (in.) Cramped-37.4/42.3
Interior Space (cu. ft.) Cramped-96
Cargo Space (cu. ft.) . . . . Very Cramped-12
Wheelbase/Length (in.) 113.1/187.4

Ratings—10 Best, 1 Worst

Combo Crash Tests	—
Safety Features	6
Rollover	6
Preventive Maintenance	2
Repair Costs	6
Warranty	8
Fuel Economy	7
Complaints	—
Insurance Costs	10
OVERALL RATING	—

Volvo V60

Volvo V60

At-a-Glance

Status/Year Series Started. . . . . All New/2019
Twins . . . . —
Body Styles . . . . Wagon
Seating 5
Anti-Theft Device . Std. Pass. Immobil. & Active Alarm
Parking Index Rating . . . . Average
Where Made. . . . . Torslanda, Sweden
Fuel Factor
  MPG Rating (city/hwy) Good-24/36
  Driving Range (mi.) Average-406
  Fuel Type. . . . . .Premium
  Annual Fuel Cost . . . . .Average-$1628
  Gas Guzzler Tax . . . . .No
  Greenhouse Gas Emissions (tons/yr.) Low-5.2
  Barrels of Oil Used per year Average-11.8

How the Competition Rates

Competitors	Rating	Pg.
Lincoln MKZ	4	187
Subaru Legacy	7	226
Toyota Camry	8	234

Price Range	Retail	Markup
T5 Momentum FWD	$38,900	6%
T5 R-Design FWD	$43,900	6%
T6 R-Design AWD	$48,400	6%
T6 Inscription AWD	$49,400	6%

Safety Checklist

Crash Test:
  Frontal . . . . —
  Side. . . . . —
Airbags:
  Torso . . . Std. Front Pelvis/Torso from Seat
  Roll Sensing. .Yes
  Knee Bolster . . . . .None
Crash Avoidance:
  Collision Avoidance . . Std. CIB & Opt. DBS
  Blind Spot Detection . . . . Optional
  Lane Keeping Assist . . . . Optional
  Pedestrian Crash Avoidance . . . . .Standard
General:
  Auto. Crash Notif.. . . . Operator Assist.-Fee
  Day Running Lamps . . . . .Standard
Safety Belt/Restraint:
  Dynamic Head Restraints . . . . .None
  Adjustable Belt . . . . Standard Front

^Warning feature does not meet government standards.

Volvo V60

Specifications

Drive. . . . . .FWD
Engine 2.0-liter I4
Transmission . . . . 8-sp. Automatic
Tow Rating (lbs.) Low-3500
Head/Leg Room (in.) Cramped-38.6/42.3
Interior Space (cu. ft.). Cramped-94
Cargo Space (cu. ft.) Roomy-29
Wheelbase/Length (in.) 113.1/182.5

Ratings—10 Best, 1 Worst

Combo Crash Tests	—
Safety Features	10
Rollover	4
Preventive Maintenance	5
Repair Costs	6
Warranty	8
Fuel Economy	5
Complaints	9
Insurance Costs	10

OVERALL RATING   —

Volvo XC60

Volvo XC60

At-a-Glance

Status/Year Series Started Unchanged/2017
Twins . . . . —
Body Styles . . . . SUV
Seating 5
Anti-Theft Device . Std. Pass. Immobil. & Active Alarm
Parking Index Rating . . . . Average
Where Made. Ghent, Belgium
Fuel Factor
   MPG Rating (city/hwy) Average-22/28
   Driving Range (mi.) . . . . Very Long-458
   Fuel Type. . . . . Premium
   Annual Fuel Cost . . . . .High-$1830
   Gas Guzzler Tax . . . . .No
   Greenhouse Gas Emissions (tons/yr.). . Average-6.1
   Barrels of Oil Used per year High-13.7

How the Competition Rates

Competitors	Rating	Pg.
Audi Q7	3	77
Honda Pilot	8	149
Lexus RX	4	184

Price Range

Price Range	Retail	Markup
T5 Dynamic FWD	$40,950	6%
T5 Inscription AWD	$42,950	6%
T6 Dynamic AWD	$46,950	8%
T6 R-Design AWD	$51,000	6%

Safety Checklist

Crash Test:
   Frontal . . . . —
   Side. . . . . —
Airbags:
   Torso . . . Std. Front Pelvis/Torso from Seat
   Roll Sensing. . . . . .Yes
   Knee Bolster . . . . Standard Driver
Crash Avoidance:
   Collision Avoidance . . Std. CIB & Opt. DBS
   Blind Spot Detection . . . . .Standard
   Lane Keeping Assist . . . . .Standard
   Pedestrian Crash Avoidance . . . . .Standard
General:
   Auto. Crash Notif.. . . . Operator Assist.-Fee
   Day Running Lamps . . . . Standard
Safety Belt/Restraint:
   Dynamic Head Restraints . . . . .None
   Adjustable Belt. . . . . Standard Front

^Warning feature does not meet government standards.

Volvo XC60

Specifications

Drive. . . . . .AWD
Engine 2.0-liter I4
Transmission . . . . 8-sp. Automatic
Tow Rating (lbs.) Low-3500
Head/Leg Room (in.) . . . . .Very Cramped-38/41.5
Interior Space (cu. ft.). . . . . Very Roomy-132.6
Cargo Space (cu. ft.) Roomy-29.7
Wheelbase/Length (in.) 112.8/184.6

Ratings—10 Best, 1 Worst

Combo Crash Tests	9
Safety Features	10
Rollover	3
Preventive Maintenance	3
Repair Costs	2
Warranty	8
Fuel Economy	5
Complaints	2
Insurance Costs	10
OVERALL RATING	**8**

Volvo XC90

At-a-Glance

Status/Year Series Started	Unchanged/2015
Twins	—
Body Styles	Wagon
Seating	7
Anti-Theft Device	Std. Pass. Immobil. & Active Alarm
Parking Index Rating	Hard
Where Made	Torslanda, Sweden
Fuel Factor	
MPG Rating (city/hwy)	Average-22/28
Driving Range (mi.)	Very Long-458
Fuel Type	Premium
Annual Fuel Cost	High-$1830
Gas Guzzler Tax	No
Greenhouse Gas Emissions (tons/yr.)	Average-6.0
Barrels of Oil Used per year	High-13.7

How the Competition Rates

Competitors	Rating	Pg.
Buick Enclave	4	89
Chevrolet Tahoe	4	112
Infiniti QX80		162

Price Range

	Retail	Markup
T5 Momentum FWD	$45,750	6%
T5 R-Design FWD	$51,150	6%
T6 Inscription AWD	$57,050	6%
T8 Excellence AWD	$104,900	6%

Volvo XC90

Safety Checklist

Crash Test:
  Frontal . . . . Very Good
  Side . . . . Good
Airbags:
  Torso . . . Std. Front Pelvis/Torso from Seat
  Roll Sensing . . . . Yes
  Knee Bolster . . . . Standard Driver
Crash Avoidance:
  Collision Avoidance . Standard CIB & DBS^
  Blind Spot Detection . . . . Standard
  Lane Keeping Assist . . . . Standard^
  Pedestrian Crash Avoidance . . . . . Standard
General:
  Auto. Crash Notif . . . . . Operator Assist.-Fee
  Day Running Lamps . . . . Standard
Safety Belt/Restraint:
  Dynamic Head Restraints . . . . None
  Adjustable Belt . . . Standard Front and Rear

^Warning feature does not meet government standards.

Volvo XC90

Specifications

Drive	AWD
Engine	2.0-liter I4
Transmission	8-sp. Automatic
Tow Rating (lbs.)	Low-5000
Head/Leg Room (in.)	Cramped-38.9/40.9
Interior Space (cu. ft.)	Roomy-119.6
Cargo Space (cu. ft.)	Cramped-15.8
Wheelbase/Length (in.)	117.5/194.8

So you're considering an electric vehicle? You're not alone! A recent survey by the Consumer Federation of America found that about one-third of potential car buyers would consider an EV. So it's no surprise that 16 major auto manufacturers have 32 new electric vehicles on the market with choices ranging from subcompacts to the luxury laden Tesla. While they're still more expensive than the corresponding gas powered vehicles, EV prices are on the way down and their benefits may warrant the added expense.

Energy from electricity is something we are all familiar with and, in fact, take for granted. We live in a plug-in world where most electrically powered products are extraordinarily convenient and highly functional. Imagine every night doing the same thing with your car as you do with your cell phone—simply plugging it in for the power it needs the next day. And then getting into a nearly silent, clean running car that glides effortlessly out of your driveway and likely has faster pickup than your gas powered car.

While there are a number of environmental reasons for buying an electric vehicle, the simplicity of operation, quiet ride, high tech feel and responsive performance are also major benefits. When you consider the complexity of a gasoline powered engine (most of us can't even identify the items under the hood!) and associated maintenance costs, the simplicity of electric power is refreshing, understandable, and very reliable. Owners of EVs report very low maintenance costs as there's very little to maintain.

SHOULD I EVEN CONSIDER AN ELECTRIC?

The big question most consumers have about EVs is: will I run out of power at the worst time possible—or anytime! Who hasn't needed a flashlight or tried to make a cell phone call only to find the battery is dead. In addition, many of us find it hard to imagine that the same type of engine that runs our blender, sewing machine or drill could possibly power a car! Finally, will I easily be able to plug this thing in at home? These concerns often dissuade people from looking further into the purchase of an electric vehicle.

The fact is, according to a recent analysis of consumer readiness for electric vehicles, 42% of car buyers meet the typical driving patterns, charging needs, and model preferences of the electric vehicles already on the market. Of households, 56% have access to charging, 95% transport 4 or fewer passengers, 79% don't require hauling, and 69% drive less than 60 miles on weekdays, well within the range of most battery-electric vehicles. Bottom-line, there's an excellent chance that an EV will meet your driving needs.

WHAT ARE MY CHOICES?

EVs come in various sizes, styles and price ranges. In addition, there are various types of EVs. The industry is trying to settle on acronyms to describe the different types, but here's a simple overview:

All Electric:

BEVs (Battery Powered Electric Vehicles) simply have a battery and an electric motor which powers the car. They are the simplest and "purest" form of electric vehicle. Because they depend solely on battery power, the battery systems have to be large which increases the cost of these vehicles. In addition to charging up at home, there are a growing number of publically available charging stations (almost 25,000 to date) in shopping centers, employee parking lots, and along the highway. The range of these vehicles is from 68-315 miles per charge.

Electric with Built-In Charging Systems:

EREVs (Extended Range Electric Vehicles) have a gas powered auxiliary power source, that can recharge the battery if you run low on power before getting home or to a charging station. They tend to have smaller batteries and depend on the auxiliary gas powered recharger in place of a larger battery. The battery range on these vehicles is from 47-81 miles. There are only two vehicles in this category and they are a bit different from each other. The BMW i3 has an auxiliary gas engine that simply recharges the battery; it does not power the vehicle. The Chevy Volt has a gas engine that can both recharge the battery and run the vehicle. At various times both the electric motor and gas motor will power the Volt. With the auxiliary recharging engines, the range is 200 miles for the BMW i3 and 420 miles for the Chevy Volt. When the Volt reaches about 37 mph, the gas engine kicks in regardless of the state of the battery.

Dual Electric and Gasoline Vehicles:

PHEVs (Plug in Hybrid Electric Vehicles) have both an electric and gasoline motor which power the wheels at separate times. They are different from the now common hybrid vehicles, because you can plug them in to recharge. If your daily mileage is low, then these can be used like exclusively electric vehicles. Because the gasoline engine will kick in when the battery depletes, the range of these vehicle is similar to gasoline powered vehicles. The electric range is 11-48 miles per charge and the gasoline engine range is 330-600 miles.

WHAT ABOUT CHARGING?

There are three basic types of charging systems, two of which will work in your home.

Level 1: This is the simplest and least expensive system to set up in your home. All you need is a dedicated circuit (nothing else being used on the circuit) and a common household outlet. Level 1 charging is the slowest method because it uses standard 120 volt household current. Your electric vehicle will come with a Level 1 charging cord that you plug into a regular household outlet. The cord comes with a control box which monitors charging. Typically, it will take about an hour to get 4.5 miles of range. Complete charging times range from 3 to 57 hours.

Level 2: This requires a dedicated 240 volt circuit, the same one you would need for an electric dryer or other large appliance. First, your home has to have 240 electrical service (all newer homes will) and second, if there is not a readily available line, it will have to be run to where it is needed from the circuit breaker box. Not only will this require an electrician, but if walls or ceilings are disturbed, carpentry, drywall and painting may also be necessary. In addition, once the circuit is available, you will need a special device to plug into the circuit which monitors the electrical charge to the car. Depending on features, these devices can range from $500-$2500. Before these costs scare you off, it is worth investigating the actual cost (you may be lucky enough to have a circuit box in your garage or very close) and determine if your utility company will offer any financial assistance (many do as they want to sell you more electricity). In addition, you need to consider the fact that this installation will save you hundreds of dollars in gasoline costs as well as being much more convenient than going to a gas station to refuel. Typically an hour's charging will provide 24 miles of driving. Complete charging times range from 1.5 to 12 hours.

Level 3 or DC Fast Charge: This feature enables the car to be connected to a public charging station, many of which have very fast charging systems. This is great if you have an EV and your office provides charging stations or you're on the road and find one on the highway or in a shopping center. You can get up to 40 miles of range with just 10 minutes of charging. Overall charging times can be as low as 20 minutes.

One of the issues the industry is struggling with is a universal plug. There are three types of fast charge plugs, one of which is proprietary to the Tesla. Tesla does offer adaptors that can be used in the various types of outlets. If you are planning to charge your vehicle at work, be sure to check out the DC fast charge plug before you buy. Final Note: Because EVs are so quiet, pedestrians may not hear them coming so the government is considering requiring some type of added noise making capacity. When driving an EV use care when around pedestrians.

FOLLOWING IS *THE CAR BOOK'S* SNAPSHOT GUIDE TO THE 2018 EVs:

This is a very basic guide to many of the key features on today's EVs. It's important to take a good, long test drive in order to make a selection that best meets your needs and to get the details behind the features that are really important to you.

You'll find the following items in the EV snapshot:

Range: The first number is how far you can go on a single charge on just battery power. The second number shows the range with auxiliary power. In some cases that auxiliary power just recharges the battery, in other cases it powers the wheels just like a gas engine. In addition to the estimated range, we have provided two comparative ratings. The first rating is the total electric range which includes the range added with an auxiliary recharging engine. The second includes the range with the auxiliary engine that directly powers the wheels. This range is compared to the range of standard gasoline engines. The ratings for electric and electric + auxiliary vehicles range compares just these vehicles. Beware, driving with a "lead foot" and using heat and air conditioning will reduce your range.

Charging Time: This is the total time for a complete charge using Level 1 and Level 2 systems. We did not include the DC fast charging time because there is significant variation in the power of public stations.

MPGe: This is the equivalent of the traditional gasoline miles per gallon converted to electricity (thus the small 'e' at the end). While it is not actually miles per gallon, it gives you a way to compare the efficiency of EVs with gas powered vehicles. We've presented the 'combined' mileage rating which combines highway and city driving. The rating following the estimate compares the mileage with all other electric vehicles running on just battery power.

Introduction: This is the year the vehicle was first introduced. The longer the production time, the more likely the manufacturer is to have worked out any bugs. On the other hand, more recent introductions will contain more sophisticated technology and safety features.

Price: This is the manufacturer's suggested retail price which gives you a general idea of EV pricing. It's important to check for federal and local rebate programs and to comparison shop. Car pricing is notoriously variable and that's no different for EVs. To get the best price consider using the services of the non-profit CarBargains program (page 57).

Size Class/Seating: This provides a general idea of the size of the car. Most consumers compare vehicles within the same size class.

On Board Charger: The greater the kW (kilowatt) rating, the faster the charger. In addition we indicate which vehicles have DC Fast Charging (Level 3) built-in which enables you to take advantage of speedy (and sometimes free) public charging facilities.

Auxiliary Power/MPG: This indicates whether or not (and what kind) of auxiliary power the vehicle may have. There are two types—engines that recharge the battery and engines that drive the wheels. For electric vehicles with auxiliary engines that power the car, we've included the EPA combined MPG estimate. The rating following the estimate compares the mileage with all other gasoline powered vehicles in *The Car Book*. See the descriptions on pages 259-260.

Crash Test Rating: Not all EVs have been crash tested. This tells you which one's were crash tested and how they performed using *The Car Book's* rating system based on government's tests. (See page 20.)

Safety Features: Safety has become critically important to today's car buyer, so we've identified 3 key safety features and indicated if the EV has those features. AEB stands for *Automatic Emergency Braking* – this system automatically applies the brakes if a collision is imminent. We do not indicate, here, if the vehicle has other forms of automatic braking technologies such as brake assist or forward crash warning. *Blind Spot Detection* is a blind spot monitor that uses radar or other technologies to detect objects in the driver's blind spot. *Lane Assist* moves you back into your lane if you're drifting. We do not indicate if the car simply provides a warning.

Warranty: Warranties vary so here's how the car's overall warranty stacks up in comparison with all other warranties.

Battery Warranty: Electric vehicle batteries are relatively new products and critical to the car's operation. As such, you want to be sure that your *battery* comes with a good, long warranty.

Interior Space/Cargo Space: This is another indication of the car's size. The ratings are relative compared to all of the vehicles in the *The Car Book*.

Parking Index: This rating takes into consideration the vehicle's key dimensions and determines an estimate for 'ease of parking' compared to other models. This is a general guide and no substitute for a good long test drive.

Sales: This indicates December 2018 year to date total sales for the 2018 version of the vehicle indicating the general popularity of the EV.

For more complete information on many of these vehicles, please see the corresponding vehicle on the car ratings pages.

Audi A3 Plug-in Hybrid

Introduction:	2016
Range:	17 mi.– Vry. Short/Aux. Power–430 mi.–Long
Charging Time:	Level 1 (8 hrs.)–Fast/Level 2 (2.5 hrs.)–Fast
MPGe:	Electric–86–Low

On Board Charger:	3.3 kW
Auxiliary Power/MPG:	Yes (PHEV)/MPG-39–Very High
Crash Test Rating:	—
Safety Features	AEB–Yes*; Blind Spot Detect-Yes*; Lane Asst–Yes*
Warranty:	4 years/50,000 mi.
Battery Warranty:	8 years/100,000 mi.
Size Class/ Seating:	Compact/5
Interior/Cargo Space:	89 cf–Vry. Cramped/13.6 cf–Cramped
Parking Index:	Easy
Sales:	2,597
Price:	$37,900 (MSRP)
Notes:	*Indicates optional feature

BMW 330e

Introduction:	2016
Range:	14 mi.–Vry. Short/Aux. Power - 350 - Vry. Short
Charging Time:	Level 1 (10 hrs.) - Avg/Level 2 (2.2 hrs.) - Vry. Fast
MPGe:	71 - Very Low

On Board Charger:	3.5 kW
Auxiliary Power/MPG:	Yes (PHEV)/MPG-30-High
Crash Test Rating:	-
Safety Features	AEB-Yes*; Blind Spot Detect-Yes*; Lane Asst-No
Warranty:	4 years/50,000 mi.
Battery Warranty:	8 years/100,000 mi.
Size Class/ Seating:	Compact/5
Interior/Cargo Space:	96 cf-Cramped/13 cf-Cramped
Parking Index:	Average
Sales:	2,600
Price:	$44,100
Notes:	*Indicates optional feature

BMW 530e

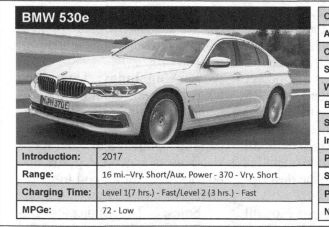

Introduction:	2017
Range:	16 mi.–Vry. Short/Aux. Power - 370 - Vry. Short
Charging Time:	Level 1(7 hrs.) - Fast/Level 2 (3 hrs.) - Fast
MPGe:	72 - Low

On Board Charger:	3.5 kW
Auxiliary Power/MPG:	Yes (PHEV)/MPG-29-High
Crash Test Rating:	-
Safety Features	AEB-Yes; Blind Spot Detect-Yes*; Lane Asst-Yes
Warranty:	4 years/50,000 mi.
Battery Warranty:	8 years/100,000 mi.
Size Class/ Seating:	Mid-Size/5
Interior/Cargo Space:	99 cf-Average/10 cf-Very Cramped
Parking Index:	Average
Sales:	8,664
Price:	$51,200
Notes:	*Indicates optional feature

BMW 740e

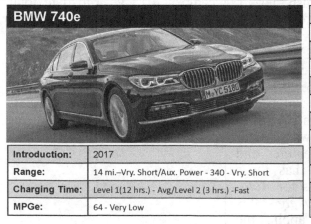

Introduction:	2017
Range:	14 mi.–Vry. Short/Aux. Power - 340 - Vry. Short
Charging Time:	Level 1(12 hrs.) - Avg/Level 2 (3 hrs.) -Fast
MPGe:	64 - Very Low

On Board Charger:	3.7kW
Auxiliary Power/MPG:	Yes (PHEV)/MPG-27-High
Crash Test Rating:	-
Safety Features	AEB-Yes*; Blind Spot Detect-Yes*; Lane Asst-Yes*
Warranty:	4 years/50,000 mi.
Battery Warranty:	8 years/100,000 mi.
Size Class/ Seating:	Large/5
Interior/Cargo Space:	114 cf-Roomy/14.8 cf-Cramped
Parking Index:	Very Hard
Sales:	339
Price:	$89,100
Notes:	*Indicates optional feature

BMW i3

On Board Charger:	7.4 kW; DC fast charge optional
Auxiliary Power/MPG:	Optional (EREV)/MPG-39–Very High
Crash Test Rating:	—
Safety Features	AEB–Yes*; Blind Spot Detect–No; Lane Asst–No
Warranty:	4 years/50,000 mi.
Battery Warranty:	8 years/100,000 mi.
Size Class/ Seating:	Subcompact/4
Interior/Cargo Space:	83.1 cf.–Vry. Cramped/2.8 cf–Vry. Cramped
Parking Index:	Very Easy
Sales:	6,117
Price:	$44,450 (MSRP)/$48,300 w/battery ext.
Notes:	*Indicates optional feature

Introduction:	2014
Range:	153 mi.–Very Long/Aux. Power–200 mi.–Vry. Short
Charging Time:	Level 1 (10 hrs.)–Average/Level 2 (3 hrs.)–Fast
MPGe:	Electric-124–Very High

BMW i8

On Board Charger:	5 kW; DC fast charge standard
Auxiliary Power/MPG:	Yes (PHEV) /MPG-28–High
Crash Test Rating:	—
Safety Features	AEB-Yes*; Blind Spot Detect-No; Lane Asst-No
Warranty:	4 years/50,000 mi.
Battery Warranty:	8 years/100,000 mi.
Size Class/ Seating:	Compact/4
Interior/Cargo Space:	80.9 cf.–Vry. Cramped/4.7 cf–Vry. Cramped
Parking Index:	Hard
Sales:	772
Price:	$136,500 (MSRP)
Notes:	*Indicates optional feature

Introduction:	2014
Range:	15 mi.–Vry. Short/Aux. Power–330 mi.–Vry. Short
Charging Time:	Level 1 (3.5 hrs.)–Vry. Fast/Level 2 (1.5 hrs.)–Vry. Fast
MPGe:	Electric-76–Low

BMW x5 xDrive Plug-in Hybrid

On Board Charger:	3.5 kW
Auxiliary Power/MPG:	Yes (PHEV)/MPG-24–Average
Crash Test Rating:	—
Safety Features	AEB–Yes*; Blind Spot Detect-No; Lane Asst–No
Warranty:	4 years/50,000 mi.
Battery Warranty:	8 years/100,000 mi.
Size Class/ Seating:	Medium SUV/5
Interior/Cargo Space:	cf– /34.2 cf–Very Roomy
Parking Index:	Very Hard
Sales:	4,434
Price:	$63,045 (MSRP)
Notes:	*Indicates optional feature

Introduction:	2016
Range:	14 mi.–Vry. Short/Aux. Power–540 mi.–Vry. Long
Charging Time:	Level 1 (3.7 hrs.)–Vry. Fast/Level 2 (2.7 hrs.)–Fast
MPGe:	Electric-56–Very Low

Cadillac CT6 Plug-in

On Board Charger:	3.6kW
Auxiliary Power/MPG:	Yes (PHEV)/MPG-26-Average
Crash Test Rating:	-
Safety Features	AEB-Yes*; Blind Spot Detect-Yes*; Lane Asst-Yes*
Warranty:	4 years/50,000 mi.
Battery Warranty:	8 years/100,000 mi.
Size Class/ Seating:	Mid-Size/5
Interior/Cargo Space:	106 cf-Roomy/10.6 cf-Vry. Cramped
Parking Index:	Hard
Sales:	231
Price:	$75,095
Notes:	*Indicates optional feature

Introduction:	2017
Range:	31 mi- Avg./Aux. Power - 440 - Long
Charging Time:	Level 1 (12.5 hrs.) - Avg./Level 2 (4.5 hrs.) - Avg.
MPGe:	62 - Very Low

Chevrolet Bolt

Introduction:	2017
Range:	238 mi.–Vry. Long
Charging Time:	Lvl. 1 (51 hrs.) - Vry. Slow/Lvl. 2 (9 hrs.) - Vry. Slow
MPGe:	119–Very High

On Board Charger:	7.2 kW; DC fast charge optional
Auxiliary Power/MPG:	No
Crash Test Rating:	–
Safety Features	AEB–Yes*; Blind Spot Detect–Yes*; Lane Asst–Yes*
Warranty:	3 years/36,000 mi.
Battery Warranty:	8 years/100,000 mi.
Size Class/ Seating:	Subompact/5
Interior/Cargo Space:	95 cf.–Cramped/16.9 cf–Average
Parking Index:	Very Easy
Sales:	18,602
Price	$37,495
Notes:	*Indicates optional feature

Chrysler Pacifica

Introduction:	2017
Range:	33 mi.–Short/Aux. Power - 570 - Vry. Long
Charging Time:	Level 1(12 hrs.) - Average/Level 2 (2 hrs.) - Vry. Fast
MPGe:	84–Low

On Board Charger:	6.6kW
Auxiliary Power/MPG:	Yes (PHEV)/MPG-32-High
Crash Test Rating:	5 stars
Safety Features	AEB–Yes*; Blind Spot Detect–Yes*; Lane Asst–Yes*
Warranty:	3 years/36,000 mi.
Battery Warranty:	10 years/100,000 mi.
Size Class/ Seating:	Minivan/7
Interior/Cargo Space:	165 cf–Vry. Roomy/32.3 cf–Vry. Roomy
Parking Index:	Very Hard
Sales:	7,062
Price	$41,995
Notes:	*Indicates optional feature

Fiat 500e

Introduction:	2013
Range:	87 mi.–Long
Charging Time:	Level 1 (20 hrs.)–Vry. Slow/Level 2 (<4 hrs.)–Average
MPGe:	116–Very High

On Board Charger:	6.6 kW
Auxiliary Power/MPG:	None
Crash Test Rating:	–
Safety Features	AEB–No; Blind Spot Detect–No; Lane Asst–No
Warranty:	4 years/50,000 mi.
Battery Warranty:	8 years/100,000 mi.
Size Class/ Seating:	Subcompact/2
Interior/Cargo Space:	71.6 cf–Vry. Cramped/7 cf–Vry. Cramped
Parking Index:	Very Easy
Sales:	2,250
Price	$31,800 (MSRP)
Notes:	*Indicates optional feature

Ford Fusion Energi

Introduction:	2013
Range:	20 mi.–Short/Aux. Power–550 mi.–Vry. Long
Charging Time:	Level 1 (7 hrs.)–Fast/Level 2 (2.5 hrs.)–Fast
MPGe:	Electric–88–Low

On Board Charger:	3.3 kW
Auxiliary Power/MPG:	Yes (PHEV)/MPG-38–Very High
Crash Test Rating:	5 stars
Safety Features	AEB–Yes*; Blind Spot Detect–Yes*; Lane Asst–No
Warranty:	3 years/36,000 mi.
Battery Warranty:	8 years/100,000 mi.
Size Class/ Seating:	Midsize/5
Interior/Cargo Space:	102.8 cf–Roomy/8.2 cf–Vry. Cramped
Parking Index:	Average
Sales:	8,074
Price	$33,900 (MSRP)
Notes:	*Indicates optional feature

Honda Clarity PHEV

Introduction:	2018
Range:	48 mi.–Average/Aux. Power–340 mi.–Vry. Short
Charging Time:	Level 1 (12 hrs.) - Average/Level 2 (2.2 hrs.) - Vry. Fast
MPGe:	Electric-110-High

On Board Charger:	6.6 kW; DC fast charge optional
Auxiliary Power/MPG:	Yes (PHEV)/MPG-42–Very High
Crash Test Rating:	—
Safety Features	AEB-Yes; Blind Spot Detect-Yes; Lane Asst-Yes
Warranty:	3 years/36,000 mi.
Battery Warranty:	10 years/100,000 mi.
Size Class/ Seating:	Midsize/5
Interior/Cargo Space:	102 cf-Average/16 cf-Cramped
Parking Index:	Easy
Sales:	18,602
Price:	$33,400
Notes:	

Hyundai IONIQ Electric

Introduction:	2017
Range:	124 mi- Very Long
Charging Time:	Level 1 (9 hrs.) - Fast/Level 2 (4 hrs.) - Average
MPGe:	136 - Very High

On Board Charger:	6.6kW
Auxiliary Power/MPG:	No
Crash Test Rating:	—
Safety Features	AEB-Yes*; Blind Spot Detect-Yes*; Lane Asst-Yes*
Warranty:	5 years/60,000 mi.
Battery Warranty:	10 years/100,000 mi.
Size Class/ Seating:	Compact/5
Interior/Cargo Space:	96.2 cf-Cramped/23.8 cf-Roomy
Parking Index:	Very Easy
Sales:	1,590
Price:	$29,500
Notes:	*Lifetime battery warranty for original owner

Hyundai Sonata Plug-in Hybrid

Introduction:	2016
Range:	27 mi.–Short/Aux. Power–600 mi.–Vry. Long
Charging Time:	Level 1 (8.7 hrs.)–Fast/Level 2 (2.7 hrs.)–Fast
MPGe:	Electric-99–Average

On Board Charger:	3.3 kW
Auxiliary Power/MPG:	Yes (PHEV)/MPG-40–Very High
Crash Test Rating:	—
Safety Features	AEB–No; Blind Spot Detect-Yes*; Lane Asst–No
Warranty:	5 years/60,000 mi.
Battery Warranty:	10 years/100,000 mi.
Size Class/ Seating:	Midsize/5
Interior/Cargo Space:	106.1 cf–Roomy/9.9 cf–Vry. Cramped
Parking Index:	Easy
Sales:	460
Price:	$34,600 (MSRP)
Notes:	*Lifetime battery warranty for original owner

Kia Niro PHEV

Introduction:	2018
Range:	26 mi.–Short/Aux. Power–560 mi.–Vry. Long
Charging Time:	Level 1 (6 hrs.)–Fast/Level 2 (2.5 hrs.)–Fast
MPGe:	Electric-105–High

On Board Charger:	3.3 kW
Auxiliary Power/MPG:	Yes (PHEV)/MPG-46–Very High
Crash Test Rating:	27 mi.–Short/Aux. Power–600 mi.–Vry. Long
Safety Features	AEB–Yes*; Blind Spot Detect-Yes*; Lane Asst–Yes*
Warranty:	5 years/60,000 mi.
Battery Warranty:	7 years/150,000 mi.
Size Class/ Seating:	Subcompact/5
Interior/Cargo Space:	101 cf–Average/19 cf–Average
Parking Index:	Very Easy
Sales:	3,389
Price:	$28,840
Notes:	

Kia Optima PHEV

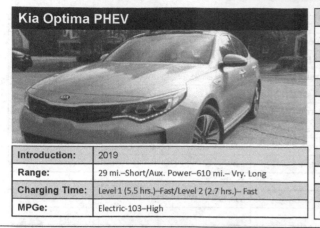

Introduction:	2019
Range:	29 mi.–Short/Aux. Power–610 mi.– Vry. Long
Charging Time:	Level 1 (5.5 hrs.)–Fast/Level 2 (2.7 hrs.)– Fast
MPGe:	Electric–103–High

On Board Charger:	3.3 kW
Auxiliary Power/MPG:	Yes (PHEV)/MPG 40–Very High
Crash Test Rating:	—
Safety Features	AEB–Yes; Blind Spot Detect–Yes; Lane Asst–Yes
Warranty:	5 years/60,000 mi.
Battery Warranty:	7 years/150,000 mi.
Size Class/ Seating:	Midsize/5
Interior/Cargo Space:	104.8 cf–Roomy/15.9 cf–Cramped
Parking Index:	Easy
Sales:	965
Price:	$35,390
Notes:	

Kia Soul EV

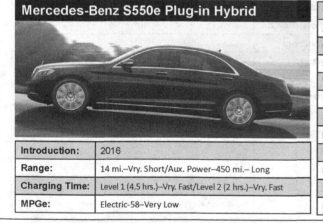

Introduction:	2015
Range:	93 mi.–Long
Charging Time:	Level 1 (24 hrs.)–Vry. Slow/Level 2 (4.5 hrs.)–Average
MPGe:	105–High

On Board Charger:	6.6 kW; DC fast charge optional
Auxiliary Power/MPG:	None
Crash Test Rating:	—
Safety Features	AEB–No; Blind Spot Detect–Yes*; Lane Asst–Yes
Warranty:	5 years/60,000 mi.
Battery Warranty:	7 years/150,000 mi.
Size Class/ Seating:	Compact/5
Interior/Cargo Space:	97.1 cf–Average/18.8 cf–Average
Parking Index:	Very Easy
Sales:	1,134
Price:	$33,950 (MSRP)
Notes:	Only available in CA, GA, HI, MD, NJ, NY, OR, TX, and WA.

Mercedes-Benz S550e Plug-in Hybrid

Introduction:	2016
Range:	14 mi.–Vry. Short/Aux. Power–450 mi.– Long
Charging Time:	Level 1 (4.5 hrs.)–Vry. Fast/Level 2 (2 hrs.)–Vry. Fast
MPGe:	Electric–58–Very Low

On Board Charger:	3.3 kW
Auxiliary Power/MPG:	Yes (PHEV)/MPG-26–Average
Crash Test Rating:	—
Safety Features	AEB–Yes; Blind Spot Detect-Yes*; Lane Asst–Yes*
Warranty:	4 years/50,000 mi.
Battery Warranty:	8 years/100,000 mi.
Size Class/ Seating:	Large/5
Interior/Cargo Space:	112 cf–Roomy/13.9 cf–Cramped
Parking Index:	Very Hard
Sales:	96
Price:	$95,650 (MSRP)
Notes:	*Indicates optional feature

Mini Countryman SE PHEV

Introduction:	2018
Range:	12 mi.–Vry. Short/Aux. Power–270 mi.– Vry. Short
Charging Time:	Level 1 (6 hrs.)–Fast/Level 2 (3 hrs.)–Fast
MPGe:	Electric–51–Very Low

On Board Charger:	3.7 kW
Auxiliary Power/MPG:	Yes (PHEV)/MPG-27–Average
Crash Test Rating:	—
Safety Features	AEB–Yes*; Blind Spot Detect–No; Lane Asst–No
Warranty:	4 years/50,000 mi.
Battery Warranty:	8 years/100,000 mi.
Size Class/ Seating:	Compact/5
Interior/Cargo Space:	97 cf–Average/17.4 cf–Average
Parking Index:	Very Easy
Sales:	1,564
Price:	$37,000
Notes:	

Mitsubishi Outlander PHEV

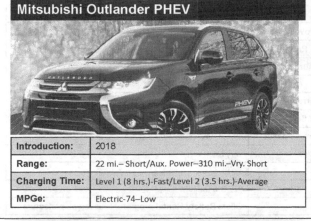

Introduction:	2018
Range:	22 mi.– Short/Aux. Power–310 mi.–Vry. Short
Charging Time:	Level 1 (8 hrs.)-Fast/Level 2 (3.5 hrs.)-Average
MPGe:	Electric-74–Low

On Board Charger:	3.7 kW; DC fast charge optional
Auxiliary Power/MPG:	Yes (PHEV)/MPG 25–Low
Crash Test Rating:	–
Safety Features	SEB–Yes*; Blind Spot Detect–Yes*; Lane Asst–No
Warranty:	5 years/60,000 mi.
Battery Warranty:	8 years/100,000 mi.
Size Class/ Seating:	Midsize SUV/7
Interior/Cargo Space:	112 cf–Roomy/13.9 cf–Cramped
Parking Index:	Easy
Sales:	4,166
Price:	$35,795
Notes:	*Indicates optional feature

Nissan Leaf

Introduction:	2018
Range:	150 mi.–Vry. Long
Charging Time:	Level 1 (22 hrs.)-Slow/Level 2 (7.5 hrs.)-Slow
MPGe:	114–Very High

On Board Charger:	6.6 kW; DC fast charge optional
Auxiliary Power/MPG:	None
Crash Test Rating:	–
Safety Features	AEB–Yes; Blind Spot Detect-Yes; Lane Asst–Yes
Warranty:	3 years/36,000 mi.
Battery Warranty:	8 years/100,000 mi.
Size Class/ Seating:	Compact/5
Interior/Cargo Space:	128.2 cf–Vry. Roomy/10.3 cf–Very Cramped
Parking Index:	Very Easy
Sales:	14,715
Price:	$29,990 (MSRP)
Notes:	

Porsche Cayenne S E-Hybrid

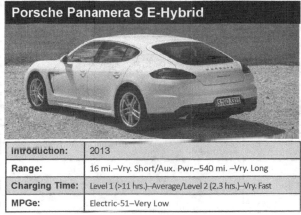

Introduction:	2015
Range:	14 mi.–Vry. Short/Aux. Power–480 mi.–Vry. Long
Charging Time:	Level 1 (11 hrs.)–Average/Level 2 (3.6 hrs.)–Average
MPGe:	Electric-47–Very Low

On Board Charger:	3.6 kW
Auxiliary Power/MPG:	Yes (PHEV)/MPG 22–Low
Crash Test Rating:	–
Safety Features	AEB–Yes; Blind Spot Detect-Yes; Lane Asst–Yes
Warranty:	4 years/50,000 mi.
Battery Warranty:	7 years/70,000 mi.
Size Class/ Seating:	Midsize SUV/5
Interior/Cargo Space:	—/20.5 cf–Average
Parking Index:	Hard
Sales:	1,022
Price:	$77,200 (MSRP)
Notes:	

Porsche Panamera S E-Hybrid

Introduction:	2013
Range:	16 mi.–Vry. Short/Aux. Pwr.–540 mi. –Vry. Long
Charging Time:	Level 1 (>11 hrs.)–Average/Level 2 (2.3 hrs.)–Vry. Fast
MPGe:	Electric-51–Very Low

On Board Charger:	3.6 kW
Auxiliary Power/MPG:	Yes (PHEV)/MPG-25–Average
Crash Test Rating:	—
Safety Features	AEB–Yes*; Blind Spot Detect-Yes*; Lane Asst–Yes*
Warranty:	4 years/50,000 mi.
Battery Warranty:	7 years/70,000 mi.
Size Class/ Seating:	Large/5
Interior/Cargo Space:	—/11.8 cf–Vry. Cramped
Parking Index:	Very Hard
Sales:	2,036
Price:	$96,100 (MSRP)
Notes:	*Indicates optional feature

Smart forTwo Electric Drive

Introduction:	2011
Range:	68 mi.–Average
Charging Time:	Level 1 (13 hrs.)–Average/Level 2 (6 hrs.)–Slow
MPGe:	107–High

On Board Charger:	3.3 kW
Auxiliary Power/MPG:	None
Crash Test Rating:	—
Safety Features	AEB–No; Blind Spot Detect–No; Lane Asst–No
Warranty:	4 years/50,000 mi.
Battery Warranty:	4 years/50,000 mi.
Size Class/ Seating:	Subcompact/2
Interior/Cargo Space:	45.4 cf–Vry. Cramped/7.8 cf–Vry. Cramped
Parking Index:	Very Easy
Sales:	1,219
Price:	$25,000 (MSRP)
Notes:	Offers Battery Rental program, *indicates opt. feature

Tesla Model 3

Introduction:	2017
Range:	310 mi.–Vry. Long
Charging Time:	Level 1 (57 hrs.)–Vry. Slow/Level 2 (12 hrs.)–Vry. Slow
MPGe:	126–Very High

On Board Charger:	7.7 kW
Auxiliary Power/MPG:	None
Crash Test Rating:	—
Safety Features	AEB–Yes; Blind Spot Detect–Yes; Lane Asst–Yes
Warranty:	4 years/50,000 mi.
Battery Warranty:	8 years/unlimited mi.
Size Class/ Seating:	Intermediate/5
Interior/Cargo Space:	–/15.0 cf–Cramped
Parking Index:	Average
Sales:	139,782
Price:	$35,000 (MSRP)
Notes:	

Tesla Model S

Introduction:	2012
Range:	315 mi.–Vry. Long
Charging Time:	Level 1 (52 hrs.)–Vry. Slow/Level 2 (10 hrs.)–Vry. Slow
MPGe:	101–Average

On Board Charger:	11 kW; DC fast charge optional
Auxiliary Power/MPG:	None
Crash Test Rating:	5 stars
Safety Features	AEB–Yes; Blind Spot Detect–Yes; Lane Asst–Yes
Warranty:	4 years/50,000 mi.
Battery Warranty:	8 years/unlimited mi.
Size Class/ Seating:	Large/5
Interior/Cargo Space:	94 cf–Cramped/31.6 cf–Vry. Roomy
Parking Index:	Hard
Sales:	25,745
Price:	$71,070 (MSRP)
Notes:	

Tesla Model X

Introduction:	2016
Range:	289 mi.–Vry. Long
Charging Time:	Level 1 (57 hrs)–Vry. Slow/Level 2 (12 hrs)–Vry. Slow
MPGe:	Electric-93–Average

On Board Charger:	10 kW; DC fast charge optional
Auxiliary Power/MPG:	None
Crash Test Rating:	5 stars
Safety Features	AEB–Yes; Blind Spot Detect–Yes; Lane Asst–Yes
Warranty:	4 years/50,000 mi.
Battery Warranty:	8 years/unlimited
Size Class/ Seating:	Mid-Size/7
Interior/Cargo Space:	120 cf–Roomy/26 cf–Roomy
Parking Index:	Very Hard
Sales:	26,100
Price:	$80,000 (MSRP)
Notes:	

Toyota Prius Prime

Introduction:	2017
Range:	25 mi.–Short/Aux. Power - 640 - Vry. Long
Charging Time:	Level 1 (5.5 hrs.) - Fast/Level 2 (2 hrs.) - Vry. Fast
MPGe:	133 - Very High

On Board Charger:	3.3kW
Auxiliary Power/MPG:	Yes (PHEV)/MPG-54-Very High
Crash Test Rating:	-
Safety Features	AEB-Yes*; Blind Spot Detect-Yes*; Lane Asst-Yes*
Warranty:	3 years/36,000 mi.
Battery Warranty:	8 years/100,000 mi.
Size Class/ Seating:	Mid-Size/5
Interior/Cargo Space:	91.5 cf-Cramped/19.8 cf-Average
Parking Index:	Very Easy
Sales:	27,595
Price	$27,100
Notes:	*Indicates optional feature

VW e-Golf

Introduction:	2015
Range:	83 mi.–Long
Charging Time:	Level 1 (20 hrs.)–Slow/Level 2 (4 hrs.)–Average
MPGe:	116–Very High

On Board Charger:	7.2 kW; DC fast charge standard
Auxiliary Power/MPG:	None
Crash Test Rating:	—
Safety Features	AEB–Yes*; Blind Spot Detect-Yes*; Lane Asst–Yes*
Warranty:	4 years/50,000 mi.
Battery Warranty:	8 years/100,000 mi.
Size Class/ Seating:	Compact/5
Interior/Cargo Space:	93.5 cf–Cramped/22.8 cf–Average
Parking Index:	Easy
Sales:	1,354
Price	$28,995 (MSRP)
Notes:	*Indicates optional feature

Volvo XC60 PHEV

Introduction:	2018
Range:	17 mi.–Vry. Short /Aux. Pwr.–500 mi.–Vry. Long
Charging Time:	Level 1 (4.5 hrs)–Fast/Level 2 (3 hrs)–Fast
MPGe:	Electric-58–Very Low

On Board Charger:	3.5 kW
Auxiliary Power/MPG:	Yes (PHEV)/MPG-26– Average
Crash Test Rating:	–
Safety Features	AEB–Yes; Blind Spot Detect-Yes; Lane Asst–Yes
Warranty:	4 years/50,000 mi.
Battery Warranty:	4 years/50,000 mi.
Size Class/ Seating:	Medsize SUV/5
Interior/Cargo Space:	132.6 cf–Roomy/29.7 cf–Roomy
Parking Index:	Average
Sales:	2,267
Price	$53,700
Notes:	

Volvo XC90 Plug-in Hybrid

Introduction:	2016
Range:	17 mi.–Vry. Short /Aux. Pwr.–490 mi.–Vry. Long
Charging Time:	Level 1 (4 hrs.)–Fast/Level 2 (2.5 hrs.)–Fast
MPGe:	Electric-53–Very Low

On Board Charger:	3.5 kW
Auxiliary Power/MPG:	Yes (PHEV)/MPG-25– Average
Crash Test Rating:	5 stars
Safety Features	AEB–Yes; Blind Spot Detect-Yes; Lane Asst–Yes
Warranty:	4 years/50,000 mi.
Battery Warranty:	4 years/50,000 mi.
Size Class/ Seating:	Large SUV/7
Interior/Cargo Space:	119.6 cf–Roomy/15.8 cf–Cramped
Parking Index:	Hard
Sales:	1,387
Price	$68,100 (MSRP)
Notes:	